ISLAM AND GENDER

PRINCETON STUDIES IN MUSLIM POLITICS

Dale F. Eickelman and James Piscatori, Editors

Diane Singerman, *Avenues of Participation: Family, Politics, and Networks in Urban Quarters of Cairo*

Tone Bringa, *Being Muslim the Bosnian Way: Identity and Community in a Central Bosnian Village*

Dale F. Eickelman and James Piscatori, *Muslim Politics*

Bruce B. Lawrence, *Shattering the Myth: Islam beyond Violence*

Ziba Mir-Hosseini, *Islam and Gender: The Religious Debate in Contemporary Iran*

ISLAM AND GENDER

THE RELIGIOUS DEBATE IN
CONTEMPORARY IRAN

Ziba Mir-Hosseini

PRINCETON UNIVERSITY PRESS   PRINCETON, NEW JERSEY

Library of Congress Cataloging-in-Publication Data

Mir-Hosseini, Ziba.
Islam and gender : the religious debate in
contemporary Iran / Ziba Mir-Hosseini.
p. cm. — (Princeton studies in Muslim politics)
Includes bibliographical references and index.
ISBN 0-691-05815-6 (cl : alk. paper).
ISBN 0-691-01004-8 (pb : alk. paper)
1. Women—Iran.   2. Muslim women—Iran.
3. Women in Islam—Iran.   4. Women's rights—
Iran.   5. Women's rights—Religious aspects—Islam.
6. Shiʿah—Doctrines.   I. Title.   II. Series.
HQ1735.2.M55   1999
305.4'0955—dc21   99-22786   CIP

This book has been composed in Times Roman

The paper used in this publication meets the
minimum requirements of ANSI/NISO Z39.48-1992
(R1997) (*Permanence of Paper*)

http://pup.princeton.edu

Printed in the United States of America

10 9 8 7 6 5 4 3 2 1

10 9 8 7 6 5 4 3 2 1
(Pbk.)

FOR THREE WOMEN

Ezzat Amoli

MY MOTHER, WHO GAVE ME THE CHOICE
TO MAKE MY OWN LIFE, A CHOICE SHE
DID NOT HAVE HERSELF

Esther Goody

MY TEACHER AND FRIEND,
WHO TAUGHT ME ANTHROPOLOGY AND
GAVE ME A HOME WHEN I NEEDED IT MOST

Zahra Saʿidzadeh

WHO SHARED WITH ME THE MEETINGS
WITH THE CLERICS IN QOM,
AND BECAME A DAUGHTER TO ME

Contents

Foreword _____

WOMEN ARE CENTRAL to the political and moral imagination in Muslim majority societies. Because of this centrality, the contest over women's roles in society and family legislation has often become a matter of high politics. In many countries, demands for Islamization have focused on such matters as women's rights in divorce, inheritance, and legal testimony. In Pakistan, for example, sections of the conservative religious establishment have been pitted against the Women's Action Forum and women's professional associations in attempting to reform *shari°a*-based family law. Islamic arguments about women that defend the authenticity of tradition seek to draw boundaries not only between Muslim and non-Muslim communities, but also between the "true" guardians of political and religious values and others who contest established political and religious authorities.

In societies as varied as France, Egypt, and Turkey, legal challenges and debates over veiling and headscarves in schools and other public places have captured the moral and political imagination of Islamists and secularists, and Muslims and non-Muslims. At times, however, the headscarf debate detracts from a second, more profound debate that has the potential for transforming Muslim thought and practice. This debate about the very nature of religious authority is especially pointed in the Islamic Republic of Iran. Iran was profoundly transformed by the 1978–1979 Islamic revolution, but it is now in the throes of a transformation at least as substantial as the first. More than half of Iran's population has been born since the Islamic revolution, and many challenge the role of religious clerics in politics. Nonetheless, debates within the clerical establishment itself remain a powerful engine for social change. Rising levels of education in Iran mean that larger numbers of Iranians, both women and men, follow these debates and participate in them today than in the past. Iranians increasingly expect their religious leaders to articulate and justify their beliefs and are more aware of alternative and competing interpretations of Islamic belief and practice.

In 1967, the late shah promulgated Iran's Family Protection Act, which strengthened women's rights, especially those involving marriage. This act was technically repealed and recast in even more liberal terms in 1975, yet by then it had become a focal point of opposition. Ayatollah Khomeini targeted it as symptomatic of the regime's decadence, and it was suspended soon after he came to power. Ironically, some of the reforms first proposed by the shah were reintroduced by the Islamic Republic beginning in the 1980s. These included state-sponsored prenuptial contracts that give women the right to initiate divorce proceedings (1982), a further liberalization of divorce procedures

(1992), a family planning program (started in 1988), and greater opportunities in the workplace and in higher education (since the late 1980s).

In this book, Ziba Mir-Hosseini explains the dynamics of *shari'a* interpretation and debate among religious scholars in Iran and how these debates shape "indigenous" feminism and the roles women play. Increasingly since the 1970s, religious scholars in Iran have vigorously discussed the roles and responsibilities of women. Particularly after the 1979 revolution, women themselves have increasingly participated in these debates. Mir-Hosseini traces the rapidly shifting contexts of the debates among the clerics, tracing their main contours and breaking new ground in depicting the arguments of religious thinkers who argue for a major conceptual departure from existing theories in Islamic law about gender and gender relations. She traces these debates through interviews with the main participants and their writings, and the give and take of arguments offered through women's magazines, the daily press, and the "small media" of literary and intellectual journals. The result reveals the main points of controversy, portraying how central religious and social issues are debated and explained in the Islamic Republic, how clerics argue with one another, and how innovative arguments are shaped and constrained by the wider Iranian public. Ziba Mir-Hosseini's distinctive contribution is to make transparent the content and contexts of religious debates about gender in Iran, offering as a complementary benefit insight into how arguments are carried out in the public sphere of today's Iran.

Dale F. Eickelman
James Piscatori

Preface _____

SINCE THE EARLY 1980s I have sought to understand how Islamic Law, the shari'a, deals with women's issues and, in particular, how women in the Islamic Republic of Iran are shifting the limits imposed on them by a regime committed to implementing the shari'a. As part of this project, I went to Iran once again in early September 1995 to research a book on indigenous forms and expressions of feminist consciousness.

After nearly three months' work in Tehran and in the religious city of Qom, I felt that my fieldwork had been exceptionally fruitful, that I had reached a turning point in my understanding of post-revolutionary gender discourses in Iran, and that I could finally locate the indigenous feminism for which, as I had strongly argued in recent papers, the Islamic Revolution acted as a catalyst.[1] Meanwhile, I was joined by my husband, Richard Tapper, an anthropologist like myself, and together we took steps to set up a new collaborative research project with Iranian academic colleagues.

We left Tehran together in late November 1995. Inside the airport, a man waiting at the customs called Richard over. At first he would not allow me to join them, but I insisted. He then went through our luggage and started to remove papers and other items, apparently without discrimination, putting them into large plastic sacks. Nothing like this had ever happened to either of us before. In a state of shock, not daring to resist, we cooperated fully, but we repeatedly asked who he was and why he wanted these materials. He would not answer Richard or look him in the face, and all he would say to me, his voice trembling with rage, was, "it is not to do with you, you are Iranian and welcome to come and go as you please, this is your country; but tell him [Richard] that he has no right to be here, he should not have been given a visa."

Ironically, although his anger was directed at Richard, the only irreplaceable material that he took was mine. As an Iranian citizen, I do not need permission to do research in my country. I had numerous notebooks filled in Persian longhand; these he took, even though I kept telling him they were mine. I had a bundle of tape recordings of sermons at women's gatherings, radio programs, and interviews with clerics, sealed with official permission to take them home; and a mass of newspaper cuttings, reports, and documents given me by Iranian women's organizations in relation to the recent United Nations Women's Conference in Beijing; all these he took. In restrospect, the search, perhaps designed to frighten and impress rather than to find anything, was a hit-or-miss

_____
[1] Mir-Hosseini 1996a and 1996b.

effort: he took the film from my camera, and other films, exposed and un-exposed, but he did not even ask to see Richard's camera. At the time we were too shocked to challenge him further. All we could think of was to get on the plane home. This proved to be his main concern too. As soon as he was sure we were through into the departure lounge, he hurriedly left the airport with his loot.

On arrival in London we immediately made official protests to the Iranian Embassy and Ministry of Foreign Affairs. After a few weeks, a small assort-ment of documents was returned to my parents in Tehran. Some months later, a deputy foreign minister gave us an embarrassed verbal apology, regretting that a mistake had been made, that the "official" had no authority for his ac-tion; but at the time I am writing this (September 1998) our other possessions have not been returned.

For a while I was paralyzed with fear, anger, grief, and guilt. What had happened is every anthropologist's nightmare. I had committed the cardinal ethnographic sin of omission: I had failed to make copies of all my notes, tapes, and documents. Worse, I was anxious for my friends and contacts in Iran, those who had allowed me to enter their space and observe, and had trusted me enough to discuss issues openly. My notes were full of intimate details about individuals I was working with, families I stayed with, places I went, anecdotes I heard, my own readings of events and press articles. I wrote for myself: they were my raw thoughts and analyses, dialogues with myself about my work; they made sense to nobody but me. I would never have chosen to share them with anyone, least of all Iranian security officers; and I certainly had no intention of writing them up as they were. I was fearful that some ignorant reader might jump to the wrong conclusions and act on them.

Two months after our return, things began to change. First, I heard that *Payam-e Zan*, a women's journal published by young clerics in Qom with whose editorial board I had had long discussions, had started to publish these discussions under the title "A Round Table on Women's Issues: With Dr Mir-Hosseini and *Payam-e Zan*." Then in January 1996 Mehrangiz Kar, an Iranian lawyer with whom I was writing a joint paper, came to London. After talking with her I felt reassured that no harm had come to anyone I had worked with closely. Next, I received the copied tapes and notes I had made before leaving Tehran, together with a collection of books I had bought in Qom, all of which I had sent overland.

I started pulling myself together and taking stock of what was left from my three months of fieldwork. This turned out to be primarily the material I had collected among the clerics in Qom, including recordings of my discussions with them—the main subject matter of this book. Still I could not envisage writing without access to my field notes. As an anthropologist I was trained to rely on these as the tools of my trade: to read and reread them, classify, re-

shuffle, try to find meanings and patterns in them, and then to reconstruct them
in my writings. What was left of my materials represented only part of my field
experiences, and at the time they had seemed relatively marginal to my original project based on discussions with women.

But as further issues of *Payam-e Zan* arrived, with more installments of my
discussions with the editors, and as I started to read and take notes on the
books on women in Islam that I had bought in Qom, the present work—very
different from the one I had originally planned—took shape. I soon realized
that I had to write the book in the form of a personal search for understanding.
Like all Iranian women of my generation, my intellectual and personal life was
deeply affected by the 1979 revolution. I write not only as an anthropologist
but also as a Muslim woman who needs to make sense of her faith and culture.
I was born into a family of Seyyeds (descendants of the Prophet). We believed
in the fundamentals of Shiʿi Islam,[2] but the spirit and values of our faith mat-
tered more than outer rules and rituals. We were taught that it was sinful to lie,
cheat, hurt, or be cruel to others; at school, we learned to read the Koran, and
we had classes in Arabic and in the religious sciences. For us, religion was a
private matter. It was not forced upon us. It was left up to us as individuals
whether we said our prayers, fasted, made vows, or went on pilgrimage.

After the revolution, all this changed and we came to know a different face
of Islam, derived from the legal mandates of the shariʿa. It was no longer
enough to believe; one had to wear one's belief in the form of *hejab*: "Islamic"
covering for women (and beards for men). The state took it upon itself to
enforce the religious mandates that had previously been the concern of the
family; the shariʿa was declared the law of land.

Although I had not been much interested in politics when a student in
Tehran in the early 1970s or later as a postgraduate in Cambridge, I supported
the 1978–79 revolution. In 1980 I returned to Iran, full of hope. In my late
twenties, newly married, my doctorate just completed, I looked forward to
teaching anthropology and living happily with my husband. But neither aim
was to be fulfilled. Like so many other Iranian women, I found myself rejected
by the Islamic Republic soon after it was established and began to restructure
Iranian society. The 1980 cultural revolution resulted in the closure of all universities, and when they reopened two years later they were "Islamized," with
no room for women like me. Not only was I educated in the West and thus not
"fit to teach," but the file on me contained a report that I had never "fully

---

[2] These are enumerated as the Oneness of God, Divine Justice, the Prophethood of Muhammad,
the Imamate of Ali, and the Day of Judgment. Beliefs in Imamate and Divine Justice are what
separate the Shiʿa doctrinally from Sunnis, who constitute the majority of Muslims. The Shiʿa hold
that the succession to the Prophet belongs to Ali, his cousin and son-in-law, and his male descendants, referred to as Imams. Twelver or Imami Shiʿa believe in the line of twelve Imams; the last
Imam, the Mahdi, is in Occultation, and he will reappear at the end of time to establish justice.

followed the rule of hejab." My marriage also began to fall apart, and I learned that the shari'a contract I had signed left me at my husband's mercy: he would neither agree to a divorce nor give me permission to leave the country. My only option was to negotiate my release in courts presided over by religious judges. I started to educate myself in shari'a family law, and learned it well enough to secure a divorce. By 1984 I was able to leave the country, and I returned to Cambridge.

As a research associate of the Department of Social Anthropology, I began a project on the theory and practice of shari'a family law, focusing on marital disputes and litigants' strategies. Between 1985 and 1989 I worked in family courts in Tehran and in the Moroccan cities of Salé, Rabat, and Casablanca. My focus soon shifted from the ways in which shari'a rules oppressed women to the ways in which women found their embedded contradictions empowering. In both countries, the court cases I witnessed and the records I examined showed women manipulating these contradictions and using the court and the law as an arena to renegotiate the terms of their marriages. Many of these women, like me, had succeeded in turning the most patriarchal elements of shari'a law to their advantage in order to achieve their personal or marital aims.[3]

My research in Morocco was the first fieldwork I had done outside Iran. Not being emotionally involved in the culture and the politics, I was able to keep some distance and be more an observer than a participant; at the same time, living at close quarters with Muslims from a different tradition gave me the intense culture shock I had not experienced when working in Iran. In both countries, however, I collected the same type of data and dealt with the same issues. My own divorce experience brought me close to the litigants (mostly women, in both countries). Meeting women outside court and asking them about their cases, I often started by relating how my own marriage broke down and how I obtained my divorce, which created an immediate bond between us. I soon noticed that each time I told my story it sounded different: I emphasized aspects of my experience that related to those of the woman I was talking to. I became increasingly sensitive to situations; to how different contexts produce different narratives, how one can control this production, how much depends on one's perspective, and how one can resolve what might seem obvious contradictions.[4]

I returned to Iran after four years' absence in April 1992 as a research fellow at Girton College, to pursue an earlier and rather different research interest, on the mystical tradition of the Ahl-e Haqq (People of the Truth) and their difficult relationship with the Islamic Republic. Nearly four years after the end of

---

[3] Mir-Hosseini 1993.
[4] Cf. Kondo 1986.

war with Iraq, I found Iran more relaxed; there was a wider range of journals to read, more tolerance of ideas, and a lively debate on women's rights in Islam. There were clear signs of the emergence of new discourses, evident in a number of articles appearing under various female and male names in women's journals. Intrigued by all this, I began preparing the project that eventually took me to Iran in autumn 1995, on the relationship between official (state) and unofficial (women's own) discourses on women's rights.

I found two journals of particular interest and significance. Both were launched in 1992 and grounded their gender discourses in Islam, but they took radically different positions. The first, *Payam-e Zan* (Woman's Message), based in Qom and run by male clerics, defended the shariʿa and the gender inequalities inherent in its legal rules. The second, *Zanan* (Women), based in Tehran and run by women, argued for gender equality on all fronts.

Zanan's stance was new in the context of Iranian politics. It advocated a brand of feminism that takes Islam as source of legitimacy, and made no apologies for drawing on Western feminist sources to argue for women's rights and a new reading of shariʿa texts. Each issue had a legal section that examined and debated the restrictions placed on women by shariʿa laws: from issue 4 (May 1992) on, the tone and style of these articles started to change, slowly but surely taking issue with the very premises on which the official Shiʿi discourse on the position of women is based, and laying bare their inherent gender bias. These articles were unprecedented: first, they made no attempt to cover up or to rationalize the gender inequalities embedded in shariʿa law; second, they had something new to say, a thesis; there was consistency in the approach and the progression of the argument. Each article built on the premises and arguments established in earlier ones. It was evident that they were written by a single person, someone well versed in the sacred sources and in the Shiʿi art of argumentation. I was curious to know who the author was.

In November 1993, I met Shahla Sherkat, editor of *Zanan*. I found that my guess was correct and that the legal articles were all written by one man, Seyyed Mohsen Saʿidzadeh, a Qom cleric whom she jokingly referred to as a "one-man band." I expressed interest in meeting him, but she seemed hesitant and reluctant, and I did not insist. I found Sherkat's own stance refreshing: she was devoutly religious, yet neither apologetic nor defensive about Islam, and openly associated herself with feminism, which was (and still is) officially reviled in the Islamic Republic. I learned that she had played a prominent role in the Islamization of the woman's press in the early years of the revolution. In 1982 she was invited to join the Kayhan Publishing Institute as the editor of *Zan-e Ruz* (Woman of Today), the women's weekly that had the highest circulation in the pre-revolutionary period, and she remained there until 1991, when she left because of unresolved disagreements over the ways in which gender issues were being addressed.

There was a similar new gender awareness among many religious women of different ages whom I came to know in Iran—although very few of them had the courage to admit it or chose to have such an active presence as Sherkat. I could also see echoes of a new awareness in myself and in other women, both in Iran and abroad, who had a secular background, although our movement was in a reverse direction: we no longer blamed Islam for all women's problems. Such developments indicated the emergence of an indigenous—locally produced—feminism. But I had difficulty in locating this feminism; its mode of expression was discursive and lucid, but by Western feminist arguments and standards its discourse was contradictory and logically untenable. Athough it was certainly not an organized movement, it was more than mere consciousness, and was acquiring voice and legitimacy. I also realized that if I was to locate and understand it, analysis of spoken or written texts was not enough; I must learn about their producers, the protagonists, and where they are located within the wider sociopolitical structures of the Islamic Republic.

Between 1993 and 1995, a number of United Nations consultancies took me to various parts of Iran, both rural and urban, where I met and talked with women from different walks of life. I also had access to women working in government, and contacted women who had contributed to gender debates through either their writings or their activities in women's organizations. In time, I made close friendships with some of these women, who came from very different backgrounds and held divergent views.

In April 1995, the lawyer Mehrangiz Kar and the publisher Shahla Lahiji organized a meeting for me with Saʿidzadeh, the cleric who wrote for *Zanan*. Both women had already started a kind of collaboration with him. Kar came to know him after he wrote in her defense when her first article in *Zanan* (on gender biases in penal law) was attacked as "questioning the shariʿa."[5] She had recommended him to the Iranian Women's Studies Foundation (of North America) as a speaker for their conference in Toronto in June 1995, "Women, Sexuality and Islam," at which I was also to speak. Lahiji was attempting to publish a manuscript by Saʿidzadeh, "The Freedom of Women in Mohammad's Time." I had just completed a paper in which I analyzed *Zanan*'s legal articles, pointing out their novel approach and their potential for shifting the shariʿa-based gender discourse onto new ground.[6] At the meeting with Saʿidzadeh we discussed my paper; he agreed with my analysis of his writings, which he was obviously having difficulty publishing. His relationship with *Zanan* was tense, and the manuscript he had submitted to Lahiji's press was unlikely to be approved by the Ministry of Guidance. We decided to collaborate: he provided me with his unpublished manuscripts to study, and I invited him to stay in London for some days on his way back from Canada, during

[5] See Chapters Six and Eight.
[6] Mir-Hosseini 1996b.

which time he also talked at an informal gathering in the School of Oriental and African Studies.

Saʿidzadeh gave me insights that I have come to value into the clerical way of life and thinking; he introduced me to debates on gender issues in Qom, and he enlightened me about the politics of women's journals in Iran—he was also writing articles for *Payam-e Zan*. Working with him brought a second shift in my views, and forced me to reexamine many of my earlier conclusions. By now, I was getting personally, even passionately, involved in the debates in a way I never had before.

It was against this background that I went to Iran in autumn 1995. My three productive months of fieldwork coincided with the United Nations Women's Conference in Beijing, the anniversaries of the birth and death of Fatima (the Prophet's daughter), and the annual Women's Week, all occasions that triggered lively public debate on women's rights in Islam; I followed all this keenly, attended numerous private and public women's gatherings, and interviewed prominent women, including the Iranian delegates to Beijing.

I also accompanied Saʿidzadeh a number of times to Qom, the center of Shiʿi religious learning and power in Iran. He arranged meetings for me with clerics who had differing views on gender. It was my first exposure to Qom and the style of life of clerics there. The strict codes of gender segregation and hejab that organize time and space meant that I spent most of my time with women. Saʿidzadeh's teenage daughter Zahra, who had lost her mother when she was five, was always present, and I became attached to her. In Qom, I stayed in the house of a pious preacher of modest means; his home was small, consisting of three connecting rooms and a courtyard that housed the washing and toilet facilities. He had six children, one of them a boy of eighteen, yet gender segregation was so effectively maintained and the space so innovatively divided by curtains that I never set eyes on this young man, nor he on me, as I was told. I also spent long hours with the women of this family and many others in Qom, many of whom saw no contradiction between Islam and their rights as women, and wholeheartedly believed in and drew power from all the rules that I saw as limiting and disempowering to women.

Through Saʿidzadeh, I established a dialogue with clerics in *Payam-e Zan*; they in turn arranged a meeting with Ayatollah Saneʿi, who had held one of the highest-ranking judicial posts in the first decade of Islamic Republic, but now devoted himself to bringing shariʿa interpretations in line with the present state of society. My tape recordings of discussions with these clerics are among the only materials that I retained—I had left copies of them in Tehran. Besides, in the first half of 1996, *Payam-e Zan* in six successive issues published its edited transcripts of these discussions. Later, extracts from my interview with Ayatollah Saneʿi also appeared in two other journals: a monthly in Iran, which welcomed the dialogue as evidence of new interpretations and of the ability of the shariʿa to accommodate women's aspirations; and an opposition weekly in

London, which mocked the dialogue as evidence of the absurdity of shari'a rules in the modern world.[7]

In 1997 I traveled to Iran twice, in very different circumstances. In January I went for a month, combining work with a visit to my family, a pattern I have followed ever since moving to England. Having completed the first two parts of this book in rough draft, I needed to update them and look for fresh material for Part Three. Sa'idzadeh and Zahra came with me to Qom and helped fill in details of the Houzeh careers of the protagonists in Parts One and Two. I revisited the places I had written about, to check the accuracy of my descriptions.

While in Iran, I followed up an application by filmmaker Kim Longinotto and myself, submitted the previous spring through the London embassy, to make a documentary film about women and family law. We were advised to discuss our project with officials at the Ministry of Guidance, who had so far failed to respond to our application. Kim and I were excited about the possibility of making a film together in Iran; we shared the same frustration with Western media images and stereotypes of Muslim women, particularly women in Iran.

Working with Kim on the film project involved lobbying British television executives for funding and Iranian officials for access and permission. I found myself in an uncannily familiar situation of shifting perspectives and self-redefinition: as well as refocusing my views on the complex politics involved in the representation of women, I once more had to confront, articulate, and honor my own multiple identities. During my debates with clerics in Qom, I had to justify my feminism; now I wanted to articulate the Muslim and Iranian aspects of my identity.

In Tehran we talked about our project to people ranging from independent filmmakers, who were anti-clerical in their outlook, to officials in television, the Ministry of Guidance, women's organizations, and so on. We needed to convince them that a film about marital problems, shot in the family courts, need not present a negative image of women in the Islamic Republic. We had to distinguish what we (and we hoped our target audiences) saw as positive from what many people we talked to saw as negative, with the potential of turning into yet another sensationalized foreign film on Iran. We argued that images and words can evoke different feelings in different cultures; for instance, a mother talking of the loss of her children in war as martyrdom for Islam is more likely in Western eyes to confirm stereotypes of religious zealotry and fanaticism than to evoke the Shi'i ideal of sacrifice for justice and freedom. In the end, we persuaded some of the authorities that if we presented viewers with social reality as complex and allowed them to make up their own minds, this could give a more positive image of Iran.

[7] See Chapter Five.

In February I left for London, intending to return in April, before the May presidential elections, to make the film while those who had approved it were still in office. I took back a case full of journals, newspaper cuttings, and notes, and resumed work on the book, reassured that my focus for Part Three was the right one.

Then in April I heard that my mother had been diagnosed with advanced cancer. I returned to Tehran to be with her, and to see what could be done. For the first time since I had left in my teens I was home as a daughter, not for work. Meanwhile the permit for the film had not materialized, so we had to postpone the project. My stay in Iran (I returned to London in late June) co-incided with the presidential elections of 23 May, when thirty million of the electorate of thirty-three million participated, and over twenty million voted for Mohammad Khatami, the candidate who argued for peace, tolerance, rationality, freedom, and the rule of law. It was a watershed, opening a new phase in the Islamic Republic: some are already calling it the Third Republic.

In recent years, largely through me, my mother had become increasingly interested in women's issues and in politics. Each time I was in Tehran, I would share with her my findings and my discussions with the clerics and with women, and I brought her journals to read. It was different this time: now I was there because of her, and rarely left home; but a lot was happening, and the world outside was brought into our house through newspapers and television, and by our neighbors and relatives. On the streets outside, we could hear busloads of schoolgirls shouting for Khatami. When I arrived, my mother was still interested in the outside world; I showed her the latest issue of *Zanan* featuring a photograph of a smiling Khatami—a rare sight in clerics. She was determined to vote for him. But she never made it to the polls; she died three days later.

This book narrates one debate among many that have paved the way for the Third Republic. The main theme is the varying notions of gender that inform Islamic jurisprudence (*feqh*) and the ways in which Shi'i clerics in Iran today attempt variously to perpetuate, modify, deconstruct, and reconstruct these notions. The theme is pursued through a series of texts representing the three dominant gender perspectives in the theological seminaries of Qom. Part One discusses the perspective of clerics from the pre-revolutionary seminary system. Part Two discusses the views of clerics involved in creating the new seminary system but not prepared to challenge directly the old ways of thinking. Part Three deals with an emerging new discourse on women, influenced by Islamic intellectuals outside the seminaries, but very much rooted in the shari'a.

Two painful losses helped to conceive and induce the book. Its present format was inspired by the loss of my field notes in 1995; knowing that my data and my inner thoughts were in the hands of people with whom I would have never chosen to share them, I found I could reconcile my academic aim of impartiality with my personal engagements in feminist discourse and Islam. The loss of my mother eighteen months later made me realize how much women of different generations live through each other, and the strange ways we are interconnected. In this book I have sought to narrate an ethnography of my engagement with a series of texts and their authors, in the hope of provoking other Muslim women to write more revealingly of their own changing engagements and trajectories. We need to know more of and about these trajectories if we are to explore the relationship between feminism and religious politics, and to articulate the emergence of indigenous feminisms.

Acknowledgments ———————————————

THE RESEARCH that eventually led to this book began when I was still a research fellow at Girton College in Cambridge. Field trips to Iran in 1995 and 1997 were funded by the Nuffield Foundation and the British Institute for Persian Studies. I am grateful to them for their generous help and support.

Between December 1995 and February 1998 I presented a paper based on the data and some of the arguments of the book in various forums: Institut für Iranistik, Frei Universität Berlin; Carsten Niebühr Institute of Near Eastern Studies, University of Copenhagen; the Middle East Study Group in London; the conference on Gender and Society in the Muslim World at Royal Holloway College, University of London; the annual meeting of the British Society for Middle East Studies at Oxford University; and the Seventh Annual Critique Symposium at Hamline University, St. Paul, Minnesota. This last paper was published as an article in the journal *Critique*. I am grateful to Maria Macuch, Connie Caroe Christensen and Lene Kofoed Rasmussen, Sami Zubaida, Vanessa Martin and Sara Ansari, Haleh Afshar, and Nasrin Jewell for inviting me to air my ideas on those occasions, and to Eric Hooglund for his careful editorial comments on the article.

My thanks are due to Dale Eickelman and Mary Murrell for their careful readings of the manuscript. Dale's incisive comments and good sense were of great value and reassurance throughout. Mary has been the best editor an author could ask for, and the book owes much to her wisdom and sensitivity. Azam Torab also read the book in draft and discussed it at length with me; I benefited greatly from her perspective on gender issues in Iran. Richard Tapper gave me the initial strength to write in a way that I would not otherwise have dared and has continued to give me every encouragement, as well as meticulous editorial advice, throughout the gestation of the book.

My greatest debt is to the "characters" in the book, whose help, trust in me, and generosity with their time made the research for this book possible. Any errors are my responsibility.

Note on Language

Transliteration, Translation, and Technical Terms

WHENEVER POSSIBLE I use familiar English forms of Persian and Arabic terms and names, for example: ayatollah, chador, fatwa, halal, Imam, Koran; I have preferred shari'a to shariah, ulama to ulema.[1] Otherwise, for ease of reading and best approximation to actual pronunciation, I have tried to follow a simplified version of the transliteration system used by the journal *Iranian Studies*, using the full range of English vowels and confining diacritical marks to the glossary and bibliography, but maintaining 'ain (') and *hamzeh* (') except where initial in proper names. Arabic terms are usually transliterated in a Persianized form. Non-English terms are italicized when first introduced.

Persian is highly allusive and allegorical, qualities encapsulated in the notion and practice of *ta'arof*, a mixture of tact and politeness.[2] Ta'arof not only structures social relations and bridges hierarchical differences, it also allows paradoxes to be sustained and contradictions to be overlooked, even in a single sentence. For a reader unfamiliar with Persian, some sentences in the texts and transcripts will seem illogical; the speaker often starts by endorsing the other's point of view but ends by demolishing it. In translating them—by no means an easy task—I have tried to capture this fluidity and to allow double meanings and paradoxes to come across. With some hesitation, however, in order to make the texts more accessible to those who do not share the same religious world, I have omitted many of the religious references and phrases that saturate the language of the texts discussed: for example, the salutations that always accompany mention of the names of the Prophet and the Imams.

Islamic sciences, like any branches of science, are replete with technical terms, specialist jargon often used to mystify rather than clarify. In my encounters in Qom, I was struck by the frequent vagueness and lack of precision in clerics' use of technical terms, and how at times this filtered through to the everyday meanings of these terms—or was influenced by them. In deciding whether to translate such terms or to keep them in their original form, I have usually preferred the former wherever a simple English translation seems possible, capitalizing it (to mark its nature as a technical term) and noting any complexities when first using it. Examples are (divine) Law (my translation of *shar'*); (divine) Lawgiver (*share'*); Lawful (*shar'i*); (Legal) Ruling (*hokm*,

---

[1] All these words have entries in the *Concise Oxford English Dictionary* 8th ed. (Oxford: Clarendon Press, 1990).

[2] For a discussion of ta'arof at both linguistic and sociopolitical levels, see Beeman 1986.

hokm-e shar°i); Principle (*asl*, pl. *osul*); Jurist (*faqih*); Ethics (*akhlaq*); Theology (*kalam*).

Some key terms call for initial discussion because of multiple and indeterminate meanings, made clear only by the context and the user's intention. One such word, *hokm* (which I have translated as Ruling), in its singular form denotes: Koranic commandment, divine law, ruling, judgment, decision, order, command, sentence, decree; in the plural (*ahkam*), it means religious rulings, principles, precepts. Two other key words are *shar°* and *haqq*. The first, when used as a noun (which I have translated as Law), can mean religion, religious law, divine law, canon; in adjectival form (*shar°i*), which I have translated as Lawful, it can mean religious, legitimate, legal, lawful, permissible, licit, authorized, admissible, jural, de jure. Haqq, in the singular, has a multiplicity of meanings: right, correct, fair, sound, valid, genuine, authentic, title, claim, justice, God, truth, rightness, reality, certainty, and so on. I have translated it as seemed appropriate in context. In its plural form (*hoquq*), it means law (as a science), or salary.[3]

In translating these and other technical terms, I often follow precedents set, for example, by Arjomand, Fischer, Kamali, and Mottahedeh. In the absence of precedents, or when the context calls for alternatives, I have improvised with Richard Tapper's help. I have tried to give priority to semantic accuracy, but a measure of technicality and arbitrariness is perhaps inevitable in any translation, so I have tried not to isolate the English terms from their originals, which are repeated frequently throughout the book.

Some key terms are kept in their original form (translated and italicized when first used), leaving the context to illuminate their meanings: *ejtehad, feqh, hadith, haram, hejab, Houzeh, khadem, khoms, khol°, marja°(-e taqlid), marja°iyat, mojtahed, Seyyed, talaq, taqiyeh, velayat-e (vali-ye) faqih*. These terms are part of everyday vocabulary in Iran as well as the jurisprudential discourse of theological colleges in Qom. See the Glossary.

Quotations from the Koran are from the Shakir translation published in Iran (*Holy Quran* n.d.), and references are by name of Sura and verse.

[3] Cf. Mottahedeh 1995a, 94.

ISLAM AND GENDER

Introduction

Gender in Islam: The Need for Clarity

Women's issues and gender relations have been central to religious and political discourses in the Muslim world since early in this century. There is now a vast literature on women in Islam, and more recently gender in Islam. The whole literature has been ideologically charged, and has become an arena for polemics masquerading as scholarly debate: arguments about Islam as the main cause of women's subjugation, or as the panacea for women's problems; and more recently, arguments that Muslim societies have denied women their rightful status, or that Muslim jurists have misconstructed the Prophet's message of egalitarianism.[1]

Gender and Islam are huge, vague topics. Each is the subject of multiple discourses and widely ranging perspectives. The same is true of their conjunction, gender in Islam, a topic too often debated through broad generalizations or platitudes. It has been addressed at three levels. The first is that of the varied interpretations and reinterpretations of the sacred texts, which are invoked as sources of authority and legitimacy for particular ideologies or standpoints on women's rights, gender roles and relations, and so on. The second level is that of local and national political ideologies with their local historical particularities, which produce their own discourses on women and gender roles. Neither kind of discourse relates closely to the third level, that of the lived experiences of individuals and local communities: actual opportunities, power, control of resources and of self, employment, education, and gender roles and relations.

Debates about gender and Islam tend either to confine themselves to one level and ignore the others; or, more often, when polemics are involved, they follow the common (conscious or unconscious) rhetorical tactic of shifting between levels without acknowledgment. Most common is the device of comparing the ideals and rhetorics of a favored system with the practices and experiences in an opposing one. Clarity and honesty surely demand that we keep the three levels separate.

Those of us who research, think, write, and talk about gender in Islam must also be clear, both to ourselves and to our audiences, where we stand personally on issues that touch our innermost feelings of self.[2] I suggest that unless

---

[1] Useful general discussions can be found in the following: Beck and Keddie 1978, Bodman and Tohidi 1998, Fernea 1985, Göçek and Balaghi 1994, Haddad and Esposito 1998, Kandiyoti 1991 and 1996, Keddie and Baron 1991, Malti-Douglas 1992, Sabbagh 1996, El-Solh and Mabro 1994, Sonbol 1996, and Tucker 1993; for Iran, see the Bibliographic Essay.

[2] Some writers show an awareness of this dilemma, e.g., Accad 1991, Ahmed 1984 and 1992, Hoodfar 1996b, and Hussain 1984 (preface).

we are honest about our own personal, individual motives in participating, there will be no movement in the debate. I am not suggesting an individual or collective psychoanalysis, but an admission that each of us has a position. I often listen to colleagues, or read their writings, with a strong feeling that there is a conscious or unconscious agenda beneath what is presented as objectivity. I also know how difficult it is to recognize and talk about one's often very complex and contradictory identities and positions.

If we are Muslims, whether or not believing or practicing, Islam is part of our identity, our way of life, a culture, a system of values. We may be at ease with it, or find our position painful and ambiguous. If we are not Muslims, Islam is the "other"; but whoever we are, since Said's *Orientalism* our position is inevitably affected by a healthy skepticism toward common Western media representations of Islam as a unitary phenomenon like no other religion, incapable of development, reflection, or self-knowledge, and above all anti-woman. Here, the shariʿa takes center stage: its mandates on marriage and women's roles have made it for some time the gendered battleground between the forces of traditionalism and modernism in Islam. With globalization, deterritorialization, and the blurring of Islamic discourses with others, the battle is no longer contained within the Muslim world.[3]

There are complex issues here that have received much attention recently in anthropology and gender studies.[4] What I wish to stress is that it is sometimes hard to distinguish the personal from the political, and what we see from what we want to see, while claiming that we have retained any academic impartiality. No meaningful discussion of gender in Islam is possible unless we are prepared first, to be clear about the level at which we are arguing and to be honest when we shift between levels, and second, to bring our own perspectives and agendas to the surface. Otherwise, we risk being locked in old polemics or in essentialisms, and end up with nothing but clichés, platitudes, and sweeping generalizations.

All these, in my view, continue to bedevil much of the debate about Islam and gender, as reflected in the unending flow of "Women in Islam" titles in secular and religious publishing projects, both outside and inside the Muslim world. Leaving aside works written by *out*siders, among those originating *in*side the Muslim world two genres prevail.[5] The dominant genre comprises studies with a strong religious tone and content, mainly written by Muslim

---

[3] See an-Naʿim 1990, Eickelman and Piscatori 1996, and Watt 1988.

[4] I have found the following discussions particularly helpful: Abu-Lughod 1993 and B. Tedlock 1991.

[5] By no means do I intend my distinctions between outsiders and insiders, or between Western and indigenous feminisms, as categorical oppositions. I see them as elements, points, in a process. I focus on texts produced by Muslims themselves not because I consider those produced by non-Muslims to be of less value or relevance to the debate but because, as we shall see, it is a question of legitimacy and belonging.

men—and more recently women—for believers in their native language; these I would call "shariʿa-based." Their perspectives and arguments range from those of patriarchy to those of gender equality, but their positioning is clear: they write to defend Islam against a perceived attack by the West, and by Western feminists in particular.[6]

The second major genre includes works with a feminist slant, written largely by women of Muslim background and culture, often in English or French and not necessarily for a religious audience. These writings—let us call them "feminism-based"—are by authors as diverse as Haleh Afshar, Leila Ahmed, Riffat Hassan, Azizah al-Hibri, Nilüfer Göle, Fatima Mernissi, Nawal al-Saadawi, and Amina Wadud-Muhsin. Their positioning is neither uniform nor simple. Some clearly locate their feminism in Islam, others make a point of distancing themselves from any Islamic association.[7]

Despite the fact that writers in both genres take an insider position, there has been almost no dialogue between them.[8] It is not just that they speak different languages, literally and metaphorically, but they also use different modes of argumentation and belong to two different scholarly traditions. Yet they have much in common. Both are responding to the changed position of Muslim women, their new gender awareness, and their aspirations for full participation and equality in society. Also, both are highly skilled in shifting between the three levels, in particular when they represent and respond to the arguments put forward by their opponents. In so doing, writers in each genre become hostages to the terms of the very discourse they intend to subvert, whether Islamist or feminist, and often end up generalizing and essentializing in similar ways.

Although few of those involved seem prepared to admit it, there has recently been a kind of rapprochement, in the sense that writers in the two genres are increasingly coming to follow the same route in their quest. Compare, for instance, Fatima Mernissi's *Le harem politique*, published in 1987, with her *Beyond the Veil: Male-Female Dynamics in Muslim Society*, published over a decade earlier. Not only is Mernissi's approach different but the way she frames her argument has changed. Earlier she sought to expose the patriarchal inner logic of Islamic texts; now she does exactly what writers in the first genre do, that is, she seeks new meanings in the sacred texts to throw a new, less

[6] For a discussion of such writings in Arabic, see Haddad 1998, and Stowasser 1993; for those in English see, e.g., Amini n.d., Doi 1989 and 1993, Khan 1995, Lemu and Heeren 1976, Mesbah et al. 1985, Motahhari 1991, and Nazlee 1996.

[7] Among them, Wadud-Muhsin and Hassan clearly locate their feminism in Islam, Afshar and Göle identify themselves as secular feminists, and the others fall somewhere in between. See Badran 1995b and 1997.

[8] Since the mid-1980s, women's networks such as "Sisters in Islam" (including Wadud-Muhsin), and WLUML (Women Living under Muslim Laws) have tried to establish such a dialogue, but neither secular feminists nor Islamic scholars have yet given due acknowledgment to the importance of their work. On WLUML, see Shaheed 1994.

patriarchal, light on gender relations in Islam. Compare, too, Haleh Afshar's early writings on the impact of the 1978–79 revolution on women in Iran with her writings of the 1990s. Whereas in the early 1980s she saw no way that women could realize their rights within an Islamic Republic, ten years later she has taken a partisan position on behalf of those in Iran whom she calls "Islamic feminists."[9]

What has happened during the past decade to bring a change of heart in Afshar and a change of style in Mernissi? I hope that these writers will at some time write explicitly about their own trajectories, and theorize how and why their conceptions of gender in Islam have changed. The change cannot be explained away by external changes. Is it a matter of tactical moves, in the sense that the end justifies the means? Or have their interpretations and understandings of Islam changed?

It seems clear that—for whatever reasons—some writers of the feminism-based genre have moved toward positions taken by some writers of the other genre: they are at least prepared to listen to them, to take them seriously, and to borrow something of their arguments and approaches. At the same time, shariʿa-based writers are making similar, recipocal movements in the other direction.[10] Here the reasons are rather clearer. One neglected and paradoxical outcome of the rise of political Islam in the 1970s was that it helped to create an arena within which Muslim women could reconcile their faith with their new gender awareness. This has happened at all three levels: textual interpretation, political ideology, and personal experience. Thus we have the emergence, now widely debated, of an Islamic feminism in the form of feminist readings of the shariʿa, with repercussions at the other levels.

My own initial premise is that gender roles and relations, and women's rights, are not fixed, not given, not absolute. They are negotiated and changing cultural constructs, produced in response to lived realities, through debates that are now going on all over the Muslim world, through the voices of women and men who want either to retain or to change the present situation. They exist in and through the ways in which we talk about them, both publicly and privately, and as we study and write about what gender relations and women's rights in Islam are and can be.

Second, I understand "feminism" in its widest sense: as a general concern with women's issues; an awareness that women suffer discrimination at work, in the home, and in society because of their gender; and action aimed at improving their lives and changing the situation. Although some Muslim women feel uneasy with the term "feminism," I retain it because I believe that it is important to locate women's demands in a political context that is not isolated from women's movements and experiences elsewhere in the world. Feminism

[9] See Afshar 1982, 1987, 1994, 1996, and most recently 1998.
[10] See Stowasser 1993, 1994, and 1998.

is part of twentieth-century politics, and only through participation in this global feminist politics can Muslim women benefit from it and influence its agenda.[11] Moreover, since 1992 there has been a growing movement among women in Iran (such as those in *Zanan*) who remain involved in the politics of the Islamic Republic and call themselves feminist, making no apologies for using the term and drawing on Western feminist sources.

Finally, I argue that Islam and feminism are not incompatible. Feminist readings of the shari'a are not only possible today but even inevitable when Islam is no longer an oppositional discourse in national politics but the official ideology. This is so because once the custodians of the shari'a are in power and able to legislate, they have to deal with the contradiction between their political agenda and their rhetoric: they must both uphold the family, restoring women to their "true and high" status in Islam, and at the same time retain the patriarchal mandates of shari'a legal rules. This tension has always been inherent in the practice of the shari'a, but when the shari'a becomes part of the apparatus of a modern nation state, its custodians may have to accommodate, even seek, novel interpretations. This opens room for change on a scale that has no precedent in Islamic history.

Perspectives on Women in Post-Revolutionary Iran

Iran is the main instance. After the 1978–79 Islamic Revolution, feminists examined the stated intention of the Islamic regime: a return to shari'a and the enforcement of hejab. Some made dire predictions about the fate of women, and that they would be condemned to the status of chattels.[12]

A generation after the revolution, such predictions have not been fulfilled. On the contrary, there have been unexpected developments. First, not only have women not been excluded from public life and politics but their participation has actually increased, although in different guises and according to different rules.[13] Paradoxically, the enforcement of *hejab* became a catalyst here: by making public space morally correct in the eyes of traditionalist families, it legitimized women's public presence. Second, there are clear signs

[11] Uneasiness with the term is shared by a number of Third World and Black women (cf. Mohanty 1991 and Johnson-Odim 1991, 316). In recognition of this, Margot Badran suggests "gender activism" (1994, 202). Although Third World feminists have shown the extent to which feminism is part of the political process, religion is still seen as not being conducive to feminism; see Mahmood 1996.

[12] This includes the bulk of literature on women in Iran from the early 1980s, which I call the "first wave." See the Bibliographic Essay.

[13] This is most evident in the field of education, where by 1996 over 33 percent of university students were female, including 49 percent in medicine. As regards women's participation in the labor market, there are divergent views. Some studies (F. E. Moghadam 1994, Omid 1994) argue that there has been a substantial decrease, others (Khalatbari 1998, V. Moghadam 1988) deny this.

of the emergence of feminist rereadings of shariʿa texts, manifested in two currents.

The first, which reflects a shift in the official gender discourse, is evident in a number of laws, some of which amount to a reversal of the early decisions of the revolutionary regime. They include the removal of earlier bans on women studying topics such as mining and agriculture, and serving as judges.[14] The most conspicuous reversal is in the area of family law. Shortly after the revolution, the Family Protection Law of 1967, which curtailed men's rights to arbitrary divorce, was dismantled and its courts were abolished, on the ground that it was in contradiction with the shariʿa. The Amendments to Divorce Regulations, enacted in 1992, in effect reinstate the rejected elements of the Family Protection Law, though under a different legal logic.[15]

The second feminist current reflects an internal tension and debate among the Shiʿi clerics and intellectuals, and among women from different walks of life, both inside and outside the country. It is here that one can detect the emergence of a new discourse on women, which is feminist in both tone and inclination. One forum inside Iran is women's journals, in particular *Zanan*, which has brought about a rapprochement between religious and secular women.[16] Others include the Majles, the Houzeh (the Qom seminaries), and women's groups and associations. Some protagonists in this debate subscribed to the early shariʿa discourse when it was still part of the Islamic opposition to the Pahlavis, and helped translate it from rhetoric into policy after the establishment of the Islamic Republic. During this process some of these women (and men) had to confront the patriarchal biases of shariʿa laws, and became aware that they could find support in feminism, regardless of its Western baggage, whereas they could meet only resistance in patriarchy, regardless of its Islamic credentials.

Iranians educated and living in the West have also played important roles in the formation of new discourses on women, through the substantial literature on women in post-revolutionary Iran. Taking a secular feminist perspective, and writing in English or French, they commonly depict the revolution as having been a catastrophe for Iranian women. Their writings have also influenced, and continue to influence, Western perceptions of post-revolutionary events in Iran. At the same time, they have enabled women inside Iran, operating within the restrictions imposed by the Islamic Republic, to formulate some of their demands, and the regime to produce a counter-discourse.

Yet these writers have so far avoided a critical engagement with Islamic premises on gender. One reason is that the general acceptance in Middle East-

---

[14] Women have been advisory judges since 1992, and in 1998 the first woman judge was appointed. A number of works have commented on these changes, e.g., Ramazani 1993, Paidar 1995 (chapter 9), Hoodfar 1994a and 1996a, and Kian 1995a and 1997a.

[15] See Mir-Hosseini 1996a, 1998a; and Paidar 1995 (chapter 8).

[16] See Najmabadi 1998.

ern studies of a modernization paradigm, with its implicit progressive and activist approach, combined with an uncritical adoption of theories of women's movements in the West, continue to blur the actual experiences of women and the politics of gender in the contemporary Muslim world.[17] Current narratives of gender in Islam are grounded in assumptions that should be reexamined in order to make room for the emergence of feminist theories based on the actual politics of gender in Muslim societies in which religion is a paramount element.

Another reason is to be found in the vexed relation between feminism and religion. Saba Mahmood singles out "two core issues around which feminism's discomfort with religion is articulated: one is the claim that religion is largely a male enterprise, and has historically granted women a subordinate position; two, is the more recent phenomenon of the resurgence of politicoreligious movements (in the US, the Middle East and South Asia) whose goals are considered to be inimical to women's interests."[18] This is part of the general, uncomfortable ambivalence many Muslims feel with the religious aspects of their identity, and with their relation to the West. As Leila Ahmed notes, loyalty has been a major issue in discourses of the Muslim world, not least in regard to feminism. Muslim women have always been aware of gender inequality, but since the nineteenth century feminist consciousness has been articulated mainly in the context of nationalist and anticolonial movements, and largely by the middle and upper classes.[19] Unlike feminists in the West who could be critical of androcentric elements in their culture and religion, Muslim feminists have been under pressure to conform. Any dissent could be construed as a kind of betrayal, which made it difficult for them to use the existing political vocabulary to express feminist demands.[20] This is no longer the case. Since the 1970s, with the growth of mass literacy and mass media, and the rise of Islamist movements with mass participation,[21] loyalty is no longer the issue, and feminist critiques and demands are very much part of the postcolonial politics of the Muslim world.

In Iran, as elsewhere in the Muslim world, women who acquired a feminist consciousness in either a Western or an indigenous form have always faced a tension between the different components of their identity: their Muslimness is perceived as backward and oppressed, yet authentic and innate; their feminism as progressive and emancipated, yet corrupt and alien. Over time, the Iranian revolution deepened the perceived divide between Islam and feminism,

---

[17] For ways in which certain assumptions, rather than actual women's experiences and cultural and historical specificities, have defined the history of relations between women and Islamic law, see various contributions in Sonbol 1996; with respect to Algerian women, see Lazreg 1994.

[18] Mahmood 1996, 2; cf. Gerami 1996.

[19] For Egypt, see Ahmed 1992 and Badran 1995a; for Iran, see Najmabadi 1991, Paidar 1996, and Sanasarian 1982.

[20] Ahmed 1984, 121–22. Cf. Badran 1997, Ghossoub 1987, and Lazreg 1988.

[21] See Eickelman 1992 and 1998.

forcing many Iranian women—both religious and secular—to reexamine and redefine the relation between their faith and feminism, thus opening a new phase in the politics of gender in Muslim societies and fostering a new gender awareness. A crucial element in this politics is that it has created a space in which a critique of the fundamental gender assumptions in Islamic law can be sustained in ways that were impossible until very recently.

Narrative and Debate in Ethnographic Writing

I write as a "native" anthropologist.[22] My involvement with the politics of gender in Iran, and indeed my own feminist awareness, did not begin until many years after the revolution. My experiences and views thus differ from those of Iranian women who were engaged in the early phases of the revolution, and whose writings form the main body of the English and French literature on women in post-revolutionary Iran.[23] I neither advocate an alternative model of gender relations as defended by clerics in Iran nor condemn their vision of gender, as their feminist critics have done. Rather, I seek to understand the key assumptions and premises in Islamic law that have so far delayed a serious engagement between the two positions.

This requires the establishment of a non-confrontational dialogue with the clerical protagonists. The main body of this book narrates my engagement with a number of texts and my interviews with their authors. In this, I hope to contribute to ongoing debates on the production of ethnographic texts. Recent ethnographic writing has placed authors back on the page, insisting that they examine how far their own identities and experiences have influenced their textual constructions of ethnographic reality, in order "to enable the reader to identify the consciousness which has selected and shaped the experiences within the text."[24] The importance of this was brought home to me when I read *Payam-e Zan*'s version of our discussions. By changing the order in which the issues were raised, with minor omissions and additions, they constructed their own text, which, as we shall see, differs from mine—as indeed our target audiences differ: whereas theirs is scholars in the seminaries and other religious people in Iran, mine is predominantly non-Muslims and secularists outside the country.

[22] I use the term not only to indicate my country of origin, but in a sense of a certain consciousness, and the way in which it interacts with the anthropological epistemology that is rooted in Western traditions. As Barbara Tedlock notes, "Just as being born female does not automatically result in 'feminist' consciousness, being born an ethnic minority does not automatically result in 'native' consciousness" (1991, 80). This consciousness, for Tedlock, distinguishes "native" from "indigenous" anthropologists.

[23] For an overview of this literature, see the Bibliographic Essay.

[24] B. Tedlock 1991, 77–78; see also Altorki and Fawzi el-Solh, 1988, 1–23.

11

The resumption of authorial responsibility in ethnographic writing in recent years has been accompanied by recognition of two important features of dialogue. First, it is in the dialogue between ethnographer and subjects that "culture" is produced. Second, dialogue, conversation, and debate actually change the participants' views and perceptions—their "culture."[25] In this book, much of which is a transcription of actual dialogues, I hope both aspects will be well illustrated: how cultural notions of "gender in Islam" are produced in these dialogues, and how all participants learn from them and change their views.

The dialogues narrated in the book represent encounters between different worldviews: between adherents of Islamic discourses on gender who are trying to respond to challenges presented by women, and Muslim women like me, with complex identities, who seek to reconcile their feminism with their faith. Some of the chapters—particularly those in Part Two—constitute an account of two different conceptual frameworks and modes of argumentation about gender issues. The clerics are guided by their own gender and life experiences, and by the theories and assumptions that inform their discipline, that is, Islamic sciences and jurisprudence as taught in the seminaries. As a Muslim woman and a social anthropologist educated and working in the West, I am guided by a different set of life experiences and academic theories and assumptions. To my knowledge, in the literature on women in Islam there is no account of such a face-to-face encounter, either between these two disciplines or between the two genders.

Religious Authority and Knowledge in Post-Revolutionary Iran

The central concern of this book, like that of two earlier studies of Qom clerics—Michael Fischer's *Iran: From Religious Dispute to Revolution*, and Roy Mottahedeh's *The Mantle of the Prophet: Religion and Politics in Iran*—is the production of religious knowledge in Shi'i Islam, and the complex relationship between the believer, religious authority, and political action. But I start at the point in time when they finish—the revolution—and I put the focus on a subject that was marginal in their work—women. Mottahedeh makes not one reference to women. In Fischer's book, the only time an individual woman appears is when he relates the expulsion of a female school principal at the wishes of a male religious leader;[26] otherwise, like Mottahedeh he invokes women only in the context of marriages among the Shi'i leadership, or of political discourses about them.

[25] For useful discussions, see Abu-Lughod 1993, Clifford and Marcus 1986, Clifford 1988, B. Tedlock 1991, and D. Tedlock 1987.
[26] Fischer 1980, 113.

The creation of the Islamic Republic has brought about major transformations not only in the notion of authority in Shi'i Islam but also in the relationship between ordinary believers and religious power. Before the revolution, the institution of *marja'iyat* encapsulated the notion of supreme authority in the Shi'i world, embodied in the person of the *marja'-e taqlid*, the "source of emulation." A uniquely Shi'i institution that emerged in the nineteenth century, the marja'iyat is the product of a historical convergence of belief, epistemology, and organization.[27] The first, belief, refers to the Shi'i doctrine of Imamate, according to which the Twelve Shi'i Imams are the main sources of religious knowledge, and the believer must look to them for guidance. During the period of Absence, following the Occultation of the twelfth Imam, the ulama act as his deputies.

The epistemological base is the Shi'i theory of *ejtehad*, which holds that, although the fundamentals of the shari'a are clear, most of its details are uncertain and difficult to discern; they are a matter of informed opinion, not knowledge; they can be accessed, with extreme effort (*ejtehad*), only by the *mojtaheds*, those with knowledge of the sacred sources, skill, and piety, to whose authority the rest of the Shi'a must submit. This submission, known as *taqlid* (emulation), is offered to the most learned mojtahed of the time, to whom the believer "refers" (Arabic *raja'*, hence marja') for guidance. Ideally, at any given time there should be only one marja', to whom other mojtaheds defer and whose rulings then are binding on all Shi'is. In other words, his leadership is recognized both by the universal consensus of ordinary Shi'is and by the clerical establishment. In practice, this is not always the case.

The organizational base of the marja'iyat derives from the fact that Shi'is pay their special religious tax—the *khoms* (fifth)—to their marja', and these funds have enabled Shi'i clerics, unlike their Sunni counterparts, to remain autonomous and independent of the state. The khoms is an annual tax levied on net income and wealth (after paying all expenses). In theory, half this tax should go to Seyyeds, orphans, the needy, and travelers, and a believer is free to administer it personally. The other half, known as the *sahm-e Emam*, the share of the (Hidden) Imam, should be paid to the marja' in his capacity as the Imam's deputy. In practice, believers often send the entire khoms to their marja', via his representatives all over the Shi'i world, and leave its administration to him. With these funds, seminaries are built, stipends are paid to teachers and students, mosques and hospitals are paid for, the needy are fed, and so on. No questions are asked: there is no compulsion on either side. Believers are free to choose when to pay their religious dues and to whom. The marja' is free to use the dues as he thinks fit. The system rests and operates on complete trust and freedom of choice.

[27] For the historical organization of the Shi'i clergy, see Algar 1969, Arjomand 1984 and 1988, Calder 1995, Mallat 1993, Momen 1985, and Richard 1991.

Although in practice selection of a marja‘ is in the hands of a few seminary scholars, the procedure is informal and gradual, and above all, it must to be seen to be free from any government or outside interference. One element is the publication of a *resaleh ‘amaliyeh* (Practical Treatise), commonly known as *resaleh*, which can be done only after the death of one's own marja‘, one's teacher and mentor, whose followers are now looking for a living mojtahed to whom they can refer. A treatise contains no legal arguments or explanations; it is a kind of compendium of legal opinions, with a fixed format, starting with Rulings (*ahkam*, pl. of *hokm*) about ritual acts such as prayers and fasting, and proceeding to those relating to contracts, such as marriage, divorce, and so on. Through a treatise, a cleric establishes not only his mastery of the fundamentals and specifics of Shi‘i law but also his fidelity to authority and tradition; the format ensures that he remains faithful to the approach of those whose path he follows.

The second element is a core group of students and supporters who can actively campaign for the emerging marja‘. This again must await the death of a marja‘; only then can his followers divert their support to a senior student who has been marked out. The process is informal, and a successor gradually emerges and establishes himself. Everything must be done by his entourage: his students, his sons, his sons-in-law. He is judged for his piety, his religious knowledge, his scholarship, his austerity, and his disdain for worldly affairs and office.

At the eve of the 1978-79 revolution in Iran, apart from Ayatollah Khomeini there were five other marja‘ in the Shi‘i world. Each had his followers and supporters among ordinary Shi‘is all over the world and among clerics and students in various seminaries.[28] They were equal in rank and religious authority; none was recognized as sole marja‘, and none had a modern state apparatus at his disposal. The revolution changed the balance forever. None of the others shared Khomeini's vision of an Islamic government built on his concept of *velayat-e faqih* (mandate of the jurist), which establishes the authority of one single jurist over all others. Yet none could overtly challenge or oppose either Khomeini or his concept, which later became enshrined in the constitution of the Islamic Republic and was ratified in the referendum of December 1979. Nor could the new notion of leadership of the Shi‘i world accommodate the old one.

As the Islamic Republic consolidated itself, a structural contradiction between the two notions of supreme authority—the marja‘iyat and the velayat-e faqih—became increasingly evident. The first has no overt political claims, having evolved through a tacit consensus between Shi‘i masses and clerics.

---

[28] Ayatollah Khoi'i (d. 1992) lived in Najaf, the rest in Iran: Ayatollahs Shari‘at-Madari (d. 1982), Mar‘ashi-Najafi (d. 1992), and Golpaygani (d. 1993) in Qom, and Khonsari (d. 1985) in Tehran; see Momen 1985, 249, and Fischer 1980, 88.

The second, the child of the revolution, exerts power over and demands allegiance from all Shiʿis. It has no precedent in Shiʿi political thought: it invests the ruling jurist with the kind of powers and mandate that Shiʿi theology only recognizes for the Prophet and the twelve Infallible Imams.[29]

By 1988, the tension between these two notions of authority intensified and brought on a constitutional crisis. There was conflict not only between clerical supporters and opponents of velayat-e faqih but also between factions within the ruling elite, who held differing views of authority. The resignation in March 1989 of Khomeini's designated successor, Ayatollah Montazeri, added a new edge to the tension. Montazeri was the most senior clerical supporter of velayat-e faqih, the only one whose marjaʿiyat was recognized. The crisis was resolved when Ayatollah Khomeini himself gave his blessing to the separation of velayat and marjaʿiyat: the constitution was revised accordingly.[30]

With Khomeini's death in June 1989, the concept of velayat-e faqih and the legitimacy of its mandate had to be renewed. Khomeini's charisma was routinized: whoever replaced him as Leader (*rahbar*) of the revolution would depend more on the state for legitimacy. Thus the Leadership had to be institutionalized and become firmly grounded in the apparatus of the modern state. The divorce between the two notions of authority in the Islamic Republic was now complete. President Ali Khameneʾi became the new Leader; Majles speaker Ali Akbar Hashemi Rafsanjani became president following general elections in July, and simultaneously a popular referendum ratified the revised constitution.

In summer 1995, when I was in Qom, the concept of authority in Shiʿism was the subject of lively debate—which history shows to be the sign of the passing of an era and the beginning of a new one.[31] Clerics fell into two main camps. Some supported the velayat-e faqih and saw a merger with the marjaʿiyat as inevitable. They argued that the old notion of authority embodied in the marjaʿ is no longer viable in today's world of real politics: it is no longer acceptable for a marjaʿ to be knowledgeable solely in religious matters and to confine his rulings to them; he must assume Shiʿi leadership on all fronts. This camp was clearly politically dominant, and hence most outspoken. Its theological arguments were published in periodicals financed by the Houzeh (the Qom seminaries), where topics such as the qualities of the Shiʿi Leader, the selection process, and the system of payment of religious dues are debated.[32] Their argu-

[29] See Arjomand 1988.

[30] For a succinct discussion see Arjomand 1992, 151–58. See also Mottahedeh 1995b, 320–22; and Akhavi 1996.

[31] Parallels and contrasts between the current debate and that which followed the death of Ayatollah Borujerdi in 1961 should be explored and documented. For an excellent account of the 1960s debate, which paved the way for Khomeini's emergence, see Dabashi 1993, 161–73. See also Motahhadeh 1985, 240–47.

[32] For instance, *Houzeh: Vizheh-ye Houzeh-ha-ye ʿOlum-e Dini* (Journal of the Religious Sem-

ment is that with the establishment of the Islamic Republic, Shiʿis have entered a new era that calls for a revision of Shiʿi organizations. They divide Shiʿi history into four eras. The era of Presence and Rule was that of the Prophet and the first Shiʿi Imam, Ali. The era of Presence and Isolation lasted from Imam Ali's death to the end of the Minor Occultation of the Twelfth Imam. The third era, beginning with the Major Occultation, was that of the Occultation and Absence of an all-powerful jurist. The era in which Shiʿis now live is that of Occultation and the rule of the just jurist, the velayat-e faqih, which shares more with the first than with the other two eras, since Shiʿis possess political power.[33] The conclusion is that there can be only one authority, that it can only be the Leader of the Islamic Republic, the *vali-ye faqih*; all other ulama should defer to his authority, and all believers should pay their religious dues to his office.

The other camp comprised adherents of the old notion of authority in Shiʿism, who favored the continuation of the old system whereby the religious hierarchy maintains a clear separation from government. They argued that choosing a marjaʿ is the personal prerogative of every believer, thus no imposition can be made and no criteria can be set. A marjaʿ should emerge gradually through the consensus of ulama and ordinary believers; any regulation would hinder a true consensus and thus deprive the marjaʿiyat of its real source of authority, which is the people and not government. This camp was probably in the majority in Qom, but without official support they were less able to be candid about their views; they aired their arguments orally, in their lessons, or less directly in their writings—in books and journals published outside Qom.[34] The camp also included some clerics closely associated with government in the first decade of the Islamic Republic; most prominent among them is Ayatollah Montazeri, Khomeini's first successor-designate as vali-ye faqih, who drew strength from the old style of politics; his classes were gaining in popularity and attracting more followers—and khoms, which in turn ensured funding for students.[35]

It remains to be seen how these debates will evolve, and which camp will prevail. Whatever the outcome, the notion of supreme authority in Shiʿism, in the form of the nineteenth-century institution of marjaʿiyat, will no longer be the same. Although the subject was not one I could directly raise in the Qom of 1995, I could sense the passing of an old era. A mood of change in the whole

---

inaries) devoted two issues (vol. 10, nos. 2 and 3, Spring and Summer 1993) to the question of marjaʿiyat, and *Feqh: An Innovative Effort in Islamic Feqh*, a new quarterly, devoted its third number (Spring 1995) to debates related to the payment of religious taxes.

[33] Najafi 1995, 8.

[34] For instance the book, banned in Iran, by Mehdi Haeri-Yazdi (1995), son of a founder of the Qom Houzeh.

[35] In 1988 Montazeri was put under house arrest; in late 1997, his classes were closed down.

system was in the air; my very presence there, my meetings with the clerics, were evidence of this, as I was frequently reminded.

The shaping of the new era in Qom is nowhere more evident than in the transformations in the traditional system of Shiʿi learning.[36] Theology (*kalam*) and jurisprudence (*feqh*) are still the two prestige subjects, and there are still three levels at which students study—elementary (*moqaddamat*, preliminaries), intermediary (*sotuh*, texts) and advanced (*dars-e kharej*, beyond texts)—but the content and organization of courses, and the relations between students and teachers, are undergoing a major shift from meritocracy to bureaucracy.

There were intermittent and uncoordinated attempts to reform the Qom Houzeh in previous decades, but the 1979 revolution gave them a different purpose and momentum. In the spring of 1981, the first Qom Houzeh Management Council was created. Its mandate was to oversee and facilitate the introduction of reforms, the transition from the old system of education to the new. This council (now referred to as the Former Council) had nine members, representing the two power centers in Qom at the time. Six were representatives of Ayatollahs Khomeini and Golpaygani (three each)—one marjaʿ, Ayatollah Shariʿat-Madari, was under house arrest; others kept their distance. The other three members represented the Society for Houzeh Teachers (Jameʿeh Modarresin-e Qom), a loose grouping that came into prominence during the upheavals of the 1960s, which led to Ayatollah Khomeini's exile; this society became a major power center after the revolution.

Although it lasted for ten years, the Former Council had problems from the outset. Old hands in the Houzeh resisted its program, and various political factions challenged its mandate and authority. The members finally resigned in 1991, and in October 1992 a new council started work, with substantially greater control over Houzeh affairs.[37]

In 1995 the Houzeh in Qom was in a transitional stage: two methods of education coexisted and competed. The old system is free of any form of bureaucratic constraints: there is no process of selection, either for students or for teachers; there are no written examinations, no graduation, and no award of formal degrees. Students can join the system at any time, any age, and any level of education; they are free to attend any lesson they wish and to remain in the Houzeh as long as they want. The capable ones in turn hold their own classes, while still continuing to attend those by the Grand Ayatollahs. Supporters of the old system argue that learning and teaching of religious sciences are a kind of duty that should be performed on a voluntary basis, without control or external constraints; their motto is "the organization of the Houzeh

[36] See Fischer 1980, Dabashi 1993, and Mottahedeh 1995a.

[37] See various issues of *Payam-e Houzeh*, which has appeared quarterly since autumn 1993. The above account is based on Firuzi 1994 and published interviews with Ayatollah Makarem-Shirazi (head of the High Council of the Houzeh) and Ayatollah Mo'men (executive director of the Houzeh).

is in its lack of organization." They fear that reform is bound to result in loss of independence and of freedom of belief and speech in the Houzeh.

The new system, which is gaining increasing currency, resembles present university regimes in Iran. There are ideological and academic selection processes for both students and teachers, set courses with defined curricula and duration, and qualifying exams and specialization in different fields. Students have less freedom to choose teachers or courses, and cannot start teaching simply by proving their academic merit. Class attendance and progress are monitored, scholarships and modern dormitories have been introduced, and student conduct outside class is scrutinized.

Ethnography of Gender Debates in Qom:
The Organization of the Book

The clerics I came across in Qom fell into two broad categories: adherents of the pre-revolutionary school, now referred to as Traditional Jurisprudence (*feqh-e sonnati*); and those who promoted what they referred to as Dynamic Jurisprudence (*feqh-e puya*). Each category includes some clerics who have taken up governmental posts, known as "government clerics" (*rouhaniyun-e hokumati*), as well as others who are solely engaged in seminary activities, known as "Houzeh clerics" (*rouhaniyun-e houzavi*). Some clerics who held government positions in the early years of the revolution now engage solely in seminary activities; others took up government posts later. Likewise, some adherents of the old school later joined the ranks of those arguing for Dynamic Jurisprudence—although the reverse did not happen. Some clerics are open to modernist and reformist currents, while others see them as a threat to Islamic traditions.

Unfortunately, I was not able to meet or talk with any of the scholars in *Jame'at al-Zahra*, the theological college for female Shi'i scholars that was founded after the revolution. The college has its origin in the activities of a small group of women in the 1960s who lobbied the Qom seminaries for teachers and courses in religious sciences. By the mid-1970s, the group and their classes became a conduit for religio-political awareness for the young generation of women who were increasingly drawn to Islam. With Khomeini's approval and funds from wealthy, traditional bazaaris, the building work started in the early 1980s, and it was officially opened in 1986. It offers boarding facilities and a wide range of courses, and attracts students from all over the Shi'i world. In the process of its transformation into the first proper female theological college in Iran, the original group lost its modernism and is now one of the bastions of the school of Traditional Jurisprudence. In 1995, al-Zahra College was like a fortress, with high walls and gates guarded by male attendants. Despite all my attempts, I did not meet any female scholar from the college; two appointments were canceled at the last minute, and I could not get permission to enter the college. One reason, perhaps, was that these female scholars did not want to engage with someone associated with the views of clerics who were arguing for a change. They also declined to work with *Payam-e Zan*, which would entail transgressing the proper boundaries of male and female segregation. The male clerics who used to teach there would enter the classroom through an underground passage, and never saw any of the students. I was told that the college has now become self-sufficient, and no longer needs male teachers; men are no longer allowed inside. I found it ironic and revealing that, while male scholars in Qom seemed to have no objection to my research and were willing to meet and talk with me, female scholars avoided me.[38]

There are three parts to this book, each dealing with texts—both oral and written—representing one of the three dominant gender perspectives that I encountered between 1995 and 1997. I present them in an order that reflects the chronology of the development of concepts, and so as to convey something of the context. Each part begins with a brief introduction to a defining text on women, and each chapter builds on and adds a new dimension to the arguments presented in the preceding one. Chapters in the first two parts begin and end with narratives of my visits to Qom in 1995 and 1997 and meetings with the authors whose texts are discussed. These accounts are intended to draw attention to the taken-for-granted, shared meanings that underlie life in Qom, the familiar routines that inhabitants take as natural. At times, I interrupt the transcripts of texts or narratives of interviews, in order to locate issues referred to by the authors or speakers within the context of wider debates on power and gender in post-revolutionary Iran.

The structure and format of chapters in each part differ, reflecting the different nature and extent of my engagement with the texts and their authors. The two texts discussed in Part One ("The Traditionalists") represent the viewpoint of clerics who see the gender model in shari'a law to be immutable and their mission to be to convince others of this truth. Chapter One concerns a text by Ayatollah Madani-Tabrizi, a senior Houzeh cleric. Chapter Two deals with a text by Ayatollah Azari-Qomi, a government cleric who was an ardent supporter of velayat-e faqih in the first decade of the Islamic Republic, but who now argues for its separation from the marja'iyat. Although I talked with both ayatollahs, my engagement with their texts is limited to selecting passages for

---

[38] After discussing the matter with male clerics and some female students, I concluded that in order to be accepted within a scholarly tradition as male-dominated and constructed as that of the Qom Houzeh, a woman must first observe its implicit rules. I found the same tendency in Cambridge among Old Girtonians, women of the first generation of female students in the University of Cambridge, who did not question many of the values of the Cambridge colleges but merely reproduced them in a different form.

full translation, and paraphrasing and summarizing the rest: our views on gender and our understandings of Islam were so different that there was little room for a constructive dialogue.

The four chapters in Part Two ("The Neo-Traditionalists") recount my discussions with the clerics of *Payam-e Zan* and their mentor Ayatollah Sane'i. Although they, too, staunchly defend the immutability of the gender model manifested in Islamic law, they admit the need for change in practice and seek new interpretations within the bounds of feqh. As already mentioned, transcripts of these interviews have been published in Persian. I use them to shed light not only on the gender debates but also on clerical modes of thinking and argumentation. I translate my own records of the interviews almost in full. Here too, I interrupt the narrative to help the reader understand and interpret the occasions. I also draw attention to omissions and additions in the published transcript, not merely to set the record straight but also to highlight passages that the clerics saw fit either to elaborate or to omit. Unlike Part One, where the authors of the texts and I could only repeat our positions, here the clerics and I managed to engage critically with each others' premises and argument— these four chapters are, in effect, coauthored.

The two chapters in Part Three ("The Modernists") contain texts that represent a theoretical break from conventional wisdoms of Islamic feqh, and my engagement with them goes further than with those discussed earlier. Chapter Seven deals with lectures by Abdolkarim Sorush, perhaps the most prominent among the new wave of contemporary Islamic intellectuals in Iran. In Chapter Eight I discuss the work of Hojjat ol-Eslam Seyyed Mohsen Sa'idzadeh, whose articles in *Zanan* provided the impetus for my research, and whose presence the reader will be aware of throughout the other chapters.

These narratives, in particular those in Part Two, must be read with a number of cautions. First, as with any other debate in the Islamic Republic in the 1990s, there were limits to the discussion that could not be transgressed, and I was never sure how far I could go. I was also anxious not to be seen as taking a Western perspective, but as someone who is not hostile to it, who appreciates and respects its values and traditions. I was keen to show that although I have lived in England for over twenty years, I consider myself Iranian and Muslim, that I understand and relate to issues as an Iranian Muslim woman, and value and respect my own religious and cultural heritage; this is my identity. Yet *Payam-e Zan*, perhaps inevitably, portrays me as representing the West; for example, when introducing the round-table participants, they write: "Ms. Mir-Hosseini, in addition to her own views as a researcher, was voicing current [that is, non-Islamist] perspectives." They made a similar point when introducing me to Ayatollah Sane'i, whom we will meet in Chapter Five.

Second, the texts discussed here are all by men. The absence of texts by women is due to the fact that Islamic jurisprudence *(feqh)*—the subject of this book—has remained a monopoly of male scholars. In Iran, as elsewhere, female scholars of Islamic studies so far have focused their energies on the field of Koranic interpretation (*tafsir*).[39] Yet it was women's voices and concerns, particularly as expressed in *Zanan*, that enabled me to formulate the questions I posed, and above all gave me the courage to articulate them.

[39] Riffat Hassan (1988, 1996) and Amina Wadud-Muhsin (1992) are prominent scholars in this field. In Iran, among the most distinguished is Monir Gorji (1994).

Part One

THE TRADITIONALISTS:
GENDER INEQUALITY

Introduction to Part One _____

MOST CLERICS IN Qom consider the pronounced patriarchal bias of shari'a legal Rulings to be immutable. The Inequality between the sexes they take for granted: it is rooted in sacred tradition, but it also makes sense to them intellectually. It reflects the world they live in, a world in which inequality between men and women is the natural order of things, the only known way to regulate relations between them.

I call these clerics, and their gender views, Traditionalist. They wield a great deal of power, and most religious texts produced in Qom represent their perspective. They all ground their arguments on the naturalness of shari'a law and its compatibility with human nature, as formulated by Allameh Seyyed Mohammad Hosein Tabataba'i and later elaborated by his student, Ayatollah Mortaza Motahhari. Their texts and views have been discussed by others;[1] my aim here is to locate them in the context of the Islamic Republic in the 1990s.

Allameh Tabataba'i, who died in 1981 at the age of seventy-eight, was the most renowned Shi'i philosopher of this century, and the first to address the question of gender and women's rights from the perspective of Islamic philosophy. Despite his command of jurisprudence, which could have earned him more prestige and authority in the Houzeh, he chose not to pursue it, but instead devoted his scholarship to philosophy and exegesis, in which he excelled and became Allameh, the highest title reserved for nonjurist scholars. His monumental, twenty-volume Koranic commentary, *al-Mizan fi-Tafsir al-Qur'an* (Balance in the Exegesis of the Koran), commonly known as *al-Mizan*, was written in Arabic between 1954 and 1972. In *Polygamy and the Position of Women in Islam*, a small book in Persian published during his lifetime, Allameh articulated all that is implicit in the writings of the Traditionalists, both those who remained in the Houzeh and those who became involved in the politics of the Islamic Republic.

Allameh Tabataba'i was teacher and mentor, recognized in both Shi'i and Sunni religious circles, and among academics both inside and outside Iran.[2] Throughout his life, he kept away from politics, both in the Houzeh and outside, yet he came to contribute to the founding political and gender discourses

[1] For example: Azari 1983c, Ferdows 1983, Ferdows 1985, Mahdavi 1985, Nashat 1983b, Paidar 1995, Yeganeh 1982, 41–48, and Yeganeh and Keddie 1986, 126–28.

[2] In the late 1950s, he began a lifelong dialogue with Henry Corbin, the French orientalist; and in 1963 he was asked to write the volume on Shi'ism for a series intended to present "Oriental religions through their authentic representatives." Allameh's text was published as *Shi'ite Islam* in 1975; see the preface by the translator, Seyyid Hossein Nasr 1975, 17–19.

of the Islamic Republic.[3] This was managed by his students, who developed and spelled out the ideological dimension of his writing; notably Morteza Motahhari, whose seminal text on women became the official discourse of the Islamic Republic on gender.

Motahhari takes his arguments almost verbatim from Allameh Tabataba'i's *al-Mizan*, but his own text, whose language and mode of argument are more accessible to outsiders, is the better known outside traditional Shi'i scholarship. Motahhari taught both in religious schools in Qom and at universities in Tehran, and during Khomeini's exile in Najaf (1963–1978) he became one of his representatives in Iran. After the victory of the Revolution in February 1979, he became a member of the Revolutionary Council; in May that year he was assassinated.

His text bridges the traditional and modern worlds of the Shi'a and is rooted in one of its divisive debates. The occasion of this debate, conducted in a women's magazine, was the enactment of the Family Protection Law of 1967. The popular women's magazine *Zan-e Ruz* was then campaigning for radical reform of the Iranian Civil Code, whose articles on marriage and divorce reflected dominant opinions within Shi'i feqh. Among prominent reformers was Judge Mahdavi Zanjani, who had prepared a forty-article proposal to replace some of the articles of Book Seven of the code, which deal with marriage and divorce. This alarmed the religious authorities, and a leading Tehran clergyman approached Motahhari to prepare a defense of the code. Motahhari agreed to do so, provided it was printed intact. This was accepted and *Zan-e Ruz*, as a goodwill gesture, printed his original letter containing the proviso. Motahhari's first response appeared in November 1966 as a direct rejoinder to the first article in Judge Mahdavi's proposal. Mahdavi's sudden death ended the debate after six issues, but Motahhari continued his contributions, which had attracted a large readership, for another twenty-seven issues. In 1974, he compiled them into a book, *The System of Women's Rights in Islam.*[4]

The System is divided into eleven parts, each dealing with a cluster of rights and obligations arising from marriage. It starts with marriage proposal and engagement, the subject matter of the first articles of Book Seven of the Civil Code, which was also the starting point of Judge Mahdavi's proposal. In the following parts, Motahhari deals with temporary marriage, women and social independence, Islam and modernity, women's human status according to the Koran, the natural basis of family laws, differences between men and women, dower (*mahr*) and maintenance, the question of inheritance, the right to divorce, and polygamy. In each part, Motahhari chooses his facts and sources selectively, especially when he invokes Western scholarship to justify the dif-

---

[3] For his views and their impact on the discourse of the revolution, see Dabashi 1993, chapter 5.

[4] Motahhari 1991, xxxvii–xl.

ferent treatment of women in Islam. Although he admits the injustices done in the name of the shari'a—the plight of divorced and abandoned women was widely highlighted by *Zan-e Ruz*—he blames this state of affairs on un-Islamic society and men who abandoned Islam.

Motahhari's arguments remain the most eloquent and refined among those that hold the concept of gender equality to be contrary to the shari'a. They provided the Islamic Republic in its early years with much-needed validation for its gender policies. In 1981, his book was translated into English, and by 1995 it had been reprinted in Persian over twenty times. The bulk of the vast post-revolutionary literature on women, especially that produced by the official Islamic Propagation Organization, not only follows Motahhari but reproduces his arguments verbatim.

The two chapters that follow discuss texts by two high-ranking clerics articulating Traditionalist views on women in the domain of feqh. Ayatollah Madani, the focus of Chapter One, has kept aloof from the politics of the Islamic Republic, turning a blind eye to state policies bearing directly on women's role in society. Ayatollah Azari-Qomi, the subject of Chapter Two, is by contrast a senior cleric who has been actively involved in politics.

1

Women Ignored: Grand Ayatollah Madani

SOME OF THE high-ranking clerics who have remained in the Houzeh since the revolution make a conscious effort to keep their distance from the politics of the Islamic Republic. They do this by retreating into the scholastic, ivory-tower world of the Houzeh, and ignoring what is happening outside. For them, the texts produced by Muslim jurists over the years have dealt adequately with women and their rights. Whatever was necessary has already been said and done. The Islamic position on women, and the relevant legal Rulings, are crystal clear. There is nothing to discuss: women have been given their rights.

Ayatollah al-ʿOzma Seyyed Yusef Madani-Tabrizi is one of these clerics. A highly respected scholar, he was born in 1928 in Tabriz in Azarbaijan. Educated in the Tabriz Houzeh and then in Qom, where he studied feqh and its Principles under Ayatollahs Borujerdi (the last sole marjaʿ) and Mohaqqeq al-Damad (a renowned scholar), he produced his treatise in the early 1980s. He is thus a marjaʿ, but only a minor one and in the old style.

I visited Ayatollah Madani one hot evening in early September 1995, on my first visit to Qom. I had arrived in the early morning with my cleric friend Saʿidzadeh and his daughter Zahra, for a meeting with the editorial board of *Payam-e Zan* (see Chapter Three), which lasted well beyond noon. In mid-afternoon I visited the shrine; when it became cooler, Saʿidzadeh and I browsed in the bookshops. I came across several books and pamphlets on women that I had not seen in Tehran. Soon each of us was carrying a large bundle—booksellers in Iran wrap purchases in paper and tie the bundle together with string. With more bookshops to go, Saʿidzadeh said, "Why don't we leave these somewhere before we go on? We could leave them in the offices of the Society for Houzeh Teachers." He once worked at the society's research and publication section, and the guards knew him. I welcomed the idea. As usual, I was having great difficulty managing my chador while carrying something; and I noticed that Saʿidzadeh seemed rather uncomfortable. Zahra, his daughter, was no longer with us, and he was obviously not at ease to be seen with me alone in Qom. In the two bookshops we had visited, he had deliberately kept his distance; only at the cash desk did he come to add some books that he thought I might want to buy. Much later, when I had learned more of Qom's unwritten laws, I also understood how inappropriate it was for clerics to be seen in the street with women and carrying bundles.

As we approached the society's building, Sa'idzadeh said, "There's a Grand Ayatollah who lives in the alley just back here; I studied under him and I have his authorization (*ejazeh*). His name is Madani-Tabrizi and his views on women are traditional, but he allows and enjoys disputation with students, and you can certainly engage him in debate and ask about women's position in Islam." It was getting close to evening prayer time; I knew Sa'idzadeh was eager not to miss his prayers, and was looking for somewhere to go, but did not know what to do with me. For my part, I was hot and felt stifled inside my *maqna'eh* headgear and chador.[1] We left our bundles of books with the guard, and turned down the nearby alley.

Ayatollah Madani's house was *jonubi* (on the south side of the street), with its garden on the sunny far side of the house. Like all other houses in the row it was a two-story building with high walls and curtained windows. But the main door was open. Sa'idzadeh shouted "Ya Allah!" and went in, as I waited outside. He came back with the *khadem*, and said that the ayatollah would see us after prayers. A khadem is a cross between a steward and a doorman, who runs errands and is in charge of receiving visitors; the word implies service in a good cause, without expectation of reward. Shrines and mosques also have khadems as attendants and gatekeepers, one of whose jobs is to keep women under control in public—as we shall see. Ayatollah Madani's khadem was a tall, grim-faced man in his late sixties; he did not look at me and gave no response to my greeting. He was obviously put out by our arrival. I thought perhaps it was because we had come just before prayer time and disrupted his routine, but I soon realized that it was not our timing that upset him, but my very presence. However, he showed us the way, Sa'idzadeh in front and me behind.

We entered a hallway. As in the residences of all distinguished ayatollahs, this area was the *biruni*, outer quarters, frequented by male visitors and students. Up a short flight of steps to the right was a reception room. A large, heavy curtain on the far wall led to the courtyard beyond. On the left-hand wall was a basin with taps, and to the right of the basin a washroom with a toilet; to the left of the basin, a door led, presumably, to the next-door house, used as *andaruni* or inner quarters where the family lived, with its own outside entrance for female guests.

We took our shoes off and climbed the steps to enter the reception room. It had a window opening onto the courtyard, but a curtain was drawn over it. Apart from carpets covering the floor, the room was simple and austere. There

---

[1] Maqna'eh (the post-revolutionary women's headgear, similar to a wimple, previously used only for prayers) and chador together now constitute the correct form of hejab. In Qom, all women wear the chador; entry to the shrines is forbidden without it; throughout my time in Qom I saw only two women on the street without chador (wearing only overcoat and scarf)—both probably visitors from Tehran. See Chapter Two.

was no furniture apart from a couple of large cushions and, by one of the windows, a low writing desk, next to which lay several large bundles of books tied together with string, like those I had just bought. The khadem turned on the ceiling fan and brought us a jug of iced water and two glasses. I thanked him but again he left the room without responding. Sa'idzadeh followed him to do his evening prayers. It was hot under my black overcoat, headgear, and chador, and the elastic band (quite a useful innovation) that held my chador in place was hurting. Sitting down facing the door, I helped myself to some water; it was Qom water, salty in taste but cooling. I felt uneasy and apprehensive about meeting a Grand Ayatollah; I didn't know what to expect. I was also offended by the way the khadem ignored me. I wondered whether to take my chador off and just keep my headgear; eventually I decided to keep my chador on, took out my fan and gradually cooled down.

When Sa'idzadeh came back into the room he sat by the door, with his back just inside the threshhold, so that he could be seen from outside. This was the way he sat whenever we were alone in a room, so as to avoid breaking the rule of *khalvat*, which prohibits two people of different sex who are unrelated to each other from being alone together in an enclosed space. The khadem returned, this time bringing tea on two individual small trays, an old-fashioned and formal way of serving it. He put both trays next to Sa'idzadeh. We both thanked him. He muttered something to Sa'idzadeh alone, and left the room. The old man's conduct had by now become insulting. I asked Sa'idzadeh the reason for it: "He's so bad-tempered he didn't even bother to answer my salaam, let alone my *ta'arof* [the compulsory exchange of courtesies]." Sa'idzadeh gently explained that old khadems like him were not used to receiving women like me in the biruni part of the house; perhaps I had broken one of the ground rules; perhaps my manners were unfamiliar; perhaps I had been too forward with my greetings; my voice was rather too loud for Qom. I drank my tea in silence, glad I had kept my chador on.

Then we heard footsteps. The servant cried "Ya Allah!" and Ayatollah Madani entered the room. We both stood to greet him; he responded warmly, and separately, and asked us to sit down. He himself sat on the same side as Sa'idzadeh, facing me—as always happened in Qom: no man would sit on the same side of the room as me. His face was kind and peaceful, and he spoke Persian with a slight Turkish accent. When we were seated—Sa'idzadeh's back now fully inside the room—the ayatollah once again, as is the custom, turned to us to exchange courtesies, first with me and then with Sa'idzadeh. He looked directly at me and inquired about my health and my family. I experienced an immense sense of relief that he was looking at me, and I responded in my normal voice. Sa'idzadeh introduced me as an Iranian researcher from the University of Cambridge in England, saying I had studied family law and marital disputes in courts in Iran and Morocco, I was currently doing research on women's rights in Islam, and I had that morning had a meeting with

Payam-e Zan. "She has came to Qom to talk with the ulama, and to find out for herself about current debates in the Houzeh concerning women's rights."

Ayatollah Madani then spoke for quite some time. He began by praising the interest and efforts of women like me, who make use of their education. He spoke broadly of the high status of women in Islam, how their lot improved after the advent of Islam, and how shari'a law guarantees all their rights and gives them full protection. He finished by inviting me to ask questions. I said I was interested in the concept of gender equality and wanted to know whether women can aspire to equal rights in shari'a law. He replied: "Shari'a not only fully endorses the principle of equality, but in effect has given women more rights than men." I said: "But there are certain Rulings that defy the principle of equality; for instance, a man's right of unilateral divorce (*talaq*), or his right to have more than one wife." He said: "Islam also enables a woman to protect her rights, she only needs to stipulate it in her marriage contract; and if she hasn't stipulated the right to talaq then she can obtain a divorce through khol'." I pointed out that, unlike talaq, which the husband can do unilaterally, in khol' a woman can obtain a divorce only if her husband gives consent, for which she must compensate him. In effect, she must buy her divorce; she must pay for it. I added that this very fact, that the right to divorce must be stipulated as a condition in her contract, is the best proof that a woman is not automatically entitled to the same as a man.

I tried to draw the ayatollah's attention to what I saw as obvious disparities in the construction of men's and women's rights and duties in Islamic law. The ayatollah tried to convince me that Islam granted women all their rights, that apparent disparities in rights and duties between men and women are natural and reflect the essence of divine justice. We agreed on the principles of equality and justice, we both believed that men and women are entitled to them, yet we kept talking across each other. The ayatollah could not see how, as he put it, "a sensible and learned person" like me, who knew shari'a Rulings and their rationale, could not concede that they were for women's good. I could not understand how someone with his analytical mind could deny the disparities and unfairness in legal Rulings that grant one party (the man) the rights of unilateral divorce and polygamy.

It became evident to me that we were not talking about the same thing. The ayatollah may have felt the same, because he suddenly stood up, picked a book from the wall-recess behind him, and handed it to me. It was a copy of his own book of Rulings (*ahkam*) on marriage and divorce, written in Arabic. He then pointed to the large bundle of books near the window and said that these were the second edition of his most recent book, in which he gave his *fatwa* (opinion, decree) on 650 Problems (legal questions); 450 of them dealt with novel issues and recently created problems, such as blood transfusion and artificial insemination, for which there were no earlier Rulings. I asked if he had given any new fatwas relating to family law or women's role in society. He smiled and said gently: "Of course not, these aren't new issues, the Rulings on them are as clear as day." He added that I would find them in the book I was holding in my hand. He then opened one of the bundles of the book and handed me a copy, together with a bundle of fliers to take to England.

I took the book and the fliers. I thanked him but asked no more questions. Our conceptions of gender and rights were so different that we were simply talking about two different realities. I could not understand how he could reconcile what seemed to me patent contradictions, illogical statements. How could he talk of equality and justice, and then endorse the restrictions that feqh places on women? How could he assert that all my demands could be accommodated within the context of Islamic law? He was also kind and tolerant, and spoke with such certainty, honesty, and integrity that my objections seemed flat and irrelevant. Yet he was sanctioning and defending all that I saw as unjust and unequal. I did not know what to make of this paradox.

It was almost dinnertime: time to leave. We made our excuses and Ayatollah Madani stood up to see us out of the room. He told me to come back with my questions when I had read his book. In the hallway, by the front door (now fully closed) stood the khadem. As I passed him, I rearranged my chador to free the books I was carrying, and walked through the door without saying goodbye—inadvertently leaving my fan behind in the room.

"The Way of Rulings on Marriage and Divorce"

Back in Tehran, I started to read the two books Ayatollah Madani had given me. The first was a study in feqh called *Minhaj al-ahkam fi'l-nikah wa'l-talaq* (The Way of Rulings on Marriage and Divorce).[2] In the introduction, Madani tells us that many people had urged him to write a book that would complete and update a current text (*al-Wasila*) on the subject. Despite his physical weakness and other difficulties, he decided to write on all bilateral and unilateral contracts, and to start with contracts and Rulings on marriage and divorce.[3] What he had given me was a copy of the second impression of the first volume, published in Qom in 1,000 copies by Isma'ilian Press. It is in Arabic: even the publication date is in the Arabic/Islamic lunar calandar (Rajab 1412/November 1990), as opposed to the solar Iranian calendar.

In line with other feqh texts on marriage and divorce, *Minhaj* is in three parts. The first, on marriage, is the longest, with fifteen chapters (445 pages). There are then eight short chapters (pages 446–528) on talaq, the husband's repudiation of the wife, the commonest form of divorce. The third part, on the two forms of divorce initiated by women (*khol* and *mobarat*), has only one chapter (pages 529–52).

[2] The book is probably destined for marriage and divorce notaries.
[3] There are twenty-four other volumes dealing with other forms of contract.

Madani starts by defining marriage, and cites *hadith* (sayings of the Prophet and the Shi'i Imams) concerning marriage as a meritorious act. He proceeds to delineate the legal Rulings and effects of the creation and dissolution of marriage, from the recitation of the appropriate formulae to the rights and obligations of spouses when the marriage is operative or ended, as well as the fate of children.[4] In so doing, he goes through the existing arguments and reasoning invoked by Muslim jurists, takes issue with some, elaborates others, and states his own.

In *Minhaj*, there is a clear-cut, definite notion of gender. It rests on a number of assumptions and legal theories about marriage, society, and male and female sexuality, validated and argued by reference not to actual practice (at least of today) but to a certain reading of the sacred texts, the Koran, and hadith. These readings are in turn legitimated and justified by the authority of eminent Shi'i jurists and the Rulings themselves. It is a closed legal system, in which there is little room for consideration of current realities of gender relations.

There is not a single reference to gender debates and consequent legal changes in the Islamic Republic. Madani's own notions of gender and marriage are those of the jurists whose fatwas form the core of the book. Thus he accepts the entire framework of Rulings for ending a marriage; he has no qualms about the notion that a man has the absolute right to terminate the marriage contract whenever he wishes. If he takes issue with the Rulings at all, he does so within the framework. For instance, he challenges jurists who say that a man cannot delegate to his wife the right to divorce herself on his behalf since divorcer and divorcee cannot be the same person. He finds this invalid, arguing that since the right to contract marriage between two persons can be delegated to one of them or to a third party, so can the right to terminate it; this person can be the wife.[5]

"Newly Created Problems"

The second book Madani gave me was a different matter. Madani wrote *al-Masa'el al-mostahdaseh motabeq ba fatwa-ye Hazrat-e Ayatollah al-'Ozma Aqa-ye Seyyed Yusef al-Madani al-Tabrizi* (Newly Created Problems according to the Opinion of His Excellency Grand Ayatollah Mr. Seyyed Yusef Madani Tabrizi—henceforth *Problems*) in Persian, a language accessible to nonspecialists, ordinary believers. Here he aired his views on new developments in the Houzeh and in society since the revolution. *Problems* belongs to a genre of legal texts common among Shi'i jurists, known as Practical Treatises, which deal with specific legal questions—Problems (*masa'el*)—arising in social life.

---

[4] See Mir-Hosseini 1993, 31–41.
[5] Madani-Tabrizi 1989, 446–52.

Madani started *Problems* as a small treatise providing shari'a Rulings on forty medical issues for which there was no previous Ruling; all forty had arisen because of recent progress in medical science, referred to him by the Imam-e Jom'eh (leading Imam) of Qom. When the treatise came out, some of "the Learned" (in the Houzeh) urged Madani to publish other Rulings he had discerned on diverse matters "for the benefit of all the ulama and all believers" (p. 18). Published in Qom by the same press that brought out *Minhaj*, the first edition of *Problems* contained 180 Rulings on "newly created Problems." It sold out after two impressions (2,000 copies each).

The second, much-expanded edition came out the day I went to see the ayatollah, 7 September 1995. It has a new introduction, in which he makes four points revealing both his approach to Islamic Law and social practice and his anxieties over opening "the science of feqh to outside influences." The first two points show his concern about the implementation of the shari'a by state institutions. The other two warn students and teachers of the pitfalls of changing the centuries-old educational system of the Houzeh. After reading them, I could make some sense of my meeting with him and of what had seemed to me a paradoxical way of thinking. These four points show how jurists like him relate to social practices, and how they are bound by the rules of their discipline.

In what follows I translate the first two points in full and the other two in part. Madani uses few punctuation marks and leaves many things unsaid; he writes in a complex and allusive style, and his language is heavy, highly specialized, and full of Arabic terms not easily accessible to a reader unfamiliar with feqh terms and concepts. I try as far as possible to preserve this style and to convey his tone and manner of presentation. (Emphasis and parentheses are as in the text, sometimes indicating an Arabic passage; my own glosses are in square brackets.)

> [This] humble [servant] finds it judicious to mention briefly a few important points that are for the good of the sacred Law of Islam and all the people of knowledge:
>
> 1. Their Excellencies, the Learned Gentlemen [a common way of addressing the ulama, always men] must be aware that the conditions and circumstances of time constantly change and evolve and that, whether we like it or not, these changes and new phenomena influence aspects of the personal and social life of human beings, and because the sacred Laws of Islam are not confined to a specific time but determine people's duties in every area of life and how to carry out religious duties and [social] interaction, people must not transgress them; that is, *to transgress the limits* [set by] *God is to do injustice to oneself.*
>
> (*Therefore*) it is necessary for Learned Gentlemen to provide Rulings for the Problems of the day, about which many questions are posed. In all circumstances, especially in scholarly [Houzeh] gatherings, they must be

mindful to adjust the conditions of life of the Dutiful and others to Islamic feqh, from ritual acts in *their specific sense* to social contracts in *their general sense*. *(If)* we want to adjust Islamic feqh to the conditions of the time, then the science of feqh will be destroyed and suffer irreparable damage.

(Observation) of this matter is very necessary and the ulama should not pay attention to public opinion or pay regard to non-Islamic institutions formed in the present age which create laws in any domain. And the ulama of Islam must try to adapt public opinion and the laws created by these institutions to Islamic feqh. If we tell non-Islamic institutions what the Koranic punishment for adultery is, [they] will regard [it] as contrary to human emotions. Now, one cannot, in order to gain their [approval], kill an adulterer or adulteress[6] by bullet or sword; it must be by stoning.

(Briefly), society must be reformed by Islamic feqh, and conditions and circumstances [of the former] must adapt to [the latter]; and thank God that Shi'i feqh, which has reached the jurists of Islam via members of the Prophet's House of Purity and Infallibility [the Shi'i Imams], has answers for all new issues and Problems. . . .

2. Their Excellencies the most Learned Gentlemen (may God help them) when discussing a shari'a Problem, whether it is fundamental or subsidiary, must pay full attention and be careful that as far as reasoning is concerned the Problem discussed does not go outside its shari'a and rational limits, subjecting it to demolition or confirmation and creating divisions among the most learned.

In addition, when the shari'a limits set by the divine Lawgiver are not observed, the Problem itself will disappear [that is, the issues must first be defined within feqh limits].

As is the custom and habit of the jurists of Islam when they discuss an Islamic Problem, before entering discussion they establish a *Principle* so that, if they cannot find a shari'a proof for that Problem, they can refer to that Principle; evidently, if that Principle becomes flawed in its reasoning, then all its ramifications are also liable to be flawed; so attention to all aspects of establishing a Principle is necessary and important. On [this] second point there are many things to be said, but for various reasons I have been brief. (pp. 5–8)

Generally, Shi'i jurists speak of a Principle *(asl)* in two contexts. The first, deductive Principles, they resort to in order to deduce the terms of the divine will by means of what are known as the four Proofs. These are: the Book (the Koran); Sunna (sayings and deeds of the Prophet and the Twelve Imams); Consensus (of Jurists); and independent Reasoning. If these will not produce a Ruling, in order to determine a believer's duty the Jurist will appeal to one

---

[6] Those who are married and have unhampered access to sexual relations yet commit the act of *zena*, sexual intercourse between sexes outside marriage.

of the four practical Principles: Exemption, which means that one is free from obligation and has no duty; Precaution, which means that although no Ruling exists one must act so that, if one did actually exist, one would have followed it; Option, that is, one has the option either to obey a Ruling or not; and Continuity, by which one presumes that what has existed remains as it was. The assumption is that there is a shari'a Ruling on every issue, and if the Muslim Jurist cannot find it by reference to the four reasons then it is his duty to discover the will of God by resorting to the procedures and principles established by the Principles of feqh.[7]

By "establishing a Principle" Madani probably has the latter in mind. As he says himself, he chose to be brief; but he is also vague and deliberately leaves much to be inferred.

3. Learned Gentlemen should not interfere with textbooks and other works and should not torment the souls of their authors by changing [their] themes, because shortening the books of [our] predecessors will reduce the level of knowledge and is harmful to the Houzeh.

(And the Learned Gentlemen) should not encourage or force the students of religious sciences to read summary books that contain only idioms. I do not find it judicious to name these types of books which are now taught in the Houzeh.

4. Gentlemen clerics and students of religious sciences must study and teach the books that were used by ulama in the past. . . . [He lists books he considers should be used in various subjects such as syntax and logic.]

(*Gentlemen students*), when you have undergone hardship and endeavored to master [Arabic] literature and Principles of feqh, then you may write a commentary on the Koran or a book on Islamic economics, because the chapters on contract law cover all economic issues; do not waste your time, but work hard in learning religious sciences, especially feqh and Principles of feqh. Studying by means of audiotapes, and attending debating sessions which are mere silence and where questioning is forbidden, does not make you learned. You are aware of the meaning of the word debate. . . . If the teacher talks and the student listens, then it is no longer a debate; it becomes a lecture. . . . (pp. 9–13)

These four points are clearly addressed to teachers and students in the Houzeh, not to the ordinary believers whose legal questions gave rise to the book in the first place. Madani is also commenting on post-revolutionary developments and changes in the Houzeh, presented as structural reforms in the traditional system of education to enable it to meet contemporary demands. Madani is obviously in favor of the old system, lamenting its passing, by warnings and advice to students and teachers. He is also anxious about the future of shari'a

---

[7] See Feiz 1995, Motahhari 1995, and Kamali 1991.

law after its implementation by state institutions. Ironically, he labels as "non-Islamic" the institutions set up in the Islamic Republic to implement the law. He is worried they might become susceptible to "public opinion" or political expediency. He is critical of jurists who, in order to accommodate current realities, are willing to go beyond old opinions in search of new solutions. He is worried that their action may inflict "irreparable damage" on the science of feqh. He argues they should strive for exactly the opposite, that is, to adapt current realities—which, as we shall see, he calls "conditions and circumstances of the present age," a euphemism for the Islamic Republic—to the science of feqh. This is exactly why he wrote *Problems*.

The second edition of *Problems* contains 650 Rulings, in two parts. The first (pages 21–296) covers 450 "newly created Problems." These concern issues that have emerged in recent times, for which there are no previous Legal Rulings. The second part (pages 297–380) covers 200 miscellaneous Problems, for which there is already a Ruling but also some ambiguity as to its applicability to the matter in question.

In Part One, 122 Problems concern women and gender roles, as do forty in Part Two. These 162 Problems provide a fascinating insight not only into Madani's thinking but also into the life and concerns of those who follow him in religious law. They show Madani's juristic vision at work, as he makes current gender realities conform to feqh logic and theories. They also reveal the anxieties and dilemmas experienced by his followers—a highly religious and conservative section of Iranian society—who try to live their lives according to the mandates of feqh. Of the 122 newly created Problems, 45 concern artificial insemination,[8] 31 abortion,[9] 25 marriage, divorce, and paternity,[10] 8 contraception,[11] 4 sex change,[12] and 9 women in society.[13]

I translate a selection of Problems bearing on gender roles in circumstances of either social change or technological progress. The Problems on sex change encapsulate Madani's notion of gender.[14] Three of them come in a separate section:

What Are the Rulings on Sex Change According to the Islamic Viewpoint in the Following Cases?

(Problem 19) True hermaphrodites, individuals who are genetically neither men or women?

---

[8] Problems 59–69, 180–81, 204, 207–10, 225–26, 239, 256, 260, 299–300, 308, 336–37, 352, 368–69, 380, 384–88, 392–93, 398, 400, 409, 435–37.

[9] Problems 30–48, 188, 319, 367, 370–71, 374, 395, 438–42.

[10] Problems 142, 206, 219–22, 224, 228–29, 240–41, 244–46, 260–62, 275, 305–6, 275, 381, 391, 396, 405.

[11] Problems 22–29.

[12] Problems 19–21 and 203.

[13] Problems 71, 74, 100, 183, 423–25, 252–54, 277, 344.

[14] For discussion by medieval jurists of sex change, see Sanders 1991.

(Problem 20) A person who is essentially a man but so far has lived in society as a woman, or even been married [as a woman?] for some years. Can his[15] penis and testicles be removed and a vagina be made for him by means of surgery? Emotionally he feels a woman and by using medication he has developed breasts and acquired a female appearance. Given all these, is [sex change] still not permitted?

(Problem 21) A person who is essentially a woman but has a small penis and has been raised since infancy as a male, because cultural values favor boys not girls; but gradually it has become evident that she is a woman. Can she be changed into a full woman by surgery? And if he feels she is a man, then what should be done? Since medically it is not possible to change her into a full man.

(Answers to 19, 20, 21) Sex change by means of surgery in a person who is essentially man or woman is not permitted; and according to the shariʿa it is not correct to remove a man's testicles and penis by surgery and make him a vagina, even if he feels emotionally a woman and has by using drugs developed breasts and a female appearance.

Likewise, it is not permitted to make a penis and testicles for a person who is essentially a woman, even if she feels a man.

But in the case of a hermaphrodite, because there is the possibility of either maleness or femaleness, therefore s/he may, even must, consult a medical specialist and determine his/her maleness or femaleness by means of surgery. (pp. 46–48)

In the next section Madani gives his juristic reasoning for his Rulings:

But the Proof that Sex Change Is Not Permissible, Briefly

(First,) sex change requires severing certain parts of the body, of either man or woman, and replacing them by other parts, and this act is not permissible in the shariʿa.

(And in other words,) destroying vital parts [of the body] or creating deformity in them is not Lawful.

(Second,) changing a person who is essentially created man or woman into the opposite sex (for instance changing and transforming men into women or vice versa) is impossible and beyond human knowledge. These two sexes (male) and (female) in the human realm; the evolutions that occur from the stage of conception to birth; the attributes of each of these two sexes in relation to their comportment; and many other mysteries hidden in the meaning of gender, are all indications and signs of the Wise Creator. No power can change them.

(In summary,) therefore, if by means of surgery and medication a man's

---

[15] Unlike Arabic, Persian has no grammatical gender; in fact, the language is free from any gender distinction.

facial hair disappears, his breasts enlarge, and a vagina is made for him, in reality he has not become a woman. Likewise in a woman, growth of facial hair and disappearance of breasts, along with the acquisition of testicles and penis, do not prove that she has really become a man. If they have resorted to this nonlawful action, they have sinned; as to religious duties, they are bound by those incumbent prior to the change in their appearance.

(In other words,) changing parts of the body does not alter the subject of maleness and femaleness, to enable us to say that the Rule may be changed. This [the impossibility of real sex change] can be inferred from certain Koranic verses, such as Sura Shura, verses 49 and 60, which say:

"He creates what He pleases; He grants to whom He pleases daughters and grants to whom He pleases sons. . . . He makes whom He pleases barren."

And all know and see that, despite all efforts and endeavors, no one has yet been able to make *"really barren"* [women] have children, or men who have gone through sex change give birth like real women; and the fact that they cannot give birth proves that real change has not taken place.

(In brief,) given what has been said, this important issue [sex] is in the realm of the infinite knowledge of Almighty God, and the created will never acquire such power. (pp. 49–51)

These two passages need little explanation. Madani is clear and uncompromising in his notion of gender and its implications for individuals. Gender is a mystery of creation that cannot be interfered with, and should be left alone. It is not determined by social roles, nor by physical and emotional attributes, but only by the sexual organs. It is a complex notion, he admits, but he rules that it cannot be changed, even if one feels that one is born in the wrong body, even if one lives as the other sex. When asked for clarification on Rulings for looking at those who have undergone sex change (Problem 203, p. 163), Madani writes, "Men may look at a man who has changed sex and has apparently become a woman, but they may not look at a woman who has changed sex and now appears as man."

Madani's Rulings on sex change are based on two postulates or, in his words, on two Principles: that it is impossible to alter God's creation, and that it is wrong to deform bodily organs. These two Principles also inform his discernment of Rulings on aspects of sexual reproduction, the subject of a number of newly created Problems, addressing three main topics: artificial insemination (45 Problems), abortion (31), and birth control (8). As with sex change, Muslim jurists have in fact dealt with the last two, deducing various Rules for them from the sacred sources and invoking various arguments;[16] if

---

[16] On sex change, see Skovgaard-Petersen 1994. On contraception and abortion, see Musallam 1983.

Madani treats them as new Problems it is because he is responding to current government policy, as well as new reproductive technology.

I translate those Problems which contain Madani's Rulings and arguments.

Rulings on Birth Control

(Problem 22) In general what is the Ruling in the Sacred Laws of Islam on tube-tying in various illnesses?

(Problem 23) What is the Ruling on male vasectomy for birth control? Considering that in a small percentage [of cases] vasectomy is surgically reversible, and this percentage increases with advances in medicine.

(Problem 24) What is the Ruling on female sterilization for birth control? Considering that in a small percentage [of cases] it is surgically reversible, and this percentage increases with advances in medicine.

(Answers to 22, 23, and 24) A number of hadith from the Prophet's House have reached us from diverse sources, encouraging and emphasizing procreation; and this humble [Madani] has mentioned them in detail in the first volume of *Minhaj*.

(But) we have no hadith on birth control and reducing the number of children for individuals.

(Of course,) it is well known that too many children bring hardship; especially in the present age, the fewer children one has, the more comfort.

(Nevertheless,) in the Sacred Laws of Islam contraception is not obligatory except in special cases, for instance, if a woman cannot give birth naturally and after several surgically aided births there is the danger of death or injury, when contraception becomes obligatory.

(Yet) if it is logically probable that a first pregnancy might result in death or injury and so on, in such a case too, contraception becomes obligatory.

(As a result,) if pregnancy threatens danger or harm to a woman, she has the absolute right to prevent it; and it makes no difference whether the harm would be immediate or delayed.

(But Lawful ways) of preventing pregnancy are the following:

1. Using the pill or injection and other [methods] which do not cause deformity, paralysis, or barrenness in women.

2. The man's withdrawal, provided it does not cause him or the woman physical harm.

3. The wife stipulates at the time of marriage that for a while, or permanently, she will prevent pregnancy, and the husband accepts this condition.

(But tube-tying) to prevent conception is permissible only if it is temporary and causes no physical harm or barrenness in the woman and it is 100 percent [certain] that she can become pregnant when [the tubes] are untied. *(Otherwise)* it is not permissible; and in [my] humble opinion a woman's use of contraception, even if temporary, is not free of ambiguity; perhaps it is not permissible, and the best ways to prevent pregnancy are 1

and 2. (Birth control) must be [done] by means that were explained, and no person has the right to compel another to do it. (pp. 52–55)

Madani's Rulings on birth control must be read as a kind of commentary on recent debates in Iran. Contraception became a contested domain soon after the revolution, partly because it had been actively promoted by the previous regime, with clinics providing a free contraceptive service all over the country. Some clerics denounced it, on political rather than religious grounds, as an imperialist conspiracy aimed at limiting the population of Muslims. After the revolution, when abortion was made illegal, contraception was not, but many birth-control clinics were closed. The discourse of the Islamic Republic promoted fertility, especially during the years of war with Iraq (1980–1988). By the mid-1980s, the high rate of population growth alarmed the authorities and brought a change of heart, which led to a total reversal not only of the early revolutionary discourse but of the policy. In 1989, the government launched a massive birth-control campaign, which has achieved some success. Among the methods actively promoted and used are both male and female sterilization. The latter is more prevalent, and these days women are encouraged to undergo the operation in hospital soon after giving birth. Abortion, though still illegal, is allowed under certain conditions: if continuation of pregnancy endangers the mother's health and life, or if the fetus is abnormal.[17]

These shifts in discourse and policy were accompanied by lively public debate over the Islamic position on birth control, and Qom clerics were among the main participants. By the early 1990s the debate had subsided, but some clerics still spoke out on the issue. They ranged from supporters of the government's campaign to those who denounced it vehemently.[18] All of them grounded their arguments in feqh and hadith, justifying their positions on the basis of the interest of the Islamic Republic and the welfare of its citizens.

Madani takes a middle position. He does not reject birth control in principle, but he does oppose its promotion, and categorically forbids sterilization. I translate further Problems relating to birth control, which indicate not just the kind of issues on which medical experts feel the need for clarification, but the gulf between Madani's religio-juristic world and the reality doctors have to deal with. There is a hint of gender awareness in the questions, which Madani ignores.

(Problem 25) Can a woman without a husband have her tubes tied?

(Answer) Tube-tying, if it is permanent and if it results in bodily deformity, is not permissible even if the woman has no husband.

---

[17] See Hoodfar 1994a and 1996a.

[18] Opponents of birth control constitute a very small minority, and their views seem not to carry much weight either at the official level or among the populace. One extreme view is that of Hoseini-Tehrani (1995), a Qom cleric whose stance opposing women's right to vote early in the revolution was rebuffed by Khomeini personally.

(Problem 26) In cases when the outcome of a pregnancy between two people would be deformed fetuses or genetic illnesses, can pregnancy be prevented by male or female sterilization?

(Answer) In such cases the prevention of pregnancy by the Lawful means I have mentioned is without problem, but tube-tying must not be resorted to.

(Problem 27) If female or male sterilization is to be permitted, who has priority?

(Answer) Tube-tying of men or women has certain conditions I have already written about. If studied, it becomes clear that priority between the husband and wife is not an issue, they can decide.

(Problem 28) Given that reliable medical sources confirm that mothers who have given more than five live births, and are over thirty-five, are likely to be exposed to physical danger, that is, high-risk pregnancy, is sterilization permissible for them?

(Answer) They may not choose sterilization, and if it is logically probable that pregnancy will expose them to physical dangers, then they may resort to other methods of contraception already mentioned. (pp. 56–57)

Madani prohibits sterilization in all circumstances on the grounds that it is forbidden to deform bodily organs. He rejects abortion, however, for a different reason. This is to be found among Problems posed by medical experts, who present him with medical facts. This must have led to a kind of dialogue, to which Madani puts an abrupt end, so as to deal with the issue of blood money.

I translate these problems in the order Madani presents them in his book. Note his use of "forbidden" (*haram*) and "not permitted" (*jayez nist*).

Rulings Concerning Abortion

(Problem 30) Can remedial abortion be carried out prior to ensoulment[19] in the following cases?

(Problem 31) Illnesses when we know for sure that the fetus will die after birth.

(Problem 32) Genetic illnesses.

(Problem 33) Infant abnormalities.

(Answers to 30, 31, 32, and 33) In the sacred Laws of Islam, it is forbidden to abort the fetus after conception, and there is no doubt and no difference among the jurists on this. Therefore, in all the above cases, abortion is not permitted.

(Of course,) it is possible to prevent conception by means already explained.

(If) the mother assists the abortion, by taking pills or other things that cause her to abort, she must pay blood money and repent of the sin she has committed; and if she has done this without her husband's knowledge, she must pay [blood money] to the husband who is the father of the fetus.

[19] See Problem 35, below.

(And if) the physician has knowingly and purposefully carried out the abortion, s/he is responsible for the blood money; if the mother has not resisted the act of abortion, she has sinned and must repent.

(It should not be hidden) that, after it is evident that conception has occurred, if the mother aborts, either by taking something or by other means, with or without her husband's consent, she has sinned and must repent. If mother and father are both parties to the abortion, they must pay blood money to the heir who was not party to it.

(In brief,) abortion is not permissible, and incurs blood money; [payment of] blood money is incumbent on the person who has performed the abortion.

(For instance,) if a physician by surgical or medical means aborts a women's child, the physician is accountable, and if the mother herself does this by taking a pill or medication prescribed by the physician, the mother is accountable. (pp. 58–60)

Madani's Rulings seem not to have satisfied those medical experts who are aware of the legal arguments put forward by other jurists, as the following two Problems suggest. They refer to the feqh theory of fetal development, which has a bearing on both ritual and legal matters. For instance, blood money payable if a pregnant women aborts after an injury depends on the stage of fetal development; as do the appropriate burial ceremonies. It is held that a human soul enters the fetus 120 days or four months after conception.[20] Some Shi'i jurists allow abortion during the first 120 days, provided there is a valid reason, such as the mother's poor health or abnormality in the fetus.[21] Madani is not among them. His prohibition of abortion is so categorical that he even rejects the consensus of Muslim jurists as to the time of ensoulment (*voluj-e ruh*) of the fetus.

(Problem 34) How do the above factors [which?] affect the fetus after ensoulment?

(Answer) Abortion is not permitted, whether after or before ensoulment.

(Problem 35) When is the time of ensoulment?

(Answer) It is impossible to determine the exact time for ensoulment. Only God Almighty knows the exact time. (But) it is said in the hadith that *four months after conception God sent two angels of creation*. Nevertheless the exact timing of allocation of the soul cannot be discerned even from this hadith. (pp. 60–61)

---

[20] Before that, the fetus goes through three stages of development in the womb, each lasting forty days: first is semen (*nutfa*), starting with conception; second is the bloodlike clot (*'alaqa*); third is the lump of flesh (*mudgha*). This is based on two Koranic passages and a hadith from the Prophet; see Musallam 1983, 54.

[21] Hanafi jurists are the most liberal, and grant a woman the right to abort without her husband's consent. Malikis are the most rigid, and prohibit abortion absolutely (Musallam, 1983, 57–59). Shi'i jurists take a middle position; see Rizvi (n.d., 95–112).

The medical experts pose more questions, in the course of which they inform him of their practice and their ethical arguments.

(Problem 36) A pregnant woman has developed cancer of the womb; treatment involves radiotherapy, which is bound to result in deformity of the fetus; may medical abortion be done before radiotherapy?

(Answer) Abortion is not permissible; and radiotherapy in this case is not permissible, because it will result in deformity of the fetus.

(Problem 37) In pregnant women afflicted with cancer (for instance, breast cancer), if the cancer is progressive, it is usual to carry out a medical abortion—irrespective of stage of pregnancy—before treatment of the mother. This is done for two reasons: first, the mother's life is in danger, and second, by not allowing termination not only will the mother perish but a motherless child will be left who needs her love.

(Problem 38) If the cancer is at an early stage, and the pregnancy in its final months, [treatment is postponed] until the fetus is capable of survival, then it is removed prematurely by surgery and placed in intensive care.

(Problem 39) If the pregnancy is at an early stage, then medical abortion is carried out and cancer treatment is started. Of course, in such cases, abortion is carried out if we know that treatment for cancer, such as chemotherapy or radiotherapy, would harm the fetus. Are the above [procedures] in conformity with Islamic Rules or not?

(Answers to 37, 38, and 39)

The answer to these problems is be found in those given to problems 36, concerning radiotherapy, and 14, concerning priority in treatment.

(In brief) in the sacred Laws of Islam, abortion is not permissible. (pp. 61–64)

The core of Madani's reasons for categorically prohibiting abortion is contained in the answer to Problem 14, which comes earlier in the book, under the heading "Legal and Penal Rulings Concerning the Medical Profession." It asks: who has priority in treatment where several patients need emergency attention at the same time? What is the basis for giving priority? Is the severity of a patient's condition the only criterion, or do the status and social worth of a patient play a role here? Madani's response is that, provided that all the patients are Muslims and believers, the one closest to death has priority. He then provides a commentary on a passage from an established Shi'a text, *al-Wasa'il al-Shi'a*,[22] and adds, "In a case where the mother is young and it is not certain that the fetus will survive after her death, can we say that we should destroy the fetus in order for the mother to survive? [I] do not dare to say that the mother must be saved, but it should be left to destiny" (pp. 39–40).

Madani's rejection of abortion under any circumstances reflects his juristic

[22] By Hasan Hurr Ameli (1625–93), a Shi'i jurist and collector of hadith; for a concise introduction to Shi'i sources of hadith, see Fischer and Abedi 1990, 471–72.

approach; that is, to paraphrase him, once a Principle is fixed, everything must then be subordinated to it. The Principle concerned is the sanctity of human life, and he adheres to the Principle so rigidly and narrowly that he puts himself in a situation where, if he has to choose between the mother and the unborn fetus, he cannot find a way out. Madani is of course aware of current practice, that abortion on medical grounds is legal. Yet he is intransigent, unwilling to compromise his juristic Principle or relax the prohibition for the sake of the mother's health or the child's welfare.

On the question of artificial insemination, Madani is equally categorical. He states his position in one Problem and then turns to the child born of such an act.

Rulings Related to Artificial Insemination

(Problem 59) It is not permitted to inject the semen of a stranger[23] into a woman's womb, whether or not with her permission, whether or not she has a husband, whether or not with the husband's permission.

(And if) in the above case insemination is carried out and the inseminated woman becomes pregnant and gives birth, the child belongs to the owner of the semen, who becomes subject to the Rulings on progeny [he is responsible for the child's welfare] and they inherit from each other; likewise, a woman who has a child by means of insemination is that child's mother and the Rulings on progeny are incumbent on her.

(Problem 60) If a woman, through lesbian intercourse, pours her husband's semen into another woman's vagina, and this woman gives birth, the child belongs to the owner of the semen and this woman is its mother and all Rulings on progeny are incumbent on her.

(Problem 61) Insemination of a women by her lawful husband's semen is allowed, if the action is done by the husband himself, and whether his wife is inseminated during his lifetime or after his death, the child born from this semen belongs to both and they are subject to all Rulings on progeny.

(Problem 62) It is permissible to take a man's semen and put it in an artificial womb in order to produce a child; and the child who results from such an action belongs to the owner of the semen and all progeny laws are established between them, but that child has no mother. (pp. 77–79)

Another forty Problems deal with further possible twists in the issue of artificial insemination. Some of them, like Problem 60, might appear bizarre to a reader not familiar with feqh literature; Madani here is referring to a Shi'i hadith: "A woman has intercourse with her husband, and then immediately connects with her slave girl in such a way that the semen of the husband pours from the woman into the vagina of the slave girl and makes her pregnant. The Imam's Ruling is that the child born from the slave girl belongs to the owner

---

[23] Arabic *ajnabi* (fem. *ajnabiya*) means foreigner, alien; here it means unrelated by marriage or kinship ties.

of the semen."[24] It is on this hadith, it seems, that Madani bases his Rulings on a new problem—artificial insemination; but again his reading of the hadith is so literal that it ignores the time and context in which the question was put to the Imam. Besides, he ignores the gender implications of new reproductive technology, though clearly his questioners are concerned with them.

Among the "newly created Problems," thirty-one concern family law and women.[25] None of them addresses the issue of the unequal construction of men's and women's rights in marriage and in society, though again concern with this issue is evident in the questions. Madani tries to make the "conditions of the time" conform with the Rulings, dealt with in detail in his first book, *Minhaj.* The results are at best irrelevant or abstruse, at times absurd. The following are the kinds of "newly created Problems" that can arise within the limits set by Madani's legal Principles.

> *(Problem 142)* Is repudiation (*talaq*) by telephone or loudspeaker permissible, if two just witnesses hear it, or must the two witnesses be present in the room?
>
> *(Answer)* In such a case, the repudiation is valid because it is not obligatory for the two just witnesses to be present at the place where the repudiation is taking place; if they hear the repudiation formula, this is sufficient, but if they are absent this would be contrary to the Principle of precaution. (p. 130)

Madani's response is detached from the legal realities of divorce in contemporary Iran. He knows that a man must go court to exercise his right to repudiation. But he ignores this, because the reality he is dealing with is that defined by feqh theories rather than contemporary imperatives.

Nine problems touch on women in society.

> *(Problem 183)* A woman, instead of wearing chador or headgear, covers her hair by wearing a wig; please state whether covering hair under a wig is sufficient in the eye of the Law. It is important to mention whether or not the sacred Laws of Islam designate a special form for women's covering.
>
> *(Answer)* Covering the hair by means of a wig is insufficient Legal covering for women, even if it prevents [men's] unlawful gaze; and it is necessary for a woman to cover her hair and body from strangers; as to type of covering, no specified form has been recommended, but mere covering is insufficient, and the shape of [a woman's] body must not be seen, and when in our age girls and women come out in special shirts and trousers which reveal

---

[24] The hadith is narrated in various sources of the second, fourth, and fifth Imams. For an account of other Rulings based on this hadith, see Rizvi n.d., 116; he sees it "as very good example of how our ulema solve the modern day problem even though they use old sources in Islam."

[25] Two relate to government-imposed requirements of marriage, such as taking a blood test; six relate to virginity, three to the father's permission for a girl's marriage, two to dower payment; three to women's rights within marriage; three to divorce, and seven to paternity.

their body and face, this is incorrect. I have discussed the issue of covering in detail on page 88 of *Minhaj al-Ahkam* and I have referred there to the views of the Jurists. (pp. 150–51)

This is the only Problem dealing with hejab. Madani's style remains scholastic. Interestingly, he avoids the term *hejab*, which everyone else, including clerics in Qom, uses for women's obligatory covering of the hair and all parts of the body apart from the face and two hands. Instead, he uses the correct Koranic term, *setr*.

The other eight Problems deal with rules of segregation arising from changes in medical tradition. I translate five of them:

(Problem 277) Can a woman [nurse], at a doctor's orders, inject blood into an unrelated man, when it is unclear whether the blood is that of a man or a woman, a Muslim or a non-Muslim?

(Answer) [A woman's] injection of blood, at a doctor's instructions, into an unrelated man, or vice versa, and the injection of a non-Muslim's blood into a Muslim, are without ambiguity [permissible], but while doing the injection the woman must not look at or touch the man's body. (p. 202)

How this is to be done, Madani does not explain. He is more forthcoming in the following cases:

(Problem 344) To complete their specialization in medicine, Muslim sisters have to travel abroad and study there. This means that they may be without Islamic hejab or possibly that their Islamic belief becomes weak and some diversions occur. Taking this matter into account, is it permissible for sisters to travel abroad or not?

(Answer) If traveling abroad entails abandoning the practice of Islamic Rulings, either for men or women, it is not permissible. (pp. 242–43)

(Problem 423) If a woman is afflicted by an acute illness and the only doctor in the village is a man, can that doctor perform all kinds of examination on the patient?

(Answer) If there is no access to a female doctor, a man can do the examination as necessary.

(Problem 424) If a woman is afflicted by a minor illness, is it necessary that she consult a female doctor or can she go to a male doctor in the village?

(Answer) If it does not entail hardship and harm to which she is not accustomed, she needs to go to town to a female doctor.

(Problem 425) Can a male doctor touch a woman's body over her clothes, regardless of the availability of a female doctor?

(Answer) Yes, it is permissible if it is without temptation or pleasure; there is no ambiguity. (pp. 284–85)

These "Islamic Rulings," which Madani dealt with in *Minhaj*, he reiterates in Part Two of *Problems*, under "Miscellaneous Problems." Over 25 percent

(58) of all these Problems relate to family law and women. Of these, forty-three are on aspects of marriage and divorce; twelve relate to rules of filiation and nursing, and three to women in society. I translate those touching on current debates, even if indirectly. They show how far Madani's religio-juristic world is detached from most people's experience of life. (The format is the same but, instead of "Problem," Madani now uses abbreviations for "Questions" and "Answers," hence "Q" and "A.")

The following two Questions relate to instances of public conduct, both of which occur, the first at any official gathering and the second at private ones, such as wedding parties.

(Q 70) Is clapping in ceremonies and lectures permissible?

(A) If not accompanied by other forbidden acts [such as dancing, merry-making], it is without ambiguity.

(Q 71) Are women's dancing in female gatherings and men's dancing in male gatherings permissible according to Law?

(A) In this case, if men's or women's dancing is like that of professionals who dance in a special way, it is haram and not permitted according to Law, because it is evidence of forbidden amusement, and if they receive payment for dancing it is haram and its usage is not permissible. (pp. 327–28)

Two further questions dealing with women's role in society touch on post-revolutionary concerns. In Question 74, Madani indirectly touches on practices and developments in female theological colleges.[26]

(Q 74) In the [Islamic Republic] some women study in the field of Propagation [spreading the message of Islam]; in order to complete the specialist course in rhetoric they have to deliver a speech in the presence of men. Can the woman's husband prevent this, and if he is not happy, is her [speaking] permissible or not?

(A) [I] wonder why specialization in rhetoric must be done in a men's gathering. Can it not be done in a women's gathering?

(And with all this) the husband can prevent her from delivering a speech, and without his consent [woman's] speech is not permissible. (p. 328–29)

In Question 100, Madani refers to the controversy over expanding sports facilities and activities for women, which had provoked the anger of religious zealots. In 1993, the first Islamic Games were held in Tehran, organized by the president's daughter, Fa'ezeh Rafsanjani, in her capacity as vice president of the National Olympic Committee.

(Q 100) What is the Ruling in the Sacred Laws of Islam on women's sport? Muslim women athletes are sent abroad to participate in international

---

[26] See Chapter Four.

competitions; in sports halls they are watched by strange men; please state the Ruling in such a case.

(A) Sport for women in places which are exclusive to them is no problem, but in the present age women's sports and competition outside the country, in particular in non-Islamic countries where participants and spectators are not bound by Islamic Rulings, is not permissible.

(What) must be mentioned is that in early Islam the Prophet did not invite Arab women to take part in horse riding and shooting, whereas riding and shooting are lawful acts that Islam legislated to prepare Muslims for war with heretics; and although the Prophet in his lifetime had many defensive and nondefensive wars with heretics, there is no record of brave Arab women participating in the competition or that he encouraged them to prepare for war. There are many things to be said on this, but present conditions and shortage of space do not allow [me to elaborate]. (pp. 340–41)

Ayatollah Madani in 1997

When I returned to Qom in February 1997 with Sa'idzadeh and Zahra, I went to see Ayatollah Madani to ask about the details of his Houzeh career. It was an afternoon in Ramadan, before evening prayer. As we entered his alley, we saw the ayatollah's khadem leaving the house; as grim as ever, he exchanged greetings only with Sa'idzadeh, while showing us into the room where, eighteen months before, I had waited alone, not knowing what to expect. It was much smaller than I remembered; and now there was a heater installed. When the ayatollah entered, he too seemed much shorter, but he was just as kind and welcoming. He recalled my first visit, and sent the khadem to fetch his notebook—and the fan I had left behind. But he did not remember my questions. I told him I was devoting a chapter to his views and had translated a section of his book *Problems*, on women. He said he was now working on another edition, dealing with further, new Problems. Since its publication, he had received many other questions, some from Iranians abroad; for instance, that day he had had a phone call from Germany with a question that excited him, about an ethical issue faced by an Iranian doctor. He discussed the legal side with Sa'idzadeh, adding that the caller had asked him to phone back with the answer as soon as possible, but he had told him to call back that evening. Sa'idzadeh said: "you did the right thing not to call Germany," but the ayatollah responded: "it's too expensive; I'd never do it." They were talking across each other. Sa'idzadeh was referring to the Mykonos trial, which was complicating relations between Iran and Germany at the time; the ayatollah was worried about wasting the "Imam's share" he receives as a *marja'*.[27]

---

[27] Mykonos is a Berlin restaurant where four leading opposition Kurds were murdered in September 1992. The trial, which came to be known by the same name, from August 1996 to April

Then the khadem entered, with my fan in one hand and the ayatollah's notebook in the other. The ayatollah put the fan on the floor near me, and started to read the question from Germany. I took out my notebook to write it down, but he said "no, just listen, it's not finished." It concerned whether a doctor who administers medicine with harmful side effects is responsible for them in the eyes of shari'a. The answer was: not if the administration of the medicine prevents a greater harm, and saves the patient's life.

When we asked permission to leave, the ayatollah said that his daughter had liked my fan, and asked where I had bought it. I said it was a souvenir from Japan, not available in Iran, and asked him to keep it, but he refused; I insisted, saying, "please accept it as gift from me to your daughter." He said: "now that you have made it a gift, I can accept," and jokingly added, "not all mullahs are grasping!"

As we were putting on our shoes in the hall, Zahra drew my attention to the khadem—I had told her the story of my first visit. He had his eyes down and his lips were moving, as though he were praying. Was it because of Zahra and me? Or because it was Ramadan, the month of fasting and prayer? I would never know. As the ayatollah was passing through the connecting door, the fan in his hand, he said: "I'll tell my daughter you've made it a gift, she'll be pleased."

Clerics like Ayatollah Madani live in a world whose gender codes and way of life Iranians like me find alien, just as they find those of our world unsettling. His world is that of traditional Shi'i authority, ruled by the power and logic of faith and piety, and still untainted by the realities of gender relations in the 1990s. It is a world of duties, where the notion of women's rights—the way I mean it—has little relevance. A woman is created to bear and rear children; in the divine plan, she has been assigned the very heavy burden of motherhood as her prime role and most important contribution to society. To fulfil this, it is both natural and logical that she stay at home and be provided for by her husband. Of course, she can study; and, if she chooses, she can work outside the home and earn money; but why should she want to do such unnatural things? They only hinder her from fulfilling her primary role.

In my world, a woman may well want to do these unnatural things: go out to earn money and not be maintained, share rights and responsibilities with her husband, choose whether or not to have children. To me, Ayatollah Madani's notions of family and gender roles are at best abstract and idealistic, and at worst impracticable and oppressive. Nor could they satisfy my criteria of causality and justice. His knowledge of women and their nature comes from texts and manuals, all written by men, all constructed with juristic logic, reflecting the realities of another age, a different set of interests.

1997, implicated high-ranking Iranian officials in the killing and brought about a political rupture between Iran and Germany.

2

Women Politicized: Ayatollah Azari-Qomi

SENIOR GOVERNMENT CLERICS were well aware that the Islamic Republic is dependant on women's political allegiance and cannot afford either to ignore or to alienate them, and some of them consequently produced a new narrative on women and gender issues. Yet they too, like their Houzeh counterparts, came from a scholarly tradition that takes the inequality of the sexes for granted. Whereas the old narrative was silent on women's social roles, the new one accepts women's participation in society and politics, but retains the traditionalist assumptions about gender.

The most explicit example of this new traditionalist narrative is a book by Ayatollah Ahmad Azari-Qomi, one of the most influential clerics of the first decade of the Islamic Republic. Born in Qom in 1925, Azari began his religious studies there in 1941 under Ayatollahs Borujerdi and Mohaqqeq-Damad, and Allameh Tabataba'i. He took part in the oil nationalization movement, and was among the founding members of the Society for Houzeh Teachers, which declared Ayatollah Khomeini's marjaʿiyat during the Qom upheavals of 1964 that ended in Khomeini's exile to Najaf. Between 1965 and 1979, Azari spent periods in prison for opposition to the Pahlavis. After the revolution he became judge of the Revolutionary Court in Qom and speaker and secretary to the Society for Houzeh Teachers; he was elected to the Majles and was a member of the Assembly of Experts (which appoints the Leader). He is best known, however, for founding *Resalat* in 1981; this is the daily newspaper that became the voice of conservative clerics, now referred to as the Traditional Right. He left the paper in 1994, after speaking out over the issue of marjaʿiyat, and returned to the seminary way of life. In the same year, he published a monograph on the notion of authority and problems relating to leaders and followers; in the introduction, he declares that the time of the Practical Treatise (*resaleh ʿamaliyeh*) is over, and he has entitled his work *Scientific Treatise* (*resaleh ʿelmiyeh*; the pun was intended).

Azari's book *Sima-ye Zan dar Nezam-e Eslami* (Woman's Image in the Islamic Order, henceforth *Image*) is an extended version of an article entitled "A Discussion of the Personality and Rights of Women in Islam" that Azari published in *Resalat* in December/January 1991/2.[1] His own researchers turned the text into a book, published in Qom in autumn 1993 in a print run of

---

[1] It also appeared in a collection of articles published in February 1992 by the Islamic Propagation Organization to celebrate the anniversary of the revolution.

50,000 by his House of Learning Institute Press. By "Islamic order" Azari means the Islamic Republic, for which *nezam* (order) is indeed now a synonym. Three decades earlier, when Ayatollah Motahhari produced his seminal text on women, nezam meant system, as evident in its title: *Nezam-e Hoquq-e Zan dar Eslam* (The System of Women's Rights in Islam).

I first learned about Azari's book a year after its publication, when I read a highly critical review in the journal *Zanan*. It was prefaced by a paragraph in which *Zanan* apologized for the delay in publication, stressing the need to respond to the book's gender thesis: "[Since] the views expressed in this book represent a current that is influential in shaping the movement and condition of Iranian Muslim women, we consider publication [of the review] to be necessary, however late. In this review, we shall become acquainted with the esteemed writer [Azari]'s most important views on women, and we shall read a critique of these views based on [Koranic] verses and authentic hadith."[2] The reviewer, signing himself Kazem Musavi, disposes of Azari's arguments one by one, with style, skill, and wit, pointing out not only Azari's errors regarding sacred sources but also how his text negates the Islamic Republic's rhetoric on women.[3] I was curious both to discover the identity of the reviewer and to find and read the book he had so entertainingly demolished. The reviewer was evidently a cleric; but not until April 1995 did I learn that it was Sa'idzadeh, my future collaborator, writing under a pen name.

I read Azari's text more or less at the same time as Madani's, in September 1995. I concluded that their gender perspectives were essentially identical. The only difference was that Azari was writing not just as a jurist but as a government cleric with his own political agenda. He sought to translate his notion of gender into policy, and above all to ensure that it was enforced. The importance of Azari's text dawned on me in January 1996, as I read the first installment of my discussions with the clerics of *Payam-e Zan*. He articulates the basic discourse that these clerics are trying to modify and circumvent; but unlike them, he states his views forthrightly.

Azari's text reveals not only the assumptions behind the Traditionalists' concern with hejab but also the kinds of dilemma that government clerics face, now that the regime sanctions women's participation in politics. It also contains an implicit debate, in that it carries its own counter-arguments in the form of alleged "objections" to traditionalist views. The final chapter also contains responses to a reader of his original article, whose questions constitute a barely concealed critique (quite different from the *Zanan* review), revealing the inconsistencies inherent in Azari's gender vision and narrative.

Image runs to 127 pages, although Azari's actual text is much shorter, since half of almost every page is filled with either a Koranic verse or a hadith in Arabic and its translation. I found it difficult to render Azari's statements into

---

[2] Editorial preamble to Musavi 1994, 36.   [3] Ibid., 36–40.

English. Much of what he says simply does not make sense to an uninitiated reader, even in Persian, let alone in English. It is effectively an oral document, highly allusive, repetitive, and rhetorical in style, based on his readings of sacred texts. It presumes and appeals to a shared knowledge of a body of sacred and popular beliefs. I decided to introduce the main arguments of each chapter, translating only those passages that epitomize Azari's perspective. I keep to the order of the original text, and place the arguments in context.

"Women's Image in the Islamic Order"

The front matter prominently includes a letter from Ayatollah Khomeini addressed to the author. First comes Khomeini's handwritten original; on the facing page is a printed transcription. The original, signed and dated 28/6/67 (18 September 1988), nine months before Khomeini's death, reads:

In the Name of God
His Excellency, Hojjat ol-Eslam Azari-Qomi

With greeting and prayer; I always liked you and still do, and never imagine that (God forbid) you might do something contrary to Islam. You are among the learned, active, and caring personalities of the revolution. By writing good matters and articles, you are trying to guide people to the right path. *I cannot say anything as regards Resalat newspaper and the esteemed Society of Teachers. Do as you, or the Society, find expedient. If I have said or written something regarding this, I acted in a way that I myself found expedient.* [emphasis added] May God keep you to help Islam and Muslims.

Both versions occupy the same page space (six lines each), and a casual reader could be forgiven for not noticing that the transcription, omitting the sentences I have emphasized, contains only those in which Ayatollah Khomeini expresses his affection and his confidence in Azari-Qomi.[4] The missing sentences clearly suggest that Khomeini wrote the letter in response to a specific question (perhaps in a letter) by Azari; but the reader is not told what the question was. Why was Azari seeking Khomeini's sanction and reassurance? Was it to do with the dispute over who was to be his successor, the next Leader? With changes in the constitution? With Khomeini's increasing frustration with clerical infighting? We never find out. Whatever the question was, clearly Khomeini refrained from giving his blessing to Azari's request.

Such selective and decontextualized quotation is a hallmark of Azari's text. It is also common in religious writings in the Houzeh and elsewhere. A new

---

[4] The same letter is produced in the front matter of Azari's *Scientific Treatise*, but there the facsimile and the transcript occupy a single page and are captioned "part of the holy handwriting of the Imam to Mr. Azari."

feature of Azari's book is that he uses Khomeini's sayings and writings more or less like holy hadith—a common practice in political rhetoric. Khomeini's sayings, removed from their original contexts (various speeches at different pre- and post-revolutionary junctures), are frequently invoked by opposing factions either to legitimize their own position or to undermine that of their rivals. They are compiled in twenty-one volumes, named the *Book of Light*;[5] these volumes and their subject index provide a repertoire of quotations that can be used to embellish almost any occasion and sanction almost any viewpoint.

For Azari, Khomeini's letter serves two obvious purposes. It shows that Azari, as a person, enjoyed the trust and affection of the founder of the Islamic Republic, and that what he writes is for the good of Islam and the Republic. Both are necessary to compensate for his relatively low scholarly rank; note that Khomeini addresses him not as Ayatollah but as Hojjat ol-Eslam, an honorific title for any middle-rank cleric, indicative of his Houzeh standing.

Azari's agenda as a government cleric is to contain the "cultural invasion," which prompted him to write a book on women in the first place. "Cultural invasion" became an issue in Iranian politics soon after the end of the war with Iraq, and served a useful purpose in the factional fighting following Khomeini's death. It is one of those vague ideological concepts that everyone is trying to find ways of confronting, and owes its power to its vagueness: it is the enemy within, which resists the ideological definition of Islam.[6] In his Introduction, dated November 1993, Azari tells us that his original article aimed to show the kind of measures that "the authorities of the Islamic Republic, and each individual," should take to counter the new "conspiracies of world imperialism" that now present themselves in the form of "a wholesale cultural invasion." He defines "cultural invasion" by opposing it. This new ploy of the enemy, he contends, requires "the people, especially the *basiji* [volunteer] fighters, to enter the trenches in defense of the achievements of the revolution." He recommends a number of "consolidation measures," and specifies three as the most important:

> First, expansion and clarification of the culture of hejab and the Islamic code of dress for women, through films, plays, publications, or other means. Because if the smallest breach is opened in this strong fortification, corruption and recklessness will expand to all other institutions and the way will be paved for the downfall of other Islamic values.
>
> Second, among the important actions that officials and ordinary people must pay attention to is the facilitation of marriage for youth. Economic measures must be taken to make marriage more affordable. . . .

[5] *Sahifeh-ye Nur*; also available on CD-ROM.
[6] See Kian 1995b.

Third, the role of the Islamic regime in containing cultural invasion in all its different dimensions is undeniable. The Islamic regime must exercise control over the press, public media, radio, and television in order to ensure that they all encourage young girls, even children, to observe Islamic dress and chador. We must make men and women in society aware of the value and special status of women in Islamic society. If a woman realizes her true status and does not lose her spiritual values then she will not be overwhelmed by West-struck culture. *Although* many women in our Islamic society are aware of their position and role on various platforms of the revolution, as the late Imam [Khomeini] said,

> "In the course of the revolution [women in our society] have proved that they can serve Islam and Muslims alongside men, *even* in social and political activities, and be vanguards in educating the esteemed society." (pp. 10–11; emphasis added)

These three points contain the key to Azari's text and his gender discourse, which center on women's appearance in public: "the culture of hejab." Before the revolution, when Islam was not in power and clerics like Azari were in opposition, the "image of woman" and her place in their Islamic order was clear-cut. She was not to be seen by strange men and her place was at home. But with the revolution she came out, and since then she has continued to play an important role in consolidating the regime. Khomeini sanctioned the first; he also had to give his blessing to the second (hence "even"). Azari has had to accept these facts (hence "although"). Yet he cannot abandon or ignore the worldview and gender discourse of the Traditionalists among whom he belongs. Women's participation in politics and society goes against the very grain of the Islamic order as constructed by the Traditionalists. At the same time, as Azari tells us, women hold the key to opposing the enemy's latest ploy: "cultural invasion." In a way, he invests women with the power to make or break the value system on which the Islamic Republic rests.

The main body of Azari's text reveals other facets of this dilemma and Azari's ways of dealing with them. The seven chapters are divided into sections, with titles accurately indicating their theme and content.

Chapter One, "The Image of Woman in Islam," contains the core of Azari's theological reasoning. It is about Fatima Zahra, the Prophet's daughter and wife of his cousin Ali, the first Shi°i Imam; and it must be read in the context of the official Iranian discourse, which portrays Fatima as embodying Islamic ideals of womanhood. This discourse dates to the mid-1970s, when Ali Shari°ati, the Islamic thinker and ideologue, in a lecture delivered in the Hoseiniyeh Ershad (then the center for Islamic intellectual opposition to the Pahlavi regime), addressed the crisis of identity faced by women in Iran, urging them—both Muslims who unquestioningly accepted traditional roles and those who aped the West and became mindless consumers—to follow Fatima's example as an ideal.[7] For Shari'ati, her life embodied the essence of Shi'i traditions and values of defiance, struggle, and protest against tyranny and unjustice.

Since the revolution, "Fatima as role model for women" has become (like "cultural invasion") a shibboleth used as a source of legitimacy for gender discourses. Fatima and her image have undergone a transformation. Her birthday (in the Islamic lunar calendar) was officially proclaimed Mother's Day, and the week it falls in is celebrated as Women's Week. She no longer stands for protest, defiance, and justice, but for chastity, piety, and submission. Iranian women are encouraged to follow her example: at times they have no other choice.[8]

To give the flavor of Azari's style and mode of argument, I translate the first section of Chapter One in full.

Fatima the Pinnacle of Exemplary Women of the World

In the perspective of the greatest divine School [Islam], woman in comparison to man has a totally equal position, and sometimes higher and more elevated. History contains outstanding examples of women who even in guarding the Prophets excel [men] in humanity.

Eve moved alongside her husband Adam, both in Paradise and in this world, the House of Trial.

Pharaoh's wife Asiyeh took the first and the most important step in protecting Moses. Likewise, Moses's sister, who took a risk in saving and educating her brother, perfomed her duty as a divinely worthy woman.

Hagar had an active role in founding the Hajj ritual, this "greatest divine congress," and protected and raised the Prophet Esma'il.

Mary, daughter of Emran, suffered the intolerable accusation of the infidel Jews, attained the status of "divine sign," and became the companion of angels. She received directly the Annunciation of the miraculous birth of Jesus.

> "And when the angels said: O Mariam! surely Allah has chosen and purified you and chosen you above all women of the world" (al-Imran, 42).

This woman did not earn this station except by self-restraint, resisting sexual urges, and taking refuge in God Almighty in the face of Angel Gabriel, who came to her as a man with a difficult mission.

[7] See Ferdows 1983, 288–90; and see Introduction to Part Three below.

[8] In 1989, in a radio program broadcast on Women's Day (28 January that year), a young girl aroused Ayatollah Khomeini's ire by choosing as role model not Fatima but Oushin, the protagonist in a popular TV serial from Japan. In a letter of the following day, the Leader of the Revolution denounced the broadcast and demanded that those involved be punished. The young girl could not be traced, but a number of senior radio officials were sentenced to jail terms (Najmabadi 1994, 366).

Sexual urges, which have been instilled in women's nature, are one of the blessings and ladders to progress and great divine trials. Mary's chastity and her self-restraint elevated her to a station such that she became companion of angels; some even mistakenly impute divinity to her.

Mary's self-restraint, alongside her knowledge, insight, and devotion, made her a divine sign and placed her among the great women of the world.

"And Mariam, the daughter of Imran, who guarded her chastity, so We breathed into her of Our inspiration and she accepted the truth of the words of her Lord and His books, and she was one of the obedient ones" (al-Tahrim, 12).

Mary is one of the two models whose name is repeatedly mentioned by God Almighty in the Koran.

God sets forth Pharaoh's wife as an example to those who believe. While silently praying to her God, she said:

"My Lord! build for me a house with Thee in the garden and deliver me from Pharaoh and his doing, and deliver me from the unjust people" (al-Tahrim, 11).

It is understood from this verse that the advancement of Muslim women is in their possession of two qualities:

First, self-restraint in the face of sexual urges.

Second, spending life in worship of the Unique Creator and the service of His creatures.

Such was Emran's daughter Mary, and in different places in the Koran she is remembered with goodness.

"When a woman of Imran said: My Lord! surely I vow to Thee what is in my womb, to be devoted (to Thy service); accept therefore from me, surely Thou art the Hearing, the Knowing. So when she brought forth, she said: My Lord! Surely I have brought it forth a female—and Allah knew best what she brought forth—and the male is not like the female, and I have named it Marium, and I commend her and her offspring into Thy protection from the accursed Shaitan. So her Lord accepted her with a good acceptance and made her grow up a good growing, and gave her into the charge of Zakariya; whenever Zakariya entered the sanctuary to [see] her, he found with her food. He said: O Marium! whence comes this to you? She said: It is from Allah. Surely Allah gives to whom He pleases without measure" (al-Imran, 35–37).

When pregnant, Mary's mother offered her unborn child to the temple—she expected to give birth to a boy who would be suitable for service in the temple but contrary to her expectation she found Mary, and it was not fitting for her to stay in the temple. She exclaimed: "My Lord! My child is a girl," not in order to inform God—she knew that "God knows" (God knew best what she brought forth, al-Imran, v. 36), but she knew it was not right to leave a girl alone in the temple because she would be in danger.

Therefore, she made this silent prayer to God:

"Oh Lord! man is not like woman, I could easily leave a man alone in the temple. Oh Lord! I leave her and her children in your protection."

God thus brought Mary under His protection and brought her up in goodness, and the guardianship of His pious servant [the Prophet Zachariah] protected her from harm of accidents and treacherous eyes and fed her with heavenly food.

But with all these qualities, Fatima is the pinnacle of all these women. She has such conspicuous qualities that throughout history no one has been able to compete with her. (pp. 14–20)

The abrupt way Azari ends the section is another hallmark of his style. He argues by fortifying his statements with Koranic verses. In the next section, "Attributes of Zahra the Gentle," he does the same thing, but this time he delves into Shiʿi sacred sources and draws on popular devotion to Fatima. He also engages in a kind of a play with words and concepts, and lists Fatima's attributes: infallibility, devotion to God, knowledge of the Traditions, self-denial, self-sacrifice, politics, hejab, housekeeping, and finally her heavenly progeny. Azari links each of these attributes with one of Fatima's names, and relates them to women in the Islamic Republic. The effect is both powerful and baffling: powerful because these words carry a load of meanings and connotations for Shiʿi believers, baffling because he is clearly putting a spin on sacred tradition to justify the Islamic Republic's policies on women. For instance, on Fatima's hejab, he writes, "The Prophet's daughter called the Jews to Islam by her hejab, in particular by wearing the chador. In observing hejab, she is a perfect example for our women. Likewise, with their hejab, our women, especially our female university students, have created fear in the World Despotism [Western countries] and in this way they are calling their Muslim and non-Muslim sisters all over the world to Islam and hejab" (pp. 25–26).

The notion that Fatima wore a chador is a far-fetched but now prevalent post-revolutionary assertion. I also heard it in Qom when discussing hejab with womenfolk of a clerical family with whom I stayed. They told me that "until recently we didn't know that both maqnaʿeh and chador were among the items Fatima brought as her dowry." They had first heard this the previous Ramadan in a sermon in the mosque. Azari compares not only the form but also the functions of Fatima's chador with that worn by women today: both constitute a call to Islam and an attack on the infidels.

The remaining two sections of Chapter One are much shorter, three pages each. In the first, as suggested by the title, "Fatima, Model for Women in the Islamic Republic," Azari expands on Fatima's other facets as a role model. He makes two points. First, "if a woman wants to find her place in an Islamic society, in the eyes of God and the Prophet," she "must adjust the program of her life in accordance with feqh." Second, in order to do so, she must model her life on Fatima's.

In the final section, "Woman's Image in the Islamic Republic," Azari draws a parallel between the pre-revolutionary era in Iran—which he refers to as "the time of idols (taghut)"—and the pre-Islamic "time of Ignorance (jaheliyeh)." His thesis is that women entered a new era with the establishment of the Islamic Republic, more or less like the advent of Islam. "In the time of idols—with few exceptions—[women] cared only for makeup and expensive clothes; and in their special dress, day and night they busied themselves with makeup and wasted their lives, and were happy that Western culture and its surrogate [Pahlavi] state had granted them this banal Western freedom. . . . The deposed Shah regarded "wearing chador" as "backward" and suitable for old women and the poor, who did not have beautiful clothes and comely bodies; he repeatedly said so" (p. 31). Azari explains women's abhorrent behavior, and its transformation by the Islamic Republic, as due to the existence of opposing forces in their nature, which are in a state of constant conflict.

> In the perspective of the Prophets, a woman, like a man, through struggle and endeavor, can preserve her piety and chastity and reach the highest state of perfection in the realm of God's guidance. Islam mentions two defects in women, one of which is their love of luxury and display, and the other is lack of knowledge and strong reasoning [capacity]; and both defects can be remedied.
>
> If a woman gives her allegiance to religious leaders and accepts their rule and guardianship, she will become higher than an angel and superior to a man.
>
> Woman, because of her nature and the natural attraction that exists in her, can ascend the levels of perfection and reach the highest peak of blessedness faster than men. Because a woman has greater patience, the fruits of her patience will be sweeter.
>
> Among the achievements of the Islamic Revolution which are the cause of pride and honor . . . is the evolution that has occurred in this class [women], which has amazed the entire world. (pp. 32–34)

As he continues, it becomes clear that Azari is talking about his own amazement and that of other clerics on discovering that the women they encountered during and after the revolution did not conform to their version of the Islamic theory of women's nature.

> A world that has imposed all kinds of corruption on women, especially sexual corruption, now witnesses that a *creature named Iranian Muslim woman* has reached such a degree of self-sacrifice, dignity, and honor that her role in fighting world oppression, if not greater than man's, is certainly

no less. Perhaps one can say that the secret of the victory of the revolution was the active participation of Muslim women.

They sent their children to the war fronts to welcome the burning bullets of the merciless enemy, and with an open face and a heart full of patience and gratitude sacrificed [their sons] for Islam. With all this, they see themselves as indebted to God, religion, and the Leader.

Women offered their services behind the front line and, side by side with men, they struggled and performed services for the revolution, the war, and the wounded. They sacrificed their youth and worldly pleasures to marry those wounded for the revolution

Our women have such political awareness that none of the ploys of world oppression will silence them or make them to give up their fight. With such brave women the Islamic revolution's stability and continuity are guaranteed. (p. 34, emphasis added)

"The Personality of Woman in Comparison to Man"

Chapter Two, "The Personality of Woman in Comparison to Man," contains what can be considered the ideological center of Azari's text. Fascinating but hard to translate, it is full of incomplete and qualified arguments, and even in Persian it is difficult to follow his intentions. I summarize key passages.

In the first section, "Woman's Delicate Constitution and Her Important Responsibility," we see Azari's version of Motahhari's theory of the complementarity of sexes and gender roles. The only difference is that Azari places the emphasis on women's independence in both spiritual and social realms.

The Creator has created men and women to complement each other. Both are independent and move toward a defined goal, but one cannot fulfill his/her duties without the other. Men and women are both human, and humans are superior to other creatures. Both have the same positive and negative qualities; both can be either just or corrupt, both can be believers or nonbelievers. . . .

On the first day of creation, God addressed Adam and Eve in the same way; both were summoned to obey God, given the mission to come to earth and accept divine guidance, and threatened with a dire fate if they strayed.

On this long road that stretches between their creation and their consignment to Hell or Heaven, [men and women] move side by side and with independent personalities, and complement each other in the division of labor and duties. Nowhere in the Koran has it been said that a woman's destiny is dependent on that of her husband. . . .

Woman has appropriated the privilege of carrying the child and rearing it for a long period. Men and women have shared and specific duties and roles in the conception and rearing of children; they also have shared and specific duties in making themselves pure and continuing human life. Both are blessed with the same divine gifts. Heavy jobs are assigned to men and light and delicate jobs to women; but they are the same in human value and greatness. The advantage of divine religions, in particular the sacred religion of Islam, over other schools is that men's and women's duties and responsibilities stem from their creation and nature; so all responsibilities are given to men. (pp. 37–40)

The next section, "Depiction of Women as Independent Personalities in Islamic Texts," argues that in sacred sources women are considered "independent entities." Here Azari counters objections voiced by those Traditionalists who still consider women's presence in public as a violation of the sacred laws of Islam. He makes a case for women's full participation under the following headings: (1) [women's] participation in politics and total submission to the Islamic ruler; (2) women's personal wealth; (3) women's [right] to inherit; (4) reward for women's pious deeds; (5) acquiring knowledge; and (6) enjoining the good and forbidding evil.

Azari invokes seven Koranic verses and one hadith of the Prophet. All seven verses imply gender equality. The first (Mumtahanah, 12) invites women to declare their allegiance to the Prophet; the second (Nisa, 32) tells men and women that whatever each earns is theirs and neither husbands nor wives should interfere with each other's wealth; the third (Nisa, 7) indicates that women, like men, inherit wealth from parents and relatives, however much there is; the fourth (Nahl, 97), the fifth (al-Imran, 195), and the sixth (Ahzab, 35) all confirm that God rewards and punishes believers, both men and women, according to their deeds; the seventh (Toubeh, 71) enjoins both men and women to help each other to keep to the correct path. The hadith also implies equality: "acquiring knowledge is obligatory for Muslim men and women."

Without making any reference to the arguments of those who invoke the same verses to argue for gender equality in Islamic law, Azari signals his consent by saying that they are the proofs of the "permission that Islam has given women to participate in politics, provided it has the sanction of the Islamic ruler." The only commentary he provides is under the last heading, enjoining the good and forbidding evil.

Men and women believers are components of an Islamic collectivity and responsible to others. If ladies always stay at home, the important duty of "enjoining good and forbidding evil"—which heads all duties—will be left unperformed. It is true that regarding the question of jehad and armed defense [women] have no duty, but even this Ruling is confined to a time when there are enough men. Women's presence in armed conflict is not obligatory, but this, and their participation in medical work, nursing, and other behind-the-lines tasks, are among their most important duties. Likewise, in early Islam women took part in treating the wounded. (p. 46)

Azari then refers to Fatima's speech in the Prophet's mosque defending Ali's right to succeed, and other instances in which women took part in political events. But suddenly he shifts ground and produces a hadith in which the Prophet recalls the important role of parents in a child's religious development, and he ends the section by giving women advice on bearing and rearing children:

> One of the main duties of a Muslim woman is, on the one hand, to care for the physical and psychological well-being of the infant and, on the other, to cultivate the hidden talents of the child; and these two important [tasks] cannot take place unless husband and wife regulate their marital relations in accordance with shariʿa customs, by complying with what is recommended and avoiding what is reprehensible. A woman gives birth to a healthy child by paying attention to matters of hygiene and shariʿa considerations, and after that, when breast-feeding and nursing the infant, she must not forget hygienic and Islamic points; and at the next stage [she must] bring them up correctly with kindness and affection—one of the characteristics of mothers. Choosing a good name is also an important matter, which is assigned to the father in order to make a positive and permanent mark on the personality of the child. (p. 48)

In the final section of Chapter Two, "Response to Some Objections," Azari offers a rejoinder to those who argue for gender equality. This section encapsulates how Traditionalists perceive women's rights, both in the West and in Muslim societies, when women work outside home, as a form of cruelty and exploitation, and how they consider any form of dress that is not chador as tantamount to nakedness. They not only fail to understand why women object to these views, they simply refuse to recognize agency in women at all.

> In capitalist countries, where their greedy men's only objective is to acquire more capital and to exploit the rest, including women, in the beautiful and magnificent name of "equality for men and women," women suffer the greatest cruelty. With the pretense that women in Eastern and Muslim societies have been deprived of their human rights, and with the conspiracy that hejab is an obstacle to women's social activities, [men] have compelled Western women, in spite of their delicate nature, to do heavy work. Women are degraded; and through the expansion of the culture of nudity they are turned into pretty dolls for the satisfaction of [men's] lust. In order to cause the fall of Muslim women too, they have instilled Doubts into their minds and have planted seeds of Doubt in Muslim societies.
>
> Here it is appropriate for me to produce for discussion a sample of these Doubts and Ambiguities and to respond to them. (pp. 49–50)

Selecting five of these, Azari devotes the rest of the chapter to refuting them. Ambiguity (*eshkal*) and Doubt (*shobheh*) are technical terms used in the Houzeh and in feqh. Eshkal is ambiguity or difficulty in the scope and applicability of a shari'a mandate, in instances when the believer's duty is not clear-cut. It may lead to a Doubt, a question that comes into the mind of a believer which goes beyond the accepted body of religious knowledge. Once a question becomes a Doubt, it must be suppressed and intellectual energy will be directed at obliterating the Ambiguity that caused it. What Azari calls Ambiguities and Doubts turn out to be women's demands for equal rights in law and society, the kinds of issues and questions that are openly debated in journals such as *Zanan*, and that I raised in my discussions with the clerics of *Payam-e Zan*, as we shall see.

First objection: Women's share in inheritance is half that of men. Therefore women do not have equal rights with men.

Response: At a time when patriarchy ruled in different human societies and woman was but a slave, the result of women's work belonged totally to men.

1. Islam gave women economic independence and the Holy Koran explicitly declares woman to possess her own wealth, saying about this, "men shall have the benefit of what they earn and women shall have the benefit of what they earn" (Nisa, 32).

2. Islam has instituted the right of mothers to demand wages from their husbands for breast-feeding and caring for their children.

3. According to Islamic instructions, a man has no right to order his wife to do housework, and a woman can demand wages for cooking and sewing and even for work she does for herself.

4. Also a woman has the right to demand that her husband pay her dower, however large.

5. Provision of complete personal maintenance for a wife is incumbent on her husband, even if she is rich. Unlike a man, who is bound to provide for his wife and children and his own parents if they are poor, [women have no duty].

Second objection: Blood money (*diyeh*) for women is half that of men.

Response: Blood money belongs to the heirs. The reason for this Ruling on the part of the Lawgiver is that heirs need resources for securing their maintenance, and because if a man is killed his heirs will lose all their resources. Therefore they need higher blood money than for a woman. But if a mother is killed, usually heirs need fewer resources.

The above objection stems from that fact that objectors consider that blood money is "the price of the person killed," whereas a free man or woman has no price.

Third objection: Why is talaq put in the hands of men, and in general what is its purpose? [Why can only men unilaterally divorce their wives?]

Response: As to why men are given the right of talaq, it should be said: First, it is possible for a woman, under the influence of caprice and transient impulse and because of her emotional nature, to free herself from the bonds of marriage and thus inflict irreparable harm on herself and her children. [She is] unlike a man who is rational in nature and does not act upon his emotions.

Second, during the marriage contract it is possible in special conditions [by inserting stipulations] for a woman to take control of talaq and to preempt the man's probable pressure [on her] or to demand that he compensate her for depriving her of protection.

Azari devotes the rest of his answer to explaining the purpose of divorce: when the marital relationship is under strain, the best solution is for the man to release his wife from the bond of marriage. He also stresses that if a women is in a brutal marriage, "the court must free her from the evil of such a man." In other words, he expresses approval of post-revolutionary changes in the law that give judges a free hand to release women from marriage if it entails "hardship."[9]

Fourth objection: The right of headship [of the family] is with men.

Response: Woman complements man and man complements woman. Women manifest the compassion and mercy of the Divine and men manifest Its knowledge and wisdom. Each is assigned tasks proportionate with their capabilities. For instance, men are used for judgment, which needs knowledge and wisdom, because women's mercy and compassion are an obstacle to the punishment of the guilty. Whereas, according to the Holy verse, "let not pity for them detain you in the matter of obedience to Allah," God has forbidden Islamic society and the judge to show compassion for the guilty.[10] Killing a murderer and leaving his children without a guardian is contrary to mercy, but it is in line with wisdom and necessary for the life of society. "There is life for you in [the law of] retaliation, O men of understanding, that you may guard yourselves" (Baqara, 179). Likewise in duties that require mercy and compassion both [men and women] are used.

Fifth objection: At various historical junctures women have experienced discrimination. One day women's suffrage and participation in elections are declared haram by the custodians of Islam, the next their participation in political life becomes obligatory. Does this not mean changing divine Legal Rulings and discrimination against women?

Response: From the perspective of Islam, confirmation and consolidation

[9] See Mir-Hosseini 1993, chapter 2.

[10] Madani refers to the same verse (Nur, 2) in the Introduction to *Problems*, relating it to punishment for fornication.

of the heresies of idolatrous governments, whether by woman or man, are condemned. Likewise, supporting and strengthening the divine regime are among Islamic instructions.

For instance, at the time of Reza Khan [Pahlavi] the tyrant, Modarres [an opposition cleric] was against women being elected to the Majles. However, after the victory of the revolution, the Imam [Khomeini] considered women's participation in elections and political action not only permissible but even obligatory.

This [difference in opinion] never implies a duality of divine Ruling with regard to women, since women's participation in non-Islamic governments amounts to supporting and strengthening the political, social, and cultural bases of the idolatrous regime; and in that regime women were but a plaything, [as] the government of the time used them for its evil purpose—to corrupt society—whereas at the present time women's role and direct participation in the advancement of the aims of the Islamic revolution are considered extremely important. (pp. 50–58)

Here Azari explicitly admits the extent to which context can affect what he calls a divine Ruling. If women's right to vote and their presence in the public sphere can be changed, then why not also their legal status in the family? It is perhaps in anticipation of such questions that Azari devotes his next chapter to marital rights.

"Duties of Wives and Husbands toward Each Other"

Chapter Three, "Duties of Wives and Husbands toward Each Other," contains Azari's views on marital relations. The first section begins:

One of woman's characteristics is her love of adornment. Women are raised in a variety of adornments. For her, adornment is among the necessities of life, and to display herself and to attract men's attention is important to her. At the same time, it is in woman's nature to be intimate with only one man, and this is a prized quality that compensates for her other weaknesses.

"The love of desires, of women and sons" (al-Imran, 14).

In the dictionary, the word for sexual desire (*shahvat*) means the lust of the self (*nafs*), and under the word yearning (*shouq*) it is said:

"Yearning is when the Self is filled with an attraction towards something."

Therefore, woman encapsulates a man's desire and yearning; and in return man is created to be drawn to women and to manage human forces.

This mutual love and attraction is the basis for the creation of male and female, on which the division of labor in the family is based. The internal affairs of the home, which revolve around pure emotions and feelings, are entrusted to someone who has them [women], and affairs outside the home, which involve reason and wisdom, are entrusted to men. And because the general management of the family needs reason, wisdom, and management skill, man is the ultimate decision maker and woman is the adviser in the internal affairs of the family and what relates to them. (pp. 61–62)[11]

To back this up Azari cites Sura Nisa, 34, which Traditionalists always invoked to argue that women should submit to men and obey them, as God has made men superior to women and put them in charge.[12] In his own translation of the verse, interestingly, Azari states that God made men superior because they are breadwinners; that is, he implicitly admits that the difference is social, not natural. But he leaves it there, and then elaborates on the notion of division of labor in the family, invoking a hadith in which the Prophet assigned matters concerning the inside of the house to Fatima and those concerning the outside to Ali. From this he concludes:

In all undertakings, the man is responsible and is the final decision maker. For example, the way a woman wears clothes and her appearance outside the home concern her husband, and in this matter a woman must obey her husband.

The first and most important quality in a good woman is to be obedient to her husband. She must in no way expose herself to the eyes of unrelated men and ruin her character under their lustful and poisonous gaze. In Fatima's words:

"The best thing for a woman is not to see and not to be seen by an unrelated man."

It might be said that:

"If it means that man and woman not only should not look at each other's faces and places of ornament but also should not converse except through a curtain or other barrier, such a command is impossible [to follow] in society."

In response it must be said: history records many occasions when Fatima talked with men, and they narrated her hadith. Therefore, the mentioned hejab and women's seclusion must be considered as "ideal and desired hejab"; or the raising of such issues by Her Holiness must be considered a response to those who criticize the severity of [imposition] of hejab and see it as contrary to the values [of the revolution]. (pp. 62–64)

Azari devotes the rest of the section to reconciling this hadith of Fatima with his own position that Islam gives women permission to take part in political activities. On the one hand, he admits that it is impossible for men and women

---

[11] Cf. Chapter Seven.   [12] Cf. Stowasser 1993, 17–18.

not to see each other in society and to avoid communication; on the other, he asserts that it is not Lawful (*shar'i*) for a woman to look at an unrelated man; and he then makes a case for men's right to chastise their wives in order to keep them in line.

In the next section, "Men's Assumption of Responsibility for the Family," Azari implies an answer to the problem, though he does not state it explicitly. First, he tells men to control their wives' movements and not to let them leave the house. Then he tells women that God has never sanctioned men's obstinacy and wilfulness. He concludes:

> Women's obedience to men is obligatory in only two matters, which come to the same thing, that is, the protection of the essence of the family, otherwise a man cannot give even the slightest command to his wife. A man must instruct his wife in what is permitted and forbidden, and cut the roots of corruption; he should not even house his wife in places where she can be seen by unrelated men. A man should not bring unrelated men to his house and let them be seen by his wife. A man must avoid buying and bringing [home] books and magazines and films whose teachings are harmful. When satisfying his own sexual urges, a man must consider the woman's right, too, and avoid lechery and socializing with unrelated women and being alone with them in a room either at home or in his office. (p. 69)

The "Culture of Hejab"

In the next three chapters, Azari's text and message become more explicit. They contain his manifesto for proper gender relations and women's rights according to his version of the Islamic Order, and his objections to the current situation and the way women appear in public, and how to rectify this. They also contain his dilemma: women's participation in politics and society subverts traditionalist notions of the proper sphere of gender relations, and "threaten society's moral fabric." The solution he proposes is to regulate women's movements in public and in private, or in his words, to promote the "culture of hejab."

In Chapter Four, "The Role of Islamic Hejab in Keeping Society Pure," Azari starts by defining hejab, both figuratively and literally.

> The protection of a woman's bounds and character is her modesty, and the importance of this issue is such that the Commander of the Faithful [Ali] recommends to his son:
>
> > "[Ensure] if you can, that she does not recognize anybody but you."
>
> Of course, observance of hejab in this way is impossible, because even Purest Fatima and her dear daughter Zeinab and the wives of the Noblest

Prophet could not abandon more important duties to reach the highest level of hejab.

The Holy Verse on the particulars of hejab says:

> "Oh Prophet! say to your wives and your daughters and the women of the believers that they let down upon them their over-garments; this will be more proper, that they may be known, and thus they will not be given trouble" (Ahzab, 59). (p. 73)

Azari then engages in a kind of exegesis that makes little sense unless read in the context of post-revolutionary attempts to promote the chador as "the supreme form of hejab." His apparent goal is to establish that the over-garment (*jolbab*) the Koran refers to is the same as the chador of the Islamic Republic. His main evidence is that the chador, like the jolbab, is a piece of cloth that women place over their headgear, and is thus the best cover and protection for a women's chastity. However, as soon as Azari has established this, he qualifies it by adding:

> It is better for [women] not to confine themselves to wearing only the chador, because, as narrated in a hadith by Omm Selma [one of the Prophet's wives]:
>
> > "I was in the presence of God's Prophet; Meimuneh [another wife] was there too. Blind Ibn Omm Maktum arrived. The Most Noble Prophet commanded: 'Go behind the curtain.' We said: 'O Prophet of God! Isn't it the case that a blind man cannot see us?' The Prophet responded: 'You are not blind. Do you not see him?' "
>
> From this order it is clear that hejab must be such that men cannot see women and women cannot see men, whereas chador is not such, so in our country and other Muslim countries where it is customary for women to go out shopping and there is no barrier between men and women, [the situation] is contrary to this order. (pp. 77–78)

Azari supports his point by producing three other Koranic verses on hejab (Ahzab, 32 and 33, and Nur, 31). He also produces a hadith of Imam Ali: "if possible do not give [women] permission to leave the house."[13] Azari relates these to contemporary issues:

> [We must therefore] restrict whatever can cause corruption or stimulate men's [sexual] desire, whether this corruption comes through looking at ears, hands, and faces decorated with ornaments, or whether it comes through looking at body protrusions, even if the skin is covered.
>
> Therefore, tight trousers and stockings that reveal the shape of a leg, using perfume—which has stimulating properties—and the sound that comes either from the throat or from tapping decorated feet, or singing by

[13] Cf. Chapter Seven.

men and women which stimulates sexual desire, all these cause corruption and are forbidden.

Such corruption might afflict people by other means, some of which are as follows:

1. Reading stimulating novels.
2. Looking at pictures that can excite and corrupt men and women;
3. Watching bad films, even if the actors are unknown Muslim or even non-Muslim women.
4. Shaking hands with an unrelated women, even through a glove; touching a woman's body, even through clothing, if it is stimulating.
5. Joking and laughing with unrelated [people of the other sex].
6. Even learning the Joseph Sura [the story of Potiphar's wife Zoleikha], if it can have a bad effect.

This bizarre catalogue, some of it directed at men as well as women, encapsulates Azari's notion of a sexual morality which not only women but men are expected to observe. When it relates to women, he calls it hejab, giving this concept a meaning far broader than the dress code: "Therefore a Muslim woman's character must be placed within such confines that she will not be vulnerable to aggression by an unrelated person, even in his imagination. . . . What has today become known as Islamic hejab, which covers women's nakedness but displays the parts that stimulate, is not Islamic hejab. Islamic hejab is what protects a woman's character from man's aggression by any means" (p. 81).

Azari ends the section by urging Muslim men to reject women who resist the kind of hejab he promotes. Men can do this at the personal level, even if government fails to impose the Ruling. "In truth hejab is a blessing by God for women, it is not an imposition, a limitation or aggression. It is because of her belief, her piety, that a Muslim woman becomes a worthy partner for a Muslim man. A woman without belief and without hejab is certainly not a suitable partner for a Muslim man" (p. 82).

In the next section, "Rulings for Looking at Nonrelatives," Azari focuses on three kinds of look (*negah*) that should be avoided in all circumstances. The first is a look entailing pleasure (*lezzat*), which he defines as "a look and a touch that transforms a permitted action into a forbidden one. Therefore, if a young man looks at his mother or sister or another relative or touches their body with the intention of pleasure; or if a man looks at another man, or even if a man or woman looks at or touches a nonhuman entity; or even if they touch their own body in such a way—this is forbidden. Only one's spouse is exempted here" (p. 83).

Second is a look that entails *reibeh*, the fear that it might lead to a forbidden act, even if pleasure or evil are not intended; for instance, looking at a woman's face with the intention of describing it to someone else. Third is a look that leads to chaos (*fetneh*), resulting in a forbidden act, even if it does not involve the intention of pleasure or evil: for instance, watching a film or listening to a story that might have bad results.

Having said all this, Azari then raises a logical question: "If the rationale for hejab is to prevent men falling into corruption, then it should suffice for men to guard their gaze; why such an emphasis on women's observing hejab?" His answer, stretching over two pages, is hard to render in English. Paraphrased, it reads:

> It is for woman's human dignity that she must observe hejab, because one of the differences between a female animal and a female human is that the former will surrender to any male by instinct. If a woman does not cover herself she may attract any man, and this is certainly not in her interest. The human female has been created to be part of an order and if she defies the rules of this order she will be separated from it and might not be able to rejoin a new order. This is what has happened to Western women. If a woman understands properly why a man is attracted to her, she will feel degraded, not respected, because the opposite sex has seen her as a means of satisfying his own sexual and animal urges. That is to say that he has considered her as a worthless animal. On this, Imam Sadeq says: "looking at an infidel's pudenda is like looking at an animal's." There is consensus among jurists that looking at an infidel woman's face and body is allowed. Some jurists object to looking at nomad or peasant women who because of their work and geographical conditions do not cover their heads or parts of their body ... because they consider it an insult to nomad and peasant women, although there is a hadith that such women must obey the rule [to cover themselves]. The fact that, according to the blessed verse of Sura Nur, a Muslim woman must observe hejab in the presence of non-Muslim women, confirms this point, although there might be other points there, because infidel women can describe the features of Muslim women to their men. From this it is clear that the benefit of observing hejab goes to women themselves, not to men. (pp. 84–86)

To deal with questions that might arise as to the proper limits of Islamic hejab, Azari devotes the final section of this chapter to answering fourteen specific questions. Seven relate to Rulings for looking at women or hearing their voice, one to the form of women's hejab, and the remaining six to Rulings for interaction between unrelated men and women. The questions are similar to Ayatollah Madani's "newly created Problems," and Azari's position and juristic answers are identical to Madani's; again, they might sound absurd or unreal to the modernized middle classes, or indeed most people in urban Iran, but they are concrete and of real concern to those who share Azari's understanding of the shari'a. To give an idea of how they are trying to come to terms with women's presence in public life, I translate five of these questions.

2: What is the Ruling for looking at a Muslim woman's image in water, mirror, glass, and television?

Answer: It is not permissible.

4: Can one look at Western women's artificial hair [wigs]?

Answer: In principle it is not barred, but it is not permissible with pleasure or fear of doing something forbidden.

8: Can ladies content themselves with wearing clothes that cover the skin and its color, and basically what is Islamic hejab?

Answer: No, they cannot. Their clothing must cover the parts which cause stimulation, in addition to covering the skin and its color. This is what is meant by Islamic hejab. Of course, as to Islamic hejab, chador is best.

9: Can unrelated men and women shake hands?

Answer: If the hand is covered and provided there is neither pleasure, nor fear, nor chaos, there is no ambiguity.

13: What is the Ruling for men and women gathered in the same meeting and laughing and joking?

Answer: It is forbidden. (pp. 87–89)

Earlier, Azari lists shaking hands between men and women, even when both are wearing gloves, among actions that can cause corruption; here, in his answer to question 9, he sanctions it, provided it is not done with evil intentions.

Traditionalists like Azari and his audience, accepting women's increased public presence as a reality they must adjust to, are clearly trying to find ways of regulating again the whole sphere of male-female interaction. The following two chapters must also be read in this light. They contain the remaining elements of Azari's manifesto for redefining gender boundaries and roles in the Islamic Republic.

Chapter Five, "The Role of the Islamic Regime in Keeping Society Pure," has two sections. In the first, Azari reemphasizes the necessity for the Islamic government to enforce hejab, as one of its primary duties. In the second, he argues that Islamic punishments are the most effective way to ensure that women comply with hejab. Both sections are short, and neither contains any fresh idea or argument; Azari repeats verbatim what he has already said in the Introduction or elsewhere in the book.

Chapter Six, "The Role of Marriage in Keeping Society Pure," also in two sections, does have fresh things to say. In the first, Azari defends *mot'eh/ mut'a*, temporary marriage, a contract with a definite duration (from a few minutes to ninety-nine years), which only Shi'i jurists recognize as valid. It legitimizes a sexual union as well as the children born into it, yet it is socially frowned on, regarded by some as a form of prostitution, and women who enter such unions are stigmatized.[14] Azari argues that it works as a kind of safety valve for society, and should be encouraged when legal means of

[14] See Haeri 1989 and 1994; Mir-Hosseini 1993 and 1998b.

satisfying sexual urges—that is, permanent marriage—are not feasible. He
writes:

> By legislating the Ruling of mot'eh, besides the intention of preserving
> public modesty in Islamic society, God has given the Islamic ruler a free
> hand to respond to social conditions. He can expand the Ruling in order to
> preserve society from sexual corruption when necessary; or, when society
> has no problem in [satisfying] sexual urges, he can limit it.
>
> Here I recommend Sunni brothers to heed the testimony of the second
> Caliph [Omar, who outlawed mot'eh] that
>
> > "women's mot'eh was permissible at the time of the Prophet."
>
> Perhaps he used his authority as leader, and clearly this was limited . . . since
> no one, not even God's Prophet, can alter the permanent divine Rulings.
> (pp. 100–1)

Azari means that Omar's ban on mot'eh was a temporary measure, imposed by
the Muslim Ruler; another Ruler can reverse it, since the Koran did not ban it.
The rest of the section explains how mot'eh differs from zena (sexual intercourse without marriage), taking issue with both Sunni jurists, who do not
recognize mot'eh, and Iranian popular culture, which stigmatizes it.

The next section, "The Special Place of Permanent Marriage," suggests that
Azari himself does not consider temporary marriage a proper one, and certainly not something that fathers can be proud of: "Compared to mot'eh, the
castle of marriage is solider, more impenetrable, and more secure. Therefore
Islam considers the marriage of nubile daughters to be among the good fortunes of a father" (p. 104). By "marriage" (ezdevaj), Azari means the permanent form, the only one popularly regarded as proper—mot'eh is never called
marriage, but simply "formula" (sigheh, short for sigheh-ye 'aqd). He then
preaches to future spouses and their parents the virtues of marriage. He touches
on issues such as the stipulation of dower in marriage contracts, choice of
partners, and equity in marriage. Again he gives neither logical nor juristic
argument, but tries to strike a balance on moral grounds. He concludes as
follows:

> Husband and wife, like two dear friends and colleagues, must lead a shared
> life, and neither should try to dominate the other, since both patriarchy and
> matriarchy are condemned and reprehensible.
>
> It is important to note that in some situations it is better to refrain from
> marriage. In the absence of [financial] means and other obstacles, it is better
> for a human being to put him/herself within the shield of chastity and absti-
> nence. If a woman sacrifices her sexual urges for Islam, the velayat-e faqih,
> and the Islamic Republic, she will be on the same level as Mary, mother of
> Jesus and Asiyeh, wife of Pharaoh. Many revolutionary sisters have sacri-
> ficed their youth and vitality at the feet of soldiers of the Islamic revolution

[the war-wounded] and have aroused the wonder of Westernized girls. Islam and its Leader are proud of those women who have waited for many years for the return of the war prisoners and wasted their youth.

It is true that God Almighty orders society and parents to prepare for the marriage of their children, and that the Prophet says:

"marriage is my practice and whoever avoids it is not among my followers."

But, at the same time, [the Prophet] says that if you are unable to marry, wait and do not fall into the trap of the evil of lust. (pp. 107–8)

With this passage, the text of *Image* ends.

Azari's position on marriage goes counter to feqh and traditionalist discourse. His statement on temporary marriage negates the Shi'i jurists' argument that the second Caliph had no right to outlaw it, as it was sanctioned by the Prophet and practiced under his rule. His advice to men and women to refrain from marriage contradicts every chapter on marriage in both Shi'i and Sunni feqh texts. Likewise, he thinks of women as social beings only when they forfeit their sexuality, hence the story of Mary; or when they are all covered, hence his concern with hejab.

Image has something new to say; it encapsulates the essence of the new narrative of the Traditionalists and the dilemmas they face in reconciling their gender views with the imperatives of the Islamic Republic. But how do women relate to such a book? What is its place in the gender debates in Qom?

"Response to Your Questions"

An answer to these questions can be found in the book itself. The final chapter, "Response to Your Questions," consists of an exchange, a kind of debate, between Azari and "a female student of midwifery." Introducing it, Azari tells us that she wrote to him posing a number of questions soon after the original article appeared in winter 1991–1992. He decided to include them when turning his article into a book, "with slight modifications to accord with the other chapters." On the surface, the twenty-one questions ask for clarification on behalf of the unnamed woman, her classmates, and her brother, but the issues raised and the arguments put forward clearly came from someone familiar with feqh idioms. The questions are both subtle and clever, drawing attention to the unrealistic nature of Azari's version of gender relations, and above all to the impossibility of policing its implementation, but Azari seems to have missed their tone, taking them at face value, as a compliment rather than a challenge.

The questions and responses are fascinating, and the effect is sometimes comic, an example of the kind of indirect, double-edged social and political criticism that has been perfected since the revolution: seemingly innocent questions, grounded in correct religious arguments and language—and thus placed beyond censure—expose contradictions in these very arguments.

Only the first two questions are distinctly serious. The first points to a contradiction in Azari's version of rights and duties in the family, and to a discrepancy between his rhetoric and lived reality.

1. In the first chapter you said: "a woman can ask her husband to pay her wages for housework or breast-feeding the children." But aren't home-making and caring for children a woman's primary duty? If so, why should she be paid wages? If not, why do men see [woman's financial demands] as selfish? Unfortunately, in marriage we see men oppressing their wives.

Anyway, can a man say he isn't financially able to pay for housework, or that he's not the kind of man to help you [in the house] or pay you anything for your housework? Does a man have such a right?

Answer: In response to this question three points must be dealt with separately.

First, a women must obey her husband in conjugal matters and meet his sexual needs and satisfy him in this respect so that he will be calm in his workplace and in society and not be tempted to fill his sexual void through sinful means.

Second, a woman must have her husband's permission to do anything outside the home; even leaving the house needs his permission, and if she leaves home without permission she has committed a sin.

Third, by prior arrangement with her husband and taking Lawful considerations into account, a woman can ask her husband to pay for part of the living expenses, such as breast-feeding or the care of children.

The last point is that maltreating a wife in the home is sinful and causes grave-pressure [punishment after death], and the Prophet says about this:

> "The best and the best-tempered among my people are those who treat their family well."

Azari falls into the trap, being forced to go beyond rhetoric and state his view that women's primary role is to satisfy their husbands' sexual needs; if these are unsatisfied then men become a danger at work or in society.

Question Two asks about conditions in which a woman can obtain the right to talaq, and receives the conventional legal answer. The remaining questions relate to facets of Azari's notion of Islamic hejab, which has to do with interaction between the sexes, pointing out the double standard for men and women in society. The questions are of two types, showing up Azari's Rulings as either impractical and constantly broken in social interaction, or as inherently gender-biased. The questioner cleverly draws Azari into a debate, implicitly suggesting that these Rulings have less to do with men's and women's natures, as he claims, than social definitions of gender, and that the former too are socially defined and changing, whether he likes it or not. Some of them are asked "on behalf of her brother," showing that, while the Islamic Republic tolerates variety and choice for men, it enforces uniformity and strict conformity for women. Here is a selection of them.

3. It's said [in a hadith] that "wearing a white headscarf is recommended." I know that if I put on a white scarf I become more attractive. But at the university I'm scared to wear one [she refers to pressure groups]; on the other hand, wearing a dark headscarf depresses my spirits; and because the chador is also black, I get depressed, as though I'm in mourning. I don't know what my duty is. Do I have permission to wear a white scarf and things like that?

Answer: Getting depressed and the like cannot give Legal Exemption (*'ozr-e shar'i*). A Muslim woman must protect herself from being molested by nonrelatives. Now this can sometimes be done by silence, sometimes by refraining from wearing perfume or makeup, and sometimes by wearing a black scarf. Therefore a woman commits a sin if she wears a thick dress in the street and market, yet [shows] her body curves or [allows] her gait or the sound of her steps [to be] stimulating. The Commander of the Faithful [Ali] scolds the men of Kufa for their womenfolk's frequenting the bazaar so that their bodies come into contact with unrelated men.

5. I ask this question on behalf of my brother. Is wearing light-colored clothes, or jeans and anorak—signs of cultural slavery—without ambiguity? If these types of clothing induce slavish [behavior], isn't it the same with suits and trousers?

Answer: Of course each nation's dress is one of its cultural markers. Therefore, wearing non-Islamic and non-national clothing is not permissible. The Prophet says, on behalf of God:

"Do not dress like my enemies, as you become like them."

In other words, we Muslims must refrain as far as possible from becoming like foreigners and infidels and be satisfied with our pure Islamic culture.

These exchanges border on the comic, but they clearly reveal Azari's ideological stance and the questioner's objection to it. Both know there is no such a thing as Islamic or national dress in Iran. Although there are local and regional forms of dress, they are confined either to rural areas or to ethnic minorities like Kurds. When Reza Shah enforced a uniform dress code in 1936, women were forced to appear in public with their heads uncovered: they could wear a European hat but not chador or scarf. Men were also required to wear European-style clothes; only clerics were allowed to retain their robes. Since then, European styles with modifications have slowly but surely gained currency in urban Iran, and when, after Reza Shah's abdication in 1941, the prohibition of the chador was relaxed and many women went back to wearing it, they usually wore European clothes underneath. After the revolution, there was another attempt to define dress codes. This time the overcoat and maqna'eh were introduced for women, whereas for men beards were encouraged and neckties frowned on and forbidden in public offices.

8. You said: "joking with unrelated men is sinful." I don't mean [indecent] joking—God forbid—but joking such as one does with one's brother. For example, in a university class—where gentlemen are also present—sometimes one of them says something funny. Although we do our best to prevent our laughter being seen by covering our faces, they betray a kind of animation. Is this kind of laughing sinful? And is it sinful in principle for an unrelated man to see a woman laughing?

Answer: The answer to this question requires a brief introduction. In interaction between men and women, what should unquestionably be avoided—and is sinful—is body contact; on this question reibeh and fear of temptation are not conditions. That is, even if a person might not be afraid of sinning, mere [body] contact is sinful and the person who does it is considered a sinner. But other acts are sinful only when they involve sexual pleasure or are a prelude to sexual relations with nonrelatives.

Therefore, looking at a beautiful flower or captivating scenery, or listening to raindrops or water running in stony passages are not only without ambiguity but they are in accordance with human nature and are good. But other acts, for instance looking at a woman who is wearing a prayer chador [white, lightweight], or looking at her when she is walking, or listening to a [female] choir and other similar acts, are sinful if they involve sexual pleasure or can result in illicit relations between them; but if they do not have such effects, there is no ambiguity in them.

It is the same with joking. So joking even with one's brother, a close relative, can be sinful if it has one of the effects mentioned. But if the joking is free of these two effects it is without ambiguity, even if it is with nonrelatives.

As for seeing women laughing, if it has one of these two effects it is sinful, otherwise it is permitted.

The question is witty and throws further doubt on whether the questioner is who she claims to be—there should be no male students in her college of midwifery. The next questions push Azari further, to define what he means by Islamic hejab, and to admit the impossibility of enforcing it.

9. Sometimes, when we're on our way to class or walking in the streets or the bazaar, although we observe full Islamic hejab, we notice evil looks directed at us. What's our duty in such instances? Must we cover our entire face or move away?

Answer: In that case a [woman] must protect herself from such looks, by whatever means she can. Now, as you said in your question, either cover yourself from the gaze of nonrelatives or leave the place at once.

13. This question too is from my brother. One of his professors is a lady who doesn't respect [correct] hejab and my brother has the habit of looking at his teacher in order to understand the lesson. But given that looking at a Muslim woman is not permissible, he's worried that he might be committing a sin; but if he doesn't look, he can't understand the lesson. What's his duty?

Answer: Your brother and his like, when choosing a course and a teacher, must think of all such matters; if he can, he must "prohibit evil" [by telling the teacher to cover herself] but if this is impossible he must abandon the course. At least he should avoid looking at his teacher; inability to follow a lesson is not an excuse for looking at her.

14. You said: "as a Muslim woman respects her hejab on the outside, she must keep her [inner] thoughts and imagination pure." What sort of thoughts are sinful?

Answer: Of course, thinking about sinful actions is not sinful in itself. However, every Muslim must distance him/herself from satanic temptation so that s/he doesn't fall into sin; and women who expose themselves to the eyes of nonrelatives have been trapped by these satanic temptations and have lowered their character to the level of animals.

The way Azari uses the question to chastise women whose hejab is not correct resembles a rhetorical device used by popular preachers, known as "flight to the Karbala desert," that is, shifting ground to invoke Imam Hosein's martyrdom. For Azari, hejab replaces Karbala. He shifts to it whenever he has nothing else to say. He disregards the whole question of intention when it comes to hejab, but not in other matters, as in the following questions.

15. Some people tell me: "your voice is soft and sexy on the phone." Of course I try to talk normally. What's my duty here? Don't I have the right to talk to gentlemen on the phone?

Answer: If you try, as you say, to talk on the phone without making your voice soft and sexy, then your telephone conversation is without ambiguity.

16. Are eyebrow trimming and removing facial hair without ambiguity, given that they beautify a woman's face? Isn't it sinful for unrelated men to see such a face?

Answer: The action itself isn't sinful, but it's sinful for a man to look at such a woman's face.

Azari's position goes against entrenched custom in Iran. Removal of facial hair and trimming of the eyebrows is a rite of passage to womanhood. In traditional families in rural and urban areas, what marks married women from girls is their trimmed eyebrows. Many families still do not allow a girl to tamper with her facial hair and eyebrows before her wedding day.

The questioner draws attention to Azari's loose use of technical terms:

17. The late Imam [Khomeini] said in his treatise: "a man's gaze at the body of a Muslim woman and a woman's gaze at the body of a man are sinful, with or without the intention of pleasure." Is the face part of the body? And why is it sinful?

In your text there's a phrase: "if a person fears falling into sin." What does it mean? Does it include desire for one's spouse?

Answer: Men and women looking at each other, except for the face and hands, even if done without the intention of pleasure, is sinful. The reason it is sinful is that there is fetneh, or potential for sexual pleasure, either all the time or most of the time. The face is exempt from this so as to avoid hardship for men and women in society, but otherwise the tendency to fetneh is stronger in the face.

The thought of being with one's spouse is not sinful, but it is sinful for a man or a woman to be with a nonrelative. In short, when someone looks at a nonrelative with fetneh, this means that s/he has taken the first step toward a sexual encounter that is illicit in Islam; and subsequent moves between these two unrelated persons can lead to a sinful act. This is the meaning of "fearing to fall into fetneh and the act of sin," and Islam by fixing a no-entry sign in this zone [contact between men and women] seeks to close the gate to sin from the very beginning.

18. When a woman sees a picture of a good-looking man, she wants to look at it again, just as when she sees a picture of a beautiful woman. She wants to see the picture for a second time to focus on the details, for instance on the aesthetic points of the eyes or nose. Is this type of look sinful? Although I'm scared to look at men or their pictures in case I fall into sin, I can't distinguish between sinful and nonsinful looking, although often, when I see a man or look at him when talking to him, my gaze is not of the types you described. Basically, is there a difference between seeing and looking? What is the difference between not permissible and sinful?

Answer: First, "not permissible" means the same as "sinful."

Second, "seeing" is possibly the first involuntary look that one casts on a nonrelative; such a look is allowed, but further looking is sinful.

Therefore, looking at a picture of someone of the opposite sex is also sinful, if it involves reibeh or fetneh, because looking at a picture is like looking at the person in the picture, and there is no difference between looking at him or his picture.

Missing the point of the questions, Azari repeats feqh phrases and conventional wisdom without examining their underlying assumptions and the contexts in which they have been discussed by jurists. When pushed further, he does not rule out the possibility of other interpretations.

19. You said: "gentlemen should pay attention not only to a woman's piety but also to her beauty and [other] qualities, and there are a number of hadith about this." Are there hadith telling women to take account of a man's attractiveness as well as his piety?

Answer: I have not yet come across such a hadith, but on theoretical grounds it is certainly possible.

20. What is a woman's duty in a marriage proposal session? Some gentlemen want to see me without my overcoat and chador; and this is indeed difficult and distressing for me; the thought that one day I might come face-to-face in the street with a man who has seen my features torments me, as it is said "it offends my honor."

Answer: Only when that person intends to marry you is he permitted to see your face and part of your features, and if you intend to marry and have a family according to Islamic Rulings you must submit to such things.

This question is interesting, not just because of its content and the answer it elicits but because of how it is phrased and the use of the word *gheirat* (sexual honor) instead of *haya* (shame).

21. I talked for about three hours with someone who had come with a marriage proposal. At the end of our talk, the gentleman complained that I did not look at him even once. I always try to act according to Imam Ali's hadith, "It is better that no man sees her and she sees no man." I looked at that gentleman only once—a passing glance. In short, his objection was that my behavior was antisocial, and seeing is different from looking. My response was, "But looking at a nonrelative is forbidden, isn't it?" Who's correct here, he or I? Of course, I'm not worried about looking at him, my worry was and is that an exchange of looks between us might have a bad effect on him [he might be tempted]. In any case, if the marriage proposal does not result in any agreement, and the man has seen the woman uncovered, doesn't this humiliate her? Basically, what is the divine Ruling on this matter?

Answer: It is without ambiguity to gaze at a woman's face, hair, and other features and beauties, when the question of marriage is involved. Otherwise gazing is not permissible and is sinful. There is no objection to your talking about physique, marriage, and its conditions, for however long a time.

This last question, both witty and revealing, concludes the exchange.

Whether we take these questions as the genuine concerns of a young woman trying to find meaning in Azari's collection of statements and wanting to know her duties in an Islamic System, or as a disguised challenge by someone who knows the juristic arguments and is trying to show up the contradictions and absurdities in Azari's text, the fact remains that Azari has no effective answers. His dilemma, which he has created for himself, is also that of the Traditionalists in Iran. He wants to keep the old interpretations and yet have women participate in political life. He knows too well that women are needed to materialize his vision of Islam; but he cannot yet conceive of them as full social beings.

Ayatollah Azari-Qomi in 1997

I went to see Ayatollah Azari-Qomi in February 1997 in Qom, after leaving Ayatollah Madani's house. I had written this chapter, and had found a published account of his career in a journal, but I was uncertain how to face him, given how critical I was of his views. We reached his office shortly before evening prayers, as Saʿidzadeh thought we might find him leading the prayers, but he was not there, so we went to his house, some alleys away. Talking with someone through the entry phone, Saʿidzadeh found that the ayatollah would receive us in his office shortly. Back we went to wait for him.

Ayatollah Azari-Qomi's office was *shomali*, on the north side of the street, reached through a small courtyard, from which Saʿidzadeh entered the main room through a corridor, while Zahra and I went directly into a small space separated from the main room by a curtain. In the small room, which was for women's prayers, there was only an old women, who said she came early to perform prayers she had missed. When the ayatollah arrived, a khadem knocked and invited me to the other side of the curtain. Zahra stayed behind. In the main room, I was introduced to the ayatollah, who was seated behind a desk, with his legs stretched out. A number of men, mostly in nonclerical robes, were sitting on the floor facing the desk; I chose a place close to Saʿidzadeh, who had already explained the purpose of our visit. A big television was on, I supposed to catch the call to prayer.

Ayatollah Azari-Qomi looked and sounded quite different from what I had expected. He was tall, good-looking, and very well dressed; his robe and turban were both white, matching his beard. He spoke with a Tehrani accent. I first asked him whether his biography as printed in one of the journals (*Sobh*) was accurate; he said he had not seen it, but he had written the details in an account of his reasons for leaving *Resalat*, the newspaper he founded early in the revolution. He then spoke openly about this separation, referring to it as "declaring my independence." He now believed that the marjaʿ must be the most learned among the ulama, and that the marjaʿiyat should be quite separate from the velayat-e faqih: the first is religious in nature, the second political. I asked who the girl was whose questions he answered in the final chapter of his book on women. He said he did not remember: the questions were submitted to the office, and his assistants referred them to him. He returned to the subject of his current views on authority, and referred me to a book in which he revises his earlier stance on the issue.

When I finally managed to bring the discussion back to women, I queried whether his views had changed from those expressed in his book. He said that people wanted to translate the book into English, as it would have great appeal in the West, since there was a chapter on Holy Mary. I told him that, in fact, this was the only chapter that I had translated in full; I did not say that I had done it for different reasons. The ayatollah added that before having the book translated he needed to add some pages to respond to the points made in *Zanan*'s review; but he no longer felt like writing; he had many unfinished works to deal with. Two issues needed to be reconsidered: contact between men and women not related by ties of marriage or kinship, and whether women can have a mandate over men. Feqh opinions on both, he argued, must be revised in the light of modern times, and he had found proofs permitting both. Permission for the second is found in Sura Touba, 71, which says "the believing men and the believing women; they are guardians of each other; they enjoin good and forbid evil"; and for the first, in a hadith which allows a woman to share a carriage with an unrelated man if she wants to go Mecca unaccompanied by a close relative. A man in the room added that there is considerable misunderstanding on this matter; it confuses the youth, who are anxious to get to know the opposite sex; whereas the shari'a permits men and women to see and talk to each other before marriage. Azari agreed that this was indeed a problem, as many marriages start without the couple knowing each other. "This is part of the culture, whereas Islam is very open; my wife told me she didn't know she was marrying a mullah! We were so confined."

The call to prayer was broadcast. I thanked him and returned to Zahra in the small room, where I counted eleven women, some with their children; the old woman had finished her missed prayers and was ready to join others waiting for the call from the men's room.

Late in 1997, Ayatollah Azari-Qomi's disagreement with his old allies, and his siding with those in the Houzeh who are questioning the scope of the vali-ye faqih's mandate, resulted in his house arrest. In an interview with an opposition radio program, he attributed his own illness and that of his wife to the psychological impact of this isolation.[15]

[15] Reported in *Mobin* (a weekly published in Iran), 12 Ordibehesht 1377. For an English digest of the news of the dispute, see *al-Moujez-an-Iran* (*Iran Briefing*) 7 (4), December 1997. He died in February 1999.

Part Two _____

THE NEO-TRADITIONALISTS:
GENDER BALANCE

Introduction to Part Two ⸻

SOME CLERICS in Qom are well aware that both practices and policies in the Islamic Republic are increasingly remote from shari'a ideals. They are sensitive to current debates about gender, and to criticisms by both secular and religious women of patriarchal bias in Islamic law. Although these clerics defend the gender model in shari'a law as immutable, they openly recognize the influence of time and place, and readily admit the need for changes.

The best label I can think of for these clerics and their views on gender is Neo-Traditionalist. Generally, they are in favor of changing the Houzeh system, and some advocate the idea of Dynamic Jurisprudence, which is gradually gaining ground as the inadequacies of the old school, now referred to as Traditional Jurisprudence, become apparent.[1] They are intent on finding an Islamic solution to the pressing issues of gender but, although they seek new interpretations of the shari'a, they dismiss equality in rights and duties as a Western concept with no place in Islam. They may vary in their approaches and arguments, but they all base their views on Ayatollah Motahhari's *System of Women's Rights in Islam*.

The most important post-revolutionary text on women is *Women in the Mirror of Glory and Beauty* by Ayatollah Javadi-Amoli, a high-profile cleric and member of the Society for Houzeh Teachers.[2] Like Motahhari's, Javadi's book coincided with changes in divorce laws, in this case the 1992 Amendments to Divorce Regulations, which reinstated some of the rejected elements of the Family Protection Law under a different legal guise.[3]

Javadi-Amoli's book, the first substantial publication on women by an eminent ayatollah since the revolution, is rooted in a convergence of three elements. The first is lessons delivered in 1989–1990 at the women's theological college, Jame'at al-Zahra, to advanced-level students who also assisted him in editing the text and in "elucidating some of the ambiguities regarding feqh and Koranic exegesis." The second was a seminar organized by Iranian National Radio and Television for which Javadi prepared a special text to fit the seminar's theme, "the high status of women in Islam, protecting their honor by amicable means in the society, and combating the Western cultural invasion."[4]

The third element was a set of "scientific questions with regard to specific Koranic exegesis," asked by Monir Gorji. A preacher and activist, Gorji was a member of the group that founded the al-Zahra College. After the victory of

---

[1] See Schirazi 1997, chapter 14.
[2] Javadi-Amoli 1993a; Glory (*Jalal*) and Beauty (*Jamal*) are among the Names of God.
[3] See Mir-Hosseini 1996a and 1998a.
[4] Javadi-Amoli 1993a, 17–18.

the revolution, as the only woman on the Constitutional Council, she accepted the council's interpretations of the shariʿa on women's rights,[5] but by the late 1980s she started to write Koranic exegesis in order to show that the Koran does not sanction the restrictions imposed on women by orthodox interpretations of the shariʿa. No longer involved with al-Zahra, she is director of the Center for Women's Studies and Research in Tehran, established in 1989, where she now holds classes. Her Koranic commentaries appear regularly in the center's journal *Farzaneh* (Sage), which was started in 1993.[6]

Ayatollah Javadi-Amoli's stance on gender is the same as that taken by Ayatollah Motahhari three decades earlier, although his mode of argumentation is different.[7] While concurring with Motahhari's thesis of the complementarity of gender rights and duties, Javadi places the issue of gender inequalities on the spiritual plane, where the real destinies of men and women lie, justifying them through a series of inferences.[8] For instance, as regards family matters he writes: "[women's] endurance of hardship might on the surface appear an evil but its immense benefit is to strengthen the family and protect its essence."[9]

If Motahhari's and Javadi's books are core texts for the Neo-Traditionalists, as I have suggested, the most active promoters of neo-traditionalist views are young clerics who run the various publications financed by the Islamic Propagation Bureau of the Houzeh. This is an independent office, deriving its income from a number of factories and assets confiscated at the time of the revolution and put at the disposal of the Houzeh.[10] In addition to specialist periodicals on Islamic sciences, the office also produces a women's monthly magazine called *Payam-e Zan* (Woman's Message). Its introductory issue (January 1992) featured a highly favorable review of Javadi-Amoli's book, recommending it to all women, especially those who want proper answers to "objections by strangers" (that is, feminists).[11]

I first came across *Payam-e Zan* at a newspaper stall in Tehran in summer 1992; and in the autumn of 1993 I found a bound collection of the first year's issues in a bookshop selling Houzeh and Islamic publications. The journal puzzled me. Some of its articles were defensive and apologetic in tone, using standard arguments to justify shariʿa legal Rulings and ignoring current reali-

---

[5] Esfandiari 1994, 63–67.

[6] In an interview in *Payam-e Zan* 6 (September 1992), she reveals her initially idealistic expectations of the Islamic revolution. She admitted the same to me in November 1995; my notes on our discussion are among the materials I lost.

[7] For discussion of *Zanan*'s review of Javadi-Amoli's book, see Mir-Hosseini 1996b, 305–7.

[8] Cf. Murata 1992, who also does an analysis of gender in Islamic thought through mystical texts, and seems to reach similar conclusions.

[9] Javadi-Amoli 1993a, 22.

[10] It is distinct from another organization with a very similar name, the government-sponsored Islamic Propagation Organization.

[11] *Payam-e Zan* Introductory Issue (January 1992), pp. 47–51.

ties. Other articles argued more subtly, criticizing traditional views on the nature of women's rights and arguing for new interpretations. For a year, the journal serialized some of Ayatollah Motahhari's unpublished material on women. There were also transcripts of interviews with women celebrities in the Islamic Republic, individuals prominent and active either on their own account or as wives and daughters of prominent men. These interviews, conducted by women, I found fascinating; they were candid and represented diverse views, including well-known establishment figures who criticized the institutional barriers that women face and their inability to voice their demands. I also found the advice ("Dear Abby"/"Agony Aunt") section of immense interest; most letters were from young teenage girls seeking both moral and practical support for problems they faced in family and society.

I came to know more about *Payam-e Zan* and its place in the Houzeh in April 1995, after starting my research collaboration with Sa'idzadeh, who himself contributed to the journal. He told me about its internal differences of opinion: all the regular contributors to the journal were male clerics, and women's contribution was limited to conducting interviews with female celebrities and helping with the Advice section. The journal's inside cover features the phrase "with the cooperation of the Sisters' Unit of the Propagation Bureau"; this meant the women working in the office, transcribing interviews and typing.

In September 1995, Sa'idzadeh arranged for me to meet Seyyed Zia Mortazavi, who has edited *Payam-e Zan* from the start, and with whose name and editorials I was familiar. The meeting turned into a vigorous discussion, as already mentioned, which we continued over three sessions between September and November 1995, and also included an interview with Ayatollah Sane'i. We tape-recorded the discussions; I kept copies of my tapes in Tehran, and later recovered them, although my handwritten notes on the debate are gone.

The four chapters in Part Two narrate my account of these meetings. I give nearly complete translations of my transcripts, removing only some minor repetitions, and adding only some necessary contextual comments.

3

Women Represented: Discussions with *Payam-e Zan*

MY APPOINTMENT with the editor of *Payam-e Zan* was for the morning of Thursday, 7 September 1995. Sa'idzadeh had organized it. As it was not proper for us to travel together unaccompanied, we went with a friend and his wife who were driving to Qom on pilgrimage; I stayed with them in a relative's house. Sa'idzadeh's daughter Zahra joined us in Qom and accompanied me everywhere.

The journal's office is in a building at the junction of two alleys, and has two entrances. The main one, which leads straight in, is used by women; the other one, used by men, opens into a courtyard with a small pool and a toilet. We passed through the courtyard, climbed a short flight of stairs to reach the veranda, took off our shoes, and entered a corridor with rooms on either side, leading to a reception area where a curtain concealed the entrance to the women's section. Sa'idzadeh guided us into the room on the left of the corridor, which had a large French window onto the veranda, and a smaller window overlooking the alley. At one end was a desk with a telephone on it and chairs nearby. At the other end were more chairs and a stand displaying copies of the journal. I sat down at the far end, near the window, with Zahra beside me and Sa'idzadeh opposite us.

The editor, Zia Mortazavi, came in. He was in his thirties, wearing a clerical cloak and a black turban marking him as a Seyyed, a descendant of the Prophet. I later learned that he was born in 1958, entered the Houzeh at the age of thirteen, and in 1992 moved to the advanced level, in which he was studying under Ayatollah Sane'i (see Chapter Five). We exchanged formal greetings, and Sa'idzadeh asked me to introduce myself.

I outlined my academic credentials and research interests and experience, giving greatest detail about my second project, a comparative study of Islamic family law in Iran and Morocco between 1985 and 1990. I explained that I approached the shari'a from an anthropological angle; I tried to understand it through practice rather than theory; and I was interested in how people relate to it and use it to solve their marital difficulties. I added that I was now researching a new book, focusing on changing notions of gender embedded in shari'a Rulings on the family. One question I was investigating, I said, was whether these Rulings can accommodate women's demands for equality. I finished by saying that since 1993 I had worked as a freelance consultant with the Food and Agricultural Organization of the United Nations on participatory development projects. This gave me opportunities to come to Iran regularly and to follow debates here about gender issues as they unfolded in women's journals. In my opinion, I added, three journals were leading the debates: *Zanan*, *Farzaneh*, and *Payam-e Zan*. I had already had several meetings with editors of the other two, to discuss their gender perspectives; now, if he agreed, I wanted to do the same with *Payam-e Zan*.[1]

Mortazavi said he welcomed the idea. So I posed my first question: "Why is *Payam-e Zan*, a women's journal, run by men? What are their motives and interests in producing a women's magazine?" After a long pause, he replied that, since it was an important question, to address it properly it would be best to ask a colleague to join us. With that, he left the room.

I became apprehensive and asked Sa'idzadeh if I had made a mistake starting with the issue of men's authorship of the journal. He assured me that Mortazavi was an intelligent and open person, and it was a good sign that he wanted to involve others in the discussion. Some minutes later, Mortazavi returned with another cleric, a man in his early thirties wearing a white turban (not a Seyyed). Mortazavi introduced him as Mr. Sa'idi from the Propagation Office, in charge of the journal's correspondence section. I learned afterward that Sa'idi was another student of Ayatollah Sane'i; born in 1961, he had studied physics at the university but left in his second year, in 1980, in order to enter the Houzeh. For his benefit, Mortazavi now paraphrased my question, adding that he had expected it; he was familiar with such criticism, when women complained that clerics in Qom were advocating and defending the rule of "patriarchy" (*mard-salari*).

My question had touched a raw nerve, and I tried to clear the air. I explained that I posed it in good faith, with no idea that they might find it offensive. As someone who studies gender and women's issues in a cross-cultural context, it was just natural for me to ask why, in Iran, clerics are putting their energies into talking for women and defending their rights. I voiced it directly, I said, because I was genuinely interested to know the answer, and was prepared to have my views challenged.

Both of them started to explain. Mortazavi said that, ideally, women should produce such a journal, but men must do it for the simple reason that there are no women in the Houzeh who can assume the task. To this Sa'idi added: "We consider the question of women important and find it imperative to address it within the Houzeh framework; the nature of the relationship between men and women is such that, if it is unregulated, women will lose and continue to be oppressed." He used the analogy of the mother-in-law/daughter-in-law relationship to stress the tension and conflict inherent in the male/female relationship.

---

[1] For accounts of the women's press, see the Bibliographic Essay.

I interrupted. I was determined not let them reduce everything to "nature." I said that any tension was a matter of social rather than natural factors, of the social construction of gender roles. For instance, not everywhere in the world is there tension between mother-in-law and daughter-in-law; in some societies the opposite is true—there is more shared interest than conflict between them. Sa'idi responded by elaborating on these "natural" differences.

As the discussion got under way, I found I could no longer take notes at the same time as trying to argue my position; I said as much, and asked if they would mind if I turned on my tape-recorder. Mortazavi agreed, and I recorded the rest of the session, which lasted nearly two hours. Not having anticipated that a debate would develop, let alone that I would be allowed to record it, I had brought only one cassette, which ran out well before the end. Throughout, we were served the customary tea and fruit; the telephone kept ringing, and Mortazavi would answer it while I continued talking with Sa'idi.

I translate my transcript with minor omissions and some comments, noting where my transcript differs significantly from that published by the journal. ZMH = myself; SMS = Sa'idzadeh; MHS = Mohammad Hasan Sa'idi; SZM = Seyyed Zia Mortazavi.

The Discussion Begins

I began by rephrasing my original question, which had set the tone for the entire discussion, and Sa'idi responded.

MHS: To eludicate this, as I said, we must consider certain factors. One is the importance of the women's issue; another is [the need] to discuss it in the wellspring of religious knowledge, whose specific geographical location is the holy city of Qom. The women's issue in an Islamic society is one of the most important and fundamental issues, which concerns everybody. It's important because the essential nature of the relationship between men and women is such that, if it isn't regulated and guided on the basis of a correct understanding, women's rights will suffer. On the other hand, if one leaves regulation of this relationship to instincts and personal inclinations, undesirable consequences will follow. For this reason, society must be based on law and certain checks must be established; it's rather like a road with slippery patches; if we put up danger signs, we protect people's safety and life. Likewise in society, because of the existence of natural conditions and special circumstances, people often stray, and this causes damage; we must prevent such damage by establishing appropriate laws and regulations.

As for the example—which you said should be opened up and discussed—I said that the primary nature of the relationship between a daughter-in-law and a mother-in-law is confrontational. In my view, this is rooted in psychology and the emotions, which are influenced by sociocultural and other factors. In principle, mothers have a strong emotional attachment to their children; a mother who brings up her child, her son, has certain feelings toward him. If she doesn't control these feelings, it'll be difficult for her to come to terms with his establishing his own independence, a new family. . . . The same kind of possessive feeling a mother has toward a son, a wife has toward her husband; she marries with the notion that the husband will be hers. It's in her nature to want him for herself.

ZMH: Are you saying you consider it "natural" for a woman to want an exclusive relationship with her husband?

MHS: Of course; it's a natural need. In fact we see that such a feeling in women comes from human nature and yields much good fruit. So also in men, sexual jealousy is natural. These form the existential and educational elements in human nature which, combined with laws, can lead to correct development. Conflict [between male and female] is natural but must be controlled by legislation. . . . The issue of women is important because it represents a vulnerable and hazardous point in society. It must be addressed from a religious perspective because we believe that what is known as the Islamic perspective on women is different from what Islam really says. One can say that Islam is misrepresented, and in fact subjected to great injustice. Many erroneous views on women stem from people's perceptions and self-interest, which they justify in Islam's name or attribute to Islam.

For example, you have probably heard that some of our religious-minded people behave as though women are inferior beings; and some even doubt their humanity. The legal tradition treats women that way and even sees women as defective in intelligence, as beings who should not be consulted, and so on. Anyway, [critics] attribute such a negative view of women to Islam. Whereas if you consider, for example, Mr. Sa'idzadeh's research, he shows how some of these negative views attributed to the Commander of the Faithful [Ali], historically weren't his, but those of his enemies. Now, we must investigate how they came to be known as hadith of our Imams. What's certain is that these hadith contradict the Imams' teachings and practices, and the humanistic principles of religion. So the Houzeh, and the mode of thinking that has come to dominate it since the revolution, are committed to clarifying these issues and tackling them from a religious perspective.

As for why men set up the journal, this comes from the sense of duty we feel; and here there's no difference between men and women. Whoever feels the duty must act. If a woman has an accident and her car is damaged, nobody says only women should help her. Likewise, we believe that defending women is defending humanity, and this duty isn't exclusive to women. Some women object, saying what sort of women's journal is this, run by

men? I think this objection betrays an assumption of an essential difference
between men and women; an assumption so gender-biased as to prevent
cooperation.

The journal is also trying to encourage women's potential, to create an
incentive for them to participate and demand their rights, and eventually to
hand the running of affairs over to them. It is our aim for women, while
observing Islamic criteria, to be able to assume key and sensitive positions
independently in society. In the Houzeh this isn't limited to our journal;
there are other efforts. Some great teachers have a particular interest in
women's issues, for example Ayatollah Sane'i. Of course there are others,
but the ayatollah has said several times that when he thinks about women's
issues, he cries about the situation; so he's trying to refute wrong and in-
human assumptions, to correct and address them through feqh, and to open
a new chapter on women's rights.

Sa'idi was making several points at once. The nature of male/female relations is fixed, governed by instinctive drives that not only create chaos but lead
to women's oppression if left unregulated: in other words, women need protection. But in addition, women need protection because of their own nature;
religion, by regulating male/female relationships, can provide women with this
protection; and women have been wronged, in the name of religion, by the
very men whose religious duty was to protect them. The journal saw its mission as presenting a correct version of the Islamic perspective on women, and
also as facilitating their participation in society; yet the logical conclusion of
his argument was that men must always be in charge.

To continue the discussion, I decided to ignore the elements in his argument
that I disagreed with and to focus on common ground. I took him up on his
final point: women's participation in society.

ZMH: I understand from what you have said that you believe in women's
presence and participation in society. Do you mean participation in a separate society? Or in a society in which men and women work together, for
instance in the same office? Do you want society to be divided into two
parts, one managed by men and the other by women?

A silence followed. Thinking that perhaps my question had not been clear, I
elaborated by relating it to government policy on gender and the kinds of
obstacles women have encountered since the revolution, all justified by religious arguments.

ZMH: Look, once women enter society, a number of [obstacles] present
themselves, which as you say are not necessarily part of religion but were
added to it; in any case, these beliefs [i.e., that women should stay at home]
are there and we see them at work. This leads to a contradiction; what is
your position on this contradiction?

The two men now understood what I was getting at. They looked at each other, and each offered the other the opportunity to respond. Finally, Mortazavi asked Saiᶜdi to reply.

MHS: In my opinion, if religion didn't sanction women's presence in society and their contact and cooperation with men, then the emphasis on the issue of hejab and gaze would be meaningless. If it was intended that men and women should operate in separate spheres, then there'd be no need for women to observe hejab.

SZM (agreeing): It would be meaningless.

ZMH: In that case, why shouldn't men observe hejab?

MHS: What?!

I repeated my question more carefully. He replied with another version of his "nature" theory, this time in a milder form, emphasizing the different psychological makeup of men and women and the need to regulate sexual relations in all societies. I agreed that in all societies, from the simplest to the most complex, relations between sexes are subject to an intricate web of regulations. He took up my point.

MHS: So we agree on the principle that regulations must exist. Now, as for why women should cover themselves and a man should guard his gaze, this is rooted precisely in their psychological and inner characteristics. The uncontrolled attraction of men to women often emanates from simple gaze, and if women didn't cover, if they didn't protect themselves, there'd be no safety for them in society. The fact is—frankly—every man, if not restrained by legal, ethical, and ideological forces, desires any woman he sees and wants to satisfy this desire by whatever means he can. So, if men aren't restrained and women don't cover themselves, women will be abused, unable to do anything, and will be transformed into objects of men's desire. So it's a woman's primary mission to preserve herself, and conduct herself so as not to cause herself trouble. She can't say, "I don't cover myself but I want to fulfill my role in society"; there can be no guarantee for her in that case.

To avoid being silenced again by such arguments, I decided that I must unpack some of the assumptions underlying the "nature" theory used to justify the gender bias in the shariᶜa; but I must do so within the limits of the permissible religious discourse.

ZMH: Despite what you say, there are societies in which women don't have hejab and yet nothing happens [the social order does not collapse]. Let me first add that some things I say are not necessarily my own opinions; I want to play devil's advocate and introduce counter-arguments. What you say is premised on two primary postulates. The first, which I objected to earlier, is that of nature and instinct. If we reduce the discussion to these, we've reached the end of the line, there can be no real debate. The second postulate is that social and ethical imperatives come second to those of nature and instinct. In my opinion, the crucial difference between humans and other creatures is that humans are essentially social beings. It's true that bees also have society, but they're governed by instinct. For millions of years bees have built their hives as they do today. The queen does the same in the same way. But human society has never been like that. So it's society that controls human instincts. In my opinion, if our instincts were not controllable then the claim that we're "the noblest creatures" would be meaningless. All these rules you're alluding to are for the control of our instincts.

I often use an example we all learned in high school. We all learned about Pavlov's experiment; whenever he fed the dog, he rang a bell so that the creature became conditioned to associate being fed with a specific sound: as soon as it heard the bell ring, it started to salivate in anticipation of food. Don't you think it's possible men in our society have been conditioned? That is, if we define woman as a sexual object, and constantly cover her so that men can't see her, this creates a situation where, as soon as men see women, they get excited. This could be the main obstacle to women finding their proper place in society and participating on equal terms.

I accept some of the arguments put forward for hejab; but there's another side to it: why shouldn't we work on men? Why shouldn't they learn to respect women and treat them as social beings? In many societies in this world men and women work alongside each other, and men don't get excited, lose control, and attack women. Let's face it, they too are human beings, with the same drives. How far can you see issues in terms of a nature/instinct imperative? How far do you think these issues can be shaped and changed by social factors? Don't you think we can discuss women's issues as social issues?

Having allowed me to finish without interruption, Sa'idi responded by reiterating his theory of human nature and its interaction with social factors.

MHS: As you said, part of this issue has a natural and instinctual dimension, shared by all humans and not affected by specific geographical and cultural characteristics. Another part is the influence of climatic, racial, cultural, and other conditions of societies. The strength of people's instinct varies in different societies. Social conditions, value systems, norms, and culture all influence peoples' perceptions and perspectives. But the principle that instinct exists in human beings is undeniable; without instinct, human survival wouldn't be guaranteed; it's a necessary stimulus for meeting a necessary need; it varies only in strength and intensity. So, if instinct is left uncontrolled and men and women are free to do whatever they want, there'll certainly be [harmful] consequences. Undoubtedly these consequences are greater for some people and some societies and less for others.

Islam has a distinct perspective on humanity. Islam sees human beings on the road between this world and the other, and embraces all dimensions of human existence, from material to spiritual and from individual to social. That is, we see no boundary between this world and the other; Islam as a whole seeks happiness in this world and the hereafter; and sees this world as a prelude to the other. When we take this into account, and when we pay attention to the universal dimensions of instinct, we conclude that in all societies human beings are such that there should be a boundary between men and women; and if women don't have hejab, harmful consequences will follow for both men and women as well as for the entire society; of course the harm will be felt more by women. Evidently, this may vary in degree and strength, but variation doesn't affect the general principle. Possibly in some societies men and women may have [weaker] drives; in everyday life they may not observe a clear boundary in their relations; and this may not lead to critical consequences. But these are exceptions, which the law ignores. As with wine, the Holy Koran says that it brings great harm for people, and little benefit. We can't allow great harm just for the sake of a little benefit. With women's hejab, we believe that not only is it not arousing, on the contrary it lowers spontaneous and irrational stimulation in men.

Let's suppose there are no restrictions in relations between men and women in terms of gaze and hejab; does sexual arousal occur more readily than when women wear chador? Obviously sexual arousal happens more quickly and easily in the former, and naturally women's immunity is less. Here we can't say men have been conditioned. I believe that if we did a social survey, and analyzed realities, we'd reach the conclusion that in the first case sexual arousal is deeper, more frequent and more encompassing than when women are covered, even if we suppose conditioning has taken place.

SZM: Even if we accept the conditioning hypothesis, the fact is that men have greater and more powerful means for gratifying their desires. So it's better that relations between men and women be restricted and controlled so that women can be protected and feel secure. Restricting relations also has the effect of preventing men from imposing their will on women in matters related to instinct.

I tried again to steer the discussion away from the abstract level of human nature toward actual practices in the Islamic Republic, by pointing to an imbalance in the way the two rules are implemented.

ZMH: How far do you think women can choose? I say this because I feel that many women are now reacting to [the imposition of hejab]. It's a social fact that whatever is imposed creates resistance. Under the previous regime, the scarf and the chador became symbols of protest; if the Pahlavis hadn't insisted [on discouraging them] perhaps they wouldn't have become symbols of protest. In the West and in many Arab countries, some women voluntarily choose hejab because they want a different identity and at the same time they want to protest against the situation, the regime. How far do you think women can have a choice?

MHS: About what?

ZMH: About the issue of hejab.

MHS: Are you talking about the rules and regulations in our country?

ZMH: No, I'm talking in more general terms. You say that when men and women participate in society, guarding the gaze and preserving hejab must be observed, that—if I understand you correctly—if these two Rulings aren't observed, women's participation in society won't be possible or there'll be consequences. Look, there's no way we can control men's gaze; there's no Ruling to force men to "guard their gaze," so it becomes an ethical and personal choice for men. Don't you think we could also discuss hejab in terms of an ethical and personal choice for women? You know better than I that hejab in the Koran has different layers and meanings; so also in the Traditions; they must all be contextualized. If we force women to cover themselves, but leave it to men to guard their gazes, aren't we discriminating? The fact is, we can't control men's gaze, no law can tell them, "cover your eyes and don't look." Instead, we focus on women and tell them to cover themselves. How do you explain this hidden inequality?

Once again Sa'idi countered my argument with a version of his theory of human nature, but this time with a hint of equity and pragmatism.

MHS: It seems to me, if we consider existing created realities, they lead us to certain musts. Naturally these musts should be clarified and mapped so that they don't cause other harm. For instance, we must protect ourselves from the cold, but this protection shouldn't restrict our mobility. This is what reason tells us. The same applies to hejab. We see that the nature of relations between men and women is such that, if left unregulated, they lose sight of their spiritual and higher goals and give free reign to their instincts. Therefore, reason dictates that we regulate the relations to prevent being swamped by instincts, so that both instinctual needs are satisfied and human interests aren't totally lost. To achieve this, the reasonable thing is for men to guard their gaze and for women to cover themselves. But if men's gaze can't be controlled, reason tells us that women must—as in the case of cold—protect themselves even more, so that they remain immune from harm by uncontrolled elements. Of course, it's important to add that if we define this requirement so as to create obstacles and difficulties for women, this isn't correct. But if women can retain their mobility while pursuing their goals in society, this is correct and acceptable. What's important is that we shouldn't sacrifice one set of values for the sake of preserving others. On hejab, I think the way it is defined by the religious regulations, even if it's unreasonable, doesn't cause difficulties for women. Second, hejab is legislated so as to facilitate women's mobility and presence in society, not to restrict them.

Again I tried to focus on policies that advocate the chador and disapprove of other types of covering.

ZMH: But the chador is restricting. One hand is always engaged [holding it to the chin] and with the other you have to carry a handbag, or briefcase; and it's difficult to write, or to drive. Generally, it's really difficult.

Saʿidi commented that the journal had an unfinished discussion on the issue of hejab; they were aware of chador's drawbacks, yet they knew that it provided the best form of covering and had fewer negative features than other forms of hejab. I responded that the chador also had a cultural and political dimension that one must not forget, but he interrupted:

MHS: Of course. One dimension of chador is hejab and the other is cultural. As a form of dress, it's rooted in our indigenous culture, thus it enjoys a kind of sanctity in our national tradition and naturally carries messages. Therefore, if we want to respect and defend our cultural values, then we must defend chador.

But as regards difficulty or comfort, we're aware that the chador has some of the difficulties you mention. The journal wanted to offer a model for hejab with the positive features of chador but without its drawbacks. You know that hejab is a sensitive subject in our society. In other countries, individuals choose hejab as a means of protest; in our society, objectors to hejab are actually protesting against something else, not the principle of hejab. The journal wanted to offer a model for hejab stemming from our religious and cultural traditions. If a model for hejab comes from outside—or even if it comes from part-cultures within society—it's a sign of failure of our culture. The model for hejab must come from the culture of religious people in our society, then no legal and religious problems will follow and it will be in line with the requirements of time and place.

ZMH: I mean, a model [for hejab] emerges gradually. On hejab, there have been a number of studies, two of which might interest you as they show the reasons for women's inclination to hejab in other societies. The first was carried out by an Egyptian woman who lives and teaches in the United States, the other by an American woman in Egypt.[2] Both show how

[2] El Guindi 1981; Macleod 1991.

and why hejab doesn't [necessarily] limit and oppress women, as some other researchers have argued. Women choose hejab because they live in a society where wearing hejab empowers them. They live in a type of society where, as you put it, when women leave home they don't feel respected or safe, and may be harassed. A woman reacts to this by covering herself and observing a certain dress code, and this signals that she is inaccessible. Another interesting point is that the majority of women who choose hejab have mothers who didn't wear it, and belong to the lower middle classes who take paid employment. Thus, choice also has a class element to it. In fact, the thesis once accepted by [Western] feminists, that hejab is a form of oppression and enslavement of women, has now been questioned. It's also my own opinion that hejab—because it is cultural—empowers women in some situations and allows them to be present in a male-controlled society; this can be a positive first step.

The other point I wanted to raise is, do you really think that a model can be given for hejab? What surprises me is that, in the seventeen years since the revolution, none of our designers has come up with a model. We must ask, why not? Look, we no longer have a national dress; it's true we have regional and tribal dresses; but not a national one. If there was one, it was taken from us [in the 1930s]; anyway, it disappeared in the past fifty years and was replaced by Western styles. We also felt ashamed of it and wanted to give it up. But no alternative has emerged, something which would be elegant and at the same time easy to move around in. The chador has a certain elegance, but it is cumbersome, for this generation and in this century. It slows you down; it's difficult to jump on a bus, and so on.

The published transcript of the discussion on hejab omits my point about different layers of its meanings in the Koran and Traditions, shortens the above passage, and expands Mortazavi's response so as to play down the cumbersomeness of the chador, on which we had all agreed. A sentence is inserted to the effect that women who are used to wearing the chador do not feel it to be restricting as people like me do. The passage ends with another new sentence, in which Mortazavi questions whether the chador is as restrictive as I had said, adding that it has both cultural value and religious merit. What he actually said (according to my tape) was as follows:

SZM: In the Lebanon and other Arab countries, the ʿabayeh [women's cloak] has all the advantages of the chador without its cumbersomeness. It stays on the head and has sleeves and is closed in front, so it covers better than the chador. This model is also seen in Iran and could be offered as an alternative. Of course, all people, men or women, are faced with different choices. Often one is prepared to put up with cumbersomeness in order to retain one's indigenous culture and values. It can't be denied that the chador has a strong cultural value and has a place in society.

ZMH: What about overcoat and headscarf? It seems to me they've found a place in society as a common form of hejab.

SZM: From the religious point of view, they haven't been opposed, and religious centers haven't rejected them. Talking of hejab in terms of religious and Legal criteria is quite different from talking in terms of socio-cultural and national symbols. If we set aside the latter factors and their advantages, [scarf and coat] present no problems from a Lawful perspective, provided they're correct in quality and extent [covering all parts of the body apart from face and hands].[3]

I tried to change the subject, with some sarcasm, which Mortazavi clearly felt. Although he did not respond, choosing to continue the debate on hejab, there was a kind of altercation between us.

ZMH: This is indeed a complex issue. As you said, it has cultural, indigenous roots. *To return to what you said about instinct and the nature of women: love of beauty exists in women, but it's a human characteristic to appreciate beauty and diversity,* which makes it difficult to present an ideal model and expect everyone to conform with it. If we give a model of hejab, some will want to modify it, for instance by cutting their sleeves in a different way or by using a different pattern or color. Whenever a system tries to impose limits, it creates conflict with innate desires. Anyway, this is a very complex issue. Permit me to change the topic. If you have nothing more to add on this, I have other questions to pose.

SZM: Allow me to add one sentence. We must make a distinction between duties that are obligatory from the religious perspective, and those that are more or less preferred but don't bring obligation. Many matters in society are presented as though they're obligatory in religion, whereas they have no religious basis and are mere invitations and recommendations.

The published transcript—which presents this exchange as part of the final session of our discussion—modifies the emphasized passage to read: "basically, a love of beauty, of attracting attention and being different from others, is among the characteristics of women." This not only eliminates my mild sarcasm but also distorts my point. A sentence is added to the editor's response, refuting my objections to the gender differences presented by Ayatollah Motahhari, which as we shall see was actually one of themes of our second session.

ZMH: But there are pressure groups; for instance, in the Ministry of Education in certain parts of the country, women must wear chador, otherwise they can't teach, or get promoted. There are pressures, impositions . . .

[3] Compare this with Azari's opinion, Chapter Two.

SZM: I said, from the religious perspective; social action is another matter.

ZMH: The very fact that you say certain things are "more or less preferred," some people interpret this as they want and give it a different value.

SZM: Is it our fault that we haven't been able to guide society properly, or is it because our communication with the public is poor and we haven't been able to clarify the issue? Is the fault in the way it's carried out? Which is it?

ZMH. The point is that the person in charge is looking at religious sources; that is, what you say becomes . . .

SZM: The religious sources you mention, their only task is to clarify religious matters; they aren't concerned with details of social reality. For example, they've nothing to do with who does what in a small office. They only give criteria and the limits; for instance, [women's] clothes must cover and not be stimulating; but they've nothing to say about color, pattern, style, etc. We can't define these in terms of religious obligations.

ZMH: Not long ago, the magazine *Zanan* had a report about why women wear black. In my opinion it was a very good report, of course from a sociological/anthropological angle. Women were asked why they wear black. A large majority of them said they don't like wearing black or dark colors but if they don't they stand out.[4] The Lebanese-style chador you describe—I have one, but I decided not to wear it in Qom, because I told myself I would be the only woman wearing it and everybody would look at me; and this wouldn't be proper. I also thought of the reputation of the person with me [Saʿidzadeh] and didn't want to attract attention. There are social pressures, even if, from the religious standpoint, there's no prohibition. The question is, how does your journal approach such issues, because your religious mission surely has a social side to it?

SZM: As for activities touching on external realities, I think the most important thing we can do is to have a correct interpretation of religion and pass this on to society. This is important to us.

ZMH: You mean, you think [correct interpretation] is fundamental?

SZM: Yes! I don't want either to reject or to endorse the action of pressure groups; we mightn't have the power to deal with social malfunctions. What I see as most harmful is not having a correct understanding of religion; and if we succeed in remedying this, I think we've taken the first step. Of course, as regards social realities, we usually draw an ideal picture for ourselves and then like to convey it to society. The second step is to clarify the distance between this ideal picture and the actuality in society. We see it as our duty to tell society how far we are from the ideal. The third step is what

[4] *Zanan* 22 (June/July 1994): 4–17.

we can do in such a situation; here we have to confront outside realities, concrete cases, which often leads to conflict. It's here that differences in approach come to the surface, creating tensions and reactions in society. If there's a weakness here, we'd like to know and to address it in a more reasonable and rational way.

MHS: On every issue, the journal has a religious point of view, derived from the values of our School (*maktab*). For instance, we defend the principle of hejab as a religious value and a Ruling; but there are other issues we approach from a cultural point of view, often from a critical angle, and we intend to introduce reforms in line with religious values. On hejab, as long as the journal hasn't found an alternative to the chador, we see it as our duty to promote it as the correct form of hejab. We don't say that the chador is the exact letter of the religious law, but we defend it on cultural grounds. We also have certain positions regarding women's employment, their participation in social and political life, the preservation of the family, and so forth. We try to clarify our positions on these issues and convey them in our journal. Most of them originate from our cultural perspective, and religion does not necessarily have a point of view on each of these issues. Although it is possible to find religious confirmation for the social positions we take, we never attribute either our social position or our approach to religion. Therefore, we are defending a certain culture [the Islamic part of Iranian culture] and see it as superior to [other parts], which we see no need to uphold and sometimes we point to their weaknesses. In short, naturally the journal has a perspective on social questions and approaches and analyzes everything from that angle.

This was the first concrete admission of a particular cultural perspective; I decided to follow it up.

By now it was evident that I had to frame my questions in a language as discursive as theirs. I also realized that I must repeat my points and arguments, as they tended not to respond at first. But they did take in each point and return to it in a different context. I continued by giving my own understanding of current debates about gender in Iran, using *Zanan* as a reference point.

ZMH: What is your journal's perspective on gender equality? I ask this because, after reviewing the women's press in Iran, I find two distinct gender perspectives. The first, represented by *Zanan*, argues for gender equality and symmetry,[5] and holds that equality between men and women is a primary principle in Islam and any laws that go against equality are in fact the product of patriarchy and have nothing to do with Islam. These are cultural issues which must be tackled from a cultural perspective; but at the same

---

[5] Here I said *tasavi*, equality, rather than *tashaboh*, similarity; only later did I realize my mistake and correct it. It was significant, as we shall see, since my discussants—following Ayatollah Motahhari—argued that Islam allows tasavi but rejects tashaboh.

time, since culture can't be isolated from religion, we must have progressive interpretations, and there's a need for Dynamic Ejtehad.

For instance, in a recent issue, *Zanan* criticizes Article 1133 of the Civil Code, which states that a man can divorce his wife whenever he wishes.[6] Given my own work in family courts, I agree with their objections and believe that men's unilateral right to divorce is a root problem. Judges in the courts also admit that this article ties their hands, that is, they want to protect women and preserve the family, but because of this article they can't. Here, then, we see a contradiction—there are inconsistencies. On the one hand, we say that in Islam the family is the most important institution and Islam wants to preserve it, on the other we have an article of law, derived from feqh, which enables a man to divorce his wife whenever he wishes. I'd like to know your journal's view on such inequalities in our civil laws. As you know, they're all rooted in feqh, in fact the Civil Code articles on the family are taken, selectively, from dominant opinion within Shi'i feqh. Do you see these inequalities as necessary, as a reflection of the nature of men and women and their relations? Do you hold that men and women should have unequal rights in the family? Should men have the right of divorce, and women not? Must women obtain their husband's permission to leave the house, to work? Must the independence that Islam grants women be submerged when she marries and becomes subordinated? Suppose we think in terms of a continuum: at one end there's the Equality perspective as advocated by *Zanan*, at the other the traditional perspective that defends all these inequalities as necessary and argues that if men and women have equal rights the basis of society will be destroyed; where can I locate your journal on this continuum?

I finished my statement without being interrupted, but I must have touched another raw nerve. A long silence followed, broken, finally, by Mortazavi:

SZM: This is my personal view. Sometimes what is done to promote equality between men and women leads to negative and unwanted consequences and only increases tension and confrontation. They [*Zanan*] have accepted that there is a conflict of interests, as though there is duality and conflict between these two beings. Despite all my admiration for the work of *Zanan*—I know how difficult it is to bring a journal out—their attempt in effect intensifies the tension and conflict between men and women; it isn't aimed at reconciling men and women in managing the family. That's the result of something done in the name of equality.

ZMH: Are you suggesting they set men and women against each other?

SZM: They intend to defend women's rights, but their method can't achieve their goal. Of course, I don't mean that women shouldn't defend

[6] See Musavi 1995.

their rights, or that they should keep silent and avoid causing conflict. It seems to me that a method which increases tension and conflict, and in practice has negative effects, is mistaken. It creates unwanted reactions, in the sense that some [clerics] think that they [*Zanan*] want to defy the fundamentals of Islam and its laws; as a result even modifications that can be achieved through ejtehad don't get a chance of an airing. My objection is to their method and approach.

ZMH: Do you have any objection to their perspective?

Mortazavi avoided answering, saying, "if Mr. Sa'idi will respond to this part, I'll benefit too." Sa'idi asked Sa'idzadeh why he was not taking part in the discussion. Sa'idzadeh muttered something about being there to learn. Then Sa'idi started to reply:

MHS: You say there's inequality in the law. Well—we don't consider the principle of equality to be applicable to all the rights of men and women. First, let me say that, in our opinion, what's important is a balance of rights between the sexes. I must say that in Islam, in constitutional laws, I don't remember them one by one, but on the whole the equality you talked about exists. Men and women have the same freedom to choose, to vote . . .

He was speaking slowly, and clearly thinking as he spoke. I tried to help him. I thought he meant the constitution of the Islamic Republic, because he had used the standard Persian term for constitution; so I prompted him: "women are treated equal to men, except on the issue of the presidency, which is also debatable."[7] But he corrected me, saying he had not meant that constitution, but basic rights in Islam. I apologized and he continued, this time with more focus. I think my intervention had made him realize we were talking of different things. I often took what he said as referring to current laws and policies of the Islamic Republic, but he was discoursing on a more general level, that of the Islamic position, and was not concerned with actuality. He continued by pursuing his earlier line once more.

MHS: In civil law, what's important is the creation of a balance of rights, not only between men and women in the family but among all members of society. Look, in an office, you can't say there's equality in rights and duties between the director and other employees; the same applies to the legal relationship between men and women. If a woman's share of inheritance is half a man's, in return she has the right to maintenance from her husband and no responsibility to provide maintenance for their children, and she's entitled to dower upon marriage, and so forth. When we discuss a legal system, we must see it as a totality and ask whether or not it strikes a balance among members of the family and society.

[7] See Conclusion, below.

So, any approach that examines the elements that make up a system of law in isolation is erroneous. It's equally erroneous to examine the law without considering other social and human dimensions of religion, that is, to separate the realm of Law from the realm of Ethics. The fact is, part of social reality is the concern of Law; the rest is covered by Ethics, and here the Law can do nothing. Islam, as a comprehensive school, pays attention to all these dimensions.

You mentioned the law that men can divorce whenever they want. First, this law does not reflect the opinion of all our jurists; some, like Ayatollah Sane'i, believe that one of the conditions for divorce is arbitration. That is, a man must first go to the court, which refers the case to arbitration; he can divorce only when arbiters have failed to reconcile the couple. There are also ethical and psychological factors; let's suppose a man can't live with his wife, and let's suppose he's the one at fault and we don't have the means to reconcile them. What should be done? If we say the marriage must continue, this has no effect except creating more hardship and suffering for the woman.

Either he had missed my point, or he was avoiding it. I tried to explain that what I objected to was the unequal right of access to divorce; this time, Sa'idi admitted that current laws were unequal, although he later tried to qualify what he had said:

ZMH: Of course he should divorce her. But why don't you consider the other side, when a woman can't live with her husband, she dislikes him or whatever; but we see that she can't divorce him.

MHS: In our feqh, she can; we have . . .

ZMH: I know that there's the option of *khol‘* [divorce initiated by a wife because of dislike of her husband]. But *khol‘* is different [from talaq]; it's a kind of contract in that the woman needs her husband's consent, and to get this, apart from his goodwill, she must forgo her dower and other rights. Talaq is legally a unilateral act, effected when one party [the husband] wills it. Look, I've done my homework in the courts. . . .

SZM: What about divorce by authority, or the option of government divorce?

I had not heard of these. I learned later that they were topics discussed in Ayatollah Sane'i's advanced lessons; they turned out to be the same thing: "court divorce." At this moment the telephone rang again, and while Mortazavi answered it Sa'idi explained to me that they had their own objections to current laws, from a feqh perspective.

ZMH: But from a feqh perspective, in the past seventeen years there's been no serious critical discussion of current laws.

MHS: Let me explain. The laws of Islam must be seen as a system, a totality. Islam perceives men and women as human beings who are rational and free in choice and action. When two human beings with freedom of choice and action want to enter a contract of marriage, what Islam does is to define the framework, that is the essentials of the contract; it leaves the rest to them. They can reach their own agreement as regards dower, place of residence, employment, and the woman's right to divorce. A woman is free to choose and define the terms of the contract as she wants.

ZMH: Wait a minute: a woman given in marriage at the age of thirteen, with no economic resources to fall back on, with all choices made [for her by others] from the moment she was born, with little alternative—how could you consider such a woman a human being free in choice and action?

MHS: This has nothing to do with Islam; these are external events.

ZMH: But these have to do with what you said earlier: ethical issues must be separated from legal issues. Separating the legal from the ethical has these results.

MHS: I didn't say these two must be separated. On the contrary, what I meant was that in fact they can't be separated. For this reason I said that, in the classification of [Islamic] sciences, certain issues fall in the domain not of feqh but of Ethics. If we want a perfect feqh, and to create an ideal society, then surely Ethics and Beliefs must also be systematically related to feqh?

ZMH: That is, you believe that Ethics must be reflected in actual feqh Rulings?

MHS: We separate Ethics and feqh for the sake of analytical discussion, otherwise they are inseparable and intertwined. If we try to sever feqh from the fundamentals of Islamic thinking and the Islamic worldview, then it will disintegrate. Scientifically speaking, we don't claim to have succeeded in including in feqh all Islamic theories and fundamentals; as a result, in various branches of feqh you sometimes come across obvious inconsistencies in [jurists'] perspectives. For instance, a jurist might adhere to a certain understanding of humanity in marriage, and to another in economic matters. This inconsistency arises from the fact that the fundamentals of Islamic Theology and thinking aren't reflected in feqh fully and in detail. Nevertheless, if we look at Islamic teachings as a system, we'll find that each element is related to the others; for instance, you can't say: "I study and implement Islamic economics, but have nothing to do with Islamic worldview and values." This isn't possible.

At this point Mortazavi intervened; the published transcript modifies the following exchanges, presenting them in a different context and omitting all references to *Zanan*.

SZM: It's impossible. As Martyr Beheshti[8] says explicitly, Islam must be seen as a system, a totality; and we cannot separate one element and judge it in isolation. Therefore, our feqh is related to our Ethics, to our theological debates and interpretations, and so on. If we separate one element from this totality and look at it by itself, then we're unable to justify and defend the Law; we lose the balance. Balance is a definite Principle, of which *Nahj ol-Balagheh* [Imam Ali's sayings] talks in terms of right and counter-right (*haqq-e lah va haqq-e ʿaleih*. That is, for every right given to one person, there's another given to the other; there's balance and justice, overall.

ZMH . . . [Pause] . . . Your perspective, then, is that of Balance. In other words, you say that when we look at the totality of men and women's rights and duties, there is a balance.

MHS: Yes, but I must repeat, our discussion isn't about current laws.

ZMH: Then what is it about? Are you dealing with current realities or not? If you are, then current laws are part of them.

MHS: Of course, naturally we are. Let's say we certainly have our own views on *Zanan*'s recent criticism of men's unilateral right to divorce; it's not that we defend this law and say it's 100 percent correct. If we want to examine it from our feqh perspective, first we place it in context and take into account other elements of marriage laws. We say that a girl who's about to enter a marriage contract is a free agent; she's free to sign or not, to stipulate any conditions permitted by religious law; nobody can force her or impose any condition that she doesn't agree to. If we have a social problem in implementing the law, that's another matter. For instance, we might have the most just labor law, but if a worker isn't aware of it and is exploited, the problem can't be solved by changing the labor law. The same applies to family law; people are generally unaware of the law and only come to confront it unwittingly. We're dealing with different issues here: one is current laws, another is their relation to feqh, another is the realities that exist outside the realm of law. It's here that we must discuss the implementation of laws and their consequences; I think we must keep these separate.

We had reached an impasse. It seemed to me that my questions and arguments had put them on the defensive. My attempt to use *Zanan* as a point of reference had not helped. My aim was to say that Muslim women, active supporters of the Islamic Republic, were demanding equality. There was no point in defending *Zanan*'s stance, since *Payam-e Zan* totally disagreed with it.

I tried to shift the focus from *Zanan* to women who had been interviewed in *Payam-e Zan*, whose standpoint they could not challenge. I referred to an

---

[8] Ayatollah Mohammad Beheshti was a political cleric who played an instrumental role in seeing the concept of velayat-e faqih included in the constitution, and later founded the Islamic Republic party; he was among the notables killed by the 1981 bomb.

interview with Marziyeh Hadidchi, known as Ms. Dabbagh, published over four issues of *Payam-e Zan* between February and September 1993. I had recently read about her life and her views with interest; she is among the religious women whose political awareness is linked to the 1963 protests that led to Ayatollah Khomeini's exile. It was she, not her husband, who went to prison, was tortured, and finally had to leave her four children in Iran to join the religious opposition abroad. She returned in 1979 in Ayatollah Khomeini's entourage, fought on the front during the war with Iraq, and was elected as deputy to the second and third Majleses (1984–1992). She was appointed by Khomeini as member of the Iranian delegation to Moscow in February 1988 to deliver his letter inviting Gorbachev to Islam when the Soviet Union was on the brink of disintegration.[9] She was elected to the Majles again in 1996. She was also the deputy of Zahra Mostafavi, Khomeini's daughter, in the Women's Society of the Islamic Republic of Iran. In the interviews, Ms. Dabbagh speaks of her personal and political life, her hope and her despair, and her assessment of women's situation after the revolution. She does this honestly and straight-forwardly, criticizing the legal situation and pointing to gender bias in the male-dominated institutions: in short, she says basically what *Zanan* is saying, although her language and the thrust of her arguments are different. For instance, on the barriers faced by women fighting for progressive legislation, she says:

> In these thirteen years the Majles has been legislating, we've killed ourselves getting a few laws passed for women. Proposed laws were opposed either by the Council of Guardians or the government, or abandoned due to budget constraints; by the time they passed they were like a toothless lion. As far as the law is concerned, I don't think we'll get what we want and make up for the injustices women have suffered in the course of human history. . . . There are educated women, such as medical doctors, but when they come and talk to me I see they're subjected to similar kinds of oppression as their illiterate sisters. Men, with all the rights they're given— whether justly or not is a matter for our ulama—are restricting our highly educated women. It's beyond my competence to say whether or not this is just, but with my knowledge of the way of life and attitudes of Imam [Khomeini] toward women, I know that these are of human making and not the laws of Islam. Islam does not say: a woman who has medical expertise must stay at home because her husband says "I do not like that you go out to treat people"; in my view there are other ways to solve the problem: Islam never tells women to stay at home and be at the service of their husbands.[10]

---

[9] The delegation was headed by Ayatollah Javadi-Amoli, whose work I referred to earlier. Javadi has written an account of the meeting and a commentary on the letter (1993b).

[10] *Payam-e Zan* 18 (September 1993): 18.

Alluding to Ms. Dabbagh's interviews, and sheltering in her legitimacy, I said:

ZMH: Somewhere in her interview with your journal, Ms. Dabbagh raises a point that touches on what we were saying. She says that many laws could have been passed in the Majles to benefit women, but there's great resistance; there's resistance everywhere, she says. Do you feel a similar resistance in the Houzeh?

Mortazavi must have understood what I was hinting at, because he said, rather sourly: "Perhaps the source of resistance lies here [in the Houzeh], after all." His remark took me by surprise. I was not sure what he meant, and my attempt to find out set the agenda for the rest of our discussion, revolving around the position of the Houzeh on women's issues. For me it was illuminating and made me realize not only the delicate position of the journal but also its importance. It quite altered my appreciation of their work, and the tone and nature of my questions must have reflected this.

The published transcript omits the reference to Ms. Dabbagh and presents the following exchanges, in modified form, as the conclusion of our "round-table."

ZMH: As I understand you, you argue that divorce must be subject to arbitration; and if marriage has broken down, then a woman can have the right to divorce. Does this mean that you don't see the right to divorce as exclusive to men? If so, such a way of thinking can open the door for change in the current laws. This is so because behind these laws is a particular perspective [on women and gender], and once there's a shift in this then the laws themselves will be modified. What percentage of ulama think like you, and how far can this way of thinking take root and flourish in the Houzeh, so as to overcome resistance? What about women's role here? Do female students in the seminary agree and collaborate with you? Do they cooperate with you?

MHS: Before the revolution a different way of thinking ruled the Houzeh. Imam [Khomeini] refers to this in his "Message to the Clerics."[11] This way of thinking presented considerable resistance and opposition to the Imam's ideas on all issues, including those concerning women. The Imam speaks of his own suffering in the Houzeh, comparing it with Imam Hosein's silent suffering. After the revolution, though revolutionary forces acquired executive and political powers, social realities remained the same; resistance continues.

ZMH: You mean the Houzeh structure didn't change?

MHS: Yes, obviously the structure didn't change, so we faced certain

[11] This fascinating speech, also known as the Clerics' Charter (*Manshur-e Rouhaniyat*), was highly critical of clerics; it was delivered in March 1989, shortly before Khomeini's death, and at the height of the debates over the notion of authority.

impasses in feqh issues, some of which have been debated in Majles and the Council of Guardians. The establishment of the Assembly for Discerning the Interest of the Regime,[12] and the Imam's direct intervention in certain situations—these are all indications of the impasses reached. Briefly, we can say that there was and still is a generation in the Houzeh who oppose the values [of the revolution] and resist them. But there's another generation that is in line with the revolution and its values; they look at the issue [of women] with a fresh perspective; in fact they differ from the first in certain fundamentals.

ZMH: You mean there's a renaissance, a revival, really taking place in the Houzeh?

MHS: In our opinion it is; although we have our views on its development in terms of speed, management, and other aspects, and how it can be improved. These are our personal views.

SZM: If you compare the present situation with twenty or thirty years ago, then you can appreciate the magnitude of change, especially regarding ways in which women's issues are perceived. You said that in the past seventeen years no serious attempt has been made in this area; to show how much has changed, I'll tell you of a remark by a highly esteemed cleric, which I alluded to in one of my editorials. Before the revolution, when changes in the curriculum of the religious schools were proposed, one of the ulama who was opposed to change expressed his opposition this way: "if we change, we'll end up producing clerics like Motahhari, who then writes a book on hejab."

ZMH: You mean writing the book on hejab was regarded as deviant?

SZM: Yes, it was seen in such a negative light. Master Motahhari says nothing extraordinary; whatever he says is in line with feqh Rulings on hejab, that a woman's hands and her face may be left uncovered. If you compare it with what's now written in the Houzeh then you can appreciate the kind of development that the Imam fostered; you must read *The Master's Responses to Criticism of the Book "The Hejab Issue,"* published recently. The story is that when the Master published his book on hejab, he sent a copy to one of his colleagues, who wrote his comments on the margin of the book and sent it back. Martyr Motahhari responded to these comments; if you read them, you'll understand what a difference there is in their outlooks; this person was among Motahhari's friends and thus open to certain ideas.[13] The very fact that the Houzeh sees addressing women's issues as a duty is itself indicative of how much has changed. The fact is, some in the Houzeh now see it as their duty to devote time and energy to resolving

[12] Also known as the Discretionary Council, Amendment to Constitution, Article 112.

[13] Motahhari 1994; it is a fascinating exchange; no one would tell me who the cleric was; rumor suggested Sheikh Abol Qasem Eshtehardi.

women's issues. If you look from outside and compare it with elsewhere, it might not seem much; but seen in the context and structure of the Houzeh, it's a lot. The only crime of Martyr Motahhari, who was seen as an outcast, was that he addressed the issue of women; the remark I mentioned was made in 1970—not long ago. Feqh and cultural issues can't be changed by sheer physical force; time is needed; there's been a major evolution, and there's no comparison with the past.

What they were saying was new to me; they made me realize how it is too easy to come from the outside and criticize without appreciating internal constraints and pressures. I admitted my ignorance of these facts and said I had no idea of the extent of change in the Houzeh's tolerance and capacity for new debates. The tone of our discussion changed, and Mortazavi referred to the types of legal questions now raised by Ayatollah Saneʿi and others in their lessons. He said one of the phone calls had been the ayatollah. He would try to get an appointment for me to see him; then I would appreciate the level of debate among the new school of thought. He mentioned that last year Ayatollah Saneʿi had dealt with women's right to divorce in the event of the husband's disappearance, starting his discussion by referring to Ayatollah Khomeini's fatwa on women's option to divorce. Saʿidzadeh cited Khomeini's famous sentence: "there's an even simpler way; if I had the courage, I would have said it." To this Mortazavi added that even the Imam, with all his political influence and standing in the Houzeh, chose not to state his own view on women's right to divorce (see Chapter Five). I asked whether Ayatollah Saneʿi's lessons were published; and if not, why the journal did not make them available to its readers. In the course of the ensuing discussion, Mortazavi returned to my first question—why men are producing a women's journal in Qom.

SZM: One of our aims is to make available to our readers the teaching that is taking place at graduate level in the Houzeh. But to render these into simple language needs time; feqh issues are very complex and one can't translate them into simple terms.

ZMH: Of course, it's extremely difficult, but it's also extremely important that these debates reach the public.

SZM: We're far from our ideals and targets; we think we've attained at most 30 to 40 percent of our goals; we have a long way to go . . .

ZMH: In my view, your journal has been very successful and has evolved in the past three years. I also think it has an important role to play, especially that your messages reach people who should hear them.

SZM: This has also been our readers' verdict; but we try not to get too proud; we tell ourselves we're at the beginning of the road and we must try harder. The criticism you raised at the beginning, about the "patriarchal" management of the journal; I must say our [women] readers don't have this impression. That is, our readers don't feel we're reinforcing the rule of men and justifying the current situation. Women see the journal as defending them; this shows that men too can play a role in fighting for women's rights. Moreover, it isn't that men run the entire journal; we have female colleagues.

ZMH: You are quite right; for instance, in England there were some men who fought alongside the Suffragettes for their rights to vote; without unity and cooperation between the sexes, it's difficult to achieve. I've no personal objection; by my question, I wanted to know why men in the Houzeh invest energy and efforts for women's rights; you replied that it's because of the importance of the issue and the duty you feel.

SZM: There is also sacrifice. I must say that the very fact that some clerics and thinkers in the Houzeh devote effort to the women's question has repercussions for them. It's not as bad as in the past, when it wasn't possible to do so without being stigmatized, but it's still looked down on. It's a kind of sacrifice.

ZMH: In terms of prestige and scholarly reputation, you mean?

SZM: Yes! At a first meeting, people often comment on it, jokingly, but it reveals their view of my work, which they see as unimportant, a low-level type of activity. Sometimes, they even question our motives [mixing with women]. On the other hand, others encourage us, value our work. If we'd started a feqh journal in the Houzeh, my status and prestige would've been much higher and I'd have had a better future. We see this work as a duty, a sacrifice, though I shouldn't say this; these are ethical and personal issues.

The other two men confirmed this. I agreed, stressing that people like me, unfamiliar with the Houzeh and its internal rules and structures, were unaware that there was a genuine interest there. I added that the low academic status of "women's studies" was not peculiar to the Houzeh. I asked about the journal's circulation and readers' reactions. They said they had recently done a readership survey, which produced some concrete facts; but in the middle of this, my tape ended. The gist was that the circulation was about 10 thousand, but the actual readership was about 800 thousand, as each issue was read by five to eleven people. Most readers were either students at high-school or university level, or housewives. *Payam-e Zan* is also read in the Houzeh, by both female and male students. Clerics also buy it for their families; they would never allow a journal like *Zanan* in their homes.

After the tape ended, our discussion continued for another half an hour or so, in an off-the-record manner. They sounded less defensive and I felt more sympathetic. I could see the constraints, the delicacy of the journal's situation, the weight of Houzeh tradition, the tyranny of feqh scholarship. I asked whether they practiced *taqiyeh*, dissimulation.[14] Mortazavi laughed and said, not in its conventional sense; they did not hide their beliefs and opinions, which are reflected in the journal; but they were mindful of the delicacy of the situation and sometimes had to restrain themselves in order not to contradict conventional wisdom in the Houzeh too openly.

As we got up to go, I told them that the meeting had been an eye-opener for me, that it had forced me to rethink my earlier views on the journal, and that I had other questions to ask. Mortazavi said they welcomed these exchanges but suggested that if we were to have another session we should be better prepared. He asked me to provide a list of questions in advance. Meanwhile, he would try to arrange a meeting with Ayatollah Sane'i.

A Visit to the Shrine in Qom

That afternoon we visited the shrine of Hazrat Ma'sumeh, the most important in Iran after that of her brother Imam Reza in Mashhad, the eighth Shi'i Imam and the only one to be buried in Iran. Both shrines receive pilgrims from all over the Shi'i world. At time of Ma'mun, the powerful Abbasid Caliph, Hazrat Ma'sumeh left Medina to join her brother in Mashhad. Legend has it that when she reached Saveh, then a Sunni town, she fell ill; knowing that she had little time to live, and that a Shi'i center was needed in those parts, she asked to be taken to Qom, where she died in the year 201 A.H. (816 C.E.). The family in whose house she had stayed built a shrine on the spot where she had said her prayers.[15]

The shrine is now a large complex with several entrances, three interconnected courtyards, beautiful buildings, and a gold-covered dome. Zahra and I passed into the women's section of the main shrine building. A curtain divides the main chamber, including the tomb and its latticed screen, into men's and women's sides. We paid our respects at the tomb, touched the screen, and then passed through the curtain to a side room where women were praying, leading to a family room, where men and women were mixed. As we sat in the side room, waiting for Sa'idzadeh to join us, I picked up a prayer book; the following was handwritten inside the cover:

> One khadem dreamed that Imam Reza told him: tell the Muslim women not to enter the Shrine without chador or wearing sheer stockings. Whoever reads this must copy it three times inside the covers of books in the shrine, then after three days Imam Reza will appear in their dreams; if they don't, after three days they will have some bad luck.

[14] Taqiyeh is a Shi'i principle that allows dissimulation of one's true beliefs and opinions when their utterance would pose a threat.

[15] For the story of the shrine, see Fischer 1980, 104–35. For other versions of the legend, see booklets about the history of Qom such as Eshtehardi 1996, 59; Wafa'i 1976, 75–83.

I promptly copied it, but only in my notebook, along with other versions that I came across in Korans and prayer books during subsequent visits.

Later, when it was cooler, Saʿidzadeh and I went to look at bookshops. That was the evening we went to meet Grand Ayatollah Madani (Chapter One), a meeting that brought home to me the significance of what the young clerics running *Payam-e Zan* were doing and saying. The very existence of their journal is an achievement.

4

Equality or Balance:
Redefining Gender Notions in the Shariʿa

MY SECOND APPOINTMENT with *Payam-e Zan* was a week later, on 14 September. Saʿidzadeh and I, accompanied by Zahra, who had come to stay with me in Tehran earlier in the week, had arrived in Qom the previous afternoon, just in time for the appointment he had made for me with Ayatollah Mohammad Ebrahim Jannati.[1]

Ayatollah Jannati, in his late sixties, is one of the new breed of Houzeh teachers, an articulate advocate of the new school, Dynamic Jurisprudence. He studied under Ayatollahs Shahrudi and Khomeini in Najaf, coming to Qom after the revolution. Since then he has kept his distance from active politics, devoting his energies to scholarly activities. His courses, popular with students, question some of the assumptions on which feqh Rulings are built. He has published several books on the theory and historical development of ejtehad, in which he argues that feqh, and in particular ejtehad, should adapt to conditions of time and place. When I talked to Saʿidzadeh in April, he included Jannati among those whose views and writings were influential in the gender debates, although they were not directly involved in them. On Saʿidzadeh's recommendation, I had read two of Jannati's books.[2] He has published two articles on puberty, taking issue with dominant opinion in Shiʿi feqh, which recognizes the age of puberty as nine full lunar years for girls and fifteen for boys.[3] Instead, he argues that no definite age can be set for girls' puberty; the determining criterion must be the onset of menses.

We met Ayatollah Jannati in his house. According to Jannati, Dynamic Jurisprudence emerged in 1986, after Ayatollah Khomeini's fatwas that legitimized music and the sale of chess sets. I tried to draw him out on current debates about women, but he remained at an abstract level, emphasizing two points: that the situation has changed a lot in the past five years, and that many issues can now be addressed in the Houzeh that were not possible before. He mentioned a lecture he was asked to give at the University of Isfahan in 1988, when female students urged him to state his opinion on whether or not overcoat and headscarf constitute adequate hejab. They pressed him, as a jurist, to

---

[1] Not to be confused with Ayatollah Ahmed Jannati, a Traditionalist, and a member of the Council of Guardians.

[2] Jannati 1991 and 1993.

[3] Jannati 1995a and 1995b.

declare that wearing light and bright colors is not anti-shari'a and that coat and scarf are enough. He did so, and his talk, widely reported in the women's press, angered some in the Houzeh. He said he had completed a manuscript on women's hejab; when I expressed interest in reading it, he said I should wait until it was published. His second point was that the way was now paved for addressing women's rights in accordance with current realities but within shari'a bounds.

I found Ayatollah Jannati open, but unwilling to engage in a discussion on women's issues. So I asked some specific questions about his feqh approach. He affirmed that the shari'a and its Rulings are eternal and immutable, but that there is a constant need to reinterpret these Rulings as new circumstances emerge. He rejected the argument put forward by some, that jurists must strive to modify the shari'a in response to the demands of the time. Instead he argued that when there is change, either internal or external, in the subject of a shari'a Ruling, naturally a different Ruling will be needed: this does not mean a change in the divine laws as such, but merely a change in the nature of the subject which gave rise to that Ruling in the first place. For instance, sale of chess sets was banned in the past because they were used for gambling, whereas now, according to expert evidence, chess is a mental exercise.

I pointed to what I considered a circularity in his argument: permitting or banning something, whether in response to demands of time and space or because of a change in the subject matter of the Ruling, entails a change in law, whatever we call it. But he would not listen. Looking back now, I realize that, rather than offering an alternative approach to law, I had displayed my naiveté: I did not know enough about Qom and how feqh arguments are constructed; as he made clear, I was in no position to offer an opinion.

The following day, Zahra and I went to the *Payam-e Zan* offices early so that I could browse through their library. Sa'idzadeh had arranged this for me when he telephoned my list of questions through to Mortazavi earlier that week.

The library was housed in the basement. There I met some women from the Propagation Office Sisters' Section, whose cooperation is acknowledged on the inside cover of each number of *Payam-e Zan*. Those I talked to were all based in Qom; one had been with the journal from the beginning; all did office jobs like typing, copying manuscripts, and dealing with subscriptions. Other women I did not meet worked as journalists, interviewing female celebrities or writing reports; they were all based outside Qom: two in Tehran, and one (Dr. Zahra Akuchakian, Sa'idi's colleague in the Advice section) in Isfahan. Several of the women working for *Payam-e Zan* were also following religious studies courses offered in the Office's Education Section in Qom. I did not know then that this was to be the only space I visited in Qom connected with the Houzeh where men and women were not segregated, even by a curtain. This was one reason why female clerics in al-Zahra College—as I had learned to my amazement—refused cooperation with *Payam-e Zan*.

I stayed browsing in the library and chatting with the women for a couple of hours. Saʿidzadeh arrived at about ten o'clock to say that our meeting was to be there. Soon Mortazavi and Saʿidi joined us, bringing their own tape recorder. As we sat round the big reading table, the "sisters" continued with their work—and I regret to say that I never thought of trying to include them in the ensuing discussion.

I formulated my questions so as to follow up the issues raised in the previous session and to try to bridge the gap between the journal and myself. I was conscious of the difference in our conceptual frameworks and approaches to both legal issues and women's rights. They tended to remain on an abstract level and to argue in terms of ideals and imperatives, whereas I was keen to bring the discussion to the level of social experience, which they called "current" or "external realities," euphemisms for issues on which they felt they had to defend the feqh position. The language they used was heavy and technical, and although I was familiar with feqh idioms and concepts, I was sometimes not sure that I understood them correctly. At times, my responses were gut reactions. I had checked my understandings with Saʿidzadeh, who reassured me that I had understood the thrust of their argument but that they were highly skilled at not giving clear and straight answers. He added that although my questions were at times rather bold—looking back, it must have been difficult for them to handle my directness—my obvious honesty and conviction had persuaded them to continue the discussions.

I had raised the three main examples of gender inequality in shariʿa laws (hejab, divorce, and polygamy). I decided to let go of hejab, a hoary political issue tied to the policies of the previous regime and the reactions of the current one.[4] Iranian women themselves are divided on the issue, and women's journals are silent. I would follow up the other two, and try to find out more about *Payam-e Zan*'s perspective—which I had labeled "Balance" in the course of the previous session—and how it proposed to redress inequalities inherent in feqh laws.

My five questions were as follows:

1. What is the Balance perspective? Please define it in relation to the other two perspectives: Equality and Inequality. How does this perspective differ from the views of Mr. Motahhari?

2. Can feqh, with its current framework, theories, and tools, accommodate the needs and desires of women in this century, given that among their aspirations are equality and participation in society? I ask this because some wonder how a system of law with an unspoken assumption of women as inferior and defective creatures can protect women's rights and improve their lot.

---

[4] It is also a contentious issue in the literature on women in post-revolutionary Iran; see the Bibliographic Essay.

3. To what extent do you think that the question of women should be addressed and solutions be sought outside the realm of religion?

4. How do you see the relationship between Islamic ethical injunctions and feqh Rulings? What is the role of custom?

5. What are your views on women's employment, their right to serve as judges, the minimum age of marriage, and men's unilateral rights to divorce and polygamy?

Mortazavi opened the discussion by commenting on the last session: if the themes had been identifed in advance, our discussion could have been more fruitfully directed, as we hoped it would be in the second session. This session too lasted around two hours; the published transcript presents it as the first session of our debate.

The Second Session with *Payam-e Zan*

SZM: As an introduction to the main axis of our discussion, I think it's essential to state two points. The first is that the gate of ejtehad is open. One specific feature of Shi'i feqh is that in relation to Problems, especially to Rulings, it has left the door open to new opinions, of course on the basis of the proper frameworks, both in sources and in tools and methodology. Obviously there are different perspectives and different opinions. Given the fundamentals in Shi'i Theology, we do not consider a mojtahed to be correct in all conditions, that is, what they understand of the divine Rulings is beyond dispute. The truth is something a jurist might or might not ascertain; the scope and type of debates that are common in the Houzeh encourage tolerance and diversity, as when a mojtahed states his opinion on a legal matter he can't say: this is definitely the letter of Islam. What is said must be viewed as the personal opinion of the individual who utters it, even if he's the spokesman of a major judicial or intellectual current in feqh. That is to say, we can't consider ourselves to represent what Islam says, given our own fundamentals and frameworks. We don't allow ourselves to do this, nor can we speak for all legal perspectives within the Houzeh. Therefore, expectations must be lowered to the level of expert opinion. For instance, my opinion or that of others can't be regarded as that of the collectivity of Muslim thinkers and jurists. This is of course true of all sciences and disciplines, not just Islamic Studies.

My second point, in line with the first, is that we have a series of definite Principles which we call the essentials of religion; denial of them is tantamount to negation of the comprehensiveness and completeness of Islam. These essentials aren't open to debate, and they're not matters of opinion [where guidance is needed]. Now, the relation between these definite

Principles and essentials and other, secondary elements of religion must be defined. Given this, if a view or perspective is found to contradict the Principle of human value, we don't accept that view or perspective, even if its authenticity is beyond question. For instance, if we come across a hadith to the effect that women are from hell, we don't accept it, as it contradicts the Principle of "nonwasting of acts" in the Holy verse: "that I will not waste the work of a worker among you, whether male or female" (al-Imran, 195). The Koran is clear that there's no difference between men and women, and good works will not go unrewarded. So, even if such a hadith is authentic, if it doesn't tally with the Principle, we don't accept it. The most we can do is a kind of explanation and analysis, for instance that it arose in certain circumstances in a certain era. But we don't accept such a hadith as stating a general interpretation on women.

I could not see what he was alluding to; but given their rejection of equality in favor of balance in our earlier discussion, I tried to discover if gender equality was a Principle, in his view as a mojtahed. For "inequality," I said "discrimination" (tab*iz), to avoid being trapped by Motahhari's distinction between "equality" (tasavi) and "sameness" (tashaboh).

ZMH: Could I ask something in this connection? In your own research, have you come across a Principle that opposes discrimination between men and women?

SZM: At the level of Genesis, we believe the world to have been perfect and just; and therefore at the stage of Lawgiving, the wellspring of laws is justice and human value (keramat). Thus, as I said before, the accusation that there's discrimination between men and women is groundless. At the level of valuation of acts, we already said that there's no discrimination between men and women. At the level of opportunities to develop potentials and fulfil talents, if we go back to essentials we see that Islam's position is also clear. Of course, there are some differences in other areas that will be discussed.

Then he suggested that we let him convene the discussion. He began by reading out my first question, asking Sa*idi to deal with it.

MHS: Well . . . the [first] three interrelated questions are in fact one. Let me start with what Martyr Motahhari says on the concept of equality. He rejects the Western concept of gender equality as mere propaganda, and says that what they mean by "equality" in rights for the sexes is in fact "similarity." You have probably studied his views; if not, it's appropriate that you do. On the difference between equality and similarity, he argues that the first entails equivalence while the second merely entails resemblance. For instance, a father might divide his wealth among his children equally according their capacities, giving one the shop, another the land to cultivate, and the third property to rent. What he gives them is equal in value, but not similar.

Motahhari doesn't believe in the similarity of rights between men and women, instead he argues that if women want to have equal rights with men and to enjoy equal fortune with men, then the similarity of rights must be removed, in order to pave the way for men and women to acquire their proper rights. Martyr Motahhari stresses that dissimilarity of rights as between men and women, within the limits set by nature, is compatible not only with justice and natural laws but also with the well-being of the family and society.

There isn't much difference between our Balance perspective and the views of Martyr Motahhari; they're the same in spirit. But we distinguish between equality and balance. For instance, in a contract, if the rights of the two parties are equal and of the same value, such a contract can't be said to be necessarily just. In other words, when two people want to share life together, their rights might be totally equal but sometimes we see that this equality isn't just. Why? Because rights must be proportional to duties; that's to say, we must divide the rights of individuals by their duties, and establish equality in the results; in clearer terms:

Women's rights : Women's duties = Men's rights : Men's duties

This is how we define "balance," and this rule is found in every equitable contract. For instance, suppose you enter a contract to run a company with someone, you get paid according to the level of your investment and the time you put in. If all were paid equally, this would be the essence of oppression and injustice.

I had agreed to let Mortazavi lead the discussion, but now, thinking that if we continued in this way we would not move beyond clichés, I decided to intervene and open up my question:

ZMH: You mean, basically you concur with Mr. Motahhari's perspective. Master Motahhari made extensive use of the studies of Western thinkers—psychologists and sociologists—in reaching an understanding of women, their psychology, and the relations between the sexes. I have read his book carefully and am familiar with his perspective. There have been a number of criticisms of the book. In fact, many of the assumptions on which Mr. Motahhari bases a number of his generalizations have been seriously questioned in the past two decades. Mr. Motahhari says men's nature is totally different from women's. Women want to be loved, men want to love; women want to be possessed, men want to possess; women are the hunted and men are hunters. This theory, he argues, is based on nature, supported by psychology. But the findings of the psychologists he refers to in his book have now been refuted. These differences are more to do with nurture, and aren't fixed but are shaped by social conditions. If women are more compromising and want to please, it's to do with their socialization; that's to say, from the moment an infant is fed, its gender is defined. If we consider these definitions as natural, then discrimination can be interpreted as divine Justice. In his book, Martyr Motahhari says: it's a kind of justice that women don't have the right to divorce; it's the essence of justice that a man can take up to four wives. Mr. Motahhari's views have been discussed critically, within the Islamic framework as well as outside it. What he does is a kind of justification.

My own criticism is that Mr. Motahhari wrote his book—as you know better than me—when a series of articles appeared in *Zan-e Ruz*; this was when the Family Protection Law was about to be introduced [1967] and there were attempts to put aside shari'a family law. That is, some saw Islam and the shari'a to be in danger. Therefore Mr. Motahhari came to the defense of the shari'a, and to some extent his arguments and justifications are the product of their time, when a Western model was being adopted without much sensitivity to the nation's cultural and Islamic roots. But we're now seventeen years into the Islamic revolution, and we're in a position where Islamic values, our basic values, are safe and defended by government, and they can be implemented, whereas in the past this wasn't the case. Don't you think that this perspective must now be approached critically, within the Islamic framework? Do you accept it totally?

Let me return, briefly, to the issue of equality and similarity—last session I wrongly referred to "equality" as "similarity." There are certain matters that reflect outright gender discrimination, and there's no way we can say they reflect equality. For instance, the issue of divorce, which we discussed last session. It's a fact that women's access to divorce is limited, whereas men have all the legal prerogatives. On the other hand, there are a number of ethical principles, rooted in Islamic Ethics and Traditions, which don't permit men to repudiate their wives whenever they wish. But we see that, when it comes to legal interpretation and legal frameworks, one particular interpretation is preferred. My question is: what has the Balance perspective to say on these changes? What I want to know is, do you accept and repeat what Mr. Motahhari says? As I said, his views are the product of a particular time and a particular state; you have a different mission now; the time and and state are different. Has there been change since then or not? That's why I posed the question.

MHS: To an extent, we recognize the influence of conditions of time and place on issues and the way they're addressed; but this doesn't mean that because of conditions of time and place one is forced to change certain things fundamentally, especially in relation to religion. We believe that in religion we have some undisputable Principles, including the Principle of justice, on which religion is based. We don't recognize as Islamic a law that conflicts with this Principle. Now the question is, how do we define justice, what's our interpretation and what do we understand by it? As regards male-female relations, when we discuss their mutual rights and duties, we have the issue of justice in mind. What you must bear in mind is that in Islam marriage is a dyadic contract in which the two parties are free. The contract wasn't founded by Islam: marriage predates Islam, which has modified its limits and conditions. In effect it has regulated the marriage contract in order to bring it into line with its objectives for the development of humanity. For this reason, we see marriage as a contract entered by two rational, free, and aware individuals. We see that Islam only determines the framework of this contract, that is the pillars of marriage. Otherwise, the rest is left to men and women to agree and do as they want. Whether it's just or not is the result of [the parties'] decisions and their own actions.

ZMH: The way you put it covers only the personal and individual aspect of legality; you neglect the social side. Don't you see any role here for the state? Do Islamic states have no duty here? Do you want to leave everything to men and women who enter the contract?

MHS: The responsibility of government is to clarify the general laws. When two persons want to set up a company, is it the duty of the law to tell them how much capital each should put in or how many hours they should work? No. The duty of the law and the state is to define frameworks and boundaries. On marriage and other similar topics, what is often neglected is that some think men and women marry on the basis of compulsion, and that all aspects of marriage are defined by the shariʿa. But many [aspects of marriage] have nothing to do with the shariʿa. There is a handful of rules and limited measures that the shariʿa requires; the rest, as regards dower, the employment of women, place of residence, and the right to divorce, can all be determined one by one. Therefore, Islam can't be blamed for actual practices in society. Islam, both specifically and case by case, isn't responsible for these. Of course I say "specifically," because Islam has a duty to define general cases.

I was not sure what he was getting at. I wanted to say that the problem as I saw it was that some people claim in the name of Islam that they have the answer for every problem; and that such a claim makes them responsible for the present situation. I put it rather vaguely and discursively, leaving myself room to modify and retract.

ZMH: What you're saying contradicts so much . . . both the Islamic perspective and . . .

MHS: Contradicts the Islamic perspective?

ZMH: Permit me; what you're saying is that Islam, the shariʿa, has nothing to do with marital relations. But this isn't the case: people believe that the shariʿa has a lot to do with these matters; they believe that their marriages are conducted according to shariʿa law. Besides, in the press, in speeches, everywhere we hear about the shariʿa, and our religious authorities see this as their mission. Take the issue of polygamy, for instance; I say this on the basis of my own research in courts, that polygamy is indeed painful and difficult for women. Although the incidence isn't high in our society [according to official statistics, 1 percent of marriages], it causes over 20 percent of all divorces. This is a kind of marital problem where the court has difficulty in bringing about a reconciliation: the marital crisis is often terminated by the husband divorcing one of his two wives. Many women are subject to polygamy and accept it, because the shariʿa allows it. This is just the problem. Or take what you say about marriage, that it's a contract between people of free will. I agree with you entirely, and I'm familiar with its feqh and legal aspects. But this contract was defined in the past, when feqh was independent of central government. You know better than me the context feqh operated in: a multiplicity of religious courts, schools, and legal opinions, people could choose judges, and so on. Now we're talking in the last years of the twentieth century, in the context of centralized government and unified legal systems. The types of state and legal system are radically different from what they used to be. The basis of the political and legal system in our country is Islam; therefore, we can't say here that shariʿa, feqh, and our government have nothing to do with marriage.

Why? Because here lies discrimination. How can we expect a woman unaware of the [legal rules] to secure her rights in marriage before entering it? Can a woman who's given in marriage at thirteen stipulate conditions? We can't separate our culture from shariʿa. In discussions of marriage proposals, people don't usually talk of divorce or of securing rights for their daughters; they want to give them away. During the contract ceremony of a close relative of mine, I told the mullah to insert among the conditions the bride's unconditional right to divorce; the groom had already agreed to it. But the mullah refused, saying: "I'll do no such thing, divorce is the man's right; you're giving the bride ideas; talking of divorce at the time of marriage is wrong, it's a bad omen," and so on. I tell you, our society is one in which such beliefs and actions exist, and women are dealt with unjustly. This isn't in line with the Principle of justice that you talk about. Since injustice exists, therefore there's a need to take legal measures, to do something to defend women. Your thesis that shariʿa has nothing to do with these "external realities" is rather hard for me to digest. In my opinion, the shariʿa has a lot to do with these matters. Perhaps I have misunderstood you.

When I had finished, Mortazavi intervened and told Saʿidi: "It seems that your point wasn't clear to Ms. Mir-Hosseini." I agreed; then Saʿidzadeh made one of his rare interventions:

SMS: For me too as a listener, Mr. Sa'idi's point is problematic. What I understood is that marriage is a contract; shari'a has nothing to do with regulating it and has only a few recommendations. If this is the case, then we must also clarify our position on its dissolution, which is also an aspect of marriage. We know that it's man who can terminate it unilaterally; there's no [dyadic] contract here.

SZM: Mr. Sa'idi, if you separate the law proper from its implementation, then the issue of government and its responsibility becomes clear. Is it the duty of government to implement the law, for instance to stop [the mullah] who wasn't prepared to insert the condition, or other such things?

Sa'idi repeated what he had already said in different words: that they were talking from the journal's perspective, that they were not defending the current situation and legal realities; that many of the issues I raised were cultural and had nothing to do with religion. If injustice is done in the name of religion, it is the fault of the people, and it is for this reason that the journal is trying to raise women's awareness, to make them aware of their rights in Islam. If that mullah did not do his duty, which was to insert what the two parties had agreed, that was his fault, he did wrong, and it has nothing to do with religion. Again for this reason, the journal tries to deal with social realities critically, to identify the unjust elements and inform people about them.

I did not challenge Sa'idi this time. There was no point. He either could not or did not want to talk in terms of the interaction between shari'a laws and actual practices. When he had finished, a silence followed, broken by a question posed by Mortazavi, leading to a discussion which developed in a way that brought to the surface our conceptual differences. It was interesting for two reasons: first, he framed his question using the word Doubt (*shobheh*)—in Houzeh terminology, Doubt (see Chapter Two) implies questioning a principle of belief; second, Sa'idi finally admitted that gender equality was accepted on all fronts except in the family.

SZM: Some Doubts were raised; if you permit, we'll discuss them. Do you want to refute "the Principle of difference" [between the sexes]? Are you saying that all these things are conventional because of nurture and socialization?

ZMH: Not at all. I'm not denying there are differences. In fact, there's recently been much discussion over how far male and female brains work differently. But let me clarify what I mean by way of the example of racial theories. Those theories that supported discrimination always said that the black race is inferior to the white, the oriental race is inferior to the Western, as proved by their smaller brains, less intelligence, and consequently lower economic and social status—all this because of race. This way of thinking perpetuated the status quo, as it ignored the root factors, such as European

domination, colonialism. Later research showed that if black children have
a lower IQ, it has to do with nurture, not nature; it has to do with socioeconomic deprivation. At the same time, this isn't to say that the black race
is identical to the white race; there are physical, genetic differences, there
might even be others. . . .

The same is true of gender differences. Here much of what has been said
about nature is based on assumptions that have never been fully examined:
that women are "defective in reason," that they can't defend themselves, and
therefore they need protection and men are their protectors. It's a vicious
circle.

SZM: So you accept the Principle of natural and innate differences? Of
course, I'm not referring to actual instances of difference, or the arguments
put forward by Martyr Motahhari, but do you also accept that these differences will have an impact at the level of lawmaking?

ZMH: I do accept that; I'm not arguing for identical rights. I think that the
mechanics of reproduction, motherhood, and the special bonding between
mother and child, all must be taken into account, and that identical rights
and duties aren't necessarily beneficial for women. I accept this, but I feel
we're getting diverted from the theme of our debate. If I raised [the question of] Mr. Motahhari's reasoning, it was because I wanted to understand
what you mean by Balance perspective. Do you view the disparities that
exist in law as a kind of discrimination, or do you want to justify them
and regard them as the essence of justice? Look, Mr. Motahhari's perspective is apologetic; [I know] it's not a matter of black and white. But if there
isn't gender equality, then we have inequality, whatever shape and form it
may take. What I'm saying is that, if we want to eliminate sexual discrimination, we first need to accept, both theoretically and strategically, the Principle of equality; then we can discuss issues such as dissimilarity of rights
and duties.

SZM: We don't refute equality; our dispute is over interpretation. The
Principle of gender equality, whether interpreted as Balance or Equity, is
undeniable.

MHS: Excuse me, sometimes we're talking of humankind irrespective of
external conditions; we say that they're equal, whether they're men or
women, or as you said white or black, and both examples can be used here
to support our position, that human beings are equal in this respect. . . .

Here I interrupted him, thinking I knew what he was coming to, and hoping to
move the discussion on; but to no avail. Sa'idzadeh came to my aid, however,
bringing up an issue implied in my questions.

ZMH: I said black and white deliberately, because I wanted to get out of
the gender dimension and draw parallels. I'm now quite familiar with your
position; if you agree, let's get down to specifics.

MHS: But I think we've a problem in the generalities of our debate that must be clarified. The Principle of equality between men and women is agreed, but in marriage men and women aren't merely two humans in terms of their natural and basic rights. This is an important point; we can't say that men and women in the family, which is formed on the basis of a contract, are equal and must have equal conditions. Although equality is admitted in its broader meaning, men and women in the family aren't simply two human beings, they have different and complementary roles, and it's natural that they have different conditions, according to their different roles. What must be done is to observe justice here; and as Martyr Motahhari said, similarity [read "equality"] can't be accepted; roles and rights can't be the same.

SMS: If we look at men's and women's rights in marriage, and if we accept the present definition that man is head of the household and has the duty of providing, then, because man has two duties (as head and provider), he's given the right of divorce. Is this what you mean?

MHS: I beg your pardon? But we haven't been discussing present social conditions.

ZMH: But we can't have an imaginary discussion! Are we talking about current legal realities or not?

MHS: Look, if we want, we can discuss the current state of society, but we must take into account the different dimensions: ethical, cultural, social, legal, and so on. We have our own critical views; but if we want to discuss as you do, then we must be more specific: for instance, why men in our society have these rights, and how their duties should be defined. This is different from our discussion in which we talk in terms of general propositions [situations on which feqh arguments are based] irrespective of external reality. Naturally, we also have a critical approach to external reality. But we don't enter into details. So I think we must decide where to locate the discussion.

I was frustrated and confused. They insisted on talking at the level of feqh constructs. They too must have been frustrated with my approach: whatever they said, whatever the force of their legal arguments from theology and philosophy, I always came back to asking their views about discrimination, which they did not accept as such, calling it difference, limitations, but not inequality or discrimination.

I took up Sa'idi's offer, and made clear that I wanted to discuss specifics.

ZMH: In your perspective, does Article 1133 [of the Civil Code], which says a man can divorce whenever he wants, contradict the Principle of justice or not?

MHS: Look, if it's the law that a man can do this whenever he wants, which it's not . . .

ZMH: It is; that's the letter of the law.

MSH: The law [of divorce] isn't a single article, to be implemented in isolation; in practice we see that a man has to go to court and the case is dealt with there. Now if the issue of arbitrators isn't taken that seriously in our legal system, that's a different matter.

ZMH: They do take it seriously; the court refers all cases of divorce to arbitration, and now no divorce can be issued without arbitration; but still men's and women's access to divorce is radically different.

MSH: I'm not sure how the courts interpret the issue of arbitration; I don't know whether they see a divorce without arbitration as invalid; or whether they just send a case as a matter of procedure. But the question is, if a man wants to [use his unilateral right to divorce] without good reason, then we must examine it and try to find ways of reconciling the couple. If this isn't possible, and a man can't live with his wife under any circumstances, what do you say we should do? Should we say that the shariʿa prohibits him from divorce?

ZMH: We discussed this last session. I said that he must be able to divorce; but I also said, look at it from the other side. If a woman can't live with her husband, we see that her legal access to divorce is very limited, unless she can get her husband's consent, for which she must give something up. The difference is there.

SZM: This isn't the case; a woman who can't tolerate life with her husband has no shariʿa obligation to continue such a life. Here the judge can effect a separation; this is the "government divorce" I mentioned last session. Government, of which the judiciary is part, has a role to play here. As I already said, we're talking irrespective of current realities; we're not defending the situation; but we want to discuss women and their position on an Islamic basis. Current realities in society aren't ideal. If they were ideal and defensible, then there would be no need for journals like ours. That's to say, current realities, at least at the level of awareness, have certain drawbacks that necessitate cultural activity. As the Imam said, the basis of Islam is government; and he sees all its laws and Rulings as a tool, as a means for achieving the general aims of government. If we look at it from this perspective, we'll see that it's not the case that members of society in their social affairs or even in their personal lives have reached dead ends that Islam can't solve.

I referred to "government divorce" last session. We might have problems in implementing it; in practice, so many restrictions might be created that the whole concept gets distorted and loses its efficacy. This is a different matter, but it's another thing to say that the way is closed.

He was showing irritation; I must have offended them in pursuing my point, so I decided to back off. After all, I had made my point.

ZMH: I just wanted to know whether the way is closed or not.

SZM: No, the way isn't closed! [Marital] life becomes unbearable [for a woman] when her husband either misbehaves or doesn't pay maintenance, and so on. If he doesn't pay maintenance, then the Islamic judge can force him to do so, his hands aren't tied. I mean, when [the judge] can go as far as issuing the death sentence for those who oppose the Islamic government; when the hand of Islam and the Islamic government isn't tied, we shouldn't say there are dead ends in the life of individuals, that life is intolerable and there's no way out. Let's imagine a society where all women are unhappy with their situation; we can't say there's no way out. The solution lies in seeing Islam as a totality and as a government: this perspective solves many problems. This is the Imam's conception, he wasn't for temporary measures; when he objected to the Family Protection Law and other issues, his objection was to the whole [Pahlavi] system, not details. Although [now] government rules and controls the laws in the name of Islam, this isn't to say that all laws in society are truly Islamic. If that were the case, there wouldn't be so many defects and corruptions.

MHS: One of the accepted Principles in feqh is the Ruling on "denial of harm." Islam doesn't allow hardship and harm. If a woman's husband doesn't mistreat her, provides for her, and is a very good person, yet she dislikes him and for this reason can't continue to live with him; if the court reaches the conclusion that the continuation of marriage is difficult for such a woman, then it will either order the husband to divorce her or itself effect a divorce. But we must ask to what extent our judges take these matters into account.

I started to say that I was aware of these things, but Mortazavi broke in to refer to an event at the time of the Prophet and the Ruling from which the feqh Principle of "no harm" originated. A man owned a date palm which was located on another man's property. The first man had no respect for the privacy of the second and refused to abide by the Prophet's instruction not to enter the house without the owner's permission, so the Prophet ordered his tree to be destroyed so that he could not abuse his right of ownership. Mortazavi then turned to me:

SZM: If Islam doesn't accept that, do you think it would sanction hardship or harm to a human being [a woman in an unwanted marriage] in the way you say? No, it's never like this. We consider justice as the basis and foundation of all laws and rules. Suppose there were only one human being in this world and one law; we say the basis of this law is justice and it has nothing to do with ties and social relations. This is one point. The second is that there's an overall balance in laws, if they're taken as a system. This is what we said earlier, and it became the basis of your questions. On laws, rules, and social institutions from this angle, I believe that our perspective, if not the same as that of Mr. Motahhari, is very close to it. I also dare say there's balance in all subsystems, like the one that concerns family relations. . . . Perhaps we can't say that this particular law is equivalent to that particular law . . . but at least at the level of family relations, if there are some limitations for women, there are others for men. There's difference in Islamic law—but it can't be taken as proof of gender discrimination.

When he had finished, Mortazavi asked Saʿidi and Saʿidzadeh whether they wanted to add something. The latter said something in a low voice, inaudible on the tape. The pause gave me a chance to think, and as Mortazavi was about to move the discussion ahead on the lines he had prepared, I made another attempt to show the contradiction in his position:

ZMH: I have a question here. This Balance perspective that you adhere to, as I understand it, has two premises: one is justice, and the other is a holistic approach; I mean, if one right is given to women, another is given to men. Now all these are premised on a number of unspoken assumptions and presuppositions; as an anthropologist/sociologist I want to come back to these, and look at them individually. If we look at the family, we see that the assumption is that men provide maintenance for women, therefore they're in charge of them. But when we look at Iranian society at large, be it rural, nomadic, or urban, we see that socioeconomic reality is such that men aren't the sole providers. Women also contribute to the household economy. In other words, the assumption that men are the sole providers has no basis in people's everyday life. Many women now work outside [the home].

SZM: Is it their [women's] duty to do so?

ZMH: We must separate [duty from reality]. Many women have to engage in outside employment, otherwise the family can't make ends meet. It's an economic imperative; these days many men are looking to marry a woman with a salary. For instance, take the case of a couple who are both teachers: both bring their salaries into the household; if not, they can't make ends meet. We can't accept the assumption that men are providers, it has no basis in the reality of such couples' lives.

SZM: Imagine a society in which it's enough when one of the two works; who do you think then has a duty to provide? the wife?

ZMH: Yes, of course, if she's earning.

SZM: No! we say she has no such duty.

ZMH: What if the man is unemployed and his wife isn't? If you consider marriage to be a partnership, then both are equally responsible.

SZM: In that case, it becomes what Mr. Saʿidi said before about the contractual side of marriage. A couple can agree that the man stays at home and the woman goes to work, on the basis of external realities; this is a different matter and has nothing to do with religion, which allows it. Our assumption concerns the primary model of marriage where one person [the man] is the provider; does the woman feel any duty here, from the religious point of view, morally?

ZMH: I don't understand what you're getting at. Are you suggesting that when a man works and can provide for the family, then the woman shouldn't feel that she too has a responsibility?

SZM: She has no responsibility to feel. What responsibility?

ZMH: You mean that she has no role to play in managing the family?

Sa'idzadeh intervened: *Payam-e Zan* had commissioned him to write a piece on maintenance in marriage, which he hoped would appear soon.

SMS: With your permission, let's take the example of a woman who's wealthy and capable of providing for herself and her children and there's no need for the husband to provide. What's his duty here?

SZM: It's the man's duty to provide; this is the shari'a Ruling, and the wife's financial situation has nothing to do with it. Here we're talking only legally; ethical imperatives and human values such as self-sacrifice, cooperation, and so on must be separated from shari'a obligations. Thus we see that, at the level of legislation, the legislature views ethical issues as beyond its realm of responsibility. Legal Rulings define the limits of duties and responsibilities. If a man can't pay and his wife is willing to forgo her right, this is another matter; but this doesn't mean the man had no duty to provide.

SMS: What is the woman's duty? We accept that the man has the duty to provide; does this mean the woman has no duty?

SZM: As a wife she has no duty.

ZMH: So all privileges here go to the man with financial means—since his power is premised on his providing? In that case, only men who are capable of providing can have authority over their wives . . .

MHS: This power is neither illogical nor boundless . . .

ZMH: . . . so a man who can't provide shouldn't have the right to headship . . .

SZM: No! this has nothing to do with whether he actually pays, but with his duty to pay. If he doesn't provide, his wife can't say that the rights he has over her are removed. She must go to the court to secure her right to maintenance; but she can't say that, because he hasn't provided, then he has no right to headship . . .

SMS: Let me add something to elucidate what you said. In feqh, it's a man's duty to provide maintenance, a kind of duty which differs from the duty to perform daily prayers and fast, in the sense that those who are unable to fulfil [the latter] are freed from them. A man can be freed from his duty to provide only when his wife forgoes her right; for this reason, a woman can always demand past maintenance. We must make a distinction between right (*haqq*) and Ruling (*hokm*). Maintenance is a right [for women] not a Ruling [for men].

SZM: Yes! For this reason, a woman may demand retribution; I mean, in certain conditions she's entitled to take her maintenance from the property of a husband who's unwilling to provide for her. The difference between right and Ruling must be made clear: a right is something that can be forgone or created, and it comes in the realm of emotions and human relations, whereas a Ruling is a command.

I tried to relate this to my fourth question, touching on the relationship between ethics and rights, but Mortazavi said we would come to this. So, after a longish pause, I tried once again to challenge the assumptions on which their model was built.

ZMH: In effect, you agree with all the assumptions underlying the feqh notion of maintenance; and you see none of them as modifiable according to changes in social conditions. One could say that maintenance in the sense you describe belongs to a time when women's position in society was different, when they didn't have economic independence, and family relations were such that men were superior and had control over women . . .

SZM: Not superior. If [correctly] interpreted, it becomes clear that the current view in society that men are superior is incorrect. The legal limits [of men's authority] are well defined. As for the issue of men's guardianship over women—which you call authority—then its limits must be recognized. Can a man prevent his wife from participating in society? Can he prevent his wife from taking up employment or following her studies? No, he can't; the journal takes all these into consideration.

ZMH: Let's look at it at the level of your model of the family. If a man knows that the household isn't going to benefit from his wife's employment or educational activities outside, then he can't be blamed for wanting [to keep her at home]. If the family isn't founded on shared economic resources and shared responsibility between the spouses, then we must discuss all these. I mean that you're talking of rights that have no real basis in the actual life of many people. When we look at existing marriages, we see that men and women who live happily together and don't find their way to court are those who don't live by [feqh] maintenance laws; they share resources and responsibilities; they have the same purse.

SZM: Is it the same in law? Or is it the same because that they adhere to ethical principles and reach an understanding?

ZMH: Because they carry the ethical rules into the legal ones; we can have different types of legality. . . .

SZM: Excuse me! Once the ethical rules are carried into the legal, then they become law and we can no longer call them ethical.

I wanted to say that during my work in the courts I had felt that the shari'a was becoming a kind of ideology for maintaining patriarchal structures, that its function was maintaining men's authority over women. In practice, only a small minority of people could live by its Rulings, which have no place in the actual life of the majority, unless marriage breaks down; then they come to court and fight their marital battles armed with the discourse and logic of feqh. But I could not say this in a clear and straightforward way without risking offense. I had already been too provocative, and I wanted to continue the discussion. So I put it differently.

ZMH: There's a type of law that is outside the domain of government and feqh, and is established and maintained by people themselves. People live according to certain laws, which aren't necessarily written down or passed by the legislator, but their relations with their spouses and children are regulated according to them.

SZM: These are a set of ethical understandings, and they can't be called law. Law is something enforceable, that is, the state and its apparatus can intervene on its behalf; otherwise, it's an ethical understanding between people and isn't enforceable. [Here the published transcript adds: *it's evident that by "law" we have in mind its conventional meaning, that is, binding religious law.*]

ZMH: I'm talking of law at a different level; unwritten law, whose sanctions aren't in the state or its institutions; ground rules that individuals enforce in their everyday intercourse. For instance, if your child breaks one of the family ground rules and does something wrong, to punish him you don't talk to him for a couple of hours. This punishment is what reinforces the family ground rules, and what makes it effective is the loving nature of relations that exist between you. So there are other types of law that might never be written down but have a place in people's lives, they know it and regulate their life accordingly. What I'm trying to say is that many of these unwritten laws that make the family and keep it going are somehow in contradiction with the law of maintenance. That is, when we look at happy and successful families, we see that they're founded on shared interests and resources. A man mightn't have high earning power, but if his wife feels that he shares what he has with her, isn't taking it [to another wife], and values her and recognizes her place in the family, then she'll put up with him and cooperate, even if he fails to keep her in the style she might wish.

SZM: The law of maintenance doesn't rule out cooperation.

ZMH: Nor does it presuppose it. You say that woman has no duty [to provide].

SZM: She has no duty, but by law she isn't prevented from doing it.

ZMH: From the ethical point of view, has she or not?

SZM: Ethically speaking, housework, such as cooking, washing, child-care, feeling responsible, and cooperating in making ends meet, are all highly regarded and can in fact gain her rewards in the other world. Doing these things is stressed in Islam and has religious merit. But is she obliged to do them?

ZMH: Yes, I say she is obliged. If she doesn't do her duties, her husband will maltreat her, beat her, take another wife, divorce her. . . .

As I was adding to the list of consequences faced by a woman who does not fulfil what I called the "unwritten laws" of marriage, Mortazavi protested and said, "this is turning into something else; this is not what I was saying." Here he was interrupted by Sa'idi, who tried to clarify the situation and take us out of the impasse; to my surprise he more or less endorsed what I had been saying, though he put it in different language.

MHS: I think if we [to Mortazavi] remember that the journal has a point of view, and discuss the issues from this angle, the debate will become clearer. You [to me] said that the law of maintenance becomes a basis for men's control over their wives; in other words, in return for this duty, husbands gain a right, and a duty is created for wives.

ZMH: Exactly; men's duty to pay maintenance is defined in relation to the wife's duty of submission; one can't be discussed without the other.

MHS: Then you asked what happens, for instance in nomadic or urban societies, when women work and naturally play a role in the household economy. From the journal's position—which is of course rooted in our religious standpoint—we believe that actions commanded by God have two levels: justice and compassion. The first defines the limits, the red line beyond which lie injustice and oppression. To operate at this level means strict observance of one's duties or demanding one's rights in full. But compassion means trying to do more than one's duty and demanding less than one's right. It's compassion that becomes the basis of cooperation and friendship. We consider compassion to be the basis for the running of society, that is, we believe that the family, the building block of society, should regulate its relations on the basis of compassion. When this isn't possible, then law and justice come into play, and people resort to law to obtain their rights.

Payam-e Zan sees it as its duty to appraise the "unwritten laws" you mentioned according to the criteria of compassion and justice. If a man in the family is tyrannical and inconsiderate toward his wife, for instance wanting to force her to stay at home despite her desire to work or to study, we see it as our duty to inform women that housework isn't obligatory for them. It's true that relations must as far as possible be based on compassion, but that takes two, and if the husband wants to demand all his rights, then the woman should demand all hers. It's not that only one party should make all the compromises; of course we want relations to be based on compassion, and as far as possible—I'll use your analogy—neither spouse should have any reason to "take up arms" against the other.

Here he was referring to something I had said in the previous session, off the record. To highlight the difference between their position and mine, I had said that they [the ulama] had placed a big stick in men's hands and then told them it was not morally correct to beat their wives. I meant that, as long as men are not disarmed, they will use the stick to get their way, by either beating or threatening to do so; it is the stick that sets the agenda, not the moral talk that they hear. The right of divorce is that stick, I said; take it away from him, since as long as he has such an arbitrary right he is bound to abuse it, and ignore your preaching.

In that session, neither of them had acknowledged my point, but now they seemed willing to discuss it and tried to bring it within their framework. Saʿidi accepted the "unwritten laws" and added that, in the journal, they have a systems approach to all issues and try to understand the relationship between the different dimensions of individual and social phenomena, to bring them into a comprehensive matrix. Mortazavi said it was worth repeating that they see Islam as a system of government and that all its laws must be seen in this light, even those which concern acts of worship. He concluded: "therefore, an external phenomenon, a human or social reality, is the result of diverse factors and to understand it one needs to study and analyze each of these factors."

I said no more, and a long silence followed, broken eventually by Mortazavi, who made another attempt to redirect the discussion. This time he also tried to include Saʿidzadeh, asking him why he was so quiet. Saʿidzadeh replied that he was there as an observer and only intervened when he saw that I did not follow their points. Mortazavi once again emphasized the importance of approaching and understanding Islam and its laws as a system in which each part is related to the others; thus it must be judged as a whole. He then said that one important focus of my questions was the premises of the system of women's rights in Islam; they had identified several premises that informed their gender perspective. He and Saʿidi then took turns to read them out and elaborate them, referring to them as principles. This was a kind of manifesto of their position on gender, formulated in response to the issues we had discussed in the first session.

SZM: The first principle, the most fundamental and comprehensive from an anthropological viewpoint, is the principle of species unity and distinctiveness. Regardless of gender difference, men and women belong to a single species. Both sexes share the same humanity. The human self is complex and can't be divided into maleness or femaleness.

The second, which relates to the social realm and to social interactions, is the principle of mutual dependence and mutual need. It forms the foundation of human relations, as indicated by Sura Zukhruf, 32: "We have exalted some of them above others in degrees, that some of them may take others in subjection." According to this verse, all members in a society are dependent on each other, serve each other, and all have mutual needs. The philosophy of difference and conflict among human beings must also be found in this mutual dependence. Another verse that relates to conjugal relations in the family is Sura Nisa, 34, which says: "Men are maintainers of women because Allah has made some of them to excel others." Unfortunately, this verse has often been interpreted so that women are dependent on men, who excel them. However, if the verse is interpreted in the light of the principle of "mutual dependence and mutual need," it indicates the relations between men and women and their places and roles within the family. Clearly, neither of these [relations and roles] in any way puts one sex above the other; that is, if men are given a certain role and place, this doesn't make them superior. Of course there are superior statuses that can be attained and have to do with one's conduct and belief. Both men and women can attain these superior statuses.

The third principle is attention to the natural and innate attributes of each sex as facts which become the subject of divine Rulings and personal and social laws; such facts are pregnancy, gestation, and so on. Unfortunately, these undeniable facts are often neglected, whereas they're what determine the laws. In our approach, we do take these into account, since it's these natural and innate differences that explain differences in rights and duties.

As for what Martyr Motahhari wrote on the psychological attributes of men and women—of course without judging each of them one by one—while we accept that there are differences in consciousness and emotions, we say that we don't have to justify and adjust Rulings, laws, and religious matters in accordance with the latest scientific theories, which are bound to change and be replaced by new ones. We regard these theories as evidence; they can be invoked in order to communicate religious truths to people who accept the language of science more easily. For instance, this has been done by Mr. Tantawi, an Egyptian exegete, who in his interpretations has tried to adjust the Koranic verses to present-day scientific theories. This method isn't accepted by our Houzeh criteria, as these theories are subject to change and those who base the validity of religious knowledge on them are then faced with a problem and have to take back what they said. For instance, if we say that one must use water in prayer ablutions because water destroys germs, we have to explain why one can't use alcohol, since it kills germs better! Whereas the real truth and reasons for many of the laws aren't yet known to us and might never be. You say that the situation has changed, and women are providers these days; this might be the case; but it doesn't mean that the basis of the laws must change. So, the theories referred to by Martyr Motahhari are, from our point of view, mere evidence and not the basis and foundation of his arguments.

The fourth principle is the principle of balance between rights and duties, which the Koran refers to, and also *Nahj ol-Balagheh* names as "the rights and duties." That is, rights bring their own responsibilities; if men are given more rights, in return they're also assigned more duties.

The fifth principle is complementarity between men and women in the family. Men and women complement each other in both personal and social dimensions. In the Koranic phrase, they're as close to each other as clothing; that is, they cover each other and make up for each other's defects. For this reason, we object to propositions which, rather than emphasizing this complementarity, focus on differences.

The sixth principle is that the family is the founding institution in society and has a special place and importance, so it must be shaped in such a way that it can fulfil its constructive function at the macro level in the direction defined by Islamic values.

The seventh is the principle of conflict of interests, an all-encompassing reality. Montesquieu's dictum on the limits of freedom—"the freedom of each person ends where the freedom of another person starts"—denotes the principle of conflict of interests. There are times when two people's interests don't coincide, and thus one must choose. At the level of legislation, this is one of the determining criteria which is also discussed in feqh. If we expand this notion to social relations, we see that it's sometimes necessary to choose between two conflicting interests; logic and reason tell us that we must prioritize and forgo one important interest for the sake of a more important one. Since the institution of the family plays an important role in shaping society, we can't legislate for its regulation regardless of wider social interests. At the level of implementation, we must also choose and prioritize, because our possibilities are limited and the principle of conflict of interest must be taken into consideration.

The eighth principle is the precedence of ethical and compassionate issues over legal ones, in both valuation and implementation. This is true even at the level of ritual acts; for instance, performance of nonobligatory prayers has more impact in taking us closer to God than the performance of those which are incumbent on us.

The ninth principle, the final one in our approach, is that the creative and legislative wellspring of law must be ascertained; the relation of human beings with this and the other world must be clarified. Without such clarification we can't have a proper analysis and understanding [of family laws], whether at the level of creation, where differences between men and women belong, or at the level of legislation, where the philosophy and purpose of Rulings are discussed. Islam is a religion that coordinates this world and the other, and if we accept the other world and the Day of Judgment as realities, then we can't deny their fundamental impact on law, human relations, and other dimensions of life.

Mortazavi finished by apologizing for taking so much time to explain the principles that inform their approach to gender, but said that they needed some elaboration. I had listened in silence, interrupting only to ask for clarification or to add a confirmatory point. It was clear they had been put together in response to my earlier objections, and were a joint effort by Mortazavi and Sa'idi. I was intrigued that they had considered my objections to Motahhari's book; although they did not say so, again they were trying to keep a "balance." In none of these nine principles could I see a new issue or a different line of argument; so I saw no point in repeating our earlier discussion, but tried to move ahead. The published transcript omits the following part of the discussion altogether.

ZMH: I think you have covered most of my questions, not one by one, of course, but all together. Only one remains, which concerns the relation between Ethics and Law—which you also alluded to—and between shari'a and feqh and current laws. If feqh Rulings derive from shari'a, and our current laws derive from feqh, I want to know how you see their connection; what are your definitions of shari'a and Law?

Mortazavi said he had considered this relationship in the above statement; and he invited a response from Sa'idzadeh, who as usual talked in such a low voice that only part of what he said is audible on the tape. The gist of his statement was that Law is derived from the shari'a, which can be likened to a timeless, fluid, and perfect totality, like a smooth-running river, from which societies in all conditions can derive their laws. Mortazavi pointed to the complexity and different levels at which these relations can be addressed. This directed the rest of our discussion.

SZM: I want to use clerical idioms; we say that these terms belong to the realm of discernment, and definition depends on the level at which it's addressed. When we say shari'a, in one sense we mean the totality of our religion, as when we say Law, we mean all religious injunctions and Rulings. But this isn't the level at which you're asking your question.

ZMH: Let me explain why I ask such a question. In my own research on family laws in Iran and Morocco, I explored the relation between theory and practice of shari'a laws at three levels. The first is the level of shari'a and feqh; I took these to be the same, since I was neither a jurist nor concerned with debates there, so I took feqh Rulings to be synonymous with shari'a— as ordinary people do. The second level is that of codified laws; in each country, family law is derived from its respective feqh school. The third level is what I referred to earlier as "unwritten laws," that is, customs and social practices that might or might not reflect shariʿa laws, people's perception of religious Rulings, and so on. Then I tried to explore the relationship between these three levels, and to do this I focused on marital disputes that end up in court. I asked the question here because I wanted to see how far my own conceptual framework and classification correspond to yours. I think some of the problems in our discussion have to do with definitions. It's likely that my definitions of shariʿa and Law don't match yours. My question might seem trivial and obvious to you, but I think it's important to address it before we can move ahead.

SZM: [The question] is very relevant. Some existing laws in the country, used by the government, in our idiom have to do with "defining the subject," not the Rulings. For instance, all procedural rules are of this kind, and they can't be called shariʿa Rulings; they are defining the subject. They might be based on custom or social necessity or other elements, but those that concern the substance of the Law, as you said, in the Islamic Republic are all derived from the shariʿa, but defined so that they can be implemented.

Our approaches to Islamic law did not correspond, but our definitions were not very different. I tried to find how far they saw these Rulings as immutable, and how they conceptualized the gap between Islamic law and social practice. I brought up the question of Dynamic Ejtehad and current thinking in the Houzeh, summarizing my discussion with Ayatollah Jannati, and asked for their views.

SZM: It seems to me the term "Dynamic" is a misnomer, an imprecise concept. We consider ejtehad to be dynamic, always and under all circumstances. It can't but be dynamic, as Shiʿi feqh must and does cater for all human needs at all times and in all places. What we can discuss is the elements that have an impact on the dynamism of ejtehad; in my opinion, the most important among them is Islam as a system of government. If Islam is to be a perfect religion and a coherent system of government, then it can't but have Dynamic Ejtehad. One of the greatest services the late Imam performed was that he insisted that government and the requirements of time and place were essential to ejtehad. He saw traditional ejtehad as dynamic but preoccupied with details and not orientated to the requirements of religion as a system of government. I emphasize that once we see Islam as a system of government, then we can have a systems approach and identify the missing links which prevent the coordination and reconciliation of some of its laws and regulations.

In the published transcript, our exchange on the new school of feqh appears at the beginning of the final instalment, with my question shortened, references to Jannati's books omitted, and Mortazavi's response much expanded, with the effect of minimizing differences between the two schools and the two types of ejtehad. What Mortazavi said was in fact in agreement with Jannati's definition of "Dynamic" Ejtehad. It was after this that Mortazavi brought up my third question:

> SZM: We have little time left, and one of your questions remains, which we decided to deal with, even though I consider it to be diversionary. I'll read the question first, and Mr. Saʿidi will respond. "Can the question of women be addressed and solutions be found outside the realm of religion?" I will say later why I think it's diversionary, or rather defective.

I did not then understand what he meant by "diversionary," *enharafi*, which denotes questions asked in order to mislead, or detours when a main road is under construction. Saʿidi too seemed rather unprepared; it took him some time to formulate a coherent response. I produce here *Payam-e Zan*'s version of his answer, which they edited so as to make better sense than what was said at the time. It summarizes his main points, although there are still repetitions.

> MHS: In our opinion, only religion can resolve women's issues in a fundamental, basic, comprehensive, and permanent way; other solutions are either only temporary or diversionary and thus can even exacerbate and add to women's problems. For instance, as with [nonrenewable resources], if we don't tame our inner desires and set up a system of control, the consequences for the world and humanity will be dire. . . . The problem of consumption can't be solved though further consumption, we must change our approach and seek a fundamental solution.
>
> If we pay attention, we see that human values are changeable and rooted in transient emotions and perceptions, so human likes and dislikes mustn't be the criteria on which we base solutions for the problems of society. We might find a solution, but be unaware of its impact on other dimensions of human life and the next generation. Human solutions are only temporary and can lead to unwanted results, unlike religious solutions. The God who has created this majestic world, who more than anyone else knows its working and determines its order, has also legislated the best Laws with the greatest benefits and least drawbacks for his creatures, offering them to us in the form of religion. Therefore, a fundamental way to solve women's and other problems is impossible except through a comprehensive implementation of all divine Laws. The more we progress in science, the more we become aware of our ignorance, and the more clearly we see the complexity of human beings, the world, and creation.

I probed further, to see how they understood these divine Laws to be translated into human laws. This led to an interesting discussion of how feqh conceptualizes the relationship between a divine Ruling and its subject, that is social reality. As we see, it rests on hypothetical cases.

ZMH: In relation to [the women's question] can the expertise and knowledge of other fields of inquiry, for instance sociology, psychology, and anthropology, be exploited? The raw material of all these laws is society, social relations, human beings. An understanding of these becomes a priority, and could be the basis for a working relationship between a Jurist and experts in those fields of knowledge. Do you think there's such a possibility?

MHS: We believe that religion must penetrate and be realized in all aspects of social and individual life; and for this reason science and religion must be intertwined. All elements of science and religion interact and influence each other. In law, we have the Ruling and its subject. Religion gives us the Ruling, the law; but it can't define its subject, which has an external reality. It's the task of science and its experts to clarify and determine whether a Ruling has a subject, and if so, whether it's one or more. So the definition and understanding of the correct subject of each Ruling is important, and for this reason there's a great deal of emphasis in the Islamic Republic on concord between seminaries and universities. We see the link as fundamental, and believe that the problems of our society can't be solved without deep and close cooperation between universities and seminaries. Neither can solve the problem on their own.

SZM: In the Houzeh, this is done as follows. The identification of the subject is necessary, but feqh doesn't see this as its duty; as the idiom has it, "it's not for a mojtahed to define the subject." In feqh, a large majority of Rulings are built on general propositions, not on external propositions, that is, hypothetical cases which might have no actual reality in the external world. In feqh, it's said that it's always assumed that the subject of a Ruling is realizable, that it can exist in the real world. It's the task of the mojtahed to apply a Ruling to its appropriate subject, and if he doesn't identify the subject correctly then he has erred in his discernment of the divine Law. For instance, drinking wine is haram. This is a Ruling, and the subject of this Ruling is wine as a substance that intoxicates. But it's not the task of the Jurist to decide what is intoxicating. Another example is whether or not playing chess constitutes a form of gambling. At one time it did, but later usage changed; so the Imam's fatwa [allowing the sale of chess sets] doesn't mean a change in the Ruling, but in the subject of the Ruling; that is, chess in our time can't be seen as gambling. This is what's meant by Dynamic Ejtehad. Thus it's important that a mojtahed discern the correct subject for the Ruling, which means that seminaries and mojtaheds can't function and exist separately from other sciences.

Now I want to explain why I said that I found your question [whether the women's question can be solved outside religion] diversionary, and in fact defective. We believe that religion has come to solve human problems; and if we pay special attention to women's issues, it's not because of their gender, but because of external and behavioral factors and the oppression that women have faced historically; Islam wanted to stop this historic oppression. So, a fuller version of your question should be: can the problems of humanity be solved outside religion?

MHS: I have another point to add in response to Ms. Mir-Hosseini's question; that is, in order to realize any ideal, one must first define it theoretically and clarify its philosophical and methodological foundations; second, determine policies and ways of realizing it; and third, evaluate the gap that exists between the present situation and the ideal. Viewing the situation from a religious standpoint, we feel this mission to construct all aspects of human life in accordance with religion, and we believe that religion has a clear directive respecting some of the stages mentioned, but with respect to other stages—which are in fact numerous—it has simply set limits and principles which we can't transgress. For instance, we don't expect religion to give us Rulings for road construction and traffic; similarly, we don't expect religion to give us laws for experimental sciences. Religion has nothing to say on specifics here, and only defines the framework within which we operate; that is, when we've reached a certain limit, we must stop; the rest is left to reason and logic. This isn't a shortcoming in religion, rather it's considered to be one of its values and merits.

SZM: Two other axes of your questions are left that must be addressed later; one of these concerns Rulings that you say show that women are thought to be "defective," a weapon the opposition uses. It must be examined to see whether it is the case or not.

ZMH: If you look at many sources and books, you will see that one of the main assumptions is that women are defective; I haven't invented it, and my question comes from reading these texts.

SZM: Yes. It's also important for us to address this question, and that's why we must devote some time to it. This issue is the foundation for a number of objections to our perspective, which you also implied in your question: "how can a system of law, with an unspoken assumption of women as inferior and defective creatures, protect women's rights and improve their lot?" This is a question that must be addressed.

ZMH: I hope you don't see this question as illegitimate?

SZM: Not at all; in fact we expected it to be among your first questions. When I said the question was "diversionary," I meant it was incomplete in the sense that in a religious framework we don't address women's questions apart from other human issues.

ZMH: That question was based on two assumptions; one, which I referred to earlier, was the relationship between religion and science; the other has to do with a feminist theory that all religions have oppressed women, and therefore if we look to religion to redress women's problems, we end up with double oppression of women. One of the findings of my comparative study of family law in Iran and Morocco—which gave rise to some controversy—is that Iranian women enjoy more legal protection in the family than Moroccan women, who live in a more secular society in which family laws are directly derived from Maleki feqh, but are implemented by a secular legal system.

SZM: This can be a good topic for discussion; we must postpone it to our next session, along with the rest of your questions, asking our views on specific issues such as women's employment and education, minimum age for marriage, and polygamy.

I agreed, but I also decided to use this opportunity to point out a flaw and contradiction in their line of argument: that some feqh Rulings are not in line with human nature, and that they in fact have a strong male bias. This exchange too was omitted in the published transcript.

ZMH: I have a question for Mr. Saʿidi, which occurred to me after thinking about last week's discussion. In your account of family relations you pointed to the tension between a woman and her mother-in-law, and said that it's natural for a woman to want the exclusive love and attention of her husband. In other words, you saw the rivalry between these two women as natural, as part of women's nature. If we accept your premise—which of course I don't, because I think the rivalry has more to do with culture than nature—then how can one reconcile it with dominant opinion within Islamic feqh which allows a man to have up to four wives and then claims that it's no injustice to women? There's a contradiction here. If it's in a woman's nature to want an exclusive relationship with her husband, then how is it that a feqh Ruling, which should be in line with that nature, goes against it? Women, like men, want to have exclusive marital relations and not to share their partner with others.

MHS: Are you invoking the daughter and mother-in-law relationship we discussed as an analogy which reveals the spirit governing the Law, or are you objecting to [my account of] that relationship?

ZMH: These examples contain a general rule, a principle. I'm referring to the principle hidden in your analogy.

MHS: The answer should be sought in the discussion on polygamy which will be considered later. First, the point is that Islam doesn't encourage men to take four wives, but it doesn't prohibit it. This is a Ruling with certain consequences; a person who takes more than one wife should know that he might be creating financial and emotional problems for himself and others. But the issue is that we must clarify for ourselves the consequences of things permitted by religion. Religion has permitted polygamy because prohibiting it would have more undesirable consequences; but the problems polygamy gives rise to are another issue that must be discussed. It must be said that [polygamy] isn't encouraged, but men are warned of its negative consequences.

We pursued the discussion for some time informally. As we were about to close the session, Mortazavi asked me a question for which I had no answer. He wanted me to compare Western and Islamic ways of life. I found myself in an awkward position, but I responded as truthfully and as honestly as I could.

SZM: Leaving aside customs and beliefs that are rooted in Eastern values, such as the importance of the family, and that aren't specific to religion, do you think Western societies have a better way of solving their problems than societies like ours? In other words, have they managed to strengthen family values and improve social relations in a better way than societies like ours?

ZMH: This a very difficult question, and I have no answer for it. But I will open the question and point out that in the West the worldview that informs the law isn't necessarily a religious one, although many aspects of family law are rooted in Jewish and Christian beliefs. In Western countries, family law has been separated from religious laws, but people have a choice; those who are religious conduct their marriages according to the mandates of their religion. As you know, there are certain similarities between Jewish and Islamic laws. Christian law defines marriage as a sacrament, and the Catholic Church (unlike the Protestants) allows dissolution of marriage only under limited conditions. This restriction has resulted in a situation where many people, despite taking their marriage vows in church, find themselves transgressing them when they face a marital crisis and a divorce.

SZM: Why do they do this?

ZMH: If you visit the courts you will understand why. When it comes to divorce, the two parties have often reached the end of their tether; they want an end to the situation, and have no qualms in putting aside their principles, religious or otherwise, and try to use the law to their advantage. This also happens in our own society; if both parties respected each other's rights there would be no need for them to go to court for a divorce. For instance, if a woman says, "I dislike this man and can't live with him," if he acts according to Islamic principles he must release her from marriage, whereas in practice we see that he doesn't and uses his feqh right to divorce as means of revenge. This man has transgressed the ethical rules of Islam, and as you said earlier, you can't force these ethical rules on people; if you do, it will produce the opposite effect. When men behave in such a way, naturally women also seek to use the law to their advantage and try to retaliate; so in practice people tend to put aside religious laws.

SZM: What is the problem in the West?

ZMH: In the West, religion doesn't regulate every aspect of society; you could say that its links with law have been severed. This has brought its own problems; there's a kind of vacuum that I think doesn't exist in our society, where I believe the religious worldview and its moral rules still solve many social problems and provide solace for people. In the West, many people don't see their religion as a source of solace, they seek a solution in other belief systems such as humanism or faiths such as Buddhism.

There's another element that must be taken into consideration, that is marriage customs. Western customs relating to marriage and social relations are different from ours; we shouldn't judge them in the light of our own customs. As a Muslim, socialized in a Muslim family and culture, but living in the West, I think on the whole one is more fulfilled in Iran; family ties are much stronger. Not all human needs are material, there are also spiritual and emotional needs which aren't so well catered for in the West.

SZM: In evaluating the two, some [Iranian feminists] put their finger on certain cases and say: this is the reality of our society; then they conclude that it's feqh that has given rise to this reality, thus Islam is an imperfect religion and oppresses women.

ZMH: This is an error; the two must be of course separated.

SMZ: We also believe the two must be separated in evaluation and analysis, that is, Islamic laws and feqh regulations have nothing to do with social realities, and if there are shortcomings at the level of practice, this mustn't be seen as the fault of Islam. These two realms are separate. But we want to know, these Western societies, which direct such criticisms at Islam, how have they solved their own problems? What do they have to offer us? Have they reduced the rate of divorce, have they mitigated its negative consequences?

ZMH: Of course, the West too hasn't been able to solve all its social and human problems. Anyway, both problems and solutions are always relative; the realization of an ideal society, the utopia we have in mind, is very difficult and unlikely. It's a human condition; societies are composed of human beings, some of whom respect the laws and principles and some don't. But I must say, those who think there are no longer any moral values in the West are wrong; this certainly isn't the case. On the whole, all divine religions have the same message; and Christian and Judaic values and ideals are no different from those of Islam; they too value and respect moral principles; but we tend to see their more negative side.

Payam-e Zan published this interchange as though it were part of the final session of our debate, in quite a different context and framework, with the effect of showing the superiority of the Islamic way of life by having me admit to shortcomings in the West. It actually began with Mortazavi's seemingly innocent question, and was a casual exchange, not part of the main debate at all; we went on to talk about divorce settlement, custody, and alimony in English and American courts, and how they differ from Iranian ones. While they kept this part, they omitted the final note on which our session was concluded, which was about my motives in research. At first I did not understand what Mortazavi meant by "motive," but he explained. The exchange is interesting in that it shows our different approaches to women's issues, but it also may explain some of his omissions and additions in the published transcript.

SZM: You asked us in the first session about our motives in addressing women's issues. It's also important for us to know about yours. Of course Mr. Saʿidzadeh introduced you; we hope you don't think our question impertinent.

ZMH: Not at all. I find it a very pertinent question, which is why I asked you earlier. To be honest, my motives are both personal and academic; I think there's always a personal element when one chooses a topic for study. In my case, if I hadn't been born a woman, in a Muslim family and society, perhaps I wouldn't have been so drawn to the study of women and Islam. As a girl, I asked myself, why are boys treated so differently and given so many privileges? I tried to overcome my gender handicap by doing well at school, entering the university and gaining degrees. In this way, I was able to break many of those "unwritten laws" and gain a degree of independence and autonomy in my life. So my primary motive has to do with being a woman, born in a specific time and environment and trying to find answers to certain questions. This isn't peculiar to me; there are many women who are intrigued by the same questions. Men are less interested in gender issues, I think, because they feel fewer limitations due to their gender.

My specialization within anthropology is in family and religion; after my work on comparative family law in Maleki and Shiʿi feqh, I became more and more drawn to these internal debates within feqh, and I find them extremely rich and interesting. As a researcher and as an anthropologist, I see it as my task to understand and discuss social issues through appropriate analysis and by means of fieldwork, which is based on observation and participation.

SZM: Eventually, what do you want to establish?

ZMH: I don't want to establish anything specific; I want to understand . . .

SZM: Merely to satisfy a sense of curiosity?

ZMH: No, I have a research position and eventually I want to write a book, a paper, to publish my material.

SZM: What do want to achieve with this book? What sort of impact do you want it to have on society? For instance, in our journal we aim to manage and direct the situation of women in society from a religious perspective. We see it as our mission to shape future trends, and even if we don't succeed, we see it as our duty to do our best in that direction. What do you want to achieve with your research?

I now understood what he meant by "motive." I also began to understand some of the earlier questions, when they asked who I was doing this research for and who was going to read it. They simply assumed that I must have an ulterior motive; perhaps a mission; they had obviously discussed the matter among themselves. This might have been the first time they had debated with a woman. My first response was not adequate; I also could not tell them that I just do not think in those terms; that I believe there is no correct way; that it is self-defeating to approach women's issues from an ideological angle and to try to impose change. Yet I had to make my position clear. The question forced me to make it clear to myself. They put me in the situation I had been putting them in throughout the debate. It was only fair to respond. I formulated a response as I talked.

ZMH: My ultimate mission, if I must have one, is the realization of women's rights as they should be, the attainment of the rights that religion grants them, the discovery of their own worth and identity. It's important to make women aware of their rights and potentials; not only women but also men, society as a whole, academic centers, all must be acquainted with the nature of women's rights. Ultimately, I think that if my book and research can remove a veil and bring about some understanding, I have fulfilled my mission, both at the personal and the professional level, and my conscience will be at ease.

This seemed to be the answer Mortazavi expected, since he responded:

SZM: After the first session, I told Mr. Sa'idi that you have a scientific fairness in debate, which is why we decided to go beyond the first session. I hope you weren't upset by our question; we were curious; we know that doing research isn't easy.

I agreed and added that in my view, apart from awareness, Muslim women's rights must be addressed within their own religious and cultural boundaries. Sa'idzadeh supported my approach to gender, saying that unlike most Iranian women he had met in the West, he had found me open to religious debate and in fact quite knowledgeable. I told them something of the politics of gender among feminists abroad, for some of whom a person like me, who tries through her research to establish a dialogue between Islam and feminism, has already betrayed feminism a priori. Mortazavi then said he wanted to know more about the feminist critique of Islam, or—in his words—to do "Doubt-ology" (*shobheh-shenasi*); he would be grateful if I would outline it. I said I had already done so; that in fact my questions about feqh theories encapsulated the essence of feminist objections.

We left further discussion to the next session. It was well past noon and we had a meeting with Ayatollah Sane'i that afternoon.

5

Women Reconsidered: Ayatollah Yusef Sane'i

BY THE MID 1980s, several clerics who had been politically active and held government positions in the early years of the revolution had returned to the seminary way of life. Of different ages and ranks, the reasons for their return were complex, and varied from personal to political. One such cleric was Ayatollah Yusef Sane'i, former state prosecutor-general and member of both the Council of Guardians and the Supreme Judicial Council, the two highest legal bodies in the Islamic Republic. Since his return in 1984 he has devoted himself to religious scholarship and teaching, acquiring a reputation for progressive opinions on family matters, for example by his advocacy of family planning and of raising the legal age of puberty.

Sane'i is one of a new kind of marja': so much is clear in a leaflet I obtained later, dated February 1994, and devoted to establishing Ayatollah Sane'i's credentials. Prepared by "a group of students and learned persons of the Qom Houzeh" [his students and followers], the leaflet opens with a quotation from Ayatollah Khomeini, printed in bold type and occupying a whole page: "I raised Mr. Sane'i like a child, Mr. Sane'i came and participated in classes and debates that I used to hold for many years; he is a distinguished person among the clerics and a learned man." There follows a brief account of Sane'i's life and scholarly achievements. Born in 1937 in a clerical family, he began his religious education at the age of nine in the Isfahan seminary. In 1951 he came to Qom to continue his studies, and he completed the required courses in four years; at the age of twenty-two he attained ejtehad, the capacity to deduce the Law from original sources. In exams held in 1955 for advanced-level Houzeh students, he won first place, being commended by Ayatollah Borujerdi (sole marja' until his death in 1961). In the same year, young Yusef Sane'i began attending Khomeini's classes, continuing until 1963, when Khomeini made his first protest against the Pahlavis, which led to his exile. In 1975 Sane'i started holding his own official classes in the Haqqaniyeh, a prestigious Qom seminary. Finally, we learn that many of Sane'i's students are active in research and teaching in the Houzeh, some having reached ejtehad; many of his students are also active in the government of the Islamic Republic.

In the rest of the leaflet, one can see old and new juxtaposed. Addressing him as marja', the leaflet then justifies and builds a case for this designation, under four separate headings: Khomeini's approval, expertise in teaching feqh, expertise in issuing fatwas, and personality and piety. We learn that Khomeini both liked and trusted Sane'i; that he was both student and follower of Khomeini, that he started teaching through Khomeini's texts and continues that approach to feqh; that in the past few years he has taught solely feqh topics, that he has completed many topics and currently teaches about divorce; that he has published his Practical Treatise and written commentaries on Khomeini's and other established feqh texts; that besides his fidelity and commitment to feqh and the great scholars of the past, he seeks solutions to contemporary problems. Finally, we read about aspects of his personality: his love for the Prophet's family, his respect for the ulama in the Houzeh, his modesty toward people, his generosity to students, his scrupulousness with religious taxes. There is not one reference to his political career, his previous tenure of one of the highest offices in the judiciary, and membership in two of the highest legislative bodies in the Islamic Republic.

The omissions betray the awkwardness and ambiguity of a transitional phase, and the hold of an old system that was—and is—adamant on keeping the Houzeh clearly separate from the government. What the leaflet does say suggests that the two cardinal procedures in the traditional selection process are still at work: publication of a treatise, and having a core of students and supporters in the Houzeh who actively campaign for the emerging marja'. Sane'i published his treatise in winter 1993, well after Ayatollah Khomeini's death; both Mortazavi and Sa'idi, who had arranged my meeting with him, were among his advanced students, and they had frequently invoked their teacher's opinions in our first session.

Our appointment was for four o'clock in the afternoon. As arranged, I had already submitted some written questions, basically the same as those we had discussed in our morning session, but milder in tone. I made my way to the meeting, accompanied by Sa'idzadeh and Zahra. On the way, Sa'idzadeh advised me not to be as forward as I had been with the clerics of Payam-e Zan; I should remember that I was talking with a marja'. I was apprehensive, never before having met such a high-ranking government cleric.

Ayatollah Sane'i's residence, referred to as his beit, consisted of two adjoining houses, one serving as his home and the other as his office, both shomali, with their courtyards opening on the north side of the street. It was marked by a placard on the wall bearing the legend "Office of Ayatollah Haj Sheikh Yusef Sane'i," and a board giving information on classes and student allowances. The street door was open, and we entered a narrow space with washing facilities, curtained off from the courtyard. The curtain was half open; we passed through and walked toward the building across the partly carpeted courtyard, where several men, both clerics and laymen, were sitting and talking. We found Mortazavi and Sa'idi, who had just arrived.

As with most north-side houses in Iran, the entrance was through a veranda. We took off our shoes and entered a hallway, past a spacious room which I assumed was used for classes and open meetings, and into a much smaller room next to it. This room was simple; at the far end of the carpeted floor, a cushion was placed against the wall on a folded blanket, as is commonly done to make sitting on the floor more comfortable. Zahra and I sat on the right, near the door, and the three men took their places opposite us, with Sa'idzadeh sitting closer to the far end, which was the ayatollah's place. I adjusted my chador and brought out my tape recorder and my notebook, while Mortazavi prepared his tape recorder. A young man brought tea on small individual trays, serving Zahra and me first. Unlike Ayatollah Madani's khadem, he was welcoming and seemed quite unperturbed by my presence. We sipped our tea in silence, waiting.

When we heard the young man's "Ya Allah!" we all stood up to greet the ayatollah. He entered the room with his eyes glued to the floor and strode to his place, at the same time motioning us with his hands to sit down. He then turned to each of us to exchange individual greetings, and was friendly and unpretentious in manner. He was wearing a white turban, marking his non-Seyyed status. When I had seen him on television in the early 1980s I had noted that, unlike other clerics, his clear face was bare, his beard almost nonexistent. Now he looked much the same, although he had aged a little; his sparse beard had turned white and he looked less severe than before.

Mortazavi thanked the ayatollah for receiving us and asked Sa'idzadeh to introduce me, which he did briefly. The ayatollah showed interest in my earlier research, and asked why I had chosen Moroccan law to compare with Iranian family law. His voice was very loud; I felt reassured and less self-conscious about my own normal voice. I explained that I was trying to understand the working of the shari'a in modern times and wanted to see the way it interacts with culture and politics; I mentioned some of the differences and similarities between the two countries that warranted the comparison, pointing out that the two Muslim countries, geographically and culturally remote from each other, adhered to different schools of law, yet family law in both is codified and grafted onto modern systems, secular in Morocco and religious in Iran. He nodded his head in approval; then Mortazavi too put in a good word for me, outlining our discussions and making two points. First, they were familiar with my point of view and my questions, which had led to a logical and fair debate over two sessions, the second lasting nearly three hours. Second, at the level of "Doubt-ology" they found my questions and the ensuing debate useful and saw it as their duty to address them in the journal.

The ayatollah complimented us on our efforts. Then he began by quoting the first verse of the Koranic Sura Nisa, in order to address my first question, about the scope and place of gender equality in Islamic law. To my surprise the session turned into another open discussion, and lasted over an hour. Although we covered much the same ground as in my discussion with the *Payam-e Zan* clerics, I found the ayatollah's interpretations to be radical, and as we will see the whole exchange took place on a different plane from the previous two.

Almost nine months later, *Payam-e Zan* published a full transcript in two installments, with minor adjustments but no change in order, as "In the Presence of Ayatollah Hajj Yusef Sane'i." Extracts from the interview also appeared in *Payam-e Emruz* (a Tehran quarterly) as "Dialogue between an Iranian Female Academic of Cambridge University and Ayatollah Sane'i," though all the questions, including those asked by Mortazavi, seemed to be from me. *Nimruz* (an opposition paper in London) reproduced the same extracts. *Hamshahri* (a daily produced by the Tehran mayor's office) published an abridged version of the same material on the occasion of Women's Week, November 1996, as "Ayatollah Yusef Sane'i's Views about Women's Rights in the Koran," without giving any details of the interview.[1] Here I translate my transcription of the discussion in full. AYS = Ayatollah Yusef Sane'i; ZMH = myself; SZM = Mortazavi; MHS = Sa'idi; SMS = Sa'idzadeh.

Discussion with Ayatollah Sane'i

AYS: In the name of God. "O people! be careful of [your duty to] your Lord, Who created you from a single being and created its mate of the same [kind] and spread from these two, many men and women [Nisa, 1]."

One issue mentioned in Mr. Mortazavi's letter is about women and the question of equality; and this is a sensible issue. Women must be equal to men as justice demands. In His legal regulations, the Divine and Wise Creator must honor this Principle, and we see that He has done so. When I say He has done so, I also need to introduce a caveat, and bring out a point which Martyr Motahhari also referred to; that is, we must make a distinction between equality and similarity. If we say that women must be the same as men, not only do we do injustice to society but we can't realize that which shouldn't be realized. But if we say that women must be equal to men, this both exists in Islam and must be realized, because equality is different from similarity.

For example, in a country where racial discrimination exists, it may be said that all whites are equal. This equality doesn't mean that we don't distinguish between those who serve society and those who betray it. A person who serves society is valued and given benefits according to his service, and a person who betrays society is punished. That is, we see a difference between loyalty and treachery, between learned and ignorant, between active and lazy. It's an error and an injustice to society to say that all should be treated the same way.

---

[1] *Payam-e Zan* 50 and 51 (May and June 1996); *Payam-e Emruz* 13 (summer 1375/1996): 41–44; *Nimruz* 383 (23 Shahrivar 1375/14 September 1996): 26 and 30; *Hamshahri* 1,115 (17 Aban 1375/7 November 1996).

From this example, I want to infer a principle relating to men and women; that is, we must demand that Islam and world legislators value each [person] according to what they deserve and distinguish between them according to their duties, their physical nature, and their human spirit.

We see that Islam has done so. The verse I recited, the opening of Sura Nisa in the Koran, says "We have created all human beings from a single being," that is, men and women are equal in creation and neither is preferred over the other. Note that the verse says, "we created your mate from the same being"; it doesn't say, "wife," but "mate," which can be either male or female; that is, they are from each other. Man is from woman and woman is from man, thus in creation there's no difference between them.

The account, in some exegeses and histories, that woman is made from the leftover matter [clay, mud] of man, or from man's left rib, contradicts the Koran and revelation and must be rejected. According to Koranic verses and hadith of the Infallible Imams, and in line with our criteria, this is nothing but a broken jug [useless]. Martyr Motahhari says that such accounts are based on biblical distortions and have reached Islam via the Israelites.

Likewise, in verse 13 of Holy Sura Hujurat, the Koran says: "O you men! surely We have created you male and female, and made you tribes and families that you may know each other; surely the most honorable of you with Allah is the one among you most careful (of his duty)." This and the other verse show that the Koran makes no distinction between men and women in creation and regards them in the same way and as equals. Apparently, Allameh Tabataba'i argued that the second verse is the best evidence of the equality of men and women. The Wise Creator in this verse says you are created different and divided into different tribes in order to know and learn from each other; and the best and the most valued among you are those who keep themselves from breaking the divine laws.

The same applies to other dimensions; as regards ownership, for instance, the Koran says: "men shall benefit of what they earn and women shall have the benefit of what they earn" [Nisa, 32]. That is, according to the logic of the Koran and the requirements of Islamic feqh, there's no difference between men and women regarding ownership rights. Of course, there's a subtle point I must mention here. In her married life, a woman is free to do whatever she wishes with her wealth and income, but if she makes a vow to give something away without her husband's consent, that vow is void, even if it's from her own wealth. Suppose that a woman who is a university professor wants to make a vow to give a portion of her salary to orphans, or as a prize to the purest—such a prize doesn't exist of course, but it should— she can't do it without her husband's consent. You may ask: "Why does Islam deprive her of such a choice? It's her money and she's free to do what she chooses." The answer is that, once a vow is made, its fulfilment is oblig- atory and this might affect the harmony in marriage, which entails coopera-

tion and calm between spouses. Therefore, Islam hasn't made fulfilment of
such a vow obligatory for women, in case her husband objects to it and the
unity in the family is impaired. Of course, as regards recommended matters
and charitable causes, here women are free to spend from their wealth. But
a vow is a pledge to God, and it's God's mercy that has made its fulfilment
nonobligatory on women [without their husband's consent]. Apart from
this, nowhere else has women's choice been limited, and their ownership
rights are respected in the same way as men's.

His reference to racial discrimination, and other examples echoing those I
had used, suggested that he had been briefed on the content of our debates. As
I listened, I could not help wondering why God should give such power to men
in the first place, for women to need their permission to make a pledge to Him.
What sort of harmony and calm is it, if only one party needs to be mindful not
to disturb it? God here seemed to be on the side of men's authority, not on the
side of women or of marital harmony. But I put aside my Doubt; by now I was
more at ease with paradoxical reasonings. He continued:

As for spiritual perfection, there's no difference between men and women.
Women can become spiritually evolved and reach a status where they become the carriers of the progeny of the Prophet of Islam. Our blessed Imams
are descended from a woman; and they were keen to be addressed as sons
of Zahra and sons of the Prophet. Contrary to the erroneous culture of the
time, which didn't honor daughters, and so as to eliminate this incorrect
logic, the infallible Imams stressed their [maternal] descent and were proud
of such a mother and woman.

Also in the stories of Belqis Queen of Sheba, and of Holy Mary, we see
how the Koran praises women. Thus women can attain the highest status in
spiritual terms, and in Islamic society there have been a number of women
who have done so; today we find women who have attained such high
status, whether through seeking knowledge and science or through piety and
obedience to God. Whatever is obligatory for men is also obligatory for
women, and in this respect too there's no difference between them.

As regards family matters, you might say that a woman's rights aren't
respected; for instance, a wife needs her husband's permission to leave
the house. One answer to such matters is that if Islam has instituted such
things, it has also instituted that the wife can stipulate from the very beginning of her marriage, as part of the marriage contract, that she can leave the
house whenever she wants to without permission. She can make similiar
stipulations with respect to choosing her place of residence, continuing her
studies, participating in social affairs, taking up teaching posts or political
appointments.

Thus Islam has solved the problem and this isn't an impasse. Otherwise,
of course, one could object to Islam. But in this way it becomes a question

of the sovereignty of the will; and Islam has given priority to sovereignty of the individual over its own laws. This is one of the advantages of Islam, which says that a woman can make a stipulation to prevent the application of the law.

Another answer is that we are talking of shared life, and as it's said, the family is like a small country which needs to be managed and organized, and one person must be in charge and make decisions. Now a man may not like his wife to go out to study or have a career; if this doesn't cause her hardship, and if they reach an understanding through consultation and considering the family interest, in such a situation the woman should give in, for the sake of family life.

Of course, this isn't to say that men can prevent their wives from studying or working so as to cause them hardship. A man can't impose his will, act capriciously, and put pressure on his wife; if he does, she's no longer obliged to obey, witness the verse "the religion does not put hardship upon you." As far as possible, family matters must be based on consultation and understanding; but if a man is peculiar and feels inadequate, wants to control his wife and punish her by telling her not to go out, and if not going out puts her in difficulty, then she doesn't have to listen to him and can leave the house. Based on the hardship verse, this doesn't make her disobedient; she retains her right to maintenance and her husband must provide for her. Thus, in family matters too it's not the case that man is the master and woman the slave.

I'm saying these things, but I don't know how much of it you want to present. Another matter often brought up is the law of inheritance, in which men's share is twice as much as women's. It's natural to ask why? Allameh Tabataba'i says, first, it's a sign of Islam's regard that, in the holy verse on inheritance, women's share is taken as the base and men's is compared to it. Second, as far as use and benefit are concerned, women in practice are better off than men. This is so because, if we suppose the entire property to be six tomans, of which the man inherits four and the woman two, now this woman is also entitled to receive maintenance from the man, so that, in addition to her two tomans she shares the benefits and interest of the four tomans her husband has inherited.[2] Thus, in reality, a woman benefits from her husband's four tomans and a man from his wife's two tomans. [Allameh's] answer is correct, and in practice women benefit more.

Now I want to go further and suppose that we have two families, each has a son and a daughter and the son inherits twice what the daughter does. If the son of one family marries the daughter of the other, this son inherits four of his father's six toman, and the daughter inherits two of her father's six

[2] One toman equals 10 rials, the basic unit of Iranian currency. In 1995 the U.S. dollar was worth about 400 toman. Clearly Saneʿi is being hypothetical here.

toman. Therefore, when they share resources in marriage, the two benefit equally. We explain it this way too, but Allamah's reasoning is the most precise. In legislating, there is a need for a holistic approach, and the legislator must take into account the nature of cases and the conditions of society, which it has done, and the problem is solved.

Ayatollah Sane'i concluded his remarks by saying that he had not formulated them properly, he had just spoken as things came into his mind. He invited me to ask questions, adding, "if we can understand, we will; otherwise we'll leave it to the legislator." Here he was talking as a Jurist, who has the duty of determining the divine Law, but without claiming authority for himself or the correctness of his opinion. By "legislator," he almost certainly meant the divine Legislator, not a human one.

I wanted to ask about this, but I did not dare; I was also trying to work out his complex mathematics on inheritance, which rested on questionable assumptions and contradicted both what he had said earlier on women's exclusive rights over their own property and income in marriage, and the fact that feqh does not recognize a matrimonial regime. The husband must pay maintenance and the agreed dower, and that is all; what he earns or inherits is his and what his wife earns or inherits is hers. Of course, in practice it is different, but what interested me was how the ayatollah chose to mingle practice and theory so as to support his point. I was also intrigued by the parallel he drew between family and country, putting one person—a patriarch—in charge in both.

I did not get an opportunity to make these points in the form of a question; Mortazavi preempted me with one of his own. He put forward his own line, that the shari'a was free of gender bias, that any problems arose from practice, that it is the Islamic government's duty to intervene and ensure the correct application of shari'a, which will solve problems in practice.

SZM: In the first part [of your speech], to show that men don't have absolute control you use the example of women's right to leave the house against their husband's decision. Women's interests must be protected; what's the role of government here, since we consider it has the right to intervene? What can government do to protect and defend women's rights and interests, so that women have security and peace of mind?

AYS: The shari'a has provided the solution. If a woman is so much valued in Islam that her will takes precedence over the law of Islam, then she must understand this and demand her rights. Of course, it's the duty of the authorities and supporters of women's rights to make women aware that they should make stipulations at the time of marriage. Suppose a woman hasn't done so, hasn't stipulated conditions in her marriage contract, and now she has a problem; there's still a way out for her. Of course, a woman should sometimes relinquish some of her personal interests and desires for those of the family, to maintain harmony and preserve the family. But if she reaches an impasse, the [need for her] husband's permission is removed according to the Principle of "no-harm." For instance, if staying home makes a woman depressed, isolates her from society, or prevents her from developing her God-given talents, and her husband puts pressure on her to stay home, then she may go out without being disobedient, and the husband [still] has to pay maintenance.

SZM: So the Islamic government must intervene in such cases to protect women?

AYS: Yes, its legal system protects women; the general Principle of "no-harm," the absence of hardship in Islam, is the protector of women. Whenever they face difficulty, the law has provided them with a way out; of course, it's in the hands of government to implement it, to compel men to pay these women maintenance. If he says, "I won't pay because she leaves home without my consent," he'll be told, "she went out because you wanted to impose your will, you wanted to punish her because you take a wife for a slave." Both the law and its executors, that is government, protect women.

Now I was convinced that Mortazavi had discussed my questions—my Doubts, as he had it—with the ayatollah in some detail. Sane'i then showed interest in knowing my point of view, but he addressed Mortazavi, referring to me in the third person (which in Persian has no gender). He said: "If she has a view, let us learn it and benefit from it, because this is an issue that is frequently raised." This was the opportunity I was waiting for, and I addressed him directly.

ZMH: With your permission, I'll approach the issue from an anthropological angle and raise two points.

AYS: Please go ahead.

ZMH: You say that women can protect their rights through stipulations at the time of marriage; this is absolutely true, but it only happens when women are aware and can choose their marriages; that is, when they have the legal and social awareness to make independent choices. But if we look at the structure of marriage in our society, we see that most marriages are controlled by families, and through [customs such as] proposal delegations, in which the bride has little say. As I said, of course, social fabrics and structures are largely at the root of this problem. Given this, can a way be opened, rooted in shari'a and feqh, to protect women's rights better at the outset by establishing a kind of equality in the marriage contract?

AYS: When you say social structure, which one do you have in mind, the traditional one, or the new one?

ZMH: Both the traditional and what we call these days . . .

AYS: . . . the urban? I'll come to that later. Let's start with traditional societies, which were restricted, closed, with little contact with each other, and family issues and problems weren't the same [as now]. Thus in traditional societies in Iran, you will not find the kind of problems you spoke of; there the divorce rate is very low; as I've said in my lessons, that's why the notion of divorce isn't fully developed in our feqh books, in hadith; because it wasn't a problem that needed addressing. Therefore, traditional societies, with their closed cultures and limited relations, didn't have problems with these laws. But if we look at the problems of contemporary human societies, it isn't the same. Today boys and girls themselves choose; especially in our Iran, we see what difficulties these choices involve. It is only necessary for the girl to be of age and able to understand the terms of marriage; she's free [in shari'a] to contract her own marriage. But this isn't incorporated in our laws at present [the father's permission is required if the girl is a virgin— i.e., if it is her first marriage]. This problem can [now] be resolved through resort to the court, which will write to the father and ask for his permission; if he refuses, then the court will grant permission to register the marriage. The present law is based on the fatwas of many jurists who saw this permission as necessary, in line with the situation of society at the time. Today the situation is different, and that's why there is such a problem. Perhaps in future our legislators will reach the stage where they find a solution for this problem. A girl who has come of age and can understand the issues involved in marriage has the right to contract it herself; there's no barrier, from the Islamic and feqh viewpoint.

But what can we do to solve [other] problems in marriage? In present society there's no way except to direct and guide; I believe that no law can support [equality]. Can you tell me of a law anywhere that has done this? If so, we can discuss it and see whether such a law could be established in Islam. I believe it's up to individuals themselves; no law can compensate for the weakness of individuals.

ZMH: You are absolutely right, but law can protect weak individuals.

AYS: How?

ZMH: By making legal what you just said; by making it part of every marriage contract that a woman has an unconditional right to study, to have a career, to have those rights that a man has in marriage . . .

I was about to say something about the Jurists' patriarchal model of the family, in which all powers are given to one man as head of household, but the ayatollah cut me short:

AYS: Suppose we pass such a law; isn't it better to give freedom? We say we leave it to this girl who wants to marry, to define her own conditions; perhaps some girls don't want such conditions. Law brings obligation; why should we limit freedom of choice?

ZMH: Do you want to leave it to individuals?

AYS: Of course we must leave it to individuals; individual sovereignty is best. But the authorities in society must direct, those responsible for women's rights must make women aware: when you want to marry, first define your terms, say what you want as your conditions in marriage so that in future you don't find yourself in difficulty. Here it's the role of the guides of society, the media, to inform women. Why must we make these things obligatory? The fewer laws we have, the better. Life can be managed better if people have more choice and greater freedom.

I was agreeably surprised by what the ayatollah said. Although he did not answer my question—I was unsure whether he understood what I meant by women's choice in marriage or deliberately took it as limited to arranged marriages—his approach was different from that of the *Payam-e Zan* clerics. He seemed aware and ready to admit, first, that Islamic laws are like other systems of law, subject to the same kinds of limitation and constraint in dealing with social realities; and second, that current interpretations no longer reflect current realities. Mortazavi then raised another of my questions, but rephrasing it so as to confirm or touch on what we had argued about that morning.

SZM: The next question is closely related; it's about the relationship between the ethical and the legal in shari'a laws. What you said attested that we give precedence to ethical issues, and that problems are better resolved by ethical rather than legal measures and actions. Are you of the opinion that legal tools must be used as the last resort?

AYS: Yes; familial problems should be solved as much as possible with serenity and calm; otherwise, the issue of hardship arises. Look, one problem in present-day society is that there's little advocacy of serenity and solidarity in the family unit. Today's society is open and expansive, subject to diverse influences and temptations, and the individual's capacities are also diverse: a film, a novel can influence a young person. What can we do to compensate? We need to resort to the same measures, that is to have films, novels that can promote family values and serenity. No law can do this for us; what can you do with a youth or a woman who is influenced by a film or a novel? So we must think in terms of creating a balance between positive and negative influences on the family.

Mortazavi had changed the thrust of my question, framing it so as to elicit an answer supporting the journal's position, that it is better to concentrate on ethical rather than legal changes. When the ayatollah had finished, Mortazavi asked me whether I wanted to add anything. I said no, and he then went on to pose my other question.

SZM: Let me ask Ms. Mir-Hosseini's next question, part of which has become clear. "Can feqh, with its current theories, framework, and tools, accommodate the needs and desires of women of this age, given that among their aspirations are equality and participation in society?" In other words, can feqh agree with women's participation in society and provide an arena for them to utilize their talents and capacities?

AYS: The Islamic Republic has shown that in practice it can; in the Islamic Republic, women are Majles deputies, university professors, hospital doctors, and even serve in the armed forces. There's no barrier to women, but if you specify the problem and the restriction, perhaps I can give a better answer. We see women present in all spheres of social and political life; their presence and participation is needed everywhere, because once we lay a basis where men and women are forbidden to each other, then we need female physicians, female nurses, female lawyers, and so on. In fact, this Principle in Islam, that unrelated males and females are forbidden to look at or touch each other's bodies, requires women to be present in all spheres of activity. This is an interesting Principle, I have just realized . . .

SZM: That is . . .

I think Mortazavi was about to explain that they had told me how the Ruling on hejab enables women to participate in society. Although Ayatollah Sane'i was excited with what had just occurred to him, repeating "the importance of this Principle has just occurred to me," he stopped and asked Mortazavi what he was going to say. Realizing his interruption had been untimely, Mortazavi withdrew and asked him to continue.

AYS: We have a Principle that men and women are forbidden to each other, that is, they must keep their distance in gaze and touch. On the other hand, women are entitled to whatever men are, that is, in case of illness, if men need hospitalization so do women; in case of crime, men's cases must be investigated and so must women's; men need scientists, so do women. Men and women are entitled to the same degree of progress and prosperity, and if we want them not to have unrestrained contact, then we must have women involved at every step and every level in society. This is an interesting Principle, which demands women's presence in every sphere.

SZM: This is an important point, it shows that Islam sets restrictions on contact between men and women because it endorses the Principle of women's active participation in society. Had Islam not allowed women to participate in society, then there would no need to say that women should observe the limits, or to define the form of participation [hejab].

AYS: No, your interpretation is rather limited; I'm saying something more than that. Islam created men and women, and then said, you must keep distance from each other, that is, unrelated men and women should not mix. In other aspects of life, from the moment they're born until they go to the grave, men need others to survive; the same applies to women. How are we going to meet women's needs? Islam says that women need doctors, security forces, judges—in my view there's no restriction on this for women—politicians, ministers, rulers. What can be done, other than having women in all these posts?

In his eagerness to have women included in society and yet to honor the Principle of segregation, the ayatollah had ignored the central contradiction. Sa'idzadeh had obviously understood the impossibility of realizing the ayatollah's vision. I too tried to take it up and see what he meant, but he did not give me much chance.

SMS: Master (*Ostad*), are there no limits, no beginnings or endings in this matter?

AYS: No, there's no limit; and this restriction [on mingling], in my view, is itself a driving force to bring women to participate in every field of life; women should enter fields concerning women, and men those concerning men.

ZMH: Should women come on an equal footing with men . . .?

AYS: Of course, on an equal footing; women have nothing less than men. What do women have less?

SMS: Excuse me, does this mean there should be one leader for women and another for men?

ZMH: You mean, a complete division . . .?

AYS: No, I'm not saying that; you can't divide the law and have one set of criminal laws for men and another for women; I am talking about implementation.

ZMH: I meant dividing society into two [zones], one for men . . .

AYS: I mean, separate all services for men and women; one hospital for men, another for women; in the police, one section for men, another for women. In short, women must be present in all aspects of running society, but women should deal with women's affairs, and men with men's. This is the best means by which Islam has brought women into society. If someone says that women should take over men's affairs or women be at their service, this is injustice to women; if men do the same, it's also injustice to them.[3]

ZMH: How about working as two equal human beings for society and for each other?

AYS: What does working for each other mean?

ZMH: Earlier you said the family is like a small country in which husband and wife . . .

[3] Ayatollah Amini says exactly the same, in an interview in *Payam-e Zan* 57 (December 1996). Mixing of men and women in public has been a major concern of the clerics, presenting the most insurmountable problem. See the Conclusion.

AYS: Forget husband and wife, they aren't forbidden to each other, and think in terms of society; there are certain affairs that don't entail intimacy and touch, such as theoretical or scientific matters which women can do for all, for instance, designing urban planning or the country's budget. But let's assume that women want to become scientists; on the one hand they must be taught, and if men are going to teach them then limits must be observed and this might cause difficulty. On the other hand, we know in Islam that women, like men, must become scientists and have equal access to knowledge and its benefits. In this way, the very restriction that Islam imposes on contact between the sexes becomes the motor for women's progress in the sense that it encourages them to achieve all those things that men achieve in society. Once a society reaches the level where men and women are free of each other in running their respective affairs, we can call such a society progressive. Of course, there are certain common affairs where there's no separation, such as legislation, science, piety, and others. Woman can become scientists and carry out studies which benefit all; the same applies to men.

ZMH: Of course, that's one way; but some might object to such a state of affairs as a form of sexual apartheid.

AYS: What's that?

ZMH: Apartheid is separation, such as existed in South Africa when the law separated the races. . . .

AYS: That was discrimation in law; any kind of legal discrimination is wrong.

ZMH: What about segregation based on gender?

AYS: That's not discrimination, it's separation. In practice each sex does its own work. Look, is it correct for a physician to do the work of an unskilled worker, or vice versa? It would lead to chaos. Each should do his/her work and be equal in law. Take the example of teacher and student, their tasks and status are different, but difference doesn't mean discrimination. The same applies to men and women, they're equal in law, both have rights to ownership, to knowledge, to work, to spiritual perfection, etc. But if we force women to become physicians and then force men to go to them, or vice versa, this causes hardship for both. Therefore we, government, must enable society to reach a degree of progress where women are involved in all affairs; this is the best solution. I don't know if I've been able to make myself clear.

SZM: Yes. What I wanted to say earlier was that Islam has accepted the Principle of women's presence and participation in every aspect of society, but has only defined the limits and the form of participation.

AYS: It has set boundaries and limitations in order to draw women into society; in order to draw them into universities, it says that women's profes-

sors shouldn't be men but women. On the other hand, it has charged government with the task of promoting women and involving them in all affairs of
society.

ZMH: Do you mean that an Islamic government must prepare the ground
for equal participation from the outset?

AYS: Yes, Islamic government must prepare the ground, otherwise it's
against shariʿa. In case of emergency, for instance, where there's no female
gynecologist, then men can perform the task. Look, it's a tragedy if we need
men for women's childbirth. But if we want to implement the law of Islam,
which forbids such a degree of contact, then we must prepare the ground for
women to become gynecologists. The same applies to other aspects of society. It's from necessity that we do this, because women's rights haven't
been respected to the extent that Islam ordained; there are no true divinely
guided states. These days we're heading in that direction.

Mortazavi agreed, adding that true Islamic teachings on women also have
not yet been adequately formulated. As he was about to link this point to my
next question, about "Dynamic Feqh," the ayatollah interrupted and asked me:
"I don't know whether I managed to develop this discussion in a way that
convinces you; do you agree with what I said?" I now saw an opportunity to
point out the contradictions in his argument, but I could also see that these very
contradictions are empowering to women in Iran today. This was, after all, my
own thesis. I thought the best way to say this would be to place it in a different
context and suggest that any kind of segregation is bound to intensify already
existing discrimination, so I told the history of single-sex and mixed colleges
in Cambridge.

ZMH: I'm convinced up to a point, but if I may I'd like to suggest other
perspectives and the type of objections others might make.

AYS: Please, that's why I asked, I want to know.

ZMH: One objection is that we live in a situation where men are far ahead
and have enjoyed many privileges, in many ways, for many centuries, so
men and women aren't starting from the same point. Human nature is such
that it's inclined to use the best opportunities and facilities available,
so we'll probably see a widening of the gap [with segregation]. I say this
because I've seen it happen where I obtained my doctorate, the former all-
male University of Cambridge in England. In this university, like many
other educational institutions with religious origins and connected to
the Church, women weren't allowed to study. This was the case until early
this century when a group of women, with the help of enlightened men,
campaigned to establish a college for women. They succeeded, and a
women's college [Girton] was created—although it was another fifty years
before women were awarded degrees. The college was built about three

kilometers away from the men's colleges, so that the sexes wouldn't mix. Now about thirty years ago, the men's colleges started to admit female students and fellows; before long, in order to compete, this women's college decided to become mixed too. But what's happened since—and to some extent proves your point—is that it's given more and more fellowships, both in teaching and research, to men. Why? Because the college realized that it must, in order to compete successfully, if it wanted to attract the best students and the best fellows. And we see that in practice, because men have historically had better access and opportunities, they do better in competitions. So if we want to retain segregation, in practice we'll end up—unintentionally—perpetuating the lower position of women today. Because those [men] who've had better opportunities are already far ahead, and there's no way women can catch up; women take one step, but men are still ten steps ahead. In that case, how can women ever, in your view, attain their rights?

AYS: Implementation [of the law] is the responsibility of the authorities, and separate from the discussion of the law and the nature of divine Laws. Yes, when it comes to implementation some do it that way. But if someone wants to implement the law in the name of Islam, then Islam doesn't allow the authorities to misuse their powers. An example of this in the Islamic Republic is the war-wounded, who've done well in international competitions because the Islamic government invested for them. We are talking about those authorities whose leader is the Prophet; he says "in this world I love three things: women, perfume, and prayers." We are equipped with that logic, which says "it's the way of the prophets to love and honor women." We are talking of authorities who know this logic and have the power to intervene; where you are [Cambridge] the power doesn't intervene in support of women, so the situation is such. But when there's a power which says it's the way of the prophets to honor women, that we Muslims owe so much to a woman, the daughter of the Prophet, Zahra, then it has to provide the stimulus for change and action. This is a problem of implementation.

I had nothing to say. He was actually making a case for positive discrimination and ways in which women can be supported. I had no dispute with this. But I felt uneasy with his methods—giving government absolute power in dealing with social practices—especially since Mortazavi once again reminded us of Khomeini's vision and approach, in which Islam is a system of governance, and all its laws are tools in the hand of government to enforce and dispense justice. Only in such a situation could equal conditions for men and women be secured. The ayatollah agreed and said it had happened in the Islamic Republic. He referred to a young girl who had won an international award in mathematics, and to Nosrat Amin in Isfahan, one of the most accomplished Shi'i scholars of this century.[4] Mortazavi then put in a good word for me, though it was double-edged.

SZM: Although she's very familiar with the Western perspective and probably finds many of its viewpoints scientific—from an anthropological and sociological perspective, at least—and has found the answer to many of her questions there, her opinion on developments in women's position [in Iran] is of value, and if you permit, we should hear it.

I was rescued by the ayatollah, who promptly said:

AYS: Let me tell her something. We don't believe that current laws to do with women are fully in line with what they should be in an Islamic state, nor are they in line with the current state of society. We believe that since the subject [women's situation] has changed, the framework of civil laws must change too. Our current civil laws are in line with the traditional society of the past, whereas these civil laws should be in line with contemporary realities and relations in our own society. You must have shown her the Imam's letter?

Mortazavi explained that, although they had not shown it to me, Khomeini's views had come up in our discussion of divorce. The ayatollah called for his assistant, and continued:

AYS: You should show her the letter; it is precise, I mean the Imam's sentence where he says, "if I weren't afraid, there's something else I would have said." Look, this is our perspective on current laws; even the Imam, who laid the foundations for this revolution, doesn't dare say what he understands from Islamic law, because of a number of narrow-minded, backward people who have a place and some kind of power in society.

SZM: The first time we discussed it, she asked whether we practice taqiyeh, and we said that what we write in the journal is our position, but we can't say everything we believe and understand.

AYS: It is not a question of taqiyeh; they [?] simply don't allow it; that's how society is, it can't cope with it . . .

ZMH: Are you suggesting that it's the culture of society that doesn't allow it? or certain perspectives within the Houzeh?

AYS: There are groups of individuals. The Imam referred to them as petrified, fossilized, devout ignoramuses; they prevent developments that go against their whims and desires; when something confronts their personal whims, they prevent it. One must go forward step by step—Islamic Rulings

---

[4] See the Bibliographic Essay. For an account of her life, see Baqeri-Bidhendi 1992; I met the latter in Qom—a Traditionalist who strongly disapproved of my views and research. The introduction to his book is a fascinating account of how Traditionalists (like Azari-Qomi) see women's demands for equality as a Western plot.

also came about step by step—and one day we'll get there. Today Islam says this, tomorrow it could be something else. I even told these gentlemen that if they want to publish what I say, they should write it as points for debate, otherwise it mightn't look good for their journal.

At this point, the ayatollah's assistant came in and was told to bring a copy of the Imam's letter about divorce. I started to say, "The point I want to make more than anything else . . ." but the ayatollah repeated: "It's not taqiyeh, or society; we are dealing with some men's personal whims and desires; it's not in their interest." I was puzzled; I had not expected him to be so outspoken. I knew about these things; I had heard how difficult the position of a marja' is, how he is hostage to his followers and cannot give a ruling that goes against their perceptions and understandings. But now for the first time I could see from the inside the delicacy of the situation, the red lines that are so firmly drawn that even Ayatollah Khomeini, the Leader of the Revolution, with all his political power and high standing in the Houzeh, did not dare to cross them.

The atmosphere of the meeting now changed; instead of the point I had been about to make, I expressed agreement with the ayatollah, and said that I had never looked at things from this angle. From this moment on, Mortazavi relaxed and allowed me to speak and pose my own questions directly. First he praised Ayatollah Sane'i's unique juristic views on matters relating to women, which have opened the door within Houzeh scholarship, then he invited me to ask my questions on divorce and maintenance. I took up his offer and went straight to the heart of the matter.

ZMH: Feqh defines repudiation as an act of *iqa'*, a unilateral act which takes effect when the husband wills. Is it possible to find a shari'a argument through which repudiation can be defined as an act that takes into account a woman's will? In other words, can a way be found to give women a say in divorce and at the same time to curtail men's arbitrary use of it?

AYS: Several things must be distinguished. Sometimes there is no harmony, serenity, and understanding in a marriage, both spouses realize that they can't continue their relationship. Here both sides desire a separation; they mightn't admit it, but when they take their case to court it becomes evident that there's no point continuing such a marriage, and a divorce will be issued. There's no problem here; it's divorce by mutual consent, though one of the spouses might take the legal initiative. A problem arises when a man wants a divorce on the basis of caprice and the wife isn't willing to terminate the marriage and isn't at fault. What are we to do here? Should we say that he can't divorce without her consent? This isn't going to solve the problem for these wives, because it won't mend the marriage. The only thing to do is to introduce deterrence by instituting a variety of penalties, like those we have for men who avoid military service [they cannot get a job or enter university]. Or if these won't work with some men who still repudiate capriciously, then we can punish them in other ways to set an example for others. About eight years ago I raised this discussion in al-Zahra College [when it still allowed male instructors], and said that by law we can deter the action of such men; but only deter, and this mightn't save the marriage; one can't force a man to behave properly.

He was putting forward the same argument as the clerics of *Payam-e Zan*, who could see divorce only in terms of men's rights, not women's, so I responded as I had to them.

ZMH: You are quite right. But let's take the other side, if it's a woman who can't continue the marriage, how can she free herself?

AYS: It's very simple; she can free herself by annulment. That's what the Imam meant when he said "I'm afraid to say it." This is the core of my opinion; I hold that in such circumstances a woman can annul her marriage herself.

ZMH: You mean, even when there's no fault in the marriage contract itself?

AYS: It's nothing to do with a fault in the contract. If she sees that she can't live with this man, and the marriage causes her harm, she can annul the contract and go to her father's house, if she wants.

ZMH: What legal form will such an act take?[5]

AYS: The form hasn't yet been defined in our laws; I said before that our laws are incomplete. This is what the Imam says; whenever marital life becomes difficult for a woman, and we see that she can't continue her marriage, she can annul the contract.

ZMH: Does she need the permission of the religious judge?

AYS: Permission is merely a precaution, so that talaq [is pronounced] instead of annulment. However, the significance of the whole argument is that there is no need, and a woman can separate. She goes to court as a matter of formality, to have the separation registered, not to establish grounds for such a separation, according to the Law as we understand it. Islam doesn't say that a woman must stay and put up with her marriage if it is causing her harm—never! It's in the letter, which is coming. The Imam, asked about the situation of the wives of those who disappeared during the imposed war [with Iraq, 1980–1988], wrote that these women can take a representative [for the husband] and divorce themselves.

As the ayatollah was talking, Mortazavi was echoing his remarks in confirmation. Then he asked me whether I had any other points to make about di-

---

[5] Shi'i law allows annulment (*faskh*) in one of two circumstances: as a result of a fault in the marriage contract itself (either in its substance or in its form); or in the absence or presence of a condition in one of the parties. The Iranian Civil Code devotes an entire section (Articles 1,121–1,132) to annulment.

vorce. I responded, "No, this argument solves many problems, it brings a very different dimension to the issue, which I hadn't come across before." Then he asked me, "What was your objection regarding maintenance?" Encouraged and excited by the ayatollah's approach, I decided to place it in a wider context, to point to some of the assumptions underlying this Ruling and to ask for his interpretation.

ZMH: As regards maintenance, when one reads feqh texts—I'm familiar with Books on Marriage and Divorce—one gets the impression that marriage, in its legal structure, is modeled on the contract of sale. I'm not suggesting that marriage is conceptualized as a sale, but the fact is that we find in the contract certain conditions and elements that are derived from the sale contract. Some jurists are explicit on this, for instance, Allameh Helli[6] defines marriage as dominion of a man over a woman, of course not over the person of the bride but over her . . .

I was trying to find a euphemism for vagina; the ayatollah helped me with "women's honor and dignity." I went on:

ZMH: . . . her honor and sexual matters. In other schools of Islamic law one finds the same definitions. The notion of possession implicit in the contract defines the rights and obligations: that is, providing maintenance thus becomes a man's duty and a women's right, and submission a woman's obligation and men's right to demand; the same, more or less, can be said with respect to dower. Since you have allowed me, I'll voice the point many people make . . .

AYS: Please go ahead, this is a free discussion.

ZMH: It's said that Islamic law sees marriage as a contract of exchange, and doesn't involve ethical and human considerations. Such a notion of marriage disadvantages and limits women. I'd like to know your own opinion here, and also on maintenance in the conditions of the present. We see that many of our women are earners, that is, economic realities are such that many families with one breadwinner can't make ends meet; for instance, teachers or government employees. Although they don't legally have to, many women bring their earnings into the family, and this comes naturally since marriage also means sharing.

AYS: That's right.

ZMH: I'd like to know your view on this: are maintenance and its underlying assumptions, as defined in traditional feqh, in line with present conditions or not? Is there room for a kind of reform and rethinking in these areas to reflect present realities of marriage?

---

[6] I said Allameh (d. 1325), when I meant Mohaqqeq (d. 1277), the Helli whose text *Sharaye'-e Islam* I was referring to. The ayatollah did not detect my error, and *Payam-e Zan* repeated it in the transcript.

AYS: Something shouldn't be misunderstood; what I say is based on the
foundations laid by our jurists; that is, whatever we have is built on what
they left. If I say with confidence that a woman has the right of annulment,
or can go to court to divorce herself, this comes from my understanding of
the work of [Helli]—in certain assumptions—and other jurists. But as for
what you said, what comes to my mind is that, if an analogy has been made
between marriage and sale, this has been for the purpose of solving the legal
problems of marriage. We must identify where such an analogy has worked
against men or women. In effect the dower isn't a payment, but a gift, and
Islam has made it an integral part of marriage, without which the contract is
void, as a sign of respect for women. It's important to note that Islam requires a man to offer his wife a gift as a way of paying homage to her in this
union—it's a gift, not payment.

But as regards maintenance, if the two parties decide they won't abide by
it, this doesn't make the marriage void, it's still correct. In a society where
the husband can't be the sole provider, he doesn't pay it, and this won't
affect the marriage. We don't say that, in order to marry, a man must provide
maintenance; a woman can say she doesn't want it, and at the time of marriage or later she can relinquish her claim to it. But it's not the same with
dower.

Mortazavi interjected his own argument on this, pointing out that it is in fact
a blessing for women, an advantage given them by law, that they are not required to assume responsibility for any part of the living expenses. The ayatollah agreed and added that it was a matter of "sovereignty of the will" (*hake-
miat-e eradeh*), a concept for which there is room in law.[7]

Mortazavi was about to expand on what we had discussed that morning,
when the ayatollah's assistant entered the room and placed a file on the floor
next to the ayatollah, who opened it and took out a page, saying that this was
a letter which was available in the official records of the Council of Guardians.
He started to read the letter aloud to us, saying that we could turn off our tape
recorders, as he would give me a copy to keep.

In the name of God the Merciful
To the Leader of Islamic Revolution of Iran
His Excellency Ayatollah al-ʿOzma Imam Khomeini

After greetings and respect, certain issues get disputed in the Council of
Guardians and eventually your honored opinion is to be followed; among
these are some articles of the Civil Code, one of which pertains to divorce:
if the continuation of marriage causes the wife hardship, she can demand

---

[7] It was only much later that I appreciated the extent to which what they were saying was
constrained by the tension and sensitivity of the situation in 1995, when no overt criticism of
traditional feqh could be voiced; those who wanted to introduce change had first to declare their
allegiance and debt to feqh and its theories.

divorce by recourse to the religious judge who, after ascertaining the matter, will compel the husband to divorce, and if he refuses, the judge himself will conduct the divorce.

Some of the jurists in the Council of Guardians reject this [that the judge can conduct a divorce] and argue that the prerequisite of hardship is related to the need to abide by the contract of marriage; even if the hardship argument [for removing a Ruling] applies here, it can only remove the requirement of the contract and create for women the right of annulment. Given that instances in which annulment can take place are limited by consensus [of jurists], and [hardship] is not among them, therefore annulment is strongly ruled out.

Other jurists hold that the argument for hardship here is not confined to the requirement [to abide by the terms] of the contract, but the root of hardship is the husband's exclusive control over divorce, and according to the harm argument we remove this exclusive control and through recourse to the religious judge and with proof of hardship, out of precaution, the husband is compelled to divorce or the judge himself effects the divorce. Please state your esteemed opinion on these matters.

In the name of God

Caution demands that first, the husband be persuaded, or even compelled, to divorce; if he does not, [then] with the permission of the judge, divorce is effected; [but] there is a simpler way, [and] if I had the courage [I would have said it].

                                                    Ruhollah al-Musavi al-Khomeini

When Ayatollah Sane'i handed me the letter, I said: "these are two very different perspectives on women and their right to divorce." He responded:

AYS: Of course, the perspective according to which women should compromise, endure, and tolerate reaches an impasse; this is different from the Imam's perspective, which represents the richness of Islamic feqh and there is no impasse. Islam and its Rulings entail mercy, kindness, and ease.

ZMH: Why do you think these types of interpretation weren't made earlier?

AYS: Because power and government weren't in the hands of Shi'a, and such efforts weren't needed. On the other hand, in the past, societies were closed and restricted, and our feqh sources were adequate for them. The situation is different now.

He then repeated the legal argument: if a woman desires a divorce, but her husband refuses consent, such a refusal is, on its own, proof of "hardship" in marriage. In that case, either the wife can divorce herself (as, according to the "hardship" Principle, the husband loses the right of divorce and the wife acquires it); or she can demand that the marriage be annulled, just as the husband's insanity or impotency give her grounds to do, according to the feqh Principle of "no-harm."

Mortazavi made another attempt to discuss maintenance, aiming to have the ayatollah confirm that it can benefit women; but neither the ayatollah nor I was keen to follow it up.

SZM: In relation to women's maintenance rights in marriage, it must also be mentioned that they have no duty to do housework and they have the right to demand payment for the work they do. That is the issue of wages in kind which has entered civil law.

AYS: The government has solved this problem, that a man should pay something to his wife at the time of divorce, as a form of compensation. If women are aware from the start of the contract, they'll set their terms: "I work and want to have my rights."

ZMH: The concept of contract, as you define it, can solve many problems.

AYS: Yes: marriage is a contract, and this solves many problems, but women must be aware, there's no other way.

Mortazavi then changed the subject and asked the ayatollah to talk about his opinion on the age of puberty, when sexual maturity is attained and religious duties become incumbent on a child. This has been a much-debated topic among jurists and others, but it was not among my questions, since I knew that, on this issue, like that of women's right to serve as judges, the journal favored change and argued for new interpretations.

AYS: In my opinion, the age of puberty, as discussed in our traditional feqh, solves many of today's problems. We believe that if, after the age of nine, a girl manifests signs of womanhood—menstruation and the rest— then she is sexually mature (*balegh*) and all the Rulings of Islam which don't require attainment of maturity are incumbent on her. But if she doesn't manifest these signs, then she is mature at the age of thirteen; statistics show that about seventy-eight percent of all girls manifest signs of womanhood by this age. Noninclusiveness is natural here, since any law must cover the majority. Other factors, such as heredity, climate, nutrition, affect the age of puberty: in hot climates and with good diet, girls probably become balegh at the age of ten or nine and a half, but in colder climates girls don't show signs of puberty before thirteen.

In my view, such a perspective takes differences into account—genetic, climatic, and so on—and is more appropriate. One must be aware that puberty isn't the same as legal majority; certain matters—economic affairs, marital affairs—all require majority, others, such as liability to punishment or the incumbency of religious duties, don't.

I think that's enough, we've tired you out!

I had wanted to ask more about the links between "majority" and age of marriage, but this was his signal that he wanted to conclude the session, and he moved as if to stand. It was approaching time for evening prayer, and we could hear movement outside the room. I turned off the tape recorder and thanked him warmly, saying that, after this discussion, as a woman I felt relieved and reassured that there was scope for women's aspirations for equality within feqh. He also thanked me for my efforts in studying and trying to understand and represent the truth of Islam, since it was not as its enemies distorted it. He wished me success, and stood up to leave the room. As I and the others stood up too, I said something casually to the effect that other Jurists had not made my task easy: I'd come across a certain deep-rooted misogyny in feqh theories, one of which concerns women's defectiveness. The ayatollah denied this emphatically and sat down again, to make a last point. We followed suit, and I turned my recorder on once more.

AYS: This goes against the logic of the Koran; I recited the relevant verses for you, which clearly state that men and women are created from the same being. There's no difference.

ZMH: Does this mean equality between men and women?

AYS: Both are God's creation, and on the creation of both, the Koran says "blessed is Allah, the best of creators."

ZMH: How is it then that the concept of women's defectiveness has entered the hadith?

AYS: Such concepts have their origin in Sunni feqh, and are rooted in hostility toward Holy Zahra. [The Sunni] enjoyed political power, and to retain it they encouraged misogyny; unfortunately, some Shi'is were influenced unwittingly. Anyway, women came to suffer for Zahra's sake, and they must be proud of it. I remember the Imam used tell [his Houzeh followers], "After my death you will suffer a lot." Anyway, every movement is like this; it needs sacrifice and suffering. To suppress Zahra, as she was a real challenge to the Caliph's legitimate rule after the Prophet, they tried to undermine her legitimacy, and in order to make it ineffective they then tried to destroy her character through history. The consensus on the issue of judgment—that women can't become judges—is a Sunni consensus. There's no such consensus in Shi'i feqh.

SZM: If you permit, Master, I'll refer to historical evidence to support what you said. That is, in order to oppose Holy Zahra, everything to do with women was denigrated in hadith. For instance, there's a herb named *khorfeh*, which Zahra liked very much and which came to be known as Zahra's herb, for at least fifty years. When the [anti-Shi'a] Umayyads came to power, the herb's name was suddenly changed to—pardon me—"stupid" (*humqa*), and it's mentioned in inauthentic hadith as a useless weed. Then at the time of Imam Sadeq, Doubt came to some Shi'is and they went to the

Imam, who said: "Fatima Zahra liked this herb and it was known by her name. God curse the Umayyads who, because of their hostility, changed the herb's name to erase the name and memory of Fatima Zahra in people's minds." They couldn't even tolerate a herb being called by Zahra's name, so one can imagine what they did with other hadith.

Ayatollah Sane'i repeated the last sentence, and stood up to leave the room. Pausing for a moment, he said: "there are so many other misconceptions and misconstructions; it's difficult to separate [the false from the true]; that's the task of the Imam." He then left the room, as briskly as he had entered it.

After the Meeting

After the ayatollah had gone, we all lingered in the room for a while, standing and talking. We had all been excited and moved by the discussion, and by the ayatollah's frankness and openness. Mortazavi said the meeting had gone much better than he had expected, and he asked me whether I had now found answers to my questions—which he still referred to as Doubts. I said this was what I called a radical interpretation of divorce; I welcomed it, and I thought all feminists would do so. Sa'idi, who had not uttered one word during the discussion, reminded me that they had said the same things that morning, and he was glad that I could see the potential of the Houzeh for myself. I thanked them for arranging the meeting and said that it had indeed offered me a new perspective.

Sa'idzadeh told me that Mortazavi and Sa'idi wanted to stay for the evening prayer, and it was time for us to take our leave. I arranged my chador and looked at Zahra to see whether she was ready to leave. Suddenly I realized how bored she must have been; she had to sit still for almost two hours, and I knew she could not follow the discussion. I teased her: "my work is over, now we can go and have some fun and ice cream." She joked back, "I can show you where to find the second; as for the first, you're in the wrong place!"

As we left the room, we saw the young man who had brought the tea waiting in the hall to accompany us out of the building. We exchanged proper polite goodbyes, and followed him into the courtyard. It was now covered with carpets and with men preparing themselves for evening prayers to be led by the ayatollah. The young man guided us over the bare parts toward the curtain, which was now fully closed. On the other side of the curtain, by the basin, were three men performing their ritual ablutions before prayer.

That evening we went to the Hidden Imam's Mosque in Jamkaran, near a village by the same name about six kilometers from Qom on the Kashan road. The mosque is renowned for healing and miracles, and attracts many pilgrims from all over Iran, especially on Thursday evenings and Fridays, when they perform special prayers in the name of the Hidden Imam. According to legend, the Imam chose the site for a mosque of his own, a place where he appeared to believers and will reappear in the Day of Judgment: another proof of the centrality of Qom for the universal government of the Imam. Jamkaran is now a huge complex, with a kitchen to feed the pilgrims, a bookshop and library to educate them, and a clinic providing medical services; there are plans for a major highway to link the mosque to the shrine of Hazrat-e Ma'sumeh.

In the mosque, inside a Koran, I found another version of Imam Reza's injunction to women to wear a chador when they entered the mosque; this time the Hidden Imam had told the writer personally in a dream.

6

Agreeing to Differ:
Final Meeting with *Payam-e Zan*

MY THIRD AND LAST meeting with the *Payam-e Zan* clerics took place on 16 November, almost two months after the previous one. During the interval I went through the books and pamphlets I had bought in Qom, and learned more about how both popular and specialist journals and books in Tehran were airing issues of gender and feqh. I found that there was indeed a lively, at times acrimonious, debate on these issues, and that there was room for dissent from both the official line on gender and the old wisdoms of feqh theories—much more than I had anticipated when my discussions with *Payam-e Zan* started.

In September, when Iranian delegations participated in the United Nations Women's Conference in Beijing, this gave a new edge to these debates. Women's Week in November, marking and celebrating Fatima's birthday, offered another opportunity to air old and new ideas on women's position in Islam, and in some cases to settle accounts. Almost every journal—daily, weekly, monthly—featured articles, editorials, and reports on women's status in Islam; personalities raised the issue in speeches, sermons, and lectures; seminars and exhibitions were held. There was an air of open debate and exchange of ideas and wisdoms.[1]

The mood was also evident in *Payam-e Zan* 44, which came out in late October. The editorial, entitled "Women's Issues: Seen from Our Corner," marked Fatima's birthday and Women's Week by drawing attention to "one principal point in studying and assessing the status of women from a religious perspective." It sounded like a response to me, containing some of the editors' cardinal arguments during our discussion: that women's rights and duties in Islam must be seen from a holistic perspective, that is, in the three realms of Theology, Law, and Ethics; and that women's issues are complex and imbedded in the shari'a, which is in turn embedded in the wider system of religion.

The same issue featured the first of two installments of an article on Allameh Tabataba'i's views on women and their rights in Islam. Entitled "Women in *al-Mizan*," it was intended to commemorate the fourteenth anniversary of Allameh's death, but it betrayed a hidden disagreement among the clerics con-

---

[1] Even the Foreign Ministry devoted a special issue of one of its publications to Women's Studies (Mosaffa 1995), to which both secular and religious women contributed.

tributing to the journal. The author, Ahmad Heidari, a young cleric whose earlier contributions to the journal were on sacred history, clearly belonged to the traditionalist camp. He not only agreed whole-heartedly with Allameh's gender position but he grafted his own arguments onto them to make a case for gender inequality in the Islamic Republic and to close the door to further debate.

The article was prefaced by an editorial note, "Our Explanation," which made a hesitant attempt to distance the journal from some of the views expressed in the article. The note was full of ambiguity and ambivalence, and seemed to me to encapsulate the journal's dilemma: the dead weight of established scholarship, and the need to find space to maneuver within it. The editor first draws the reader's attention to Allameh's high position and achievements as thinker, philosopher, mentor, and scholar, and the hidden levels of meaning in the work he left behind. "Although today one might not be in total agreement with Allameh's views and perspective on women, one can neither dismiss nor bypass them." He goes on to qualify them, making three points. First, Allameh's views on women must be seen in their context of pre-revolutionary Iran: today they might seem outdated and outmoded, but in their own time they were daring and pioneering, paving the way for reform and correction of negative popular beliefs about women. Second, *Payam-e Zan* sees its "first mission" to be to introduce and present "in a scientific [objective] way various perspectives, analyses, and studies on women." Critical appraisal is of secondary importance, that is, the journal does not necessarily agree with the views expressed in its articles, or at least sees them as open to question; as, for example, with Allameh's view that women are banned from positions as judges and leaders and from taking part in Jehad. Third, Allameh Tabataba'i's conduct, in his personal life and in relation to his wife, are the best examples of how one can honor women and respect their humanity. I was particularly intrigued by this last point, implying that Allameh did not practice what he preached in the sphere of family law; that is, he did not do what he considered to be allowed according to the shari'a. I was determined to raise this in discussion—though when I did so, as we shall see, it was not well received.

I had prepared myself for a vigorous final discussion with *Payam-e Zan*. We arrived in Qom in time for our meeting, which was scheduled for ten o'clock as before. Besides Zahra, Sa'idzadeh also brought his young son Ali. This time we gathered in a room next to the editor's office, sitting again around a table. We exchanged greetings. I congratulated Mortazavi on issue number 44, commenting positively on his editorial. He said that it was the first in a series in which he intended to clarify the magazine's position; he also intended to publish the text of our discussions. I hoped we would take up the discussion where we left off, by addressing the assumptions on which feqh Rulings on marriage and divorce are constructed. My meeting with Ayatollah Sane'i had led me to believe that I could be more open with my views and questions.

The session did not turn out as I anticipated. Mortazavi proved less willing to engage in discussion, and directed all his skills to avoiding the very question whose importance he had acknowledged when suggesting we meet again. Interestingly, the other participant, Sa'idi, proved more forthcoming and willing to go beyond surface matters. The session lasted over two hours. *Payam-e Zan*'s version, most of which appears in the penultimate installment, in number 48 (March 1996), omits much of what transpired; a small section, concerning the journal, appears at the end of the last installment, in number 49. As will be seen, it was these omissions and rearrangements that give their version such a different impact from mine. The session began with Sa'idi's paraphrase of the question left from the previous session.

The Final Session

MHS: The question is: "How can solutions for women's issues be found in feqh, which perceives women as defective? You say that it is your religious duty to defend and secure women's rights, but how can this be done within a legal system and worldview which sees women as naturally defective and accepting of oppression?"

SZM: [a long pause] Right. With Ayatollah Sane'i's explanations, surely the problem has been resolved [for you]?

ZMH: To a large extent; to a large extent . . .

SZM: What isn't resolved then?

Taken aback by his abruptness, I tried to link the question to issues that had emerged in previous sessions, including that with Ayatollah Sane'i. I did not succeed, as we shall see; the crucial question was to be avoided—Mortazavi used his skills to devalue and sidestep the question, while I tried to justify and salvage it. This struggle occupied a good part of the session.

ZMH: [Pause] What isn't resolved . . . in fact . . . that is . . . a new perspective and thinking on women's issues. What I understood from Ayatollah Sane'i is that hadith or assumptions [depicting women as inferior] are based on a different worldview; that there's a need for new thinking; that religious thinking doesn't regard women as defective. But there are people [jurists] with such views. Have I understood correctly?

SZM: Yes! Doesn't this solve your problem? If you accept that these ideas are additions to religion, while our feqh does not endorse them, then your question should have been answered. Perhaps it isn't acceptable to you? Perhaps you think this isn't really the case? Or perhaps we're reinforcing your Doubt!

I said that although jurists present and justify their traditional understanding of gender roles in feqh as natural and ideal, it is in fact a theological construct; that feqh rules on family and gender roles are still informed by the assumptions and views of adherents of the gender inequality perspective; and that it is their views which constitute the well-known, accepted opinion of the jurists.

ZMH: The only question that arises is that feqh is made up of the views, understandings, and perspectives of the jurists. Can we say that their understanding is now changing . . .?

My question was received in total silence. At last, Mortazavi invited Saʿidi to respond. He was clearly not ready, and I made another attempt to clarify and to draw Saʿidi into the discussion. My attempt brought about a kind of altercation with Mortazavi.

ZMH: What I mean, Mr. Saʿidi, is that this [new] perspective is perhaps a minority one within feqh; that is, what Ayatollah Saneʿi says is only one opinion; there are surely others?

SZM: I don't understand your objection exactly. Are you suggesting that what existed in the past [feqh as a science] was simply the understandings of Jurists? that if their understanding changes, [women's] problem will be resolved? I want to know if you have any other proposals, since you're in effect finding fault with the past of feqh.

ZMH: I'm not finding fault with the past of feqh. I simply say that many of the laws which relate to women are based on certain assumptions and theories, that if we unpack them we'll see that one of them is that women are defective. Or if we look at the legal structure of marriage, we'll find that it is defined like a contract of sale. You know better than I the kind of legal assumptions and arguments underlying feqh rules. The question I posed was, given that these assumptions themselves have been one source of discrimination against women, without examining them, what can one expect feqh to do to help women? It's not only my question; it's that of many other women.

SZM: We don't see it this way. We don't accept that, because the Jurists viewed women as inferior and defective in nature, or because women had a lower position in society, then [Jurists] defined contracts and Rulings on that basis. Never do we find in feqh a definite assumption or an explicit Principle of women's defectiveness. No Jurist has ever said: since women are inferior, let's define their rights in marriage in this way and their rights in divorce in that way.

ZMH: How, then, do you explain the discrimination and inequality that exist between men's and women's legal rights?

SZM: We don't consider these [differences] as discrimination. You've taken it as definite, a priori, that feqh perceives women as defective, inferior, dependant on and secondary to men, and that this is why it defines women's duties differently from men's. Of course, we don't defend all instances of difference, but in general terms we see no discrimination. When you start from such a premise, then naturally you reach such a conclusion, that the only way to explain difference in rights and duties is to presume that jurists see women as defective.

ZMH: I didn't start from that as a premise, rather I inferred it by looking at ways in which feqh defines women's legal rights; otherwise, why should there be so many restrictions and limitations on women?

SZM: First, there's never been an assumption in feqh that women are born defective, and no legal Ruling is based on such an assumption. Second, many cases of what you call gender discrimination, we don't accept as such. As we discussed earlier, according to our "Balance perspective" we see these differences as based on a division of labor and of roles. Each person has rights and duties in accordance with his or her role and place in family and society; and difference here has nothing to do with women being defective. There are also restrictions on men on certain areas. Restriction has nothing to do with defectiveness. We can't say that the source of all laws in society is people's defectiveness or inferiority. We've already explained the basis and foundations of our perspective.

ZMH: Look, feqh is a legal system, and like any legal system it holds within it a distinct model of family and gender relations. In legal systems, rules don't come from or exist in a vacuum; when one talks of a [family] model, one is talking about the nature of these rules, the assumptions behind them, the premises on which they are built, from the rights that are bestowed on one party to the obligations that are placed on the other. Of course, as I already said, I'm voicing a question that many women are now asking. Your answer doesn't satisfy these women, because they see it as a kind of justification. Let's return to specifics; you want to remain on the general level but I want to be specific. We often have no problem with generalities . . .

SZM: No! We do have a problem with generalities. You say that what exists in feqh, and the views expressed by our Jurists, are all based on the assumption that women are defective. Here we disagree, and this is a general issue. Possibly we could find a certain Jurist who subscribed to such a view, as shown in his fatwas, but we can never say that feqh and the work of Jurists are based on such an assumption. You can't find a single instance premised on women being "born defective."

ZMH: I said "defective in reason." . . . On women's defectiveness in reason, there are a number of hadith. Aren't there?

SZM: We're talking about feqh, not hadith; that is, about bilateral and unilateral contracts, laws that regulate our personal and social life. Can you find an instance in which it's argued that women are defective? Can you invoke one single juristic argument to this effect?

ZMH: I don't have the command of feqh to able to invoke it.

SZM: [You can't] because there's no such a thing!

ZMH: Even if there were, I'm in no position to articulate it!

We had reached deadlock. Mortazavi saw my question as a kind of affront, an attack on feqh and its practitioners, which made it his duty to defend them. He asked Saʿidzadeh to arbitrate between us, and this proved a shrewd move which rescued us from the impasse: Saʿidzadeh shifted the blame to Sunni feqh and Shiʿi hadith.

SZM: Mr. Saʿidzadeh, you be arbiter here, and tell us whether you've come across such a feqh Principle. To be on equal ground with Ms. Mir-Hosseini, let me say that I too don't have a total command [of feqh]. I don't deny that we [Jurists] have our own prejudices and biases, which stem from our social and personal situations, or that we might get influenced by society's negative views of women. We don't defend these. But this isn't part of the juristic method, and I can't think of a single Principle which implies that women are defective. There are a number of Principles in feqh that imply a protective view of women, and see women as in need of protection and support. In your studies, Mr. Saʿidzadeh, have you ever come across a Principle that implies women's defectiveness and inferiority?

SMS: In the name of God. I haven't come across one in Shiʿi feqh; but in Sunni feqh, when discussing retribution for a [murdered] woman or blood money (*diyeh*) for women, many Jurists, especially Hanafis, say that blood money for a woman's is half that for a man because she is defective. But I think Ms. Mir-Hosseini is referring to hadith in *Nahj ol-Balagheh* and others which speak of women's defectiveness. Also, when discussing women's judgment, it's argued that women can't assume the position of judge because of their emotionality and lower capacity for reasoning. Allameh Tabataba'i, in *Al-Mizan*, like other exegetes—mostly Sunnis—says, with respect to Nisa, 34, that men's superiority to women has two dimensions: one ascribed and the other natural. Among those which are natural, men's superior reasoning capacity is mentioned. Generally, with respect to reasoning and rationality, men are seen to be advantaged.

SZM: But I meant something else; as a Principle in feqh, as a criterion for discernment, as part of the juristic method . . .

SMS: No, no! We don't have it as a Principle, or a criterion . . .

SZM: On what you said about Sunni feqh, I would like to refer Ms. Mir-Hosseini to an article in *Jomhuri Eslami* [a daily newspaper, close to the Houzeh] yesterday and the day before, on the Wahhabis' reactionary views

on women. We never defend the kind of attitudes that exist, for instance, in
Algeria, Saudi Arabia, Yemen, and elsewhere, which are very much influenced by Salafi and Wahhabi thinking. In fact, such attitudes give Islam a
bad name, and question the very legitimacy and validity of such Islamic
movements. Some go as far as denying women freedom of movement, and
say that if they go out then it's lawful to kill them. This isn't what Islam
says. In fact, as Ayatollah Sane'i said, to a large extent Sunni misogyny has
to do with animosity toward Hazrat-e Zahra; this is a historical fact and has
nothing to do with feqh. We don't defend such attitudes but oppose them
very strongly. I remember a sermon at Friday Prayers by a revolutionary
Sunni cleric, who was invited to Iran; he said that among the things that
should be avoided at all cost is giving women social responsibility and a
position in running the affairs of society: it is forbidden (*haram*). This was
his important advice to our government! But we don't defend such views;
they aren't a Principle in our feqh.

I said the issue was now clear; my tone on the tape is conciliatory: I think
I must have "swallowed my doubt" (as we say in Persian), since I too wanted
to get out of the impasse for which I felt partly responsible—I had been tactless
in my critique of feqh theories and their underlying assumptions. Sa'idzadeh
added that even in Sunni feqh women's inferiority did not constitute a Principle. Mortazavi's tone of voice now changed. He was no longer cold and dis-
missive, and to my surprise he now admitted that the inferiority of women,
though not a Principle, was indeed a presumption in feqh. He explained why
and how.

> SZM: This is what we call a post hoc explanation. Many things have been
> taken for granted in Islam, for instance the ban on women acting as judges,
> and then reasons have been sought. If you see that there's a consensus
> among Jurists, and none of them has said explicitly that a woman can act as
> a judge, it is because, in giving a fatwa, a Jurist must provide his own rea-
> soning and can't say that he follows others. To find reasons, he appeals to
> anthropological arguments, such as difference in nature between men and
> women, which have nothing to do with feqh. A Jurist must go directly to the
> [four] Proofs [Koran, Sunna, Consensus, and Reason] and our feqh doesn't
> depend on devices employed by Sunnis, such as Equity, Public Interest, and
> so on.
>
> As for the view of women as defective in reason, we have our arguments
> and objections, which we can discuss, if you wish.
>
> ZMH: No, I wanted to know whether it exists as a Principle; with what
> you said about post hoc explanations, the issue is now clear to me.

It was indeed. Clearly, feqh thinking did presume women's defectiveness,
but they were unwilling to address it. But Sa'idi intervened to give the issue

a new twist, exposing another layer hidden in my original question. I summarize his remarks, which were long and repetitive (the printed version was edited, too).

MHS: If you permit, I'd like to make a point. You start with the assumption that fatwas are based on a perspective, a worldview; this is logical and valid. But if you infer from this that differences in laws pertaining to the sexes derive from a perspective that regards women as inferior or different in essence from men, then this inference, in our opinion, is erroneous. Differences in rights and duties between the sexes don't arise from differences in their nature or essence, but from differences in their roles, and have to do with contracts that regulate relations between the sexes. Feqh establishes a framework with a fixed and immutable axis within which men and women are assigned specified duties and in return enjoy certain rights. Let's take the case of the marriage contract: Islam has set certain criteria for men and women to follow, and [feqh] allocates men certain duties for which they can demand certain rights in return. If [men's and women's] rights in this contract differ, it's precisely because their duties differ. In a contract, it's natural for the party with fewer duties to enjoy lesser rights; so you must take this into account, the fact that we stressed [balance] . . .

ZMH: Excuse me, there's a problem here. Are gender roles defined solely by nature, or do social factors also play a part? I want to return to social realities; I'm sorry, but just as you relate to issues from a feqh perspective, I do so from a social one, and like you this has to do with my training.

As Sa'idi was repeating the previous session's arguments, I responded in kind, pointing out the gap between the notion of marriage as defined by feqh rules and marriage as practiced by people; contrary to what they claimed, feqh rules do not promote harmony in marriage but imperil its stability; they maintain both men's control and women's subordination. My attempt to reiterate this point led to an interesting exchange—although, as so often, we sometimes did not seem to understand each other.

ZMH: When marriage isn't valued as a partnership and a woman is told that it's her right to be maintained and provided for by her husband, then she starts having expectations that her husband can't fulfill. A man who can't keep his wife in the style that she wants loses authority and manhood in his wife's eyes. Only rich men can perform their [feqh] duty fully and properly. This is one effect, but there's another: women who are good and have no such expectations and invest everything—including their earnings—in their marriage, feel insecure. There are many proverbs in our own [Iranian] languages which capture such women's anxieties; I'll tell you one in Mazandarani [which my grandmother used to say]: "never let the man have two pairs of trousers," that is, never let your husband's wealth exceed a certain

level; demand and spend what your husband brings. Why? Because otherwise he could destroy the family; he might be tempted to take another wife,
which would make you miserable and he might divorce you.

You say that difference in rights and duties in marriage is because men
and women have different roles in society, not because of a difference in
their natures. What I'm saying is that rights and duties in marriage rest on
the presumption that the man will provide—his duty of maintenance, in
return for the woman's duty of submission—and that this presumption is
now challenged by social realities. Men are no longer the sole providers, and
probably in many marriages never have been; what do you say to this?

MHS: Religion has a set, concrete framework, and within it has established a balance between the rights and duties of individuals. Now if one
party fails to perform their duty then naturally their rights will diminish; if
a man doesn't provide maintenance, then his wife can demand it or provide
it for herself . . .

ZMH: Do you accept that legal rules can have an impact on the structure
and stability of the family? I give you an instance: since the enactment of the
law of "wages in kind,"[2] many men can't easily divorce or take another
wife; they now have to think twice. Do you accept that such legislation can
have an impact?

MHS: Is this legislation Islamic or not?

ZMH: It's a very new legislation. It has no precedent in feqh.

MHS: But it is within Islamic criteria. As I said, religion defines the limits
and boundaries of musts and must-nots, and within this permitted zone
you're free to have whatever contract you want.

ZMH: But the extent of the "permitted zone" you talk about is very important; you can make it as narrow as these four walls or as vast as the
universe.

MHS: We make it no more or less than what religion has ordained. In the
marriage contract, religion has defined the musts and must-nots for each
party: a man must pay maintenance and dower and a woman must submit.
If the man doesn't fulfill his duty, the woman is released from hers, and vice
versa. There exists, then, a reciprocal relationship between the two [parties]
and religion defines the limits. As for the social issues you pointed out, they
have nothing to do with religion, although they have to do with the religious
community. That is, like you and others, we have our own criticism, which
is the very basis of our work. We believe that current criteria are not in line
with our religious values; men and women don't think of marriage as a
reciprocal contract; we see it as our task in the journal to make them understand that marriage is a contract in which each party is free to define his/her

---

[2] See the Introduction, above.

terms within the framework set by Islam. At the time of marriage, a girl must envisage the kind of problems she might face in the future, and acquire certain rights from the beginning and make them part of her marriage contract. We're working toward such aims. Islam defines the generalities, then laws are legislated on that basis. For instance, take blood money; some might say that difference [between men's and women's blood money] in Islam has to do with difference in essence between men and women; but no, it has to do with their roles.

ZMH: If their roles change, then might that law change?

MHS: Laws of Islam don't change the roles. As you know, law is legislated for society as a whole, and there is balance in the law itself, therefore it's I who must adjust myself to the law; I can't say: I want to live this way, so the law must change.

SZM: If people want to change the law because of changes in roles, then everything will collapse.

ZMH: You mean, the roles must remain as already defined . . .?

MHS: In addition to fixed limits, Islam has set mutable axes which can change with a change in roles. For instance, on the question of blood money, as we already said, it's wrong to conclude that a lower payment for women implies lower human value. Apart from being a fine for the murderer, blood money fills the economic vacuum created when a human being is killed; it has nothing to do with putting a value on human life.[3]

Now this was an old argument that *Zanan* had successfully challenged in a number of articles, starting in June 1993 with Mehrangiz Kar's "The Position of Women in Penal Laws of Iran." Kar gave this paper in 1992 at the First Seminar of Women's Social Participation, organized by the Tehran Governor's Office and Shahid Beheshti University as one of the first official attempts to bring together religious and secular personalities, men and women, with something to say on women, so as to highlight their "high status" in Islam and society. Kar's paper analyzed the Law of Islamic Punishments codified in 1991, and listed—without comment—instances in which men and women receive different punishments for the same crime.

Then in September 1993, *Zanan* featured the first of three installments of an article ("The Position of Women in the Penal Laws of Islam"), under a woman's name, putting a feqh perspective on the biases alluded to by Kar. In October *Zanan* published a harsh critique of Kar's paper—under the name of a woman but actually (I was told) written by her husband, a young cleric in Qom—and a response to it by Sa'idzadeh. The critique was meant to rebut earlier legal articles in *Zanan* written by Sa'idzadeh under various pseudonyms, but the author singled out Kar's article—not only because Kar, as a

---

[3] For another version of this argument, see Chapter Two.

secular feminist, was a safer target, but also because the author probably found it difficult to challenge the earlier articles, which were all argued within acceptable feqh boundaries. It was this exchange, and the tone and line of argument in *Zanan*'s reply, that persuaded me that the author of all the earlier articles debating women's rights from a feqh perspective was one single cleric—who turned out to be Saʿidzadeh.

I had not mentioned Islamic penal laws in my questions, and had not even invoked them as instances of gender discrimination during our discussions, because in my view the two sides of the feqh argument had been adequately dealt with in print.[4] But Saʿidi had now referred to the matter twice, rejecting the idea of gender bias and using the same arguments as in the case of the marriage contract, none of which I could accept. I had to address the issue, though I did not know why he persisted in raising it.

ZMH: You've brought up this issue, which I didn't want to include in these debates. You say that difference in blood money is due to economics, that gender plays no part, that blood money is meant to fill the gap created when someone is killed. Suppose I kill Mr. Saʿidzadeh; if it proves to be murder, Mr. Saʿidzadeh's next of kin can demand retribution (*qessas*), but if he murders me, retribution can only take place if my next of kin pays half his blood money. If gender isn't a factor in these laws, then why should my next of kin pay half his blood money before receiving justice? We have the same human value, and economically speaking I earn more than Mr. Saʿidzadeh; if gender isn't the determining factor, how else can one explain the difference? What I understand from these laws is that they're based on a single presumption: woman's economic value and contribution to the society is half man's; but this is no longer valid.

MHS: You must place your economic value, or in other words economic role, within the context of Islam's legal system. You mustn't think in terms of [the value of] your own person, but in terms of the legal duties that will be left unfulfilled in your absence. In the legal system of Islam, more roles and duties are assigned to men than to women; for instance, if a man is removed, eight cells in the economic matrix are left empty; if a woman is removed four cells are left empty, to be filled with blood money, as the law defines men and women's roles. Of course there can be exceptions, which by definition the law doesn't have to deal with. The law says that we assign men this role and women that role, and we compensate for the loss of each accordingly. The most important element in examining feqh Rulings is that they must be taken as a whole; Doubts [about gender bias] arise when Rul-

---

[4] For gender biases in Islamic penal laws, and the gist of Saʿidzadeh's arguments, see Mir-Hosseini 1996b, 306–8; for a translation of passages relating to women in the Islamic Penal Code, see Afkhami and Friedl 1994, Appendix II.

ings are seen in isolation. For instance, blood-money Rulings can't be separated from Rulings on inheritance, maintenance, and so on. They're elements that interconnect and interlock in a system.

I was intrigued by Sa'idi's economic matrix and his metaphor of empty cells, and that he could not see that what he had just said was a clear demonstration of gender bias in feqh, with its fixed notion of gender roles. We were back to square one, where we had started two months before. Obviously, they had not accepted my primary point, that there was another reality outside feqh definitions, and that what they called "exceptions" were in effect practice. After a pause, I tried to point out the duality and tension between the religious and the legal in feqh, and to return to inequality in marriage. Unlike our earlier sessions, this time I no longer confused shari'a and feqh.

ZMH: I accept that if we adopt a holistic approach, and look at the totality of religion—the theme of your [new] editorial—gender inequality can take a different meaning, and one might argue that it's no longer discriminatory. But I want to return again to social realities and to look at current legal rules—some of which are those of feqh, while others are rooted in its concepts and values—and see whether or not the balance you mention is maintained there. I look at Islamic legal rules at three levels. The first is shari'a, the divine, which is of course balanced and just. The second level, which is lower, is feqh, where humans intervene. A Jurist, after all, is human and is influenced in his understandings [of divine law] by his time, his environment, and his own outlook. The third level is the country's legal system and the ways people relate to law.[5] There's an exchange between these levels; if Muslims want to live by shari'a mandates, their understanding of these mandates is what feqh provides, and the means of implementing them are legal tools. Can we say there's balance at all levels?

For a simple example, I'll raise the issue of polygamy. According to our laws, a man must have his first wife's permission to take a second wife, and a marriage notary can't register a polygamous marriage without court permission. This is the situation at the third level. But at the second level, feqh—that is, our understanding of shari'a—we see that it allows a man to take a second wife whenever he wants; there are no conditions or restrictions there. Many men who want to take a second wife appeal to this level, that is, they do a temporary or permanent shar'i marriage [as opposed to the legal kind, which requires court permission], and face the first wife with a fait accompli. The notary who does the contract for them has done nothing wrong, either in the eyes of feqh or in his own religious conscience. If the couple want to legalize their union, they go to court and petition for registra-

[5] Cf. my earlier definition in Chapter Four.

tion of their shar'i marriage. This takes some time, but if there's no conflict between the two parties, the court registers the marriage with little fuss. You can't imagine what harm this does to the first wife; her happiness is over, and often her marriage as well.

I was alluding to the ruling of the Council of Guardians, which removed the punishment set by pre-revolutionary legislation for all parties concerned.[6] I went on to describe marital disputes involving polygamy, where the court almost always fails to bring about reconciliation. I fortified my argument with the statistics I had invoked in the previous session, elaborating on women's suffering and men's impulsiveness, and how men can ruin their first marriages thanks to "transient emotions," which are usually attributed to women. I finished by saying that this discrepancy between the levels of understanding and implementation of the shari'a leaves room for exploitation in practice, and that many men have no qualms in putting aside their religious consciences for the sake of self-interest or personal whim.

Sa'idi began to respond, but Mortazavi intervened and asked for my own analysis of this "duality." He clearly understood what I was hinting at: that translating a religious vision into practice is neither straightforward nor a one-way process, that it often produces the very results that the visionaries intended to eradicate in the first place. Employing their own tactics, I made a general statement. But Mortazavi reiterated his question, which I again tried to avoid by focusing on polygamy and how the law dealt with it before the revolution. This led to another altercation.

> ZMH: My analysis ... after all, the law, I believe, should protect the weak; and social conditions mean that woman is the party in marriage who needs more legal protection.

> SZM: Where do you locate the problem: in the action of the marriage notary, or in the legal organizations that should protect women?

> ZMH: I see the problem ... Look, in the past [between 1967 and 1979] the Family Protection Law restricted polygamy and in practice tied the hands of marriage notaries. But this is no longer the case, and such marriages can acquire legal validity. Of course, people could do a shar'i marriage in the past, but it could not be legalized. So part of the problem concerns procedural and legal rules defining marriage and women's rights within it. The other part goes back to human nature. When one party in a relationship is given more rights, then they'll feel powerful and want to use

---

[6] The Family Protection Courts simply did not deal with polygamy. Registration of a second marriage without court permission was an offense punishable by six months' to two years' imprisonment for all parties involved, including the second wife if she was aware of the situation. In 1984, the Council of Guardians declared this punishment contrary to shari'a. See Mir-Hosseini 1993 and 1998a.

their power. It makes no difference whether that party is male or female, or whether the rights are granted by shari'a, society, or custom; it often results in oppression. The point is that, in our country, in Islam, the family is of immense importance and women's rights must be addressed in the framework of the family. I'm one of those who believe it's no service to address women's rights outside the family context; and I think that Iranian women, Muslim women, also want this. But sometimes we see that current laws are not only the cause of women's oppression but destructive to family stability.

I have no solutions for this, Mr. Mortazavi; I have only questions.

SZM: But you made an objection; it must be clear whether you are objecting to feqh, to the laws of Islam, or to the actions and policies of the authorities and organizations. These must be distinguished.

ZMH: We can't distinguish them in an Islamic Republic . . .

SZM: We can, strictly. In my opinion, we can easily separate them; even those who don't think like us, and don't accept our view of Islam, make a distinction. The person you mention, who considers it legitimate and in accordance with shari'a to contract a [second] marriage, this is because he hasn't accepted the rule of Islam.

ZMH: On the contrary, if you ask him, you'll find that he accepts it in his heart; but his self-interest leads elsewhere.

SZM: Islam can't be blamed for this. . . . I want to be more general. The problem you raise isn't confined to family laws, we find it elsewhere too. If someone accepts the rule of Islam, then they can't infringe the laws of its government. If people infringe these laws and feel that they've done no wrong in the eyes of shari'a, it's because they don't accept the rule of Islam and the legitimacy of the laws legislated by its government. If that man had such a belief, then he wouldn't go against the rules mandated by the Islamic government. . . .

ZMH: If everyone had a perfect religious conscience, then our society would be paradise; but it doesn't work like this. . . .

SZM: [impatiently] I'm not talking about religious consciences, I'm talking about different perspectives. When we say Islam is in government, this means that the Islamic Ruler is free, whenever the interests of Muslims and Muslim society demand, to legislate new laws, or to stop the implementation of others, even if they're among definite Islamic laws. That is Imam [Khomeini]'s perspective and we look at problems from this angle. For instance, if the Islamic Ruler finds it expedient, he can stop men from taking more than one wife. This was also expressed by Allameh Tabataba'i. Or on divorce, as Ayatollah Sane'i explained, the Imam's view was that if man's exclusive right to divorce puts a woman in a difficult situation, this right can be removed and a woman can terminate the marriage unilaterally.

In my view, the questions you raise can be resolved if we accept Islam as a system of government that gives the Islamic Ruler a free hand. From a religious point of view, this ruler is well versed in Islamic sciences; from an executive point of view, he's just and gives priority to the interests of Islam and the people. The point is, some people don't accept the very basis of Islamic government; for them, Islam is confined to rules of worship, to do with prayer, fasting, and so on. This is a great injustice to Islam. There's a fundamental difference between the perspective which holds, for instance, that whoever finds oil can exploit it and need only pay the khoms on it, and the perspective which holds that oil, like any other resource, is the property of the Islamic government. This difference has ramifications in all affairs of society, from economy to the family. I refer you to articles my colleagues and I have written on broader issues dealing with the Islamic state and its sphere of authority.

We have tools at our disposal to address these problems; Islam even allows the Islamic Ruler, if he finds it expedient and in the interests of Muslim society, to change obligatory Rulings, let alone polygamy, which is only "permitted." We aren't questioning the Principle, but its application. One can't say that polygamy is always against women's interests; there are times when it's a form of protection for them: in time of war, for example.

If we'd said—as some do—that we can do nothing until the coming of the Hidden Imam, then I admit there would be no solution. But this isn't our perspective. We don't reduce religion to the private sphere and say marriage falls there and has nothing to do with the Islamic state. We approach Islamic laws from this perspective: although we adhere to current laws, this doesn't mean we endorse each one as a manifestation of the ultimate truths in feqh. No one, even the Leader [Ayatollah Khamene'i, the new vali-ye faqih], claims that all existing laws are this. We therefore say explicitly that, first, we defend the current system of laws as a whole and see it as in line with Islam, but we don't defend every single law. Second, we don't confuse what's happening outside [in society] with Islam; it isn't Islamic law that's unjust, even if the entire society understands it wrongly and applies it wrongly. Third, we see all the laws of Islam, even its Rulings on worship, from the perspective of a government that can assess their suitability, justice, and impact on society.

As for the example of blood money that was brought up, if anyone can complain it should be men—I'm not joking. I was really disappointed to see an article in *Jame'eh Salem* by a lawyer, Ms. Shirin Ebadi, who tries to deal with this complex issue emotionally and rhetorically on a single page. It's amazing that a lawyer, an educated woman, can treat Islamic law in such a way. She questions the justice of the law by saying that when a man murders a woman, her relatives must raise the money to pay half the murderer's blood money before they can get justice. This gives quite the wrong impression, and shows the writer's gendered perspective. If we look closely at the law we see that the philosophy behind it is to protect women as a class. We must put the law in its context and examine it in relation to other laws, most importantly the law of maintenance, by which men must provide for their wives and children. Islam doesn't say that a man who has murdered a woman shouldn't receive the sentence of retribution, what it says is that the impact on the family he leaves behind must be contained by demanding half his blood money for his retribution. If no blood money were required, the same people would have objected . . . that a family is deprived of its provider and women aren't catered for. If I'm using a rather emotional [unscientific] argument, it's because the article itself did.

Mortazavi said more on the philosophy and logic of blood money: it had nothing to do with putting value on human life, nor with gender; if understood properly, the difference revealed Islam's compassion for women as a class. I now understood why the issue had become one of our debating points; it arose from the article whose author Mortazavi referred to by name. This was the first and only time Mortazavi put aside his reserve and named an author. In the printed transcript he omitted names, referring to the journal as "alternative" (*digar-andish*), a semiofficial derogatory term used since the early 1990s, implicitly acknowledging the existence of a secular perspective.

The latest number of *Jame'eh Salem* (Healthy Society), marking the United Nations Women's Conference, featured several articles on women, including the offending one by Shirin Ebadi. I had read a copy but did not recall the article, although I knew the author and was familiar with her work and her arguments.[7] She had been one of the first women judges, appointed in the early 1970s. After the revolution, when women could no longer serve as judges, she took early retirement and began to practice as a lawyer, and to teach. She has written several books dealing with women's and children's rights, and in 1997 she received a prize from Human Rights Watch. Her article in *Jame'eh Salem*, "The Female Right to Life," is indeed, as Mortazavi said, only one page long. Written in a legalistic and rhetorical language, it is a critique of the Law of Islamic Punishments, enacted in 1991. Ebadi starts by citing Article 3 of the U.N. Declaration on Human Rights and Article 2 of the Islamic Declaration on Human Rights, then the texts of Articles 209, 210, and 213 of the 1991 Law, to show that capital punishment of a man who murders a woman is contingent upon the ability of the latter's next of kin to pay blood money. She cites an actual case in which a brutal husband killed his young bride simply for disobeying him; when he was arrested and brought to justice, the bride's father

---

[7] I had met her earlier in the year at a conference in Paris on "Women's Strategies in Iran" where we both presented papers; see Yavari-d'Hellencourt 1998.

had to sell his only possession, a small house in a poor locality in Tehran, in order to raise the half blood money required by law. Ebadi concludes:

> Given what the Holy Koran says in Verse 32 of Sura 5, "whoever slays a soul, unless it be for manslaughter or mischief in the land, it is as though he slew all men," can we not amend Article 209 of the Law of Islamic Punishments? Given the Holy verse "We have created you of a male and female, and made you into tribes and families that you may know each other; surely the most honorable of you with Allah is the one among you most careful (of his duties),"[8] how do we explain Article 209 of the Law of Islamic Punishments? Are women not God's creatures, that they can be killed so mercilessly?[9]

Perhaps what annoyed Mortazavi most was Ebadi's style, and her references to the Koran in criticizing feqh Rulings. He became defensive and made statements contradicting his earlier assertions: that feqh laws can accommodate change, and that the Islamic Ruler is in a position to put aside or legislate new ones when necessary. I tried several times to interrupt, but he asked to be allowed to finish, and when he did, I hinted that perhaps the time for change had come and the very premise on which he built his defense of feqh laws had already been shaken.

> ZMH: A question. I repeat: what happens if a woman who is the family provider is killed? Should the blood money for her still be half that of a man? Because what you've said so far rests on your model in which men are the sole providers of the family . . .
>
> SZM: Are you talking about individual cases [exceptions]?
>
> ZMH: I'm talking about economic and social change. It's no longer [exceptional]; and I made this point several times. At present, in Tehran and other large cities, and in many families, both spouses are earning; men are no longer the sole providers. This is dictated by economic imperatives, and working women who bring their income into the family are increasingly part of our social reality. We see in the Islamic Republic that women are present in every sphere of activity; the very changes introduced by the Islamic Republic are increasingly paving the way for women's participation and advancement in society. Today about 50 percent of our medical students are women, tomorrow they will be doctors, practicing all over the country. This is an impressive statistic, which we must be proud of. When you encourage women to enter society, when they acquire knowledge, skills, and degrees, then you can no longer tell them: "because you're a woman, your value in the economic system is half that of a man." The economy has its own rules

[8] Sura Hujurat, 13.
[9] *Jameʿeh Salem* 22 (September 1995): 24.

and imperatives. The question is: when economic relations and structures change—which they have—and in turn transform social and family relations—which they have—what happens [to your argument] then?

SZM: We already discussed all this in previous sessions. Whatever changes, the question that must be addressed is this: is a woman obliged to provide or not? You must first answer this question.

ZMH: As I said before, the point isn't whether she is obliged or not, it is that she is contributing, otherwise the family can't make ends meet. Marriage in practice is a partnership.

SZM: The point is that she isn't obliged to; Islam has taken her under its protection by not placing such a duty on her. She's free to contribute if she wants to, but she has no obligation. This puts a woman in a better position in marriage, as she retains a claim on her husband; as we see, women who know that they don't even have to do housework, can tell their husbands that they do it out of charity. There's no need to change this [maintenance law] for the sake of change in economic relations. Besides, women were also economically active in the past; as Mr. Sa'idzadeh has shown in one of his articles on women's activities in early Islam, most of the medical work was done by women. Women's economic activity is not a new thing.

Sa'idi added to this that the law must deal with general cases, that we must also have an overall view, that society suffers more when a man is lost. He repeated his metaphor of empty cells in society's economic matrix, and ended by reiterating the journal's position: it defends neither all current laws nor the present situation, and its very existence has to do with the recognition of a need for change.

I remained silent; I saw no point in repeating my own arguments. There was a basic differences in our approach to the women's question, to feqh Rulings, and indeed to social reality. Obviously, they must have felt the same, since Mortazavi suggested that we return to the beginning of the discussion: my question on the relationship between feqh theories and tools and women's oppression. He proposed, for the sake of brevity, to read a section of the editorial note that he had just written to appear in the forthcoming issue, to follow up the previous editorial, which I had commented on before sitting down to our discussion.

The source of many laws and Rulings—both personal and social, whether they come under the general categories of contract, penal, or even worship—is that set of events and circumstances that are outside the realm of human essence and humankind. Many of these are merely relative and conventional, and accord with personal and specific social needs, and meet the interests of individuals and society; they do not stem from human essence and identity. Therefore, differences in laws and Rulings, even if they lead to differences in social status, are never evidence and proof of the existence of difference in the human identity of mankind and womankind.

In other words, we regard matters which are merely conventional and relative as outside the realm of human essence and identity.

This seemed to be what I had been arguing all the time. To make sure I had understood him, I interrupted: "you mean, you find them to be outside nature?" He agreed: "yes, we regard them as totally outside nature." To take the point to its logical conclusion, I said: "so, because they're based on convention, [laws and Rulings] can also change?" To this Mortazavi assented twice, before continuing to read the rest of his article.

And in this identity, neither [gender] is dependent on the other, nor is it lower in degree than the other; and in that set of Koranic and religious directives which addresses this identity, this humanity, the self and human-kind, is the same for men and women, and difference is meaningless. For instance [this applies to] the Principles of Unity of God, Prophethood, and Resurrection, and basically whatever pertains to belief. This is so because matters relating to belief are directly connected with human self and es-sence, and since there is no difference at that level, it would be meaningless to say that the kinds of belief women have in God are different from those men have. If we accept that the most fundamental and most important reli-gious values are those relating to beliefs, which is certainly so, then we must admit that, in the holistic approach to women's issues, in an anthropological dimension, in the most fundamental of [Islamic] values relating to beliefs, there is not the remotest chance of sexual discrimination, and difference between the two sexes then becomes meaningless.[10]

SZM: I want to stress that the location of our discussion of men and women must be clarified. Are we talking about their conventional situation, based on their social positions? You might say these are liable to change.

ZMH: Yes, because as you say yourself, it's relative and conventional, and change is an inseparable part of social conventions, structures . . .

SZM: But in the system in which Islam places [men and women] there are escape routes, there are many solutions. We have Principles such as "denial of harm," "public interest," and so on; these are "ruling Principles" which overrule others. Feqh isn't only about praying and fasting, paying mainte-nance, or obeying your husband; from our perspective . . . the hand of the Islamic Ruler, the judge, will be freed if they see that enforcing a law or a right results in corruption; then it can be stopped by means of the ruling Principles; there's no problem that can't be solved.

---

[10] *Payam-e Zan* 45 (December 1995), editorial; also 48 (March 1996), in the third installment of the transcript of our debate.

I agreed with this point, and said so; but Mortazavi went on to qualify and in effect to contradict what he had just said.

SZM: But we can't say that since women's position has changed, and since they have income and play a role in providing, then men's obligation of maintenance must change. No, there can be no change in generalities.

ZMH: There's a contradiction in what you say; on the one hand you say that [feqh Rulings] are based on conventions and are thus open to change, on the other, you say that there can be no change in generalities.

SZM: When I say convention, I mean it goes back to [men and women's] social position . . .

ZMH: A position which might change . . .

SZM: No! what I'm saying is that it concerns the position Islam endorses for women; it has nothing to do with their identity or human essence. It has to do with men as providers and maintainers of the family. Woman has no such duty in the system Islam recognizes, this is a protective Principle for women, which Islam has legislated.

ZMH: Isn't this based on convention?

At this point Saʿidi intervened to provide an answer, revealing the extent to which they could allow themselves to envisage change in feqh Rulings. His answer did not clarify the problem for me, but added a further dimension.

MHS: We accept change in social roles; and believe that people's roles vary over time, in different conditions and societies. But change in roles never necessitates change in legal generalities. Look, legal generalities are immutable, they are derived from the perspective and worldviews of a school. If we look at the present situation, where you say both men and women have to work to make ends meet . . .

ZMH: I don't attribute any value to it; as an anthropologist, I don't say it's either good or bad; I just say it's happening: it's a social fact.

MHS: Fine, it's a social fact, but we don't have to change legal generalities for its sake. Of course, the appearance and form of the law might change; for instance, the form of the marriage contract might change but not its substance; a phrase can be added or omitted, but this doesn't change the nature of the marriage law.

SZM: It might be said that woman should pay 10 percent of [family] expenses.

MHS: They can make this part of the contract; but there's no need for the generalities of the contract to change. In present conditions, a couple can easily lead their lives within the bounds of the [shariʿa] contract. If a woman is prepared to put up with a lower standard of living, the husband can be the only provider. If women work it's because they want to improve the quality of their life; but they don't have to work. I'd even go further and say that although the institution of the family is sacred in Islam and we value it immensely, this doesn't mean that marriage is only for the formation of a family. Islam has set a wider and freer framework than this; people can live together for a variety of reasons and don't have to conform to the present definition of the family; marriage can take different forms and serve different purposes. In my opinion, we must only make clear what belongs to Islam; the rest is to be determined by human reason, which can shape what Islam ordained in any mold or form. This is the task of reason, of science; and the purpose of the laws legislated by government is to mold shariʿa to the needs of society and the time.

There were several inconsistencies in Saʿidi's argument, I thought, but his position was clear: that the hegemony of feqh Rulings in family and society must be maintained, regardless of changes over time in economic and social roles. In arguing that Islam provides a much wider and more liberal framework and allows men and women to form relationships without observing social conventions, he certainly had in mind temporary marriage. This was a topic I was determined to avoid discussing with them, not just because it is a sore issue, where the gap between theory and practice has become increasingly evident since the revolution, but also because I wanted to provoke discussion of women in feqh as social beings and as equal partners in marriage. I was determined not to engage in any debate over the presumed differences in male and female sexuality, which inform many feqh theories and Rulings on marriage, as well as a mass of writings by critics of feqh gender theories.[11] Interestingly, *Payam-e Zan* also seemed to want to avoid the topic: the published transcript omits this part of Saʿidi's remarks. It also omits the following exchange, ignited by my sarcastic comment on the last element of his argument.

> ZMH: Or to mold needs according to shariʿa; that's what you mean, to be precise.
>
> MHS: It's the same thing.
>
> ZMH: Not really, there's a great deal of difference . . .
>
> MHS: What you mean is the same as what I'm saying, but our idioms are different. Society needs laws to regulate its affairs, and the shariʿa is fluid— not in the sense that it has no basis or constancy, but in the sense that it can cover and accommodate a variety of needs and circumstances.

The interaction between shariʿa and social practice was the theme of my earlier research; my findings in effect supported what Saʿidi said, although

---

[11] See Chapter Three for temporary marriage: even traditionalists like Azari admit the problem. See also Mir-Hosseini 1998b.

I started from a very different premise and ended with a different set of reasonings. I saw no point in telling him that in the process of shaping society these laws also come to take its shape; that once you start altering the "appearance and form" of a feqh legal Ruling to accommodate changing social roles, then what he called the "generalities," in effect a set of patriarchal Rulings, are bound to be affected; that once women are providers and men cannot repudiate them whenever they wish, then the very model that these "generalities" help to uphold becomes irrelevant—thus its laws are negotiated, and often bypassed.[12] By now I was convinced that no matter what arguments and evidence I put forward, they could not bring themselves to admit that a single feqh Ruling—let alone the concepts embedded in the Rulings—needs modification, apart from those already modified by legislation in the Islamic Republic.

Mortazavi made crystal clear what had remained implicit in Sa'idi's argument, that is, the question of authority:

> SZM: I recently wrote a conference paper, about seventy pages long, entitled "Imam Khomeini, Government, and the Sources of Mutation and Constancy in Rulings." There I posed the question of whether we have any fixed Rulings or not; and if we admit that Islamic rules are mutable, what the source for this mutation is. The question is general and covers family law as well as other branches. We have many hadith of the Prophet and of the Infallible Imams attesting that, although the original Ruling remained constant, the Prophet acted differently because of a social need. It was not always a matter of life and death, but merely social or popular interest that caused the Prophet to allow it. For instance, we have numerous hadith [of the Prophet] to the effect that meat sacrificed [during Hajj] mustn't be removed from Mina [small village outside Mecca, where the first and last stages in Hajj rituals take place]; it must not be stored but left for consumption. But we see that Imam Sadeq says that this was a temporary Ruling, since there wasn't enough then, as Muslims were fewer and sacrificed less and meat was needed for distribution and consumption then and there. But now that more sacrifices are made, pilgrims are free to do as they wish. In this case we see that the Principle of "Sacrifice in Mina" remains constant but the Ruling, "not removing meat from Mina," alters.
>
> Now the question is, during the Absence [of the Twelfth Imam], who should decide that a Ruling should change, for instance that women should contribute 10 percent to maintenance? We see no problem here when there's a Just Government; when Islamic Government is in power, its hands aren't tied, and there can be change. To sum it up in one sentence, we don't see any impasse when Islamic Government is formed.

[12] See Mir-Hosseini 1993.

This neatly concluded our discussion of change in feqh theories. However, the published transcript adds a short paragraph, as a transition to what comes next:

> Meanwhile, those who object, for instance, to repudiation, maintenance, and so on, must say how they themselves solve these problems; we'd like to know how these problems are solved in the West. It would also be good to know your opinion about possible solutions for such problems.[13]

These questions—which Mortazavi never asked in this form and context—are followed in the published transcript by what I had said informally, at the end of the previous session, in response to his question about maintenance in law and practice in the West. Then, it had led to another question: he wanted me to compare Western and Islamic ways of life. Our discussion (see Chapter Four) had been amicable, and ended with my talking about my own motives and approach. The transcript, however, omits the latter part of that discussion and slightly alters the earlier part, adding two paragraphs to Mortazavi's response, in defense of Ayatollah Motahhari's nature theory, thereby turning the discussion into a critique of Western practices; I am both represented as a critic of the West and rebuked for failing to understand Motahhari and current feqh debates.[14]

This concludes *Payam-e Zan*'s penultimate installment of the transcript. To a careful reader of the Persian text, the passage does not make sense and has clearly been taken out of its original context. The question is, why? I can think of three possible reasons, which are not mutually exclusive.

The first is that the editor had to keep a balance, that is, to present the debate without offending sensibilities in the Houzeh, where overt criticism of feqh and questioning of its theories and assumptions are taboo. The only way they could air the debate was by ending it with their defense of Islam and condemnation of the West. This explanation is supported by the fact that they made similar alterations in transcribing other parts of the debate they found sensitive and critical, and also by the way they introduced me to Sane'i and to their readers.

The second reason is that, if this part of the debate were published as it actually unfolded, readers would soon see that the journal not only had failed to answer my question but had avoided it completely. The way out—the face-saver for them that could also be justified as protecting me—was to turn my question into a Western critique of Islam, so that it could be dismissed as biased and uninformed, not as representing the concerns of a Muslim woman but as Western objections to Islamic law. They resorted, in other words, to the old tactic of answering one criticism with another.

The third reason is hermeneutical. The alterations, additions, and omissions reflect how the clerics actually understood this part of the debate and then

---

[13] *Payam-e Zan* 48 (March 1996): 21.   [14] *Ibid.*, 23.

aimed to communicate it to their readership. Whereas I felt that my question had been evaded, they thought they had addressed it adequately during the three sessions, and thus sought to end the debate in a way that would make this clear to their readers. They saw nothing wrong or unusual in altering the order in which it unfolded or in taking sentences out of context. In the Houzeh style of teaching and scholarship, context is secondary to a concern to establish the general point, either legal or moral.

The second and third explanations for the alterations in the transcript are supported by the way the debate now continued and concluded, none of which was published, except my final question about the journal, and their answer. After Mortazavi's statement, Sa'idi reminded us that our time was nearly up and asked whether there would be another session. I said that as I was returning to England soon this must be our last session, and that I had only one more question.

> ZMH: I wanted to know your own personal views on issues we have discussed, such as men's unilateral right to divorce and polygamy, the minimum age at marriage, women's need to ask their husband's permission to work.
>
> MHS: My own personal view, or the journal's?
>
> ZMH: Both, if they're different. I'm interested to know whether you personally consider polygamy to be just or not. I'm familiar with feqh arguments in its defense, but I want to know whether you would apply them in your own life.

There was no response; Sa'idi sounded as though I had committed sacrilege. The question was in fact among those I had submitted in September, but now I phrased it differently. I was intrigued by Mortazavi's introductory note to the article "Women in *al-Mizan*," where he suggested that Allameh Tabataba'i's practice did not accord with his views on gender: I was genuinely curious to know why. As the pause grew longer, I thought it might help to express my own personal position on the issue. This was not a wise move and added to the complication; Mortazavi took it as an insult to feqh, to personalize its aims and truths.

> ZMH: I'm a Muslim woman; but I'm not prepared to become a co-wife. I believe this would be unjust to the other one, and I know myself well enough to know that I wouldn't tolerate a co-wife. So I take a personal position on this issue, and don't see it as contradicting my faith.
>
> SZM: In a particular situation, one mightn't permit oneself to exercise such a right; as with many other rights and Rulings that people's circumstances don't allow them to practice; for instance, I have the right to buy a village or to hire a train to come and go between Tehran and Mashhad.[15]

---

[15] The shrine of Imam Reza, favorite destination for Qom clerics.

ZMH: But [that's different, since] you can't afford it . . .

SZM: Whatever; I don't do it, and I don't consider it in my interest to do it. So whether people do something or not has nothing to do with the law. But you want to take [our personal opinions] as evidence whether we find [polygamy] unjust or not . . .

I was frustrated: I could see how he was going to avoid this question, like the previous one, by sidetracking the discussion, so I interrupted and asked rather pointedly, "Why not?" Saʿidi attempted to clear the air: "She's talking from an anthropological point of view, she wants to know . . . " But I did not let him finish his sentence, and expanded my question.

ZMH: Why is it nothing to do with law? Isn't the law made for the people? Isn't it for regulating people's lives? If so, how can you say what people do has nothing to do with what the law says?

SZM: [Polygamy] isn't compulsory, it's a right that I have if I determine that [its exercise] is advisable, otherwise—for the very reasons you gave yourself—I might decide it's not, and I won't do it. So, first, there's no obligation; second, each individual can choose. For instance, a woman can consider her best interest; as you said: "I'm not prepared to marry a man who has another wife and I won't allow my husband to marry another one." The point is that Islam has left the option open, for both society and individuals. I'm merely saying that from a shariʿa point of view if the interest of society demands, or if the Islamic Government permits, a man can take two, three, or more wives. Do you object to this or not? Are all problems solved in societies where such a predicament is not imposed? In the West, for example?

ZMH: Problems take different forms . . .

Before I could complete my sentence and say that it is essential to make a distinction between men's legal right to polygamy and promiscuous behavior, Mortazavi resumed his defense of polygamy.

SZM: After all, this is reality. What will happen if we ignore such a fact? You tell us to take account of social reality, of what's happening on the ground. If we don't take it into account, then we'll have a situation like the one in the West: a man has a wife and a woman has a husband, but what is actually happening? . . . Is women's honor preserved there? True, a man can't take another wife, but there's no sanction against their doing what they want.

ZMH: There are sanctions; marriage often collapses if a man is unfaithful to his wife or vice versa.

SZM: No, I mean they have no problem satisfying their needs elsewhere, destroying the foundation of the family, do they? Do we really want this?

Does this serve the interests of women and the family? Should we refuse to support women who don't have providers [husbands] and say that the law must protect only women with husbands? The point is, if properly understood, [polygamy] is for women's protection . . .

He was recycling an old argument, which I had heard so many times I knew each line by heart. It runs: men are by nature polygamous; Islamic law is in line with nature and for the good of society and individuals; so, if properly understood, men's right to polygamy maintains order in society and protects women. The argument rested on the very assumptions I had tried so hard to deconstruct during our discussions—clearly without affecting Mortazavi. But this was not what annoyed me. I was furious that, when it came to men's right to polygamy, he was finally prepared to consider social reality and practice on the ground. Not letting him finish his sentence, I said sarcastically:

ZMH: Your perspective on this issue, Mr. Mortazavi, is that of a man. Mine is that of a woman and I make no apologies for it. That is, as a woman I see it as my right—not my defect!—to think like this. The fact is, there's a vast difference between our perspectives.

Clearly my direct insistence on asking their personal views was unacceptable, even though I had shared mine with them. I thought that it was the end of our discussion. But Sa'idi intervened to give it a new lease of life. He first made it clear that we were talking at two different levels, then rephrased my question so that Mortazavi could respond without compromising his loyalty to feqh. (Note that, like Mortazavi, he avoided using the word "polygyny" (*chand-zani*), as though it were taboo.)

MHS: Her question is something else. She's not talking about feqh or the law; she's talking about an external proposition, that is, you and I as configurations of customs, ethics, and emotions. Now, she wants to know, how does this created configuration view the issue?

SZM: With conditions, I accept [polygamy] for society—[this is] not personal.

MHS: She's not talking at the level of society, but at the personal level; if I've understood her, she wants to know our own personal standing on this. I think we need to articulate our personal feelings to clarify the issue; if you'll allow, I'll give a response and let's see if it answers the question.

We believe that in principle one man and one woman are enough for each other; this is a natural and normal rule, and we also see that it's often like this in society. When the emotional relationship between a man and a woman is deep, neither feels the need to go elsewhere. None of us, therefore, in normal circumstances, would think of wanting more. But one might find oneself, both emotionally and socially, in a situation where, despite all one's resolution, one might do otherwise. You said you wouldn't do it; I say one can't swear such a thing; one might be in a situation where it might be a wise thing to do so. If you want my personal feelings, I say that the thought of [more than one wife] has never entered my mind.

The anthropologist in me was so impressed with the way Saʿidi had dealt with my question that I was happy to continue. I could not help but agree with his answer: one does things in life which might not always be in line with the rules one advocates. I knew many feminists—including myself—who had broken the very rules they set for others. I said: "this does answer the question." Mortazavi promptly added:

> SZM: This can't be taken as proof of our rejection of the Principle; you can't say that because we see monogamy as the norm then we don't believe in the Ruling on polygamy.
> ZMH: That's a different subject, which I didn't raise.

My formulation of the question and statement of my view of the injustice to women must have put the editor in an impossible position. Whatever answer he gave would have taken us back to feqh theories and assumptions, which he was not willing to discuss. Perhaps that was why he then invoked Ayatollah Saneʿi's view that Islam does not encourage polygamy but merely permits it, explaining that those hadith which apparently recommend its practice relate to temporary marriage and the second Caliph's prohibition of it. Thanking Mortazavi for his explanation, I made it clear that I was not talking about the Ruling sanctioning polygamy, but about interpretations—and abuse—of the Ruling:

> ZMH: The reason I asked the question was that, as a woman, I know its acceptance is difficult for women. I wanted to know your views as a religious thinker and whether you view monogamy as a norm. As for what you say about depending on circumstances, this is a different matter; I'm not concerned with the Ruling [on polygamy] but its consequences, which is a different subject altogether.

Mortazavi referred me, for a learned and balanced discussion, to the forthcoming issue of *Payam-e Zan*, and the fourteenth and final installment of the serialized translation of a book by the Lebanese Shiʿi leader Ayatollah Fazlullah.[16] I had read the earlier installments, including the latest one on temporary marriage, and found nothing new in Fazlullah's position or his arguments. They were another version of Motahhari's theory, and did not deal with the point I was raising: that the issue is not whether or not polygamy is practiced,

---

[16] The first installment appeared in *Payam-e Zan* 32 (November 1994), as "Islam, Woman, and a Novel Search"; the Arabic title of the book is *Taʾammulat Islamiya hul al-Marʾat* (Islamic Reflections on Women).

nor whether it should be allowed only in certain conditions and times, but rather that the very fact that its permissibility is defended on religious grounds serves to change the balance of power in marriage in favor of men. Men might not be able to afford to take another wife, but the fact that the shari'a grants them such a right enables them to control women both in marriage and in society.

I saw no point in elaborating my remarks and telling him I was familiar with Fazlullah's views and found nothing new there. By now our lines of argument and our positions were clear. So instead I asked Sa'idi about the journal's Advice section, where his initials had appeared since July 1994 as one of two advisors (the other was Zahra Akuchakian, in her full name). I had asked about this—my favorite part of the journal—after my tape ran out at the end of the first session; Sa'idi had agreed to discuss the letters in detail in the next session, but we never got round to it. Now, noting again that time was short, he explained how the journal answered letters. They receive ten to sixteen a month; each one is individually answered, in accordance with the journal's perspective, and most are also printed; sometimes details are altered to protect the writer's anonymity.

Mortazavi then proposed that we close the discussion with a summary statement. Sa'idi said it was neither easy nor necessary to do so, since we had covered a variety of issues and the whole discussion existed on tape. He asked me whether I thought the discussion should be viewed from a particular angle. I said that I too needed to listen to the tapes. I had no further questions; I added that I now needed to look at their journal afresh in the light of what we had discussed, and to rethink and reevaluate my earlier views. Half-jokingly, the editor said:

SZM: Apparently, your judgment is that our perspective is androcentric!

ZMH: After all, you can't escape your gender! You're a man and I'm a woman—here, at least, I think there's no disagreement between us! I believe men's and women's dispositions differ to some degree. Many feminists, many women don't accept this. I think women's view of the world is different; of course, that's no reason to say one is superior to the other, but the simple fact is, our social conditions and experiences are quite different.

Obviously my earlier remark, which nearly ended the discussion, had touched the same raw nerve as my very first question, two months earlier, about men producing a women's journal, and raised the same issues we had started with. Now, surprisingly, both men began to talk about their own personal views, and offered a new defense of feqh and its practitioners. The following exchanges—understandably omitted in the transcript—not only throw light on the clerical way of life and the way knowledge of feqh is depersonalized, but also help to explain how and why these clerics see themselves as women's guardians.

MHS: We consider it a duty to defend women. We note that sometimes, when talking with women, we're keener than they are in defending their rights. In our eagerness, perhaps at times we go to extremes.

SZM: This is how we feel about [defending women]; women sometimes don't believe or even accept how far we go.

MHS: This is at the level of theory; in practice, in our personal life, the same is true; personally, I pay great tribute [to my wife].

SZM: [jokingly] This is one of our objections to Mr. Sa'idi, that he takes his *"Payam-e Zan* policy" so far at home that the journal's work suffers. . . . So we find it unfair when we're accused of being men and having a male point of view.

ZMH: It's not an accusation; it's a fact.

MHS: In the lives of ulama, one comes across some astonishing models; Ayatollah Musavi Ardabili [a high-ranking government cleric] talks about one of the ulama, who lives in Tehran, I believe, whose wife literally didn't move a finger in the house throughout their married life; he had no expectations of her. Sometimes expectations might not be articulated but implied; he did neither. That is, the [ulama] stick so close to [religious] laws that they tend to ignore customary norms, and don't even demand reciprocity in rights and duties. This is the practice of our ulama; but unfortunately society tends to see the negative side.

SZM: Excuse me: this came out at the start of our discussion; and it's a perception that also exists outside [the Houzeh]; of course, we're just debating here. It's really unfair that an entire scientific trend in feqh, and the thinking and practice of Jurists, should be questioned in such a way. It's unfair to say that the ulama, in deducing the terms of the shari'a and issuing their fatwas, were influenced unconsciously—some even say consciously— by their patriarchal worldview. This is most unfair. When we read about the life of the ulama, we see that their practice wasn't like this, that is, there's a great distance between what's in their fatwas and what they do in real life.

ZMH: Why? What's the distance for?

SZM: Distance in the sense that they say, "this is a right [waivable] not a Ruling [obligatory]; I forgo my right so that no injustice is done to my wife; I want to protect and defend her, I even take on her burden." If this is their practice, then how can it be said, regarding their methods of ejtehad, that their rulings are influenced by a hostile attitude to women? This is a gross injustice to feqh and the practice of the Jurists. I don't say that they haven't been subject to unconscious influences; after all, they weren't Prophets or Infallibles. It's possible to find [biases] in feqh, the influence of environment . . . but our entire feqh doesn't rest on this; it can't be said that Jurists in general had a gender bias and saw women as inferior, defective in reason, and so on. This is a real injustice to us; and our hearts burn that there should be such criticism, that we couldn't articulate our views and spread our message, that such criticism is allowed of the history and working of our feqh and our jurists.

I was baffled by what I was hearing; the two men now seemed to be arguing for a distinction between what Jurists say in their fatwas and what they do in their lives. Not only had they abandoned their holistic approach but they also indirectly negated their own assertion that feqh marital Rulings are not oppressive to women but are meant to induce conjugal harmony. If so, why value and praise the Jurists for not practicing them? But there was no way I could ask these things without creating another misunderstanding. But I wondered if the editor had taken my questions on feqh theories as echoing the concerns of *Zanan*, and perhaps that was why he became defensive and had effectively closed the door to debate throughout this session. To make it clear that I was not echoing anybody, but had my own opinions, I asked:

ZMH: Why do you think such views have come about? Is it a misunderstanding? Is it to do with negative propaganda? ... [pause] I don't, of course, share such perceptions, but from what you say it seems that they exist.

SZM: It's largely because what a Muslim does in the name of religion is considered to be what Islam says. Since the Jurists are the definers of Islam, people attribute action [outside Houzeh] to our jurists and the Houzeh. It's largely this; [turning to Saʿidi] can you think of anything else?

MHS: I'm not following—how did it come about in society or in scientific circles?

I took Mortazavi's double-edged response and Saʿidi's use of "scientifc circles" to be a reference to the recent events in the universities and the widening rift between the Islamic intellectuals and clergy.[17] Aware of the delicacy of the situation, I said that I was not concerned about "scientific circles" but with the populace and how such a [negative] perception of the clergy came about. To this, Saʿidi gave a long reply, pointing out the interplay of three factors: negative propaganda about clerics, which has colored popular perceptions; people's expectations of the clergy, who are constantly in the public eye and are often not expected to behave like other mortals; and finally, the misconduct of some clerics, reinforcing negative public stereotypes. This was another sore point I thought it wise to avoid, and I changed the topic to ask about their vision for their journal.

ZMH: May I pose a final, hypothetical question: how do you see your journal five or ten years from now? Your first issue came out four years

---

[17] See Chapter Seven.

ago; your journal is dynamic, responding to current issues; true, your perspective is fixed, but social issues are variable. Given your past experience and your goals, what sort of issues do see your journal addressing? What will the format and the pages of the journal look like in, say, five years' time?

SZM: We can't say, of course, how our journal will be in the future, but we can say how we'd like it to be; if we identify its weaknesses and say how we want to eradicate them, then it'll become clear. First, it must become more up-to-date; although you said we're in touch with current issues, I think our journal is far behind, if women's issues and problems are to be examined in a fundamental way. Even if we can't offer a solution, we must identify problems and show their importance. The journal is defective in this respect. Second, the research and scholarly side must be enhanced so that new answers can be provided for social questions such as polygamy, temporary marriage, and some of those you also raised; although not new in principle, the answers must be justified and explained in today's language.

I also have a personal wish, which comes from my conviction that Islamic Principles, Laws, and Rulings are in line with human nature and instincts as well as social needs. If we can introduce them in a language that people can understand, then they'll reach the conclusion themselves that this is what they really want. People now feel there's a gap between what Islam says and what they want, and this must be bridged. For instance, on the question of blood money that we discussed, if we probe and understand [its philosophy] we see that it provides an ideal solution and responds to society's needs. It's my personal wish to be able to communicate the teachings of our religion, the wisdoms we find in our sacred sources, in a langue that's meaningful to people of this age. I feel that sometimes we fail to do this, and for this reason I don't see our journal as successful and up-to-date.

Sa'idi also volunteered his vision. This too was abstract and idealistic, but couched in a "scientific" language. His gist was: the journal first needs to clarify its aims and define the ideal situation [for women]; then to look at the situation on the ground and find a good analysis of the nature and causes of changing realities; and finally to offer directives and solutions for women's situation, at both theoretical and practical levels, in line with the already defined ideal. To this Mortazavi added: "our readers find the journal commendable but we're not content."

I did not know what to say. I was touched by their conviction and sincerity, but I felt uneasy with their idealism and dogmatism. In a mumbled, halting sentence, I said:

ZMH: Insha'allah, you'll succeed in all your aims. . . . I hope you'll find answers, within an Islamic framework, for women's question and the problems that many women now experience.

Mortazavi thanked me and Sa'idzadeh and wished us success in our endeavors. An uneasy silence followed. On my part I was unhappy with the hesitancy of my last remarks: I had failed to express my appreciation of the important role the journal was playing in putting women's issues on the Houzeh agenda. Breaking the silence, I praised the latest issue once again, and asked Sa'idzadeh what his vision was for the journal. Mortazavi welcomed my move; and I repeated the question.

SZM: Mr. Sa'idzadeh, please speak without taqiyeh.

MHS: We'd better turn off the tape, so he'll find the courage.

SMS: The courage is there!

I asked Sa'idzadeh—seriously—whether he wanted the recorders off; he laughed and said: "leave them on, it's all right," and went on—his voice just audible on my tape:

SMS: From the moment it began its work until now, the journal has been successful regarding its content, its contributors, and its readers. Like Ms. Mir-Hosseini, I think the latest number is excellent; Allamah Tabataba'i's views are aired, there's also Mr. Akuchakian's article [see below].

ZMH: Also your [Mortazavi's] own editorial . . .

SMS: I agree; I particularly liked Mr. Akuchakian's article because of its realism, due to his participation in the Women's Conference in Beijing. I believe that at the beginning the journal was rather detached from real issues, was concerned with abstractions and didn't raise women's basic problem; but it's changing and progressing nicely. As I used to tell you [Mortazavi], I believe that if the issues are raised through free debates, without giving the impression that what the journal says is what Islam says, and allowing those who disagree with the journal's perspective to express their views, good results will come from such disagreements.

Only this part of Sa'idzadeh's answer is included in *Payam-e Zan*'s transcript. Taqiyeh once again got us out of deadlock, paradoxically enabling us to conclude our debate more meaningfully—and honestly. The fact that we could joke about it eased the tension. Thinking back, I realize that taqiyeh made the whole debate possible in the first place; its legitimacy enabled each of us to retain our integrity, to hold on to our convictions without having to express them fully, by allowing more to be implied than could be stated. Ironically, the new function of taqiyeh in the Islamic Republic, where the Shi'i establishment wields power, seems to be to conceal progressive ideas that might weaken its hold.

Sa'idzadeh made his view clear, but he allowed its thrust and force to be expressed by an article he "particularly liked" in the journal itself. This was "Lessons and Recollections: Notes and Thoughts on the World Women's

Conference in Beijing September 1995" by Ahmad Akuchakian, one of a new breed of clerics who bridge the gap between Houzeh and university. In his early thirties, and with a British Master's degree in Communication and Development, Akuchakian is a member of the Qom-based Research Group on Religious Thought and Development. In this capacity he was invited to join the Iranian delegation to the Beijing Women's Conference. I had met him only a week earlier, when Sa'idzadeh and I went to hear him speak in a gathering to celebrate Women's Day in Tehran University; he was delayed by a car accident on his way from Qom, and arrived too late to deliver his speech; but I had a brief discussion with him about the conference and his participation.[18]

In "Lessons and Recollections" Akuchakian begins with some background to the conference and the motivations of the Iranian delegation, then proceeds to assess critically the matters raised in the conference and the issues that arose: "Many of these issues are familiar, and have been addressed by our society and our thinkers; some are new and unfamiliar for both us and other nations. What is common in both types of issues is their urgency and the necessity for enlightened, realistic, and comprehensive solutions to them."

He argues, then, that such issues can no longer be simply ignored or dismissed as impertinent; rather, their universality and pertinence must be admitted. They cover various aspects of gender rights in law, family, and society, and their links with the development and prosperity of Muslim societies. The article ends by asking a number of questions: why have both centers of learning in Iran, Houzeh and university, failed to address women's issues and role in society in a fundamental and comprehensive way? Why has no alternative to traditional models emerged since the revolution? Why do women themselves ignore their own human and female value and lack the confidence to demand their rights in the family and to take part in social activities? Why and how are aspects of the culture that restrict women's sphere of activity justified by false reference to religion? Finally, what can be done to separate them and how can limitations placed on women in the name of religion be addressed? The final paragraph is a critical assessment, unusually explicit for *Payam-e Zan*, of ways in which women's issues have so far been approached: "The time has now come for us to think seriously about all these issues, and to admit that clarifying and interpreting them, and providing realistic, progressive, and comprehensive answers to them, are far more necessary than the kind of activities to which many organizations dealing with women have unfortunately given priority."[19]

---

[18] I had a follow-up interview with him in Qom the next day, as described below.

[19] Akuchakian 1995. The same number featured another report on the Beijing Conference (Shirazi 1995), which toed the official line, praised the Iranian delegation for their firm stance, and blamed others for their antagonism. Akuchakian's article continued for one more installment without being completed, whereas Shirazi's continued for another twelve, the last appearing in *Payam-e Zan* 56 (November 1996).

Sa'idzadeh invoked "Lessons and Recollections" because it said what he did not dare to say himself; this was his taqiyeh, as Mortazavi clearly understood.

SZM: I fully agree; [to start with] we want to publish these debates. In fact, provided that certain principles are respected, we're very much in favor of free debate, whatever the limitations. One question [Mir-Hosseini] asked early on was whether or not we practice taqiyeh. We don't do taqiyeh in what we say, but we might do taqiyeh in many things we don't say, to avoid putting the very basis of our work into question; we're mindful of current realities [Houzeh sensibilities, political imperatives]. . . . We regard some approaches as breaching "scientific ethics"; if I referred to Ms. Ebadi's article it was because, in my opinion, it breached the limits of scientific discussion. Once it comes to polemics, then nothing can be achieved; for instance, take this number of *Zanan*. Despite all their hard work, they sometimes deliberately confront and challenge current values. It's no longer scientific debate. Such confrontations should be avoided.

He was referring to *Zanan* 25, which had evoked strong reactions and controversy when it came out in late summer. It was challenging on at least three grounds. First, the leading article was a report on the World Women's Conference written "exclusively for *Zanan*" by Nayereh Tohidi, an Iranian academic based in the United States. Second, the cover featured an attractive portrait of filmmaker Rakhshan Bani-E'temad, wearing the latest fashion sunglasses and leaning on a camera, her hair only partly covered by a colored scarf. Finally, it contained several articles on the poet Forugh Farrokhzad (1935–1967), acclaiming her too as a filmmaker. In the Islamic Republic, Farrokhzad is the archetype of the "Islamically incorrect" woman: her poetry is strongly feminist and rich in sexual imagery, and her life has been seen as a symbol of decadence and all the "evils" of secular feminism.

Having followed these developments closely, I was anxious for *Zanan*'s survival, fearing that all these apparently well-orchestrated pressures might be a prelude to its closure. Being in contact with *Zanan*, I knew that number 25 was an act not of defiance, as Mortazavi put it, but of conviction: another phase in *Zanan*'s growing gender awareness, a new stance that had to be taken to broaden its readership and link with women both inside and outside the country, a token of its increasing tolerance and respect for women's achievements, whether religious or not. I could not resort to taqiyeh and keep quiet. I had to say something.

ZMH: But sometimes it's also necessary to challenge current values; I don't mean what *Zanan* is doing [is right or wrong], I mean it's necessary for someone to break the dam, to confront tradition. It has always been like this; look at the revolution itself: if the Imam had always acted and expressed his opinions within the bounds of "current conditions" [the Houzeh], the revolution would have got nowhere.

SZM: The Imam could do that; he said "Islam needs sacrifice, pray for me to be its sacrifice." He really could; but I must take my own situation into account and weigh the words I'm about to utter. I don't say we must always watch our step; if so, we have to say that the present situation is fine, and keep silent. I am saying that some people step beyond the bounds of the scientific domain, and one feels antagonism; and when the situation becomes hostile then nobody is prepared to have a scientific debate. I mentioned this in the last session, and I also said, outside the session [probably to Saʿidi] after the first one: "this debate looks like going in a scientific way, although we might be accused of having a male perspective." But with many others [*Zanan*] [scientific debate] is not possible; they say we're here to defend men, and they have a very negative and often nonscientific perception of us. I'm not suggesting that our work is extremely courageous or that we couldn't have done more; but there are matters that we must take into account, as the Imam said [on women's rights to divorce], "there are other considerations above these, and if I didn't fear them, I would have said [women can divorce themselves]." Otherwise, the essence of what we want to say will be lost and the service we want to render becomes impossible.

I was well aware of the ill-feeling between the two journals, but I had no idea that each knew exactly how the other viewed it. I still wondered why the journal was willing to debate with me, and why Mortazavi considered my approach "scientific" (*ʿelmi*), as they put it. Was it because I was able to speak their language? Because I agreed to debate within the feqh framework? Because they believed my good intentions? Because I showed understanding and appreciation of their work? My arguments on gender were basically similar to what he objected to in *Zanan*—but I had neither the political nor the religious credentials of women like those in *Zanan*.

Among women's journals in Iran, I made it clear that at present I saw only *Payam-Zan* and *Zanan*—in their different ways—as significant; I also gave them my frank assessment of other women's journals: some I considered to be less concerned with women's problems than with propagating their version of Islam, others were trying to find a niche in clerical and international arenas, while the government sought to appropriate the whole debate. They all, I thought—with the exception of *Zanan*—ended up in one way or another justifying the gender inequalities in feqh laws. I repeated that the first step to finding a solution for women's questions within an Islamic framework is to admit and recognize that there is a problem, not to continue with defensive and apologetic arguments. I asked again whether they could envisage any dialogue between the two journals. Mortazavi responded vaguely, and asked me which I thought more successful, their journal or *Zanan*.

ZMH: In the long run, I think you'll be more successful; but without *Zanan*, I think you wouldn't have such success.

SZM: Why?

ZMH: I think a journal like *Zanan* has great courage; it's true that it touches on raw nerves, but it also breaks many barriers. All this indirectly paves the way for you.

Mortazavi interrupted: "They pave the way for us?!" I tried to explain tactfully what I meant by "paving the way." I said that, since *Zanan* does not shy away from dealing with social realities, it touches on some sensitive issues; that *Payam-e Zan* then finds itself able to address these issues more effectively within the feqh domain. I did not add that otherwise *Payam-e Zan* would continue to deal with gender relations as they are constructed in feqh texts and Houzeh discourses; that *Payam-e Zan* owed its raison d'être to challenges raised by women whose voices are heard in *Zanan*, challenges that had impelled the Houzeh to launch a woman's magazine in the first place, to seek new answers for old questions. Sa'idi's and Mortazavi's responses seemed to take as evident what I had left unsaid:

MHS: The task usually has two phases; questioning the present situation, and offering solutions. Sometimes, someone questions the situation quite well, attacks it forcefully, but offers solutions which may be no improvement; that is, they jump from the frying pan into the fire. Sometimes, someone raises issues in a wise and measured way, but if one has nothing better to offer one should refrain from questioning the present situation. You ask why our journal doesn't take a more critical stance. Because attacking and questioning aren't enough to solve problems; they merely create a cultural vacuum and Doubt, and the space opened up will be filled with false ideas. So one must be more rational in questioning the present situation; we see that shari'a laws didn't repeal the laws of Jaheliyeh wholesale, but replaced them one by one.

As for cooperation between the presses, I think it's a good idea, but it needs strong motivation . . .

ZMH: Of course, it might never happen. If there's freedom, then different views and perspectives can be aired and coexist happily. What you say in your journal is not the last word, you're opening space, a debate; some might agree and some might disagree; but opening the debate itself is significant.

SZM: We see the situation as conducive to scientific debate; the way is open. After all, we clerics are used to disputation; but when these debates are extended into society, then more subtlety and caution are needed. That is, if we want to move from the present situation toward the ideal, we must define our path with more care and patience.

MHS: On what you said, a point came to my mind. Dr. Shariʿati raises an issue in one of his books—I suppose in his *Father, Mother, We Are Accused*—which I think is interesting. The book is about a young man who is critical of the ways [and religion] of his parent's generation. Shariʿati says the criticism is not very different from the defense; this young man's rejection of his parents' ideas and ways stems from the same premise as that on which his parents accept them. They have a single perspective; the only difference is that he attacks and his parents defend. Neither has a correct understanding [of Islam], and both are turning in the wrong orbit. We sometimes have the same problem in social debates, that the whole debate is premised on incorrect notions. In the first session, when you compared *Zanan* and *Payam-e Zan*, we said that in our view it's important to deal with the present situation in a rational way, not to insist on criticizing it or to justify and defend it but to evaluate it against a correct model and to validate that which is in line with the ideal and change that which is not.

SZM: In future, in the long term, basic change in women's situation can only come by adopting a route that's rational and religious and acceptable in our legislative circles; in other words, by the same route that you say imposes restrictions on women, that is, in the name of religion and feqh. These restrictions can be removed only by the same way they are instituted; not by attacking, but by offering alternatives. The impact of this route is long-term and quite different from taking a purely critical stance. Not only *Payam-e Zan*, but any organization that wants to succeed in any cultural and scientific issue, not just the women's question, has no option but to follow such a rational route with patience and tolerance. We see it as our duty to adopt such an approach, although we think we've succeeded only partially, 10 to 20 percent.

On this note our discussion ended. We then talked about how it would appear in the journal. I said I hoped they would preserve the give-and-take so as to show how issues had developed. Mortavazi said they would publish it as a dialogue, but tidied up: they would smooth out repetitions and introduce a thematic order; for instance, all parts relating to the journal itself in our first and final sessions would be grouped together. He then suggested having photographs to accompany the transcript. I said we should take them sitting around the table, to show us debating. Mortazavi said he wanted to be left out; when I asked why, he merely said he wanted to be excused. I persisted, but he would not give a straightforward reason. Finally I said, either we had a picture showing all of us, or I too would remain faceless. Saʿidzadeh told me later that the editor's excuse was that he did not want to take credit for himself: another token of his modesty and self-sacrifice. I did not say that I had my own reasons for not wanting to appear in a photograph alone in *Payam-e Zan*. This was my taqiyeh, and I now understood its value.

A Second Visit to the Shrine

I stayed in Qom for two more days; I needed to complete my tour of the bookshops and Sa'idzadeh had made two more appointments for me, one with Ahmad Akuchakian, the cleric whose article Sa'idzadeh "particularly liked," and the other with a woman teacher from al-Zahra College. Only the first interview materialized. Sa'idzadeh found me a hired car and a driver for those two days, and I went to Akuchakian's house with Ali and Zahra; Sa'idzadeh was not present during the discussion. I remember little of the house, other than that it was unusually modern. Akuchakian received us in his study; it was the only time in Qom that I talked to a cleric at home with him behind a desk and myself on a sofa; all other times we sat on the floor. He looked and sounded rather like Sa'idi; young, wearing a clerical robe, talking a language full of social science jargon.

Early the following morning we went to Hazrat-e Ma'sumeh's shrine; Sa'id-zadeh suggested that I could hear the lessons of Ayatollah Vahid Khorasani, who held his classes in a room in the shrine complex. As we came up, a couple of families who had just arrived, or perhaps had spent the night in the shrine, were finishing breakfast on the wide veranda connecting a row of large rooms, whose name in blue tiles read "House of Study" (*Dar ol-Ta'lim*). I looked inside: it was huge, covered with carpets, with a pulpit at the far end; about fifty men were seated facing the pulpit, mostly in clerical robes. Zahra and I positioned ourselves on the veranda at the point nearest to the room, while Sa'idzadeh and Ali went inside.

When the lesson was about to begin, I could see through the open door that the room was getting fuller; boys as young as seven were coming and going. A khadem appeared, to clear away people who were eating on the veranda. As Zahra and I ignored him and sat on, he returned to tell us to leave; I told him we wanted to hear the lesson inside. He looked shocked, mumbling that this was not the place for women. We still did not move; after a while he came back, and this time shouted at us to clear off, his voice full of contempt. I lost my temper and shouted back. I can't remember exactly what I said, but it was to the effect: "Who are you to tell us clear off from a place that belongs to a woman, to my ancestor, Hazrat-e Ma'sumeh? If you're her khadem, you're here to serve her visitors. If there's a school here, it's because she prayed and sanctified this spot. We're both Seyyeds; her father's inside, taking notes for me. I'm a scholar myself; who are you to tell me I can't sit here and listen to a religious class?" I was astonished by my voice and my rage, and I am now ashamed that I boasted about my status as a Seyyed and a scholar. But it worked: the khadem apologized and left us in peace.

I was now so angry that I could not hear anything; I could not contain myself, I had to move, to do something. We got up and left. Zahra was impressed that I had told a khadem off. She had never seen a khadem apologizing to a woman. Shrine khadems are notorious bullies; I myself saw them many times insulting women, not permitting them to enter the complex because their hejab was faulty, or being rude and contemptuous to poor old women who spent most of the day inside.

I relate this incident because it was then that I realized how far I had come during my engagements with the editors of *Payam-e Zan*. As in the shrine, I was no longer just an observer; I had finally made a break from the personal detachment so firmly instilled in me by my 1970s social science training. I was putting my status and my education to use, and at the same time I had learned to use both my Islamic and my feminist identities to challenge authority and change a situation I could not accept.

That was my last visit to Qom in 1995. A week later I flew back to London—and lost my notes.

Payam-e Zan in 1997

In February 1997 I went back to *Payam-e Zan*. I had written to Mortazavi from London, thanking him for publishing our debate, and telling him I was using it as material for a book I was writing. I telephoned him on my arrival to say I was coming to Qom, but we did not fix a time, and when we arrived, neither Mortazavi nor Sa'idi was there. Sa'idzadeh stayed with the "brothers," while the old caretaker who used to serve tea ushered Zahra and me into the "sisters'" section. We went through the curtained door, which by now had become for me a symbol of both connection and separation, a passage and a barrier. The "sisters" remembered me well; they had transcribed the tapes and typed them out. I asked what they thought of them: whose position did they agree with, mine or the magazine's? But it was clear they had not engaged with either. Perhaps the discussion was too "scientific," as *Payam-e Zan* put it.

When Mortazavi arrived, the old man's wife took Zahra and me back to the other side—I now appreciated how privileged I was to be able to move so easily between the two sides. We exchanged news and discussed the aftermath of our debate. I told him about the publication of extracts by *Nimruz*, resulting in my being denounced by some Iranian opposition women in Paris who saw the debate as legitimating the Islamic Republic, and who objected that I had no right to talk to clerics about women's rights in Iran, that I was incapable of challenging them properly and exposing them. I also mentioned that the periodical *Sobh* had made allusion to our debate in one of its regular denunciations of "feminism," when it produced a quotation from an Arabic journal which, in a discussion of feminism in Iran, mentioned the interest of Qom clerics in the issue.[20]

---

[20] *Sobh* (Morning), now a monthly, started as a weekly in 1995. The editor, Mehdi Nasiri, a former editor of *Kayhan*, is still a scourge of Modernists and a major critic of the feminist line taken by *Zanan*.

Mortazavi said that last year, after our debate, *Payam-e Zan* had decided to hold further such "roundtables," beginning with three eminent Houzeh teachers. They had started printing the one with Ayatollah Amini (a high-powered cleric, secretary to the Council of Experts) on ethical aspects of gender relations and family in Islam; they intended to discuss legal and theological dimensions with Ayatollahs Sane'i and Javadi-Amoli, respectively. He said that, after a year and a half's work, he had just finished a redaction with commentary of Ayatollah Sane'i's advanced lessons on the Book of Divorce; the book—in Arabic and six hundred pages long—was not yet published, since the ayatollah wanted to add further points. So far Sane'i had completed three other Books: Maintenance, Marriage, and Inheritance, the last finished just this Ramadan. He also mentioned that Ayatollah Sane'i had praised him in the presence of his classmates for the paper he had submitted to a meeting to commemorate the five hundredth anniversary of Moqaddes Ardabili, an eminent Shi'i jurist who argued that there there is not enough proof to support the feqh ban on women's judgment. The first installment of the paper had appeared in the latest issue of *Payam-e Zan* (59), making a strong case for women's right to serve as judges. He added that they had begun to cover Majles debates on bills relating to women, starting with the one proposing that dower (*mahr*) be revalued on divorce to take account of inflation since the time of marriage, however long ago. Now he saw the importance of lobbying politicians and Majles representatives, and considered the journal's mission fulfilled if it could correct the perceptions of a few of them.

I agreed and congratulated him on his article on women's judgment, but did not comment on the interview with Ayatollah Amini, which I had found amusing as it covered just the questions that Mortazavi had found offensive to feqh when I had raised them. I did ask him why he had been so hostile in the last session of our debate. He denied having been hostile; but I had just finished transcribing the tape and insisted that at times his tone was really abrupt and unfriendly. He protested that it had been a debate, but hinted that perhaps my questions had been rather intrusive. By now I had a greater appreciation of how far—in Islam as elsewhere—power and authority define knowledge, the right to interpret the sacred texts.

Without commenting on the omissions, additions, or changes of order in *Payam-e Zan's* transcript, I told Mortazavi that my account of the discussions kept to the order in which the issues were raised and tried to contextualize them. I also told him that in the process of translating the transcripts, I came to realize the main common ground we shared: we both approached women in Islam in terms of their social, not their sexual roles—which had been the focus of previous literature. Though we often talked across each other, and little got resolved, the fact that we could sustain a debate showed that dialogue was possible, not just between different disciplines but between two contrary points of view.

Part Three

THE MODERNISTS:
TOWARD GENDER EQUALITY

Introduction to Part Three _____

THE WIDENING GULF between the Islamic Republic's ideals and rhetoric and its policies for dealing with social reality has gradually brought about an awareness that the mere establishment of an Islamic state is not a solution to all problems. Unlike the clerics whose views on gender we have examined so far, other thinkers are prepared to go beyond old feqh wisdoms in search of new answers for new questions. They are part of a modernist and reformist current that remained dormant during the years of war with Iraq (1980–1988)—now referred to as the First Republic. Their reemergence, which coincided with Ayatollah Khomeini's death, is marked by increased tensions between different visions of Islam.

These "Modernists" include clerics, laymen, and laywomen, and display a refreshing pragmatic vigor and a willingess to engage with nonreligious perspectives.[1] Some inherited the notions of Islam that Ali Shari'ati made so appealing to the youth in pre-revolutionary Iran, often described as "Islam without the clergy." Others subscribe to the views of modernist clerics such as Ayatollah Motahhari, who advocated reforming the clerical establishment. They no longer reject an idea simply because it is Western, nor do they see Islam as a blueprint with a built-in, fixed program of action for the social, economic, and political problems of the Muslim world. They argue that the human understanding of Islam is flexible, that Islam's tenets can be interpreted to encourage pluralism and democracy, that Islam allows change in the face of time, space, or experience. Debates stemming from their ideas are now aired in a variety of journals and periodicals, some of which are close to the Houzeh or the government.[2] Some modernist clerics whose writings appear regularly in the press, such as Mojtahed Shabestari, Hojjati Kermani, and Mohsen Kadivar, show a genuine willingness to reassess old positions and a tolerance for alternative views.

Yet nearly twenty years into the Islamic Republic, no influential male Modernist—whether cleric or layman—has yet seriously addressed the issue of gender in Islam. If the Neo-Traditionalists are still under the spell of Motahhari's text, as I suggested earlier, Modernists seem to be equally mesmerized by Shari'ati's seminal *Fatemeh Fatemeh ast* (Fatima Is Fatima), which embodied the religious intellectuals' approach to women's questions on the eve

---

[1] See Boroujerdi 1994; Cooper 1998; Schirazi 1997, Part 4; Yavari-d'Hellencourt 1995.

[2] For instance, *Naqd va Nazar* (Critique and View), *Houzeh va Daneshgah* (Seminaries and Universities), *Kayhan-e Andisheh* (Intellectual Kayhan), *Nameh-ye Farhang* (Cultural Letter).

of the revolution.[3] Their silence today, or perhaps the absence of an alternative, suggests that Shari'ati's text remains uncontested for them.

Fatima Is Fatima is an edited version of a public lecture delivered in April 1971 in the Hoseiniyeh Ershad, a celebrated religious institution that became a center of religious opposition to the Pahlavis during the 1960s and 1970s. The text can be divided into two parts. In the first (pp. 6–108), Shari'ati examines the "women's question" and the dilemmas that Muslim women face in this century. He criticizes both Muslim women who unquestioningly accept their traditional role, and modern, Westernized women who, by aping the West, become mindless consumers. He sees the latter as a new form of humanity—"woman is a human being who shops"—and blames the colonial policies of the West. Having understood women's pivotal role in maintaining the fabric of Islamic societies, the West set out to alienate them from Islam so that Muslims could be dominated. But Muslim men and the narrow-minded clergy, who continued to misrepresent Islam, are equally to blame: they also conspired to deny Muslim women their truly Islamic rights. Educated women, denied their humanity, were left with little option but to look to the West.

In the second part (pp. 108–205), Shari'ati discusses the solution to be found in the person of Fatima: daughter of the Prophet, wife of Ali, and mother of Hasan and Hosein. The picture he draws of Fatima's life is romanticized but rather gloomy: more than offering a clear and tangible model for emulation, it epitomizes Shi'i ideals of silent suffering and covert defiance. As he has it, Fatima died of grief at the injustice following her father's death—when Ali was denied his right to the caliphate—at having her patrimony taken from her, and at her failure to gain support for Ali's claim.

The text ends without providing a coherent answer to the crucial question Shari'ati considered to be facing Iranian women of the 1970s. His rhetorical style and revolutionary tone arouse the emotions without seriously examining the question of women in Islam, a subject dealt with directly on fewer than ten of the two hundred pages; and even there, Shari'ati neither elaborates on women's position in shari'a nor does he engage with proponents of shari'a discourses on women. Instead he uses the occasion to elaborate his own interpretation of Shi'i history, to condemn those in power for distorting it, to denounce Iranian society as one of pseudo-Muslims whose ways have little resemblance to true Islam, and to blame clergy and intellectuals alike for not enlightening people on true Islam. Although he criticizes narrow interpretations of the shari'a, he remains imprecise and evasive himself. He offers no concrete solution, only a romanticized revolutionary vision; not surprisingly,

[3] The text has been translated into English, and has received attention in the literature, see e.g., Ferdows 1983; Hermansen 1983; Yeganeh 1982, 46–51; and Yeganeh and Keddie 1986, 127–30. For a sample of his lectures in English, see Shari'ati 1979; on his ideas and their role in the revolution, see Dabashi 1993, 102–46; on his life and his influence, see Rahnema 1994.

his book was eclipsed with the establishment of the Islamic Republic, which adopted Motahhari's text with its feqh arguments.

In the final part of this book, I examine the approaches and ideas of two scholars who have recognized the need for a breakthrough in feqh theories on gender. Chapter Seven deals with lectures on women by Abdolkarim Sorush, who has become the most prominent of the new wave of Islamic modernists in Iran. Although he is not a cleric, nor can he be regarded as an exponent of gender equality, I decided to devote a chapter to his ideas for two main reasons. First, his approach to sacred texts has not only enabled women in *Zanan* to frame their demands within an Islamic framework, but has also encouraged clerics for whom gender has become a "problem" to address it from within a feqh framework. Second, it is in response to the challenge implicit in Sorush's ideas that some clerics have had to admit that their understanding of the shariʿa is subject to change and that they must find new arguments in feqh, or else they must abandon the claim to rule in the name of feqh. Although in 1995 no Houzeh cleric could admit it, all were in some way or another affected by the ways in which Sorush's ideas undermined the very basis of their exclusive right to religious authority. In spring 1996 Sorush came to England for a lecture tour; I started to attend his lectures and had an extended discussion with him. Hearing him in person, and seeing the reaction of students to him, I was further convinced to devote a chapter to his views.

Chapter Eight deals with work of Hojjat ol-Eslam Seyyed Mohsen Saʿid-zadeh—the most vocal clerical proponent of gender equality. His articles in *Zanan* provided the impetus for my research, and the reader will have been aware of his presence throughout the book. He entered briefly in the Prologue; he introduced me to Ayatollah Madani (Chapter One) and to the clerics in *Payam-e Zan* (Chapters Three to Six), and it was his critique that persuaded me to read Ayatollah Azari-Qomi's work on women (Chapter Two).

I could find no other cleric with similarly radical ideas on gender. Other prominent clerics—such as Fahim-Kermani, Salehi-Najafabadi, and Musavi-Bojnurdi—approach gender in Islam more or less from the same premises as *Payam-e Zan* and do not challenge "nature theory." The most prolific among them is Ayatollah Musavi-Bojnurdi, member of the Legal High Commission when family law was revised soon after the revolution, now an influential adviser to the Majles on family law and a regular participant in conferences. In his fifties, Ayatollah Bojnurdi has bases in both Houzeh and university, where he taught law and philosophy. Interviews with him have been a regular feature in the women's journal *Zan-e Ruz*, which continues to echo the official discourse on women. His views also have been aired in two other women's journals close to government, namely *Neda* (published by the Women's Society of the Islamic Republic of Iran, headed by Ayatollah Khomeini's daughter Zahra Mostafavi), and *Farzaneh* (the first women's studies journal in Iran, whose director, Massoumeh Ebtekar, became the first woman minister in Khatami's government). In *Neda*, Bojnurdi recently addressed the expansion of feqh grounds for restricting men's right to unilateral divorce, and in *Farzaneh*, the compatibility between feqh and human rights.[4]

Given the theme of these interviews, and that Ayatollah Musavi-Bojnurdi was more outspoken than before, I thought of devoting a chapter in this book to his views. Back in Tehran in January 1997, I went to meet him in his house. The meeting was arranged by the editor of *Farzaneh*. I learned that he had studied in Najaf, was Ayatollah Khomeini's student, and came to Iran at the time of the revolution; Ayatollah Khomeini sanctioned his ejtehad in 1981. He visited England several times. I showed him the copy of *Neda* that contained the interview with him about feqh grounds for divorce, and tried to engage him in discussion, but he was reluctant to talk about the assumptions behind feqh rulings, referring me to his interviews in *Zan-e Ruz*, which I knew well. His views were progressive, but I could find no real argument: I made the mistake of saying that they read to me like a mélange of *Payam-e Zan*'s and Ayatollah Ebrahim Jannati's positions. This did not help our discussion: later I learned that he and Jannati had both been in Najaf and were rivals. I tape-recorded our discussion but decided not to use it since it did not shed any new light on the issue of gender equality.

[4] Musavi-Bojnurdi 1996a and 1996b; see also Fahim-Kermani 1992 and 1995, and Salehi-Najafabadi 1996.

7

Challenges and Complicities:
Abdolkarim Sorush and Gender

I BEGAN STUDYING the works of Abdolkarim Sorush in autumn 1995, after the second of my debates with *Payam-e Zan*, and following the disruption of his lectures by the Ansar-e Hezbollah, "helpers of Hezbollah."[1] On 11 October, Sorush was invited by the Islamic Students Society to address a meeting in Tehran University; as he began his lecture, he was attacked and injured by about a hundred youths from off campus, members of Ansar. Their leader, in a debut public speech, claimed that Sorush's ideas were subversive to Islam and undermined the velayat-e faqih, vowed that he would no longer be allowed to disseminate them, and demanded a public debate with him. Another meeting at which Sorush was to speak had been disrupted in a similar manner in Isfahan University in June. On both occasions, the authorities had ignored student warnings. Press coverage was polarized: some papers condemned the attacks as blatant violations of constitutional rights to freedom of thought and speech; others applauded the legitimate right of Hezbollah to intervene if necessary.

Abdolkarim Sorush is perhaps the most influential and controversial thinker the Islamic Republic has so far produced. In the early years, his lectures were broadcast regularly on national radio and television; I remember watching him in television debates with secular and leftist intellectuals, using Islamic mystical and philosophical arguments to demolish Marxist dogmas. I was curious to find out for myself what it was in Sorush's ideas that now, sixteen years into the Islamic Republic, put him on the other side of the fence and enabled women like those in *Zanan* to reconcile their faith with their feminism.

As I made my way through Sorush's vast corpus of publications—over twenty books—I could see why and how his ideas created such varied passions and reactions. He is a subtle and original thinker, who has found a new language and frame of analysis to reexamine hallowed concepts. He approaches sacred texts by reintroducing the element of rationality that has been part of Shiʿi thought, and enabling his audience to be critical without compromising

---

[1] A group of religious and political zealots who emerged in the spring of 1995, becoming prominent through their violent disruptions of Sorush's lectures. The group is small in numbers but reportedly enjoys the support of Ayatollah Ahmad Jannati (a member of the Council of Guardians) and has links with the Revolutionary Guards and the Ministry of Information (Intelligence).

their faith. He is making it legitimate to pose questions that previously only the ulama could ask.

I could see some interesting parallels and differences between Sorush and Shari'ati. Both have been immensely popular with the youth, distrusted and opposed by the clerical establishment, and dismissed by secular intellectuals as lightweights. But their visions and conceptions of Islam are fundamentally different. For Shari'ati, the most important dimension in Islam was political; he sought to turn Islam into an ideology, to galvanize revolutionaries, and to change society. For Sorush, on the other hand, Islam is, as he puts it, "sturdier than ideology"; all his thinking and writing are aimed at separating the two.

Abdolkarim Sorush is the pen name of Hosein Dabbagh, born in 1945 in a pious but nonclerical family in southern Tehran.[2] Sorush was among the first graduates of Alavi High School, established by a group of pious bazaaris in the late 1950s with a curriculum integrating modern sciences with traditional religious studies. He then studied pharmacology at Tehran University and, after completing his military service in 1972, he went to England to continue his studies. Obtaining a Master's degree in analytical chemistry from London University, he went on to study history and philosophy of science at Chelsea College. While in London, he joined a group of Iranian Muslim students who held meetings in a building in West London,[3] where Shari'ati's funeral service was held and where Ayatollah Motahhari spoke when he came to London. Sorush was close to both men, and was a regular speaker there. He returned to Iran just as the Pahlavi regime was about to collapse.

In 1981 Sorush became one of seven members of the Council for Cultural Revolution, appointed by Ayatollah Khomeini when the universities were closed in order to contain the students and to eliminate leftist groups from the campuses. The council's task was to oversee the Islamization of higher education and to prepare the ground for the re-opening of the universities. This occurred in 1983, after a massive ideological purge of students and teachers; and Sorush started teaching philosophy of science in Tehran University. Not longer after, he resigned from the council, disagreeing with the direction it was going.[4] Since then he has held no official position within the ruling system of the Islamic Republic, although his lectures continued to be broadcast until the late 1980s and he remained close to centers of power, acting as adviser to several government bodies until the early 1990s.

[2] For details and dates, I have relied on "A Biography of Dr. Abdol Karim Soroush" dated July 1996, available at "Seraj Homepage," a website "dedicated to coverage and analysis of his ideas": www.seraj.org.

[3] After the revolution the Iranian government bought the building (*imam-bareh*); it is now called Kanun-e Touhid (Center of Unity) and is run by students closely linked to the Iranian ruling establishment.

[4] In an April 1997 interview with the Seraj website, Sorush responds to criticism about his role in the cultural revolution, which is a sore point and a major reason why he is rejected by secular intellectuals.

In 1984 Sorush began teaching courses in philosophy of religion (known as modern theology), comparative philosophy, and mysticism to both university students in Tehran and Houzeh students in Qom. In 1988, he started a series of weekly lectures in Imam Sadeq Mosque in north Tehran, on *Nahj ol-Balagheh*, the collection of Imam Ali's sermons and hadith. In the early audiences were members of the political and religious elite, including some government ministers. By autumn 1994, when the lectures were suspended, the audience was different: younger, and largely students. Not only had Sorush acquired a following among students who found his ideas and approach intrinsically appealing but he was beginning to set the tone for more public debates.

Disruption of his lectures began in April 1995, after the publication in *Kiyan* of his lecture "Liberty and the Clergy." He argues there that the clergy as a group functions as a guild, with religion as their source of livelihood, which limits both their own freedom in interpretation and that of others.[5] This article was denounced as "subversive to Islam," and brought the Hezbollah back to campus.[6] After the attack in Isfahan in June, a letter of protest signed by 104 writers and university teachers was sent to the president of the Islamic Republic.[7] With the emergence of the Ansar following the October incident in Tehran University, Sorush was no longer able even to give his regular university lectures. The showdown came in the spring of 1996. He wrote an open letter to the president, calling on him to "remove this rot" and to ensure freedom of speech and thought.[8] But to no avail. In mid-May, Ansar members surrounded Amir Kabir University in Tehran, where Sorush was due to talk in a meeting to mark the anniversary of Ayatollah Motahhari's death. Clashes ensued between the students and Ansar, arrests were made on both sides, and Sorush sent a message announcing his withdrawal. Soon after, unable to teach and fearing for his life, he went abroad on a lecture tour, not returning until April 1997.

As with Shari'ati, most of Sorush's writings are edited texts of public lectures, delivered in a variety of forums. If read chronologically, these volumes reveal the development of not only his ideas but his relationship with the Islamic Republic. Up to 1983 they mostly constitute a critique of the leftist ideologies espoused by Iranian intellectuals and groups then politically active.[9] After 1983, Sorush's writings show his concern with themes in

---

[5] Sorush 1995b.

[6] Another spur to the disruption was probably Robin Wright's article calling Sorush the "Luther of Islam"; "An Iranian Luther Shakes the Foundations of Islam," *Guardian*, 1 February 1995 [reproduced from the *Los Angeles Times*].

[7] *Kiyan* 25 (1995): 61.

[8] For the English text see "Seraj Homepage."

[9] For a list, see ibid., "Publications of Dr. Soroush"; in the Bibliography I have given the date of the first edition (when available). Some were written in England, including a book called *The Dynamic Nature of the World*, in which he expands on Molla Sadra's idea of "quintessential motion" to develop a philosophical approach to two fundamental tenets of Islam: Unity and Resurrection. Ayatollah Khomeini read this book on Ayatollah Motahhari's advice, praising it when he saw Sorush in Paris before taking power in Iran (Sorush 1994f., preface, p. 29).

philosophy and epistemology. They include translations of English books on philosophy,[10] a volume of collected essays and lectures on ethics and human sciences,[11] as well as several articles in cultural periodicals.

The breakthrough in his work came with his seminal articles on the historicity and relativity of religious knowledge, "The Theoretical Expansion and Contraction of the Shari'a."[12] These articles—in which Sorush distinguished religion from religious knowledge, arguing that whereas the first was sacred and immutable, the latter was human and evolved in time as a result of forces external to religion itself—appeared intermittently between 1988 and 1990 in the quarterly *Kayhan-e Farhangi*, published by the Kayhan Publishing Institute, which had come under the control of the Islamic faction shortly after the revolution. The heated debate that followed the publication of these articles led to a kind of intellectual coup and the birth of an independent journal, *Kiyan* (Foundation) in October 1991.[13] Sorush's writings form the centerpiece in each issue of *Kiyan*; they reveal the concerns and thinking of a deeply religious man who is becoming increasingly disillusioned by the domination in the Islamic Republic of what he calls "feqh-based Islam."[14]

This began a new phase in Sorush's writings, comprising volumes of collected essays, largely published originally in *Kiyan*; most are edited texts of lectures and talks delivered in universities and mosques in which he expands his epistemological arguments to develop a critique of government ideology and policies of the Islamic Republic and to argue for democracy and pluralism on religious grounds. Each volume bears the title of one of the essays, and has gone through several editions and impressions.

In the vast amount of his published work I could find nothing on women, apart from two paragraphs, both merely asides commenting on the incongruity between texts taught in the seminaries and the current state of knowledge and worldviews.[15] So I looked for his unpublished work, and acquired recordings of two lectures in which he had addressed the issue of women, both of them in the series on *Nahj ol-Balagheh*. The first was delivered in Imam Sadeq Mosque in January 1989; Sorush used the occasion of Women's Day to com-

---

[10] Such as Alan Ryan's *The Philosophy of the Social Sciences*; E. A. Burt's *Metaphysical Foundations of Modern Physical Sciences*, D. Little's *Varieties of Explanation in Social Sciences*.

[11] Sorush 1994a; the volume also contains the texts of lectures delivered on two successive anniversaries of the formation of the Cultural Revolution Commitee, June 1981 and 1982.

[12] Published in book form in 1991; by 1994 it had gone through three editions, selling over 20,000 copies; Sorush 1994d.

[13] For the emergence of the independent press, see Yavari-d'Hellencourt 1995. In 1995, *Zanan* shared premises with *Kiyan*, in both senses: office space and intellectual orientation. In 1997 *Zanan* moved to new premises, and its gender position came to be viewed critically by *Kiyan*. See Mir-Hosseini 1996c.

[14] For his political thought, see Vakili 1996 and Wright 1996; for his contribution to modern Islamic discourse, see Boroujerdi 1994 and 1996, Cooper 1998, and Matin-asgari 1997.

[15] Sorush 1994d, 81–83 and 1994e, 39.

ment on Imam Ali's harsh views on women, contained in a sermon delivered after the Battle of the Camel, led by Ayesha, the Prophet's widow; it reads:

O people! Women are deficient in Faith, deficient in shares and deficient in intelligence. As regards the deficiency in their Faith, it is their abstention from prayers and fasting during their menstrual periods. As regards deficiency in their intelligence it is because the evidence of two women is equal to that of a man. As for the deficiency in their shares that is because of their share in inheritance being half of men. So beware of the evils of women. Be on your guard even from those of them who are (reportedly) good. Do not obey them even in good things so that they may not attract you to evils.[16]

As Sorush recited and translated the sermon, some women in the audience—as in all mosques, the women's section was curtained off from the men's, where Sorush was speaking—cried out in protest, to be promptly silenced by a man shouting: "it's the Imam's words the Doctor is quoting: do you object even to them?"[17] But the protests continued and only stopped when Sorush asked to be allowed to finish his commentary and explain. His commentary, however, betrayed his ambivalence on the issue of women in Islam, and also suggested that he was not prepared for such a reaction, nor for a man to shout the women down. He had intended to confine his discussion of women to one session, but the reaction persuaded him to continue the following week. He repeated and elaborated the content of the discussion in his second lecture, and I shall discuss his views in that context.

The second lecture was delivered in Isa Vazir Mosque in Central Tehran in 1992, as part of an extended commentary on Imam Ali's letter to his son, known as the Will, the closing sentences of which contain the Imam's advice to his son about women. Again Sorush had intended to devote only one session to the theme of women and gender relations, but at his audience's request he continued for four more sessions. Although he was more explicit in his views, and expanded on what he had said in 1989, his position on gender, and the thrust of his arguments, remained the same. In 1995, *Zanan* gave me an abridged transcript of the 1992 sessions, prepared earlier for publication as "The Perspective of the Past on Women"; but they never carried the article and, so far, neither lecture has appeared in print.[18]

The main part of this chapter consists of selected passages from the 1992 sessions, which touch directly on gender and reveal Sorush's perspective. I

---

[16] *Nahj ol-Balagheh*, Sermon 78, pp. 150–52; for the event, see footnote comments by editor; see also Abbott 1942a, and Spellberg 1991.

[17] I later asked Sorush who the man had been. He said he was sitting close by but he thought it was the first time he had come to the mosque. He had asked Sorush to talk to his son, who had a number of questions to ask, but he never came again.

[18] Earlier parts of his commentary on the Imam's Will have appeared in Sorush 1995c and 1997a. Perhaps later volumes will include the texts of his lectures on women.

conclude with extracts from an interview with him in London in October 1996, when I was able to discuss the 1992 sessions with him, to ask about the audience, and raise my objections to his gender perspective.

The 1992 lecture was spread over five weekly sessions from 8 October to 5 November, each lasting nearly two hours. The audience of about one thousand, including many university students, was both more numerous and younger than that which attended his 1989 lecture. The sessions have an informal but uniform structure. On the tapes, as Sorush is speaking, one can hear children's voices, greetings by new arrivals, and so on. He begins each session with a short Arabic prayer, the same as in 1989 before his commentary on the *Nahj ol-Balagheh*, then summarizes the main points covered in the previous session, before reviewing and developing them further. When he has finished, there is a break, during which those who have questions submit them anonymously and in writing; the session ends with Sorush reading out and answering a selection of these questions.

Sorush is a gifted orator; his voice is calm and mesmerising. He talks without a script, and often without notes. I present a summary of each session, retaining the order in which he introduces his points and using his words as much as possible. There is a clear structure and purpose to each lecture, during which he takes his audience through layers of religious concepts and philosophical arguments, interjecting Koranic verses, hadith, and mystical poems. He does this knowledgeably, clearly, and honestly. His style and language are as important as what he has to say. His command of literature and his memory are formidable; he appears to know by heart the Koran, the *Nahj ol-Balagheh*, Rumi's *Mathnavi*, and Hafez's *Divan*.[19]

Sorush's Lectures on Women

From the opening summary, we gather that the previous session's theme was ethics and religion. Sorush repeats two points: that political ethics are separate from religious ethics, and that although religious ethics are primarily personal in nature, they can be a source for a sound political ethics. Imam Ali's letter to his son is one such source. Addressed to a future leader, it contains the Imam's advice on several political and social matters. Sorush recites and translates the closing sentences:

> Do not consult women because their view is weak and their determination is unstable. Cover their eyes by keeping them under veil because strictness of veiling keeps them [good]. Their coming out is not worse than your

[19] The first time I heard Sorush in person, in Imperial College, London, in May 1996, the large Iranian audience was electrified; later I attended his lectures on Rumi's *Mathnavi*, which he clearly knew by heart, talking without notes.

allowing an unreliable man to visit them. If you can manage that they should not know anyone other than [you,] do so. Do not allow a woman matters other than those about herself because a woman is a flower, not an administrator. Do not pay her regard beyond herself. Do not encourage her to intercede for others. Do not show suspicion out of place because this leads a correct woman to evil and a chaste woman to deflection.[20]

He continues:

> In an earlier discussion on *Nahj ol-Balagheh*, we said it contains words that are uncongenial to women, and infringe cultural notions and democratic values that have come to fill human societies in the past two centuries. For this reason, words that were once acceptable—that no commentator found forbidding to interpret or to justify—are now problematic. They demand a new interpretation or a new defense. Our forebears had no qualms in either interpreting or defending such words. . . . As such a position for women wasn't contested, no one doubted these words. . . . But today women—even men—don't accept or believe in such a position.
>
> *Nahj ol-Balagheh* contains two kinds of statements on women: those based on reasoning and those not. Taken at face value, both are offensive to women. Among the latter, for instance, is the Imam's address to the people of Basra after the Battle of the Camel. He says: "You were the army of a woman and in the command of a quadruped. When it grumbled you responded and when it was wounded you fled away."[21] Or: "As regards such and such woman, she is in the grip of womanly views while malice is boiling in her bosom like the furnace of the blacksmith."[22] Or: "Women is evil, all in all; and the worst of it is that one cannot do without her."[23] These statements contain no reasoning. But in other statements the Imam has reasoned; they include those famous ones: that women are deficient in belief, in reason, and in worldly gain, because they do not pray or fast during menses; the testimony of two women equals that of one man; and their share of inheritance is half a man's. In this part of the letter that we have recited, the Imam also advises his son not to consult women because their views are weak.
>
> Put together, these statements suggest that seeking women's advice and involving them in affairs of society should be avoided; that is, it's Muslim men's duty to keep their women secluded, to control them, and not to allow them a say. If we add feqh rulings, the picture that emerges is even more devastating for women. There's no denying that in an Islamic society women are granted fewer rights and fewer opportunities than men.
>
> If one of the ulama of a century ago could be reborn and see the conditions of our society and the women, undoubtedly he'd have a fright. Such a

---

[20] *Nahj ol-Balagheh*, pp. 434–35, Letter 31 (Will).
[21] Ibid., p. 81, Sermon 13.   [22] Ibid., p. 257, Sermon 154.   [23] Ibid., p. 539, Saying 235.

level of women's [public] presence—which isn't by any means ideal—
would be unthinkable for him. The very fact that it's now accepted that a
woman's presence in society doesn't violate her womanhood and Mus-
limhood is due to the immense changes that have occurred in the realms of
thought and practice; these have also found their way into our religious
consciousness and our society. Women's presence in society is now as natural and logical as their absence once was. This tells us the extent to which,
in our understanding and practice of religion, we act unconsciously and
involuntarily; this isn't to be taken negatively but in the sense that we're
guided by elements that aren't in our control. They do their work, shape our
lives, our minds, our language. . . .

You know, and I have already said, that there have been several reactions
to these hadith of the Imam and similar ones. These reactions are instructive,
too. Specific justifications have been made; for instance, some of our clerics
say that the Imam's comment on women's deficiencies was made after the
Battle of the Camel, and was due to the insidious role that Ayesha played in
it. Such hadith, they argue, refer only to Ayesha or women like her. Some
say the Imam uttered such words about women because he was upset and
angry. Neither argument works. We must remember that reason derives its
validity and universality from its own logic, not from what its user wishes
to impose on it. That is, once we contend that a certain hadith of the Imam
was influenced by anger or an event, then we have to admit the probability
that other emotions and events influenced other hadith. In that case, no
hadith can ever again be used in the sense that they have been so far. Likewise, we can't say this hadith referred only to Ayesha. Its logic and content
convey universality: it's not only Ayesha but all Muslim women who inherit
half a man's share, and so on. . . .

But the explanation we gave [in 1989] about those hadith of the Imam
that are based on reasoning was that once a hadith is based on reasoning then
it must be approached through its own reasoning. In fact, the credibility of
such a hadith is contingent on the force and validity of its reasoning, not on
the authority of its utterer. This has been our method in dealing with all
sacred texts. For instance, we read in the Koran: "If there had been in them
any gods but Allah, they would both have certainly been in a state of dis-
order" [Sura Anbia, 22]. This is a reasoning whose acceptance doesn't rest
on its being the word of God but on its force and soundness, so that it can
become a backbone for our thinking. . . .

One can take issue with the Imam's reasoning and say that if women
don't pray or don't fast at certain times [during menses], this isn't a token
of deficiency in their faith. It's in fact the very proof of their faith, as His
prophet tells them not to pray at such times. Obeying His prohibitions is like
obeying His commands. In God's eyes what matters is the spirit of an act,
not its form. . . . As to women's deficiency in material gain, it's true that

their share in inheritance is less, but this isn't proof that they're less than men and we can't conclude from it that women shouldn't be consulted, or assigned certain social and political status. No logical connection can be made here. If they inherit less, it's because they are told so.

Such an approach might work, of course, with ahadith based on reasoning. But what about the others that aren't? Our solution here is to say that these hadith are "pseudo-universal propositions" (as logicians have it); that is, they reveal the conditions of women of their time. In addition, since what an Imam or a sage says is in line with the society in which he lives, we need a reason to extend it to other epochs. . . . Here we're faced with two jurisprudential principles and positions: one holds that shari'a idioms—whether legal or ethical in nature—speak of societies of their time and thus we need a reason for extending them to other societies or times; and the other argues the opposite, that we need a reason *not* to apply such ahadith and Rulings to all other societies and times. These two positions can't be reached from the words [of sacred texts] but only when we examine them from outside and apply our own reasoning to them.

Contrary to the Imam's advice, today in the Islamic Republic women are consulted. As for women's entry into Parliament, the problem is theoretically resolved: women don't directly decide for Islamic society. Although it seems to me the ulama's thinking on the issue hasn't changed, since the argument put forward then against women's entry into Parliament was that the Prophet said that a society ruled by a woman is doomed.[24] Both Shi'i and Sunni ulama have argued that if women are in Parliament, their votes will be counted among the rest and thus they can influence the passing of a bill, which is a kind of velayat for women, although it isn't personal. At present, as you know, in our country the Majles is [only] the adviser of the vali-ye faqih. The notion of legislation as understood in other parts of the world doesn't exist in our country; that is, the Majles doesn't have an independent view, and the vali-ye faqih can alter its decisions or act counter to them. So you could argue that women's presence in Parliament doesn't contradict the Prophet's hadith. It bans women from velayat, which at present only the vali-ye faqih exercises. But what about the ban on consulting women? As far as I remember, before the revolution when the Houzeh opposed women's entry to the Parliament, they made no reference to such arguments or ahadith, either because they didn't find them acceptable or [they didn't think it] suitable to invoke them.

Anyway, these words exist in *Nahj ol-Balagheh*, and solutions must be sought for them, and the search for solutions, as I said already, is decisive

[24] The hadith reads, "the people who elect a woman to leadership, or entrust the running (*velayat*) of their affairs to a woman, will never be victorious or saved." Mernissi based a whole book (1991) on it; for Sa'idzadeh's discussion, see Mir-Hosseini 1996b.

and can't be confined to words. If we challenge their authenticity, then our entire [corpus of] sacred sources will come into question. If we say they're pseudo-universal propositions, then not only women but men and many other rulings based on them will be affected. If we accept them as they are, then we must resolve the consequences of their incongruity with our present society. What we can say is that there's a kind of absolute neglect regarding such ahadith. They aren't addressed seriously, so no serious solutions are found for them. This is because the hold of democratic values and notions of human rights is so strong that men and women don't allow themselves to think of contradicting them and prefer to keep silent in the face of incongruities. This isn't limited to our time, nor to religious knowledge, but [it's true of] all times and all branches of knowledge. It's also the case in science. A cultural view, a theory, sometimes takes such hold and captures minds and imaginations to such an extent that no one dares think otherwise. So, in every era, part of religious thought, views, or ahadith is overshadowed and ignored, and another part is highlighted and welcomed.

All we can say is that such issues must be left for history to resolve, in time. When our minds tell us not to think about this issue [women in sacred texts], then we can't hope to find a suitable solution. In the past, this and many other issues were so much in line with popular culture that there was no need for thinking. In our time such ahadith have been dealt such devastating blows that no one finds it expedient to tackle them or to confront such a formidable torrent. The most we can do is to become familiar with the problem and its cause and leave the solution to time and later thinkers.

On this note, Sorush brings the session to an end. He has repeated essentially what he said in 1989 about the Imam's famous words on women's deficiencies, applying his theory of "Expansion and Contraction of the Shari'a": descriptive, explanatory, and normative, all at once. He argues both that understanding of sacred texts is time-bound and that the ulama's opinions are influenced by what he calls "extrareligious knowledge." Changes in knowledge render natural and Islamic some matters that were once considered "unthinkable" and "non-Islamic." He despairs at the ulama's unwillingness to admit this at a theoretical level and to take consciously planned steps to revise their understanding in the light of current realities. He also implicitly criticizes the institution of velayat-e faqih by pointing to the contradiction in having a parliament yet subordinating it to the rule of vali-ye faqih.

Despite this heady stuff, and Sorush's fresh approach, listening to him I could not help thinking that he too, as a religious intellectual, was avoiding the issue by skirting around any discussion of women's legal rights in Islam—the domain of feqh. This may have been a concern voiced by his audience,[25] since,

---

[25] The recording of the first session ends with Sorush's talk, a reading and recitation of a mystical story from the *Mathnavi*. If there was a question/answer follow-up, as in other sessions, it was not recorded.

even though he had declared the theme of women closed, he returned to it at the next session, a week later (15 October), because "some friends, especially sisters, asked for more." But once again he skirted around feqh and moved instead into religious literature to shed light on the sources from which Jurists derive their conceptions of women's rights. This time he framed his discussion in the context of changing conceptions of the human role and place in the universe, and asked why there is such a focus on women's rights in Muslim societies. He demonstrated that there is nothing sacred in our understanding of the shari'a, which is human and evolves in time and is filtered through our own cognitive universe.

The recording begins with the usual prayer and summary of key points from the previous discussion, before Sorush continues:

Friends know that in our time certain views have emerged about mankind, women included. In our society in recent decades these views have centered on women's legal rights. The problem facing our thinkers has been to explain to believing Muslim women why certain differences in rights between women and men exist in Islamic thought. Confronted with the notion of gender equality, they try either to explain these differences away or to argue that Islam upholds sexual equality but rejects similarity in rights. Some have argued for differences not in rights but in the duties of each sex, stemming from the differing abilities of each sex and the natural division of labor. Others have tried to explain by connecting differences in rights to physical, psychological, and spiritual differences between the sexes. . . .

The nub of the matter is that it's assumed that equality between men and women—which women demand in our time in various parts of the world—means equality in legal rights. Here I want to explain the exact meaning of this [notion of] equality between men and women—in the sense that some are now seeking—and then see whether the common understanding of women's rights and duties in Islam admits such a notion of equality; and how most of our ulama, thinkers, and jurists have conceptualized women and their status and the basis for their views. I stress, it's not for me to judge but only to offer a historical report of understandings that have so far existed. Nor do I claim that the door of understanding is closed, that no other understanding will emerge on this issue. Nevertheless, what has existed so far must be recognized and known.

We can have two views, both of which are rooted in our conception of women's purpose in creation. . . . In a nutshell, one holds that woman is created for man: her whole being, disposition, personality, and perfection depend on union with man. The other view denies such a relationship and holds that a woman has her own purpose in creation, her own route to perfection. . . . The first view—that woman is created *of* and *for*—sums up past perspectives, including those of Muslims. Both qualifiers [of and for] are important.

In poetic and mystical language, Sorush discusses at some length what these qualifiers entail, how they create asymmetry in rights and shape relations between the sexes. A woman is created to mediate man's perfection, to prepare him to fulfill his duty, to enable him to manifest his manhood, to make him worthy of God's call. This is the essence of womanhood, and that is why she attains perfection through union with a man. But for a man, union with a woman is not the end but only the beginning of his path to perfection. Sorush opens two caveats: to say that woman is created of and for man does not mean she is created for, or to be at the mercy of, man's whim; and to say that woman's perfection rests on union with man does not necessarily imply marriage, although formation of a family is one manifestation of such connection and an arena for complementarity and mutual perfection.

On the second view, which he says has captured the hearts and minds of Muslim women of our time, Sorush is less eloquent or forthcoming:

> [The] second view, demanding equality between the sexes, says nothing more than that woman is not created *of* and *for* man. This philosophical and existentialist conception, of course, defines the scope of women's legal rights, shapes their status and relations between the sexes, and so on. Here I don't want to discuss the implications of such a conception for women in the sphere of gender relations, nor shall I enter philosophical and legal discussions. These are to be found in the works of the late Motahhari and other thinkers such as Allameh Tabataba'i. Perhaps what can be said in defense of difference and nonsimilarity [of gender rights] has been said in these works, and I don't intend to add anything here. Nevertheless, I will make one point. One of those who judiciously understood yet denied [the implications of the two views] was Ayatollah Motahhari: in his book *Women's Rights in Islam* he clearly states that in the Islamic view woman isn't created for man. But I should say that this is not the general presumption of our ulama. An understanding of equality between man and woman won't be possible unless we understand the basis correctly and know contemporary men's and women's understanding of it. This is the formulation of the problem, the two claims that confront each other. . . .

Having identified the core contradiction in the gender discourses of contemporary Muslim thinkers, such as Motahhari, Sorush delves into religious literature to show the kinds of theories and master narratives on which they are based. He observes that although no Muslim thinker has said in so many words, "woman is of and for man," they all subscribe to the thesis; he offers three kinds of evidence for this; first, that religious sources are male oriented: whatever their genre, they solely or primarily address men, even when they deal with apparently genderless themes, such as rules for praying or ethical issues such as lying or cheating. In this, Sorush says, scholars have followed the example of the Koran, which most often addresses men. For instance, many of the blessings promised in paradise—such as black-eyed perpetual virgins—appeal only to men.

The second kind of evidence is the way religious literature describes marriage. Here again, men are treated as the main beneficiaries, even though marriage is by definition a joint affair. He examines legal and ethical sources to list the kinds of benefit Muslim scholars identify in marriage, ranging from immunity from Satan's temptations to achieving the peace of mind that enables men to prepare for greater duties in life, such as gaining knowledge and serving God. He also relates ahadith of the Prophet, that "women are among Satan's army and one of its greatest aids"; and a story from Rumi's *Mathnavi* that when God created woman, Satan rejoiced, saying "now I have the ultimate weapon for tempting mankind"—meaning, of course, men.

Similar is the sort of advice given to men on how to respect women's rights and pay them their dues. Sorush reads a passage from Feiz Kashani's *al-Mohajjat ol-Beiza* (The Bright Way), a book on ethics and morals. Feiz, a sixteenth-century Shiʿi scholar, defines marriage as a kind of enslavement, and a wife as a kind of slave, advising men: "now you have captured this being, you must have mercy on her, cherish and respect her, etc." Sorush points out that it was in the light of such a conception of marriage and women's status that scholars read and understood the hadith, and shows the internal flaw in such understandings. He recites ahadith attributed to Shiʿi Imams, telling men not to teach women Sura Yusef from the Koran, but Sura Nur instead, and to forbid women to go to upper floors of the house, in case they are tempted to look down at unrelated men passing in the street. "The point is not what the real meaning of these ahadith is, nor whether or not they are authentic. The point is, what meanings have been attributed to them [by] our religious scholars [who] have taken them seriously. My point is phenomenological, not theological. I don't judge, I simply say that in Islamic culture and history they've been taken seriously, and religious scholars have based their views on them."

Sorush's final argument to show the absolute hold of the "woman is for man" thesis is from mystical and philosophical literature. He cites two contrasting passages, one from the celebrated Sufi Ibn Arabi (d. 1240), the other from the philosopher Molla Hadi "Hakim" Sabzevari (d. 1878), and argues that they reveal the same conception of women, although expressed in two different idioms. Inspired by a hadith about the creation of Eve from Adam's rib, Ibn Arabi says that, like a rib, woman has the inborn ability to bend in her love without breaking: she is the symbol of divine love and mercy, created from "affection," and love toward man is implanted in her essence. Thus woman's role and destiny is to bend in love; in so doing she joins man and makes him whole again. Man's love for woman, on the other hand, is like the love of the whole for a part; looked at this way, man's love for woman does not infringe his love for God. Compare this, Sorush tells his audience, with Hakim Sabzevari's view that women are in essence animals; God gave them human faces so that men will be inclined to marry. "I apologize to the sisters present here for the insult implied in these words, but it's important to know them. Today in our society there's an unacceptable cover-up, even by our Muslim thinkers, who hide what's been said. . . . There's no reason, no point in hiding it, it'll be clear to those who care to think and search. It's important to face it with an open mind, to know better the dark tunnel we've come through, and how to contemplate our future."

His excursion into religious literature ended, Sorush concludes his talk with three further points.

> First, in the sphere of women's rights we cannot think and talk only in feqh categories, of forbidden and permitted acts; we must also think in terms of interpreting religious texts, of man's and woman's purposes in creation, of traditions and social customs. Second, if Muslim scholars defined women's status in a way we find unacceptable today, it is not because they wanted to humiliate women or undermine their status, but because that is how they understood and interpreted the religious texts. Women in the past accepted their status not because they were stupid or oppressed but because they had no problems with such understanding and interpretation. In the past two centuries, however, the myths and theories that made such understandings acceptable to men and women have been challenged by scientific theories, including evolution. Changes in our worldview have also made women's legal rights an issue in Islam. Finally, the problem cannot be resolved by providing new justifications to defend an outmoded worldview, hoping women will be lured back into accepting them; after all, acceptance is a matter of belief rather than reasoning. What we can do is try to understand the basis for, and implications of, old and new views on women. Only then can women clarify for themselves where they stand in relation to each view, and where they want to be.

Sorush invites his audience, in particular the women, to do this. The session continues with Sorush answering four questions. Two invoke a Koranic verse and a hadith to negate the "woman is for man" thesis, to which Sorush replies: "true, there are also many others, but so far the other side is stronger, in the sense that their reasonings and evidences dominate." A third question asks for comment on women's status in present society; he answers that this can best be dealt with by a sociologist. After a lengthy pause, Sorush reads out what must be part of the final question: "In our history, women have said nothing about themselves." He responds with a critique of feminism:

> Yes, it has been the case, and even if [women] said [something] their voices haven't reached us. There are several theories here. The argument of feminist movements—that now exist in the world as so-called supporters of women, demanding equal rights between men and women on all fronts—is

that differences between men and women, which their rights are based on, result from socialization. That is, boys and girls are socialized differently: boys are taught they are superior to girls, sexes are assigned different roles, they are valued differently, this sets a pattern and men and women have come to accept their roles; this has been the case in most societies from the start, and so on. I once witnessed a debate abroad between one of these feminists and an opponent, who argued that you must explain why this pattern was set in the first place, why men and women accepted it, and why it continues today; perhaps there's a reason for it, perhaps there [really] is a difference between the sexes—not [necessarily] that one is better than the other—but why do you want to deny difference?

This leads into a digression on the philosophy of history; Sorush affirms his own view that "the history of mankind has been natural," and asks whether the fact of women's oppression at certain periods can be taken as contrary evidence. Although he admits that his theory cannot be falsified, he seems to imply that history will show men's domination to be natural, too.

That last question seems to me to haunt the three sessions on gender relations that follow. They are more discursive in style and full of incomplete statements and arguments. Unlike in the first two sessions, Sorush pursues neither a central argument nor a sustained critique of old readings of the sacred texts, but tries instead to make sense of the Imam's words, to provide the basis for debate and a new positioning. This he makes clear at the outset. In his summary of the previous discussion, he repeats his criticism of current understandings of the sacred texts, voices his skepticism of the new view, which he sees as seeking to "put women in men's place," then continues:

The old view has passed its test, and religious societies that lived by its rules have revealed what they entail for men, women, and the family. On the other hand, societies that have opted for the new view, putting women in men's place, have also shown their hand. In both camps, many now feel the need for revision. But since these views aren't philosophically neutral, revision is always slow and painful. They're tied up with a mass of baggage, and it's impossible to remain impartial when dealing with them. . . . Until very recently—in the West, too—men have been the main theorists on women's nature and role in creation and society. This must make us cautious. When women replace them, they too are tied to their own baggage, however different. This is one of those rare cases where the door of judgment is closed to us, as both science and reason can be influenced by our emotions. You can't apply cold reason to an issue in which your entire being is immersed. There can be no guarantee that mistakes made in previous centuries won't be repeated. . . .

I say all this to affirm that we must rely here on Revelation and seek guidance in the words of religious leaders and those pious ones who are free of such baggage; the path of human reason here passes through the path of divine Revelation; if we explore and invest in this path, perhaps we'll obtain worthwhile results.

Having set the tone and the theme, Sorush returns to the closing sentences of Imam Ali's letter to his son, quoted earlier. He relates them to the concepts of hejab, sexual honor and jealousy (*gheirat*), and worth (*keramat*). On hejab he is brief, confining himself to two points: that its form and limits have always been bound up with culture and politics; and that what God permits, man should not forbid. To drive both home, he relates what Ayatollah Motahhari told him about how he began research for his book on hejab. Motahhari said he was afraid to enter a minefield of divergent opinions, but as his research progressed he found an astonishing degree of consensus among Shi'i and Sunni jurists: all—bar one Sunni—held that women's hands and faces need not be covered. He also found that all fatwas recommending stricter covering were issued after Reza Shah's unveiling campaign. Sorush leaves his audience to draw the moral from the anecdote: that advocating chador as the "superior form of hejab" has more to do with culture and politics than sacred texts. "We all know that chador is not 'Islamic hejab,' but it's rare to find a cleric who allows his womenfolk to venture out without wearing one. What Motahhari said on hejab—which was what he found in feqh texts—shocked the ulama of his time, who interpreted it as a license for promiscuity."

On the second concept, jealousy (*gheirat*), Sorush is more explicit. He first defines jealousy as "preventing another sharing what one has," and distinguishes it from envy (*hesadat*), which he defines as "wanting what belongs to another." The first is a positive ethical value that is extrareligious and should be encouraged, he argues, but the second is negative and should be controlled. He refers to another hadith of Imam Ali: "the jealousy of a woman is heresy (*kofr*), while the jealousy of a man is part of belief,"[26] and tries to shed light on what heresy can mean in this context. It has an ethical rather than religious connotation, arising from the asymmetry inherent in the way the sexes relate to each other. Women are entrusted to men, they become not only part of men but part of their honor. Men can take more than one woman as spouse at the same time, while the opposite cannot happen. Without asking whether such asymmetry is defined by laws of nature or culture, Sorush ends the session by saying there is another jealousy, manifested in creation, but he will leave it for next week.

In the next session (28 October), Sorush continues with the theme of jealousy, but on a mystical level. He starts with Rumi's interpretation of a hadith about divine jealousy and relates it to love (*'eshq*), devoting the entire session to this. Here he is in his element, weaving his own narrative into a rich body

[26] *Nahj ol-Balagheh*, p. 515, Saying 123.

of mystical concepts and poems to make a case for love, which he argues must be treated with jealousy, that is, protected from those who do not have it.

I find this session the most engaging and important, and yet the most difficult to assess. I am taken by Sorush's eloquence, his perception, and his courage in tackling such a delicate issue in a mosque. He makes a strong case for love, keeping it out of the feqh domain—yet I am puzzled by the clear male bias in his narrative. I can't decide whether he is telling his audience the whole story or is talking in innuendo. He begins by pointing to a duality, a paradox, in Persian literature, which reflects a cultural ambivalence toward the subject of love and women. Love is the main theme in Persian literature, yet one is never sure whether the writer is talking about divine or earthly love. "Our poets have perfected the art of ambiguity. In our culture, the same ambivalence can be seen when women are concerned. . . . It's enough to look at our own current society. I suppose there are few societies in the modern era for which sex and women are such a problem, yet we pretend the issue is resolved, that no problem exists. It's enough just to see the places that come under certain people's control; the kinds of separation and segregation [imposed] speak of the obsession, of the state of minds, and show the size of the problem and the distance that must be crossed for it to be resolved naturally." He talks about the role of earthly love in the lives of those such as Ibn Arabi and Hafez, and recites poems in which they talk of their love. He relates the story of Ibn Arabi's falling in love with a learned and beautiful Isfahani woman in Mecca, and her influence on his mystical development.[27] He also tells two stories from the Koran that speak of women's love for men: those of Zoleikha for Yusef (Sura 12) and the daughter of Sho'eib for Musa (Sura 28). He relates both stories in detail, seeing their message as endorsing the naturalness of attraction and love between men and women.[28] Unlike others, he emphasizes not Zoleikha's cunning and her attempts to seduce Yusef but his beauty and ability to resist temptations. God put love for him in her heart; he is so beautiful and desirable that other women, having at first blamed Zoleikha, sympathize with her when they see him, and plead with him to respond to her love. The two stories, he says, must be taken in conjuction with Sura Nur; he recites verse 31, which deals with women's covering and chastity. He asks, can love between men and women be recommended on ethical and religious grounds, or must it be condemned? In either case, what are the consequences, and how should a religious society deal with it?

[27] On his return from Mecca (1214), Ibn Arabi wrote a small collection of love poems, celebrating their mutual friendship and her beauty and learning, but a year later he found it advisable to write a commentary on these poems, explaining them in a mystical sense. See Nicholson 1911, 8, for an edition of the poems and a commentary.

[28] For both stories and their treatment by Muslim exegetes, both traditional and modern, see Stowasser 1994, 50–61.

In the rest of the session, Sorush presents a broad review of love in the history of Islamic thought. On the one hand are the moralists, who denounce love and tolerate no mention of it; on the other are those who recognize its blessing and power and resist denouncing it in the name of religion. Mystics argue that earthly love is a passage to divine love, a metaphor leading us to the Truth; but this is also an attempt to theorize a successful experience. The force of their argument is such that even philosophers have to contemplate love, although some reduce it to sex drive.[29] Those who readily issue fatwas dividing love into halal and haram, not only mistake lust for love but also forget that love, as Sufis argue, is involuntary; it is in its nature to undermine the will, thus it is not a matter on which there can be a feqh ruling. Instead of condemning it, our thinkers should contemplate love—whether earthly or divine—and propagate it. We must not let love be treated as a disease, something that defiles. It is healing and purifying, and can cure both individuals and societies of many afflictions and excesses. Feqh, more oriented to piety than love, must approach mysticism, which is more inclined to love than piety. Then they can overcome the duality, the rupture, in our cultural history and moderate the excesses of both.

Concluding his review, Sorush returns to jealousy. What he says here, it seems to me, not only reveals his male bias but undermines the case he has made for love.

> Thus man's jealousy toward women isn't only about honor but also about love. It's said that women are the repository for love and men the repository for wisdom; we can put this better, and say that women are objects of love, and men are not. If we accept that great loves have led to great acts in history, then we must admit that women have played a great role, and it's unwise for women to try to be men; they can't, they can only forfeit their womanhood. This is to negate one's blessing. It does [neither sex] any good, if someone, or a group, doesn't appreciate their worth and their place and also if others try to dislodge them from their place.

Sorush seems to have forgotten that only a moment earlier he told his audience two Koranic love stories in which, as he himself pointed out, men (Joseph and Moses) not women were the objects of love. Or does the lapse betray his own ambivalence?

Also puzzling, I find, is Sorush's final observation on love in contemporary Iranian poetry. He says he will only touch on it briefly, inviting his audience to do their own research and draw their own conclusions. Love still dominates our poetry and occupies our poets' minds, he says, but its manifestations are no longer pure and spiritual. In the past the poet was part of a closed world

---

[29] He refers to Molla Sadra's *Asfar*, which has a chapter on love, and Molla Hadi Sabzevari, who defines love as sexual gratification.

defined by religious values: "even if the poet chose to fix his gaze on the earth, the sky above him cast its shadow on his world." This is no longer the case; he makes the point by reciting a poem by Forugh Farrokhzad, where she says she never wanted to be a star in the sky or to be the companion of angels, she never separated herself from the earth.[30] This identity—never wanting to be part of a celestial world—Sorush argues, is evident in her approach to love and somehow degrades it. Adding "some of her poems, if you don't know they're hers, you'd think they're by a mystic," he recites one of her love poems, but stops as he reaches lines in which she expresses yearning for her lover, saying that a mosque is not the place for it.[31] He ends his defense of love by returning to the mystical realm, where earthly love is a metaphor for, and a means of experiencing, a greater truth.[32]

In the final session, Sorush concludes his commentary on Imam Ali's words on women with a discussion of *keramat*, which he glosses as "the limit, the purpose, the proper place of each being." He approaches the concept from a philosophical angle, placing it in the context of the two competing worldviews discussed earlier. The first, to which the Imam's words belong, accepts the world and its order as designed by the Creator, and has no dispute with the place assigned to His creation. The second, which makes the Imam's words difficult to digest, sees the world and its order as accidental, and wants to define the role of creation. The first view (that of Islamic thinkers) sees women as created for men and the roles of the sexes as noninterchangeable. In the second (that of modern times) women aspire to men's place in the order of things. Sorush embarks on a long discussion, examining the pros and cons of each of these worldviews. Critical of both but not totally rejecting either, he resorts to the Koran to shed light on women's place in the divine order of life. As he continues, it becomes clear that his own understanding of the Koranic position is in line with that of Islamic thinkers whose texts he earlier analyzed critically. He recites and elaborates on a Koranic verse: "And one of His signs is that He created mates for you from yourselves that you may find rest in them, and He put between you love and compassion; most surely there are signs in this for a people who reflect" (al-Rum, 21). Earlier, when speaking of love, he found a kind of symmetry in the ways men and women relate to each other; now he finds asymmetry and complementarity:

> The most important role for women, as understood from this verse, and as recognized by most of our ulama, is to restore to man the peace he has lost,

---

[30] The poem is "Ruye Khak" (On the Earth), in Farrokhzad 1991, 24. For her life and poetry, see Milani 1992, 127–52.

[31] "ʿAsheqaneh" (In Love), in Farrokhzad 1991, 55.

[32] The audience questions ask for clarifications, and elicit no new points. For instance, one asks why the Prophet and Imams were polygamous, and why Ghazzali reached such high status without love.

to correct the imbalance that prevents him from fulfilling his role. This is the role assigned to woman; this is the status bestowed on her by creation. You can, of course, disagree and believe that woman is malleable and can assume whatever role she is given, and man likewise; who says woman should be confined to this role? she can have better roles in society. . . . Fine, this is a theory that some maintain today. But as I said, what we find at the root of Islamic thought is that men's and women's roles are assigned, defined, and not interchangeable; in this view, woman fulfills her role in society through man, that is, she restores to men, the main actors in society, their lost balance and peace.

If we accept this as a proper understanding of religious texts, then, when the Imam says: "don't allow a woman matters other than those about herself, because a woman is a flower, not an administrator," he means that [gender] roles in society are not changeable. Those who say otherwise are those who say we [are the ones who] define roles, that people can be prepared for roles through socialization, education, etc.

Typical to his style, Sorush now poses a question and a counter-argument that subvert the claims of conventional understandings. "But if we accept the view that [gender] roles are defined and their limits set, we face the question: what are these limits? Who says these limits have been correctly defined? How do we know the roles men and women have played so far are the male and female roles they should have played? This is an important question. In theory, we might accept that man should remain man, and woman should remain woman, but who has defined what men should do, and what women should do? We have three sources to consult: religion, science, and history."

To find the answer, Sorush invites his audience to consult each of these sources, telling them to focus on history, which he sees as natural, as reflecting the human nature in which men and women have shown their characteristics. He expands his response to a question a few weeks earlier about the philosophy of history.

I know you'll object that women weren't allowed to find their own status. But this objection isn't valid, whether in this case or in others. We must ask why and how men succeeded. . . . We can look at history from an ethical angle and reach certain conclusions; but if we suspend ethical judgment and look at history in terms of possibilities, we'll reach different ones. I suggest that if women occupied a position we now see as oppressed, then they saw this as their proper place in life; they didn't see themselves as oppressed and didn't ask for more, as they saw their keramat, their worth, as being women, not as being like men. We can't impose our own values on the past, and assume that what we now consider to be injustice, or essential rights, were valid then—that's the worst kind of historiography. I suppose we're at the start of a new epoch; in fact it began almost two centuries ago, with the rise of protesters, who see themselves as making and designing their own world. It remains to be seen how.

Although science, the second source, Sorush argues, can tell us more about the characteristics of each sex, it cannot give us the final answer. Religion, whose answer he has been exploring in these lectures, is no longer consulted, since: "men and women of this age—whether religious or not—now inhabit a world where they give an absolute value to expressing dissatisfaction and protesting at their lot. They're not prepared to hear the clear answer of religion, nor does anyone tell them. So we must only wait for the third source—history—to make our places clear to us. It's only then that humans can hear and understand the delight of surrender to God's will."

So Sorush concludes his discussion of women and gender roles. He talks for another half an hour, dealing with questions, but makes no further points.

Sorush in London

In October 1995, when I first listened to recordings of these lectures in Tehran, I did not know what to make of them. I was taken by Sorush's rational approach to sacred texts, by his eloquence, by his willingess to see different sides to an argument, by his courage in opening up and speaking of taboo subjects (such as Farrokhzad's love poetry) in a mosque, to an audience for whom women like her had been demonized in the past seventeen years. On the other hand, I found his own position on gender problematic, and was frustrated and annoyed by what I saw as skilled evasion of any kind of serious debate over women's legal rights. I could also see that his position, and to an extent his approach to women's issues, was very close to that of Shariʿati. They both criticize not just old understandings of women's status in Islam but also the advocates of equal rights; both refuse to enter the realm of feqh.

I decided there was no way I could include Sorush among the supporters of gender equality in Islam. Clearly he subscribed to the view that in the divine order of things women are for men, as they are men's "calm," their anchor. I shared my misgivings about Sorush's gender position with Shahla Sherkat, editor of *Zanan*. She conceded that she had pressed him to let her publish a transcript of his lectures, but when the text was prepared Sorush delayed approving it for publication. Finally, she herself abandoned the project. She gave me a copy of the transcripts.

I could not understand how and why Sorush's ideas had inspired women in *Zanan*, who like me objected to his gender position.[33] Only later, when I was

[33] I found it liberating and promising that, despite its devotion to Sorush's ideas, *Zanan* validated Forugh Farrokhzad, whose poetry Sorush had described as "too worldly"; see *Zanan* 16 (Winter 1993), 20 (Autumn 1994), and 25 (Summer 1995)—the issue discussed in Chapter 6. It is

well into writing this book, did I understand that I must shift my focus. It was not his position on gender but his conception of Islam and his approach to sacred texts that empowered women in *Zanan* to argue for gender equality, just as they also, I realized, made possible my debate with the *Payam-e Zan* clerics, even though they did not agree with his approach to the texts any more than I agreed with his gender position. The tension in the last session of our debate—I now realized—had partly to do with my increasing self-confidence in locating my objections within an Islamic framework, which I had internalized by listening to Sorush's tapes and reading his work in the intervening months.

Between May and December 1996 Sorush gave a number of talks in London, mostly in Persian and to audiences largely of Iranian students, including a series of eleven lectures on Rumi and mysticism. I attended most of these talks, and whenever I had a chance I asked questions and tried to draw attention to gender issues. The opportunity to hear Sorush in person helped me place his 1992 talks on women in the context of his wider analytical method and his later thinking. By now I could see how his approach to Islam could open up space for a radical rethinking of gender relations, among other issues. Yet whenever I or other women in the audience asked him pertinent questions, he was evasive. For example, at a Middle East Forum meeting at the School of Oriental and African Studies, London, in June, I asked him why he had not addressed women's questions in print. He replied that it was not easy, they cannot be addressed without discussing human rights, and anyway women do it themselves. In September, at a seminar in London, "Obstacles to Development in Iran," organized by the Islamic Society of Iranian Students, where Sorush was one of four panelists—all male—I asked why none of the speakers had said a single word about women's rights or gender issues. Again Sorush's answer was vague, in line with his 1992 talks.

After listening to the 1992 tapes again, I still could not decide what he was actually saying. There were different layers. Although I agreed with some points, I could not accept others. Sometimes he seemed to be arguing in line with the Traditionalists. I agreed with his identification of the main contradiction in the Islamic Republic's discourse on women, but his own arguments seemed to me just as problematic. What Sorush was arguing, and urging on Muslim women, was to resolve the contradiction by accepting the role they were given in creation, their "position." He called this "the step that must be taken." To me, this was the voice of a conservative philosopher, not a reformer and thinker trying to reconcile democracy and Islam. Didn't he consider gender equality, too, to be part of democratic and human rights?

Then in October I had a private meeting with him, in which I raised my

---

interesting that in early 1998 Sorush gave a series of thirty-five talks on Hafez and his philosophy, in which one of the main themes was the importance of earthly love.

objections to the gender position he took on the tapes, and tried to draw him into a more specific discussion. I started by summarizing his arguments and the issues he raised in the 1992 talks, interjecting comments of my own. Dealing with Imam Ali's views on women, he says we find them difficult to accept because they reflect an old worldview. He criticizes the two ways they are now dealt with (casting doubt on their authenticity; interpreting them as only concerning Ayesha), saying that neither will solve the problem. He suggests dealing with them by reasoning; but this, I said, is not enough.

AKS: Enough for what? That depends what conclusions you want to draw. In that talk I laid an important foundation whose implications for religious literature, in my view, can't be appreciated now. I said that unquestioning obedience to the words of a religious leader when he reasons isn't obligatory. In certain situations we follow and submit unconditionally: we're Muslims and pray as the Prophet says; here there's no room for questioning. But this isn't the case when there's reasoning in the words of a religious leader.

ZMH: That is, we can refute it?

AKS: Of course we can. If not, what is reasoning for in the first place? not just to persuade but also to evaluate. If Imam Ali reasons with us, he invites us to reason back, to use our critical faculties. There I tried to present a counter-argument, and pointed out that we can't deduce from the Imam's words that women are defective in faith [because they don't pray or fast at certain times]. If we say that, then we must also say that those who can't afford to go on Hajj pilgrimage are also defective in faith; but we say that it's not obligatory for them.

Such a foundation can be a torch for you when entering the religious literature, to put aside fear and clarify matters for yourself. You can say that such reasonings satisfied the logic of people of that age, or that since the reasoning is false it's impossible that the Imam would deduce such a Ruling from it. What conclusion you draw from these arguments depends on your own perspective and intentions. That's the essence of what I said there; it can have many applications if we use it consistently and methodically.

I continued with my summary, and pointed out that, despite the many insights he provides into the old view, there is a kind of fallacy in his arguments, particularly as regards what he calls "the new view."

ZMH: When it comes to discussing the new view that "woman is not for man," you oversimplify a complex debate and reduce women's demands for equal rights to "wanting to take man's place," which in your discourse becomes not valuing God's design for humanity. It's in this context that you introduce the concept of keramat to define the true place and boundaries of created beings, and you examine it in the context of two competing worldviews: the old and the new. You criticize the ulama's understanding of women's role, but as you go on, it becomes evident that yours isn't very different. You too hold that in the divine order of things women are for men, as they are men's "calm," their anchor. What do you mean by this?

At this point, I quoted a passage from Ayatollah Javadi-Amoli's book, where he, like Sorush, bypasses feqh Rulings and tries to place the whole gender debate on a spiritual plane—even invoking the same Koranic verse.[34] Unaware that Javadi-Amoli was Sorush's most articulate and powerful clerical adversary, I pointed out how Sorush's position and understanding of gender in sacred texts, even some of his arguments, resemble those of Javadi, whose approach is theological. As I blundered on, Sorush kept repeating (probably in disbelief): "ʿajab! ʿajab!" (how odd!). I went on:

> You close your discussion of women and gender roles by inviting your audience to look for the answer in history. That is, you tell them implicitly that women's roles in society will be the same as before, since there is a reason why they have played such roles so far. There are several problems with this argument. History has many narratives: the one you are talking of is written by men; the history of mankind might be natural, as you say, but that doesn't mean it's just; there's no reason to say that the Lawgiver wanted it to be this way, or that it will always remain such; slavery was with us for much of our history, and other examples abound. Gender equality is a Principle, a prevailing value of our age; whether it's here to stay, or a passing fashion, is another matter. The question then is why you, a religious intellectual, also choose to ignore it. What does Revelation have to say on this? What is your own understanding?
>
> Incidentally, you employ a rhetorical device—like the ulama when they talk of pre-Islamic views and practices. You criticize past thinkers' outlandish views on women, which somehow diverts attention from a discussion of current views. For instance, you quote views such as those of Feiz Kashani [woman is an animal created so that man will be inclined to mate] . . .

AKS: He takes it from Ghazzali.

ZMH: And Feiz develops it. That is, you give the men in your audience a false sense of generosity and pride that they don't think like that, and women a sense of gratitude that they aren't thought of that way. I don't know whether or not you do this deliberately, but it sets the tone and the course of the debate. You also do the same when dealing with feminism: focusing on excesses and preempting a debate.

AKS: [laughing] you're rather angry!

ZMH: I do find what you say infuriating! I can't accept the basis of what you say there.

[34] Javadi-Amoli 1993a, 38–39.

AKS: And what is that basis?

ZMH: Perhaps if there's an anger, it's because of the ambivalence in what you say. You say there's a status for women, there's a purpose, but you never say clearly what they are. You reduce this purpose for woman to being man's calm, his anchor in life. But the same could be said of men. And there's more to feminism, to women's demand for equality, than what you told your audience; there are many debates and positions within feminism; no one says that women are identical to men, difference is now brought into the picture, some even argue that apart from their bodies women differ from men in psychology and the way they relate to the world.

AKS: Look, there's a need for these debates, they've mellowed feminists, earlier they went too far and these [religious] counter-arguments gradually made them aware that woman should demand status by keeping her womanhood. I'll give some general explanations and hope they address your questions.

First, we must make a distinction. The majority of our ulama—even men of politics—when talking about women, their guide is feqh, that is, their ideas, their images come from a set of Rulings they have in mind, then they create an image of women to reflect it.

ZMH: But behind these Rulings lie worldviews, value systems. . . .

AKS: Exactly. I mean, we have two points of departure: if your guide is feqh then you define women as such to conform with its Rulings. I claim to be the greatest critic of such thinking. Among the objections I have raised is that feqh, as the lowest-ranking religious science, shouldn't become the center of religious thought. I took the basis of this argument from Ghazzali, and expanded it in a lecture I gave at Harvard last year, entitled "The Place of Feqh in Islamic Teachings." . . . One of the main differences I see between pre- and post-revolutionary Islam is that our present Islam is feqh-based, whereas before it was spiritual. That Islam was appealing; Islam since the revolution no longer appeals, it displays a stern legalism. In my last article in *Kiyan*, based on a talk I gave at UNESCO, when I reach feqh I say it's a kind of stern legalism that brings alienation.[35] . . . Of course, it isn't easy to talk of feqh in these terms . . . [but I continue to do so] since I see it as one of the ills of current religious thinking, precisely because of what you mentioned: feqh holds within itself a worldview, but some ignore this, take its Rulings as immutable, then go on to define women accordingly. In a recent article, I argue that a religious Ruling is not the same as a feqh Ruling; I discuss [the ulama's] understanding of religious Rulings as like feqh Rulings.[36] This fallacy must be eradicated.

I want you to know how I think on such issues. Feqh is not my point of departure, and the question of women . . .

[35] Sorush 1996a.   [36] Sorush 1996b.

ZMH: But you can't totally ignore or bypass feqh.

AKS: No, I'll get there in the end. The question is where feqh should be placed, at our point of departure or at our destination. To enter a debate on the women's question via the path of women's rights is incorrect, and I consciously don't pursue it. Not because I don't believe in them or want to ignore them, but because I believe that this isn't a starting point and will lead us astray. I start from your question: what's the status of women? Women's status mustn't be reduced to law; it's much broader. In the past, women's status wasn't what we say. Look at the religious literature. When I first quoted what Hakim Sabzevari said on women, some [ulama] got angry, and denied the authenticity of my quotation. In the text Molla Sadra wrote that several types of animals are created, one of which, woman, is created for men to mate with. Then Hakim Sabzevari comments on the text, saying the great man made a just point; he relies on it too in his interpretations of the religious texts: men are guardians of women because women are animals whom God gave human faces. . . . Someone even wrote that I made this up. I had quoted it from memory, but when I checked, it was correct; I have given the reference in an article which came out in *Sturdier than Ideology*.[37] It's important that someone like Molla Sadra had such views, I tell you our jurists thought the same.

ZMH: Some still do.

AKS: I'd be surprised if it were otherwise. What school teaches them otherwise? These texts are still taught in the Houzeh, there isn't one on human rights. They base their logic, the Principles of Jurisprudence, on these philosophers' views. Unless a people's understanding of the women's question is changed, there'll be no basic change; women will remain less than second-class citizens; if they're given rights, it's from charity or necessity. Look, this is the milieu in which I'm talking, as a person; this is where the status of women must be corrected; in my opinion, we'll get nowhere by haggling about women's legal rights.

ZMH: Mr. Motahhari, and today others, didn't think like this.

AKS: I accept that. I'm talking about the dominant rule; they're exceptions, all influenced by outside [the Houzeh]. I don't believe one can enter a legal debate with these gentlemen [ulama]; they can produce a hadith to silence you, but not if we start with broader concepts. We must first establish whether woman is human or, as Hakim Sabzevari says, animal; how God conceives of them, regardless of their place in relation to men. Is association with women defiling or enhancing to men? We must say that men can attain spiritual growth through love and friendship with women. This is a path I've been following in recent years in my teachings on Hafez. Hafez believes that humans aren't brought into the world to be ashamed; they've

---

[37] Sorush 1994e, 39–40. The passage is reproduced in a footnote.

a right to exist and must honor this right. Someone like Rumi or Ghazzali didn't think this way. If we can correct such ideas then we can easily take the next step. That's why I see legal debates as secondary, and favor theoretical and philosophical debates. At present in our society, among our students, we have a problem: how to look at women with religious eyes. Once ideas and views change, laws will change. . . . In the West too, ideas on these matters changed first, then women's place in life, in work, and family changed accordingly. *Zanan*, or anyone who works on women, should devote 70 percent to these broader debates and 30 percent to legal ones.

ZMH: Do you know that so far *Zanan* has had no article on [philosophical rather than legal views on women]?

AKS: Yes, that's a failing. Not many dare to write on this. It's also a difficult matter.

ZMH: It's a problem. There aren't many women competent to deal with theoretical debates on Islamic grounds. Women in the Houzeh seem to have no qualms about its views on women; some are even worse than men. To some degree this is to be expected: women who enter a patriarchal institution must accept its values in the first place, otherwise there's no place for them. Perhaps this is a stage; women in the Houzeh can't enter such debates at present. Some [religious] women, such as those in *Zanan*, haven't the expertise and others [non-religious] refuse to frame their discussions in Islamic terms. Male religious intellectuals, such as yourself, won't enter gender debates at all; for instance, there isn't a single reference to women's questions in *Kiyan*, which considers them outside the realm of concern for religious intellectuals.

AKS: No . . . but they're involved in other debates; perhaps one day they will; perhaps they think there's no need, since there's *Zanan*. But I accept that in the realm of religious intellectuals, the women's question is neglected.

ZMH: Why do you think it's neglected?

AKS: Women are always seen through the eyes of feqh. . . . Women themselves—including socially active intellectuals—tend to define themselves through a series of feqh duties. This is an important point.

ZMH: Of course, only some—that is, they've accepted . . .

AKS: I don't mean they shouldn't accept feqh; after all, a Muslim man or woman has a set of duties they must fulfill. What I mean is that they don't know their own "existence," as existentialists would say. I see the difference between old and new men, old and new women, as lying in self-knowledge. That is, in recognizing what it is to love as a woman, to be anxious as a woman, to demand rights as a woman. These they [old women?] lack; they think it's a sin to think about men, and don't see themselves as having the right to know. This is the problem: we must first make women aware of themselves. It's extremely difficult. It's like swimming in acid, which is heavy and burns your limbs. It takes a long time to explain to these women that there are some issues that have nothing to do with religion; these are meaningless taboos which are not imposed by God and His Messenger, you have imposed them on yourself and have distorted human relations. What is a woman with this image of herself to do with equal rights? That's why I say: debates on rights should come later. In our society, delicate theoretical work is needed, and when women know themselves, then you can say: now define your relationship with men, define your status, and yet remain Muslim and live according to the shari'a. These relations [defined in feqh] aren't sacrosanct, they come from minds with distorted worldviews; many arose in situations when women didn't undertake social responsibilities. In our society, women work and are present, but some still want to enforce outmoded ethics. No one says where they came from, what era they belong to. The only thing that's done is to tell girls not to wear this or that.

ZMH: It's after all a transitional stage . . .

AKS: Of course, but this transitional stage must be paved with awareness, for us to reach more fundamental issues. . . . We must change the image humans have of themselves. . . . In my talk on Houzeh and university,[38] I said [to the ulama]: if you have a Women's Day in this country, then you must also declare that you reject what Hakim Sabzevari says; you publish it in your books, yet without criticizing it, and if you don't, someone like me will—and then you'll protest. . . .

If you ask the same question about men—what's the purpose in their creation?—I would say: I don't know; certainly there's a purpose, but we don't know.

ZMH: Then why do you raise it [when it comes to women]?

AKS: Permit me. I mean that one level of the story goes to God, but at the other level, if you ask the question in broader terms—that is, what's the purpose in creation of mankind, which is divided into two sexes?—my answer is: what men, what women are we talking about? men or women of yesterday or today? The answers differ. In my opinion, men and women should know each other and define their relationships. The only thing I can say is that we think women can be this or that and assume this or that role. Now whether [what we think] really is their purpose, I don't know. One thing is that in religious thought the greatest status a creature can be accorded is to be on the road to his or her spiritual perfection, not to be a director or a prime minster. In my talks I made it clear that, contrary to Ghazzali's view—that women are among Satan's army and their very essence is to prevent men from reaching God—I say that it's to help men. It's important for women for such a status to be recognized; on that basis their

[38] Lecture delivered in May 1992 in Isfahan University; see Sorush 1994e, 21–43.

rights will be regulated. Looked at from a religious viewpoint, I think this is the story, and it's worth saying it, since when it's accepted that women bring men closer to God, then we must ask, what women? A woman who doesn't know herself and has no place in society? or a woman who's found herself and has social rights?

ZMH: These things must be debated; they haven't yet been. When our religious intellectuals don't bring them up, then the field is left to the ulama and those who address them outside the realm of religion.

AKS: If there's moderate thinking in the realm of religion, then I think women have a very good position. I know some women who have good places and use them properly, depending on their tact and knowledge.

ZMH: Look, what you say implies inequality; the very fact that you think women must have a place . . .

AKS: No; why inequality? Obviously, if it isn't there you must talk about it for a long time in order to establish it. Don't you accept this? Second, women *are* different from men, this difference is undeniable, so their roles are different.

ZMH: Certainly. But when we say that women's purpose in creation is to restore peace to men and enable them to get closer to God, then it follows that they should stay at home to care for the children, to cater for his needs, enable him to fulfill his role and duties, and so on.

AKS: This is one job woman can have, and it's an important one. If a woman can only do this, she shouldn't feel ashamed; it's a valuable job and men should be grateful. But it's not right to make it an imperative [woman should only do this, or never do it]. These days it's thought that a woman should feel ashamed to be a housewife, when her husband is doing well in society. In my view, it's no less important than any other [role]. Many of our mothers lived like this, burned like a candle and gave light to others. One characteristic of our society is that it doesn't allow exclusive roles for women; they can work and perform roles, which bring changes in defining their rights in relations with men, etc. We see that these things have happened, and changes are coming about naturally. But a proper basis for them must be established, it mustn't be allowed to take a pragmatic and unconscious course. We must start from a basis that's acceptable to people themselves, that is, from what Rumi and Ibn Arabi said. True, they were people of their time, but their insights can come to our aid. Rumi says: "Love belongs to the world of humans and doesn't define relations between males and females of other species." We must start from here, or what Ibn Arabi says, or some of the ahadith of the Prophet; then you can open the way and proceed step by step. But I admit that the issue hasn't been tackled from this angle; or if it has, little work has been done; or it took a legal turn, or certain considerations intervened, or they wanted to introduce something in line with feqh Rulings, which to me is a misguided approach. I accept what you say, that the debate is in the hands of those who didn't know how to approach [the ulama] or the nonreligious ones.

Now let's see what secularists have done in recent years. What they did at the time of the Constitutional Revolution [1906–1909] was very positive and achieved things without which women would have little place in our society. . . . They yielded their fruit at the time of the Islamic Revolution; nobody then imagined women demonstrating in the streets. But now the secularist slogan is faded; they've nothing new to say. Unless we go to the roots, nothing will change. . . . What we want from secularist thinkers is to contribute to debates at root level, for instance what elements of feminism they accept.

We talked for a while about the recent work and ideas of those dealing with women's issues in Iran and outside, and about gender developments since the revolution. I said that, judging from my own work in Qom and following the debates there, I felt that we were on the threshold of a major shift in discourses and perspectives on women. Sorush reiterated the necessity to go to roots and fundamentals, and develop theoretical grounds, but saw little prospect of this: "our society—both men and women—is now too ideological . . . even intellectuals still take their models from feqh, they haven't severed that umbilical cord." He admitted that some important changes have taken place in large towns, but was not optimistic that they would lead to a fundamental shift in perspective, since "they need theoretical backing," and this was missing.

To me, Sorush's ambivalence on gender comes from the very framework and agenda he set himself. Like Shari'ati, his refusal to address the issue of women through feqh leaves him little choice but to talk in abstractions. This brings his views and position on gender close to those of Javadi-Amoli, despite vast differences in their visions and approaches to Islam. Both men bypass feqh—Javadi-Amoli taking a theological turn and Sorush, as he puts it, a "phenomenological" one—and they end up with similar readings and understandings of sacred texts when it comes to gender.

8

Gender Equality and Islamic Jurisprudence: The Work of Hojjat ol-Eslam Sa'idzadeh

THIS CHAPTER introduces the approach and writings of Hojjat ol-Eslam Seyyed Mohsen Sa'idzadeh, the cleric with whom I collaborated during the research on which the book is based. Sa'idzadeh greatly influenced my thinking and the way I came to understand the debates about gender in Qom. I have assimilated some of his views, but at the same time I believe my questions and way of thinking have affected his. Moreover, both *Payam-e Zan* and Sa'idzadeh used me as a catalyst in their relations with each other; I articulated direct questions and criticisms that they could not. For all these reasons, the format and organization of the chapter are somewhat different, and I have kept my own comments to a minimum.

I begin by providing some background to his intellectual career and his approach, drawing on his articles in *Zanan* and the paper he wrote for the Iranian Women's Studies Foundation Conference in Toronto in June 1995, entitled "Correspondence between Feminism and Islamic Religious Issues." The latter is significant because, as his first work to be published outside Iran, it is free of the constraints of censorship, and also because it marks an important stage in his thinking: for the first time he makes an overt attempt to reconcile feminism with Islam. Then I present extracts from our discussion in London (most of which I tape-recorded), which clarify several themes implicit in his approach and writings. This was after he had delivered his conference paper, which was published a year later.[1] Finally, I summarize one of his most recent writings (May 1997), to show the direction his thinking has been moving.

Sa'idzadeh is typical of a new breed of clerics who have matured with the Islamic Republic. Born in 1958 to a lower-middle-class family in Qa'en, a small town in southern Khorasan, he began his religious studies at the age of ten at Qa'en Seminary. In 1973 he moved to Mashhad to continue his studies, and in 1976 to Qom. During the revolution, he took part in anti-Shah demonstrations, and was arrested. He was among the first graduates of the Qom Law

---

[1] Sa'idzadeh 1995b. The Iranian Women's Studies Foundation holds its meetings in Persian; it is largely composed of Iranian women who live in exile and are critical of the Islamic Republic's policies on women. They regularly invite speakers from Iran; Sa'idzadeh was the first man to be invited, see the Preface.

School (Madraseh-ye Ali-ye Qaza'i-ye Qom), set up in 1979 to train judges for the Revolutionary Courts. Becoming a judge in 1983, he served in Kermanshah until 1986, when he resigned to return to seminary life in Qom and to resume his studies at the advanced level. He was active in the cultural section of the Society for Houzeh Teachers until February 1995, when he took up a post in Tehran as adviser and researcher for the Ministry of Justice. He has certificates from fifteen ayatollahs attesting to his proficiency in Koranic exegesis and hadith.

Sa'idzadeh has written on a variety of subjects from theology to history, publishing articles in Iranian journals since 1984. He has published two books: a two-volume history of Qa'en, his hometown, based on research after his return to Qom, and a study of Resurrection.[2] The latter, based on research when he was still a judge in Kermanshah, first appeared in 1984 as series of articles in *Manshur-e Baradari*, the journal of the Feda'ian-e Islam, a radical religious group, which resumed publication after the revolution. He began researching women's issues in 1988, and has written extensively on the subject but little of this work has been published so far, most of it in *Zanan* and *Payam-e Zan*, after a cleric friend who produces a research bulletin introduced his articles to both journals. His first five articles in *Zanan* (in 1992) appeared under the name of his wife, Mina Yadegar Azadi; subsequent ones bore his own name or pseudonyms, male and female.[3] He used his wife's name, he explained, to give her a start in the field, but when the articles proved controversial, she no longer wanted her name associated with them, fearing the controversy might cost her her job as a secondary-school teacher. Meanwhile, as he grew increasingly interested in the topic himself, he realized that pseudonyms saved him from censure in Qom, so he could get on with his studies.

Sa'idzadeh's writings in *Payam-e Zan* appear under his own name. They are on diverse topics from female literary personalities to women's education and occupations.[4] Among them there are attacks on cultural imperialism and feminism that show little trace of the stance he takes in *Zanan*. Between February and May 1995 a four-part unsigned article appeared in *Payam-e Zan*: "Feminism: Repeat of Unsuccessful Experiences"—a critique of radical feminism from an Islamic perspective.[5] I read the first three parts in Tehran, seeing them as an attempt to discredit *Zanan*'s feminist aspirations. When I learned that Sa'idzadeh was the author, I was stunned by the inconsistency: I could not understand how he could simultaneously defend and attack a single position. I saw the article as a betrayal of *Zanan*, and kept asking how he could contribute to two journals with such divergent political orientations and gender views. But he saw no contradiction in this, and repeated, mantra-like: "you must separate ideas from actions."

[2] Sa'idzadeh 1990 and 1992a.
[3] For an analysis of his earlier work in *Zanan*, see Mir-Hosseini 1996b.
[4] Sa'idzadeh 1992b, 1992c, 1993a, and 1993b.   [5] Sa'idzadeh 1995a.

As our collaboration continued, and I learned more about the intellectual trajectories of clerics, the politics of gender, and of women's journals in Iran, I came to understand that the inconsistency was an illusion. I also came to understand what Sa'idzadeh meant by his mantra, and that his critique of "cultural invasion" and feminism in the *Payam-e Zan* article was in effect a necessary step in the evolution of his thinking. His contributions to *Zanan* did not mean that he endorsed or identified with *Zanan*'s political views; rather, it was the only forum in which he could express his own views without disguising them in the complex circular style prevalent in Houzeh writing. It was in *Payam-e Zan* that he felt his arguments were understood; in his articles he was trying to mediate between the two perspectives, rather as I later tried to do in my own debates with clerics. In his thinking, style, and mode of argument, Sa'idzadeh identified with the Houzeh, and he enjoyed excellent rapport with *Payam-e Zan*. Contrary to what I had first assumed, he was not *Zanan*'s cleric, and his relations with them were tense.

Sa'idzadeh calls his approach the "Equality perspective." He contends that it has always existed in Islamic jurisprudence and that many eminent jurists have adhered to it, alongside the dominant approach, which he calls the "Inequality perspective." He sees his achievement—his "art"—to be in articulating this approach coherently and shaping it to accord with twentieth-century realities. He grounds his arguments in a commentary on theological and jurisprudential issues, with the premise that the theologian and the jurist, in understanding the doctrines and in inferring shari'a Rulings, cannot detach themselves from their own worldview, which in turn reflects the state of knowledge, politics, and social customs of the age and milieu in which they operate. He further argues that apart from some minor religious Rulings (relating to biological differences), Islam regards men and women in the same way, thus it can accommodate feminism, which articulates women's aspirations in this century. He defines feminism (*feminizm*—there is no Persian equivalent) as "a social movement whose agenda is the establishment of women's human rights. Feminism endeavors to free women from an unwanted subordination imposed on them by androcentric societies; it recognizes that women are independent and complete beings, and puts the emphasis on the common humanity of the sexes, not their differences."[6]

In contrast to clerics we have met earlier and most shari'a-based arguments, Sa'idzadeh sees women's gender roles as defined and regulated more by familial and social circumstances than by nature and divine will. Some of his primary postulates, as articulated in his Toronto paper, are:

- Equality does not mean parity and identity of rights and duties, but it means that gender is not used as a criterion in their determination. Gender is not the basis for perfection or defectiveness of men or women, but to

[6] Sa'idzadeh 1995b, 33–34.

connect them. God has created both sexes perfect, their difference is not for separating them but for connecting them. Even in a case where a Ruling (*hokm*) apparently pertains to one sex only, again its subject is humankind with that specific sexual attribute. For instance, if sex-change could enable men to become pregnant, Rulings relating to pregnancy have not lost their relevance.

- Gender is a social and human concept and does not enter the divine realm, thus it could never have been a consideration for the divine Lawgiver. Sexual markers recommended by religion cannot be taken as proof of gender roles. For instance, Islam recommends that women keep their nails long and colored, and that men keep them short and plain. Such recommendations are not intended to separate the sexes nor to create gender roles. Because the length and color of nails are matters of custom and social habit, religion endorses them as sexual markers of beauty. When people change their customs, whatever becomes a marker of feminine beauty—even if it goes contrary to this recommendation—religion will endorse it, as with earrings. In the early years of Islam, only men pierced their ears and wore earrings; now in Muslim societies it is a women's fashion, but in the West men also wear them. In other words, these customs are recommended to satisfy men's and women's sense of beauty, not to create and enforce discrimination and separation between them.

- A distinction must be made between two matters: belief in religion and following its Rulings; and discussing religion and proving or disproving its axioms and Rulings. In that case a person who speaks of Islam does not have to be a Muslim or to believe in it. Discussing Islam is a matter that bears no relation to people's belief or practice. Likewise, motives for discussion or appealing to religion are not necessarily indicative of people's belief.

- A substantial number of hadith and feqh theories obstruct the way to establishing equality between the sexes. A majority of jurists and all hadith specialists have sacrificed the Principle of equality in Islam to endorse a set of theories resting on assumptions that are no longer valid but still remain part of feqh.[7]

Sa'idzadeh has set himself the task of demolishing these theories, arguing that it should be done from within feqh itself, using its own language and mode of argumentation. His approach and style of writing are those of feqh texts. First, he introduces the issue—for instance, women's right to serve as judges—and places it in its feqh context, by reviewing the divergent positions of jurists, both Shi'i and Sunni; he then scrutinizes these opinions in the light of Koran, Hadith, Consensus, Reason, and the practice and custom of the time; finally he refutes those that are contrary to the Principle of equality and elaborates on those which accord with it.

[7] Ibid., 31–34.

During his stay in London in June 1995, I talked with Sa'idzadeh about his ideas and writings. Our discussion ranged widely, although we mostly focused on the politics of gender in Iran and Islam; hejab was the only issue that he was not willing to discuss. At the time, I was trying to understand the gender discourses of the Houzeh, of which I knew little; looking back, I am embarrassed by the naiveté of some of my questions.

I reproduce here those parts of our discussion that bore directly on the ideas in two of his recently completed writings: his Toronto paper, "Correspondence between Feminism and Islamic Religious Issues," and the manuscript *Women's Freedom at the Time of Mohammad.* He gave his consent for this, provided the Islamic atmosphere of our discussion is preserved. I have retained our words as far as possible, but altered the sequence in which the themes were raised in order to smooth out repetitions; we returned to some of them many times.

ZMH: Can you date the emergence of the "Gender Equality perspective"?

SMS: There are traces of the perspective in the thinking of many Jurists, although I have not come across anyone who has thought it through systematically. I started to do it myself in 1988. I have a section on this in my [Toronto] paper,[8] where I say that since it deals with justice and basic human and Islamic Principles, it cannot escape the attention of Jurists; and I take the legitimacy of my argument from this, saying it's what every Jurist says. I give two examples: Mohaqqeq Helli, author of *Sharaye' al-Islam*, one of the best feqh texts, was the greatest seventh-[thirteenth-]century Shi'i Jurist. In the Book of Inheritance he says that the absence of any stipulated legacy in a will implies equal shares for male and female heirs. That is, if someone leaves a legacy to his children, his sons and daughters get equal shares. Basing his reasoning on the Principle of equality, Helli argues that females should get the same shares as males. He sees [fixed] inheritance ['ers, according to which women's share is half] as an exception. We must understand why Islam made [fixed] inheritance an exception; and once we understand the reason for this, we'll see that Islam has based everything on equality. I wonder why some [Jurists] leave the Principle aside and focus on exceptions.

ZMH: Why do think the Principle is left aside? If the spirit of Islam is based on justice and human equality, why shouldn't jurists adhere to them?

SMS: Of course, Islam is based on justice and human equality; it owes much of its advancement to equality—equality in every sense. But Jurists tended to leave gender out and focus on the rest; whereas I say we must oppose gender discrimination in the same way we oppose racial discrimination, since it discriminates between humans, and whatever does this is condemned—be it color, gender, or race. . . . The Jurists—some of them—have

[8] Ibid., 36–43.

come to build a theory on a trivial instance, on a special, exceptional case for which conditions are even defined. [But] we can't base a theory on an instance and ignore the Principle. For instance, Mohaqqeq Helli is explicit on the Principle of [gender] equality.

ZMH: But not when it comes to marriage, which he defines as "a man's dominion over woman's sexual and productive faculties."

SMS: In marriage he talks on the basis of the ownership axiom, and since there is a clash between the two, he leaves equality aside. Because of his jurisprudential thinking, he is forced to abandon the Principle. As I said, jurists have sacrificed the Principle of equality to feqh theories, whereas I say we must sacrifice the theory for the sake of the Principle; equality is such an unequivocal Principle that we can't leave it aside for the sake of a set of feqh theories.

ZMH: If these theories go, then there'll be little left of feqh; it's like removing the framework of a building.

SMS: No! the building will remain, one pillar replaces another. Like these historic builidings in England, their foundations are kept intact but simply fortified and updated.

ZMH: To make them habitable . . .

SMH: For today's life-style. We do the same. Sheikh Ansari is a more recent jurist who adhered to the Principle, and his approach to hadith is rationalist. He died about two hundred years ago; he's called the Seal of the Mojtaheds, and his books are among the best texts taught in Shi'i seminaries. On Shi'i hadith that permit a man to look at the entire body of a woman he intends to marry, he argues for women to be permitted the same. This permission is granted [by jurists] on the grounds that in marriage a man is like a buyer and is paying a high price (*mahr*, dower), so he must see what he is buying. Therefore, Skeikh Ansari says, there's a stronger case for granting a woman permission to look, not only because she's the other party to the deal, but also because, unlike the man, she's in no position to revoke the deal if she isn't happy with it [i.e., he has the unilateral right to divorce]! This is a critical view, premised on the notion of equality, in which Sheikh Ansari invokes the reasoning of ahadith to grant men and women equal rights in the matter of "permission to look" prior to marriage.[9]

ZMH: Are you seriously suggesting that the Equality perspective has precedents in feqh?

SMS: Yes! But articulating it this way is my own contribution.

ZMH: Don't you think this articulation is to some extent due to changed conditions? We live in an era when there's a heightened awareness of gender discrimination.

[9] Ibid., 42–43.

SMS: That's true; space and time have affected my thinking consciously and unconsciously, as with all other Jurists. Feqh and Interpretation of the Koran are affected by situations. Not only are jurists unconsciously affected by them, they must be consciously taken into account.

There is an echo here of Sorush's theory of "Expansion and Contraction of the Shari'a," which I missed then, as I was not conversant with it. In Iran later that year, I soon learned that Houzeh politics did not allow any cleric openly to admit such an influence. Like many other clerics, Sa'idzadeh has read Sorush's work, has followed the critiques, and thus must have been quite familiar with the debate, and was appropriating it into Houzeh scholarship and its Aristotelian logic. Had I known this, I would have put my questions differently. They seem now too naive. As we shall see, in contrast to Sorush, Sa'idzadeh argues for feqh as the starting point and the key to the question of women in Islam.

ZMH: In your writings you state things like "religion must be separated from the interpretation of the religion" or "Islam is not the same as the views of Muslims." How do you establish such a separation? Where do you draw the line?

SMS: Islam is what the Prophet brought people from God. This is all I recognize as Islam; we don't have any other Islam. What Companions of the Prophet said isn't Islam, nor are the interpretations. For 1,400 years, discriminatory interpretations on women have been produced; these aren't religion but interpretations of religion. I defend my position against those who say I'm questioning religion. I say I don't question religion, only erroneous religious thoughts.

ZMH: What makes your thoughts correct?

SMS: By proving their interpretations invalid, in effect I prove the validity of my own. If I tell you, "whatever I told you up to now, and you recorded, is wrong," this means what I'm saying now is true.

ZMH: Not necessarily. You must still prove the validity of what you say.

SMS: On the basis of ahadith I prove their readings are invalid. My teacher used to say that Ayatollah Borujerdi counted five hundred instances of fatwas given by Shi'i jurists that had no religious backing but were accepted by people as the religion. . . . I too will show that these [views on women] are fabricated; they are interpetations.

ZMH: Like others, you seek to prove the truth of your views through religious texts. You too are ultimately interpreting.

SMS: I too am interpreting.

ZMH: So why do you say that "religion is separate from interpretation of religion"?

SMS: What should I say, do you think?

ZMH: I don't know. It's a problem for me.

SMS: You can explain a speaker's statement in two ways: when a speaker says, for instance, "there is no partner for God," you can say that the statement suggests the existence of a partner for God in the speaker's mind. But I say that it's in order to prove His unity. . . . The kind of objections you make are not valid in logic.[10]

ZMH: For me, reading your work as an outsider, what you say is an interpretation, however different from conventional ones. Why should we accept what you say?

SMS: I believe my understanding is valid; I'm a realist; they're in the wrong.

ZMH: In other words, you claim legitimacy for your position; where do you get it from? From feqh, the Koran, or your own belief?

SMS: I take this legitimacy from the Koran, ahadith, feqh, and rational proofs and incontestable scientific principles. Truth (*haqq*) is a matter of reason; when you explain and justify something logically, it'll be accepted. I can reason and convince; for instance, when I prove that the concept of maintenance rests on a theory of ownership, everyone accepts it; since, once that theory is removed, the Rulings on maintenance are dismantled. It's clear and straightforward.

ZMH: What you're doing, in effect, is to question theories that underpin feqh Rulings on women. This I can accept, since these Rulings rest on a set of interconnected theories, some of which are explicit and others remain implicit. Earlier you said the Inequality perspective rests on several theories. What are they? Can you name them?

SMS: Yes, as far as my memory allows. The most important is the theory of women's defectiveness, which is evident in laws of inheritance, penal law, and testimony; also in some constitutional laws, such as the conditions for presidency and leadership of society. Another theory, which sees relations with women in terms of ownership or slavery, affects marriage and divorce. The theory that regards women as stupid and says they should be kept that way has a bearing on areas of economic participation and educational opportunities. Another regards women as inferior beings and bears on mysticism and the attainment of spiritual perfection: a hadith is invoked, according to which many men have attained spiritual perfection but only four women—meaning no other women will attain it in future.

ZMH: Isn't this what Javadi-Amoli tries to modify in his book, *Women in the Mirror of Glory and Beauty*?[11]

[10] He was referring to the Aristotelian logic (as developed by later thinkers) in which mutually exclusive statements are either contraries or contradictions; see Mottahedeh 1995a, 91.

[11] Javadi-Amoli 1993a; see Introduction to Part Two above.

SMS: Yes, but he deals with the issue sentimentally, not systematically; he doesn't address the theory directly.

ZMH: How can he, when he endorses the concept of unequal gender rights? This theory is but a component in a system. Are you saying that none of these theories is corroborated by Koran and hadith?

SMS: Exactly; there are verses and ahadith against them. Once it's proved that these theories are founded on erroneous grounds, in inheritance, testimony, marriage and divorce, and the other laws, then women can't be put at less than their human level. There are more of these theories that I can't remember now. . . . I've made many notes on them, but used only part of them in my writings. For instance, I've tackled "women's stupidity" in articles in *Payam-e Zan* which you haven't referred to in your own paper;[12] and "women's defectiveness" in articles on women in penal law and women in judgment, and in my response to Ayatollah Yazdi's views on maintenance—all these appeared in *Zanan*.

In June 1993, Ayatollah Yazdi, head of the Judiciary, expressed in his Friday sermon the conventional Shi'i view that the wife's right to maintenance does not include the expense of major medical treatment. Sa'idzadeh's comment in *Zanan* led to a letter of response from Yazdi, published in the following issue, in which he modified his assertion. Missing the thrust of Sa'idzadeh's argument, which questions the conventional boundary between moral and legal in laws about maintenance, he simply said that he was talking in strict legal terms; of course, morally a man is responsible to pay for such expenses. The next issue of *Zanan* carried a long article by Sa'idzadeh in which he responded by drawing attention to contradictions in Ayatollah Yazdi's position and the assumptions that lie behind his notion of marriage and marital duties.[13]

ZMH: I particularly like that exchange and referred to it in my paper; I think it shows clearly how those who adhere to the Inequality perspective accept these theories.

SMS: That's why I say my thinking is different from others: I've critically addressed these theories as a whole and systematically, and nobody else has done this; they've simply tackled details and instances, not the premises on which they're based; so they've fallen into contradiction. For instance, Mr. Yazdi says [in response to my criticism] that relations between men and women are regulated by human not commercial values and criteria; if this is so, then we can't defend conventional definitions and rules of maintenance, which say a man isn't responsible. If we defend the human values on which marriage is based, then why shouldn't he be legally responsible

---

[12] Sa'idzadeh 1993b, continued in two later issues; I had not yet read these articles.
[13] Sa'idzadeh 1994b, Yazdi 1994, and Sa'idzadeh 1994c.

for his wife's medical treatment? You can't separate the two; that's why [advocates of gender inequality] have reached a dead end; their statements are only meant to appease, when challenged. The question that must be asked is: why have the Jurists deduced these Rulings sustaining gender inequalities?

ZMH: Why? This is one of my questions, too.

SMS: I deal with this in the conference paper, in a section on "Sources of Difference between the Perspectives." It's a good paper; I worked hard on it, but they didn't appreciate it. I'll read the section for you, but first let me read out the four principles on which I base the "Equality perspective":[14]

1. Humans as subjects: I mean, humans as the subjects of God's rule; instances where other things than humanity have a role to play, are exceptions and rare.

2. The contractual nature of Rulings: I mean that every religious Ruling addressing people is a contractual, not a natural or innate one. It's evident that there are also exceptions to this Principle, but they are so few that a Principle can't be derived from them.

3. The force of Reason: this Principle is opposed to that of unquestioning obedience in the sense that humans have the capacity to understand the reasons for God's commands.

4. Separation between givens and interpretations: according to this Principle, a separation must be made between God's commands and other commands, even if they come from the Prophet, the Imams, the Companions; likewise a distinction must be made between data and their interpretations. In other words, the same as we discussed earlier: religion is distinct from its interpretations.

ZMH: Has the Prophet given other commands, separate from God's?

SMS: Of course: he received and gave personal instructions, pertaining to him or his household.

ZMH: Such distinctions are not made in hadith literature, certainly not in the way ahadith are invoked.

SMS: It shouldn't be like this. God's commands must be separated from others; and since this hasn't been done, it's believed that everything in the Sunna is God's command. That's one problem.

In the Prophet's practice three things must be separated: the Prophet's personal actions, his actions as leader of the Muslim community, his actions as intermediary between God and people. He brought people a religion, the way of Islam, and said, God told me to convey this [to people], but when it comes to executing and obeying God's commands, the Prophet himself is

---

[14] Sa'idzadeh 1995b, 88–89.

like any other Muslim. His position as leader is separate from his Prophet-hood; this separation is made in the Koran. A person can have two positions simultaneously but they shouldn't be confused. For instance, in our own time, Imam Khomeini was both theoretican and founder of the Islamic Re-public, he became the vali-ye faqih, and at the same time he was a marja'; and so it was first said [in the constitution] that the vali-ye faqih must also be a marja'. Later it was realized that the two positions were quite distinct from each other; and they were separated in amendments to the constitution. This is also what I mean when I say that an idea, a thought, must be sepa-rated from its carriers.

As for why jurists have understood the sacred texts as endorsing gender inequality, this has to do with their assumptions. In the paper, I refer to three such assumptions and premises, and criticize them: men's headship over women, which stems from an incorrect understanding of Sura Nisa, 34, and women's stupidity and weakness. Then under the heading, "Why These Assumptions," I write: "Acceptance of unsound and undocumented as-sumptions of the kind mentioned is the result of a number of basic factors: acceptance of existing written collections as religious texts; lack of atten-tion to vernaculars and idioms at the time of Revelation; incorrect arrange-ment of existing texts and subsequent imitation of that arrangement by later jurists; selection of incorrect methodologies in deducing Rulings; ambiguity in defining the boundaries of law, religion, and Islam; sacralization of exist-ing collections; ignoring factors of time and space; and so on." Each word is carefully chosen and can be substantiated; I then discuss nine of these, with examples.[15]

ZMH: My knowledge of feqh is limited, but I know that Muslim jurists strive to keep the sacred texts intact; they construct their precepts and theo-ries so as to reflect and protect religious truths; that is, they keep human interference with the sacred texts to a minimum so that God's Will can be translated into law.[16]

SMS: That's so in some cases but not others. In fact, I can even quote a hadith for what you said: "Jurists are the stockade of Islam." I accept this, but their problem is that they've exceeded their mandate and constantly broken the limits, by adding things to the religion. I've no objection if Islam is introduced as it is.

ZMH: Some say that in Islam there's no need for clerics as a class of "official interpreters"; in other words, every Muslim can access the terms of the divine law.

SMS: No, what I'm saying is different. There's a need for expert knowl-edge; thus Islam needs qualified interpreters, the Jurists, and the ulama. But

[15] Ibid., 96–111.   [16] Cf. Mernissi 1991, 125–29.

the question is whether this knowledge should be in the hands of one group [clerics] or not. I say that the door of research is open to all, and their findings can be followed provided they are based on correct methods. In other words, knowledge of religious texts isn't confined to one group. This is so since both ejtehad and taqlid have a rational basis, to the extent that anyone who masters the knowledge can discern the terms of divine law through the correct procedures discussed in the science of feqh and its Principles.

ZMH: What you say seems to me to go against the Shi'i doctrine of taqlid. As Shi'is, we must follow the rulings of a mojtahed in all matters that come under "branches" of religion, that is, all matters of ritual and law, unless we ourselves have reached the level of ejtehad. It's only with respect to belief in "roots," that is, tenets of the faith, that we must be convinced by reason.

SMS: You're confusing several issues here. First, taqlid doesn't require suspension of one's critical faculty, it means you accept the authority of a person who is expert in matters of religious law. Such acceptance has a rational basis and exists in every field of science; for instance, I'm not an anthropologist and I accept your judgment in certain matters. This is quite different from ta'bod, which means devotion, blind, unquestioning acceptance. Taqlid in Arabic comes from the root of "putting something on one's neck," by which one can be guided; that's to say, you choose to put it on and you can take it off when necessary. True, we're required to follow the practice of the Prophet, but we're also required to do so using our rational faculties; the problem is that religion and its laws have often been approached through ta'bod rather than taqlid.

Second, a mojtahed isn't in a position to issue a religious command. All he can do is merely state his opinion that an action is good or bad, in line with Islam or not; the rest is left to the believer. This is what the Council of Guardians is supposed to do, to say whether the laws of the Majles are in line with Islam or not; the rest is left to other authorities in the Islamic Republic; that is, when something becomes law, then it enters the realm of government. A mojtahed can act in four capacities, or have four stations:

Ejtehad: at this level, his opinions are simply relevant to himself
Fatwa: at this level, he transmits his opinions to others, who may choose to follow them
Marja'iyat: at this level, he can accept and administer religious tax, the Imam's share
Qezavat: at this level, he can act as judge (*qazi*).

These are the four capacities in which a mojtahed can act, and they must be kept separate. Each station is different. In today's world you can't mix the four together. You can't expect somone to function at all four levels and master all branches of law—there's a need for specialization in feqh, as in all other sciences.

ZMH: Somewhere you argue for a radical revival of the "tools and basics of feqh." You say that the tools the Jurists have at their disposal are unsuitable for life today. I take it you're talking about *osul al-feqh*, that is, the methodology and concepts on which Islamic Jurisprudence rests. But the argument is that these are rooted in immutable precepts, that is, they're grounded in sacred texts.

SMS: First, the tools a Jurist works with today are like those used by craftsmen of a century ago, like the simple crucible. They haven't evolved to match progress in other scientific fields. Second, humans make tools, not God. God has given us the capacity to make tools, the power to think and make choices; but all tools and concepts in all crafts and sciences are made by us, humans. . . . Feqh too is a science and can't be exempted from the need to evolve in time and space. I've dealt with this in the introduction to my discussion of divorce in *Zanan*, where I say that feqh is like any other human science and that one basic criterion for its soundness is the absence of contradictions in its concepts and legal Rulings.[17] Neither tools nor concepts in feqh are sacred, it's like any other science and must evolve.

Most of the jurist's tools are rooted in rational matters, such as philosophy, logic, Arabic grammar, and syntax. There is nothing inherently Islamic about them; the first two came from Greek and other sources. Islamic theology has drawn heavily on Greek and Iranian philosophy and logic, and you know that both sciences have expanded and have evolved, especially in the past two hundred years. Feqh is partly taken from these sciences, and partly from sacred texts: Koran and hadith. Here too we use our rational faculties, on which the two sciences of Exegesis and Hadith are based. The former enables the jurists to interpret the sacred texts in accordance with conditions of time and space, the latter establishes the methodology by which the authenticity of hadith can be discerned. Both sciences have a human and rational basis. For example, we need to know both the occasion and the context for any particular hadith or Koranic revelation and use them in line with cardinal Principles of Islam. Among the established Principles of Islam are equality and common humanity, the right of choice, and freedom of the human will. There are many ahadith that show the influence of time and space in Islamic injunctions. For instance, some people protested to Imam Sadeq: why do you wear expensive clothes and allow them, when Imam Ali neither wore nor allowed them? The Imam replied: then the door of fortune hadn't been opened to Muslims and people were poor, now the situa-

---

[17] The article (Musavi 1995) appeared under one of his pseudonyms, and his introduction was also omitted.

tion is different and Muslims are prosperous. Also, Jurists sometimes invoke ahadith in such a way that their true meanings are missed.

The second theme in our discussion was the manuscript, *Woman's Freedom at the Time of Mohammad*, which Sa'idzadeh had given me in Tehran in April to read and comment on from a feminist perspective. He argues that at the time of the Prophet women enjoyed many freedoms they were later denied, and were active and vocal in demanding their rights and objecting to male control. The manuscript, finished in spring 1994, is about 120 pages long, including over 30 pages of references and footnotes. Shahla Lahiji had agreed to publish it at her Roushangaran Press, but the plan was abandoned when the text did not pass Ministry of Guidance censorship.

I found this work of interest for two main reasons. First, it was the first critical and objective account of women's situation in the early years of Islam written by a cleric in Persian. I could see intriguing parallels and differences between his account and those by Nabia Abbott, Fatima Mernissi, and Leila Ahmed.[18] Second, it was quite different in style from other works of his that I had read: it contained no feqh argument, being based entirely on hadith literature. This puzzled me, since in his other works he was highly critical of others' reliance on hadith, and I had assumed that the Koran was the major source for his Equality perspective. He states in the introduction that the work is based on years of reseach and is the fulfilment of a wish to complete a themetic study of the Prophet's practice.

> Now that women have a major share in social participation and the development of countries, and now that some of these countries are governed by the Islamic [ideology], women's status and their share in political and social matters can be determined only by following the model provided by the Prophet. . . . Analytical and logical study of the Prophet's practice can shed light on various social, economic, and political aspects of the time of Presence, and provide policy makers in Muslim countries with a wealth of insight and knowledge.

I told Sa'idzadeh I had three general comments on his book.

ZMH: First, on the basis of works by orientalists, a number of Muslim feminists argue that Arabian society before the advent of Islam was undergoing a transition from matrilineality to patrilineality, that Islam facilitated this by giving patriarchy the seal of approval; and that Koranic injunctions on marriage, divorce, inheritance, and whatever relates to women both reflect and affirm such a transition.[19]

SMS: What is the difference between patrilineality and patriarchy?

---

[18] Abbott 1942b, Ahmed 1991, Mernissi 1991; see also Stern 1939.

[19] For concise accounts of the debate on the position of women in Arabia at the advent of Islam, see Smith 1985 and Spellberg 1991.

ZMH: Patrilineality means descent traced through only, or primarily, the father's line, whereas patriarchy refers more to the power that men have over women—usually as fathers, but not necessarily.

SMS: I've come across [that argument]; some speakers at the Toronto conference expressed similar views, but I didn't think it appropriate to say what came to my mind there. For instance, they said that one proof that Islam sanctioned the transition is the shari'a requirement that women keep an 'eddeh [waiting period a woman must observe on termination of marriage before remarrying, ranging from two menses to longer, depending on the type of marriage and mode of termination or whether she is pregnant or not]. But I don't think you can demonstrate that Islam sanctions patrilineality or facilitated the transition. Why? Because on the Day of Resurrection everybody will be called by their mothers' names: that's in the Koran. If Islam requires women to keep 'eddeh, this is to do with determining filiation, not with sanctioning patrilineality or matrilineality. Women had to keep different forms of 'eddeh in pre-Islamic Arabia, sometimes as long as a year, and what Islam did was to reduce it to three menses. There were also some rites associated with it, all of which Islam banned, such as that women had to cover themselves with dung, or be secluded. As with the Sassanids [ruling dynasty then in Iran], Arabia was a highly stratified society, with a distinct class of aristocrats and nobles; and experts known as Allameh and Nasabeh, who could trace and establish descent, using a combination of sciences from medicine to physiognomy. Many books on the subject are left from that period. In fact Arabian horse-breeding, which later entered Iran, was a branch of that science. The establishment of filiation was important to define this class of nobles and separate them from commoners, and since the Prophet aimed to remove these distinctions, Islam also clashed with this science of genealogy. I don't think Islam has a specific position on this. We can say that Islam is against hereditary distinctions and has nothing to do with patrilineality.

There were many types of union in pre-Islamic Arabia, some of which were accepted by Islam and continue to be practiced to this day, such as permanent and temporary forms of marriage. So we can't say that injunctions on marriage can all be explained by Islam facilitating or endorsing patriarchy.[20]

ZMH: You also say in your book that contrary to [conventional wisdom], the pre-Islamic culture of Arabia wasn't backward; what do you mean?

SMS: I mean that it was a liberal and open culture, rather like present Western culture. How it came to be called Jaheliyeh (Time of Ignorance) I don't know. Of course, it's referred to as such in the Koran, but we must find out when and why it was first called this. The point is, we must establish

[20] Cf. Robertson Smith 1885 and Stern 1939.

what is meant by "ignorant" (*jahel*). Is it similar to the way Western culture
is referred to these days in Iran: the Great Satan, or the banal? The assertion
that a culture is banal is untenable; no culture can be banal. If we say today
that everyone in the West is ignorant, nobody will accept it. It's too sweeping, every culture can have positive and negative aspects; and we must clarify what aspects we're talking about, and what the basis of our judgment is.
In the Koran, whenever Jaheliyeh is referred to, it's with the definite article
"al-," which suggests a certain meaning was intended: "ignorance" in the
sense of something not done according to wisdom.

ZMH: My second comment is that, in my view, much of the material and
evidence you produce [based on hadith literature] contradicts the main thesis of the book, that gender equality is an indisputable Principle in Islam.
You have a section entitled "women's protest in the first decade," in which
you list the complaints that women took to the Prophet; we see that as Islam
gained ground, women's sphere of activities got narrower, and their conditions started to change—they lost some of the rights they had before and
that's why they were objecting. For instance, women were excluded from
participation in wars and decision making, whereas at the beginning some,
like the Prophet's first wife, Khadija, played a very decisive role. Also the
Prophet's practice, especially his own plural marriages after Khadija's
death, suggest that perhaps the Prophet himself was not much in favor of the
kind of equality that women were demanding then.

SMS: Point taken; but the answer is crystal clear, it's in the book. Look,
my arguments mustn't be taken separately from each other—especially in
that book. There I have a discussion on "violation," where I argue that the
actions of Muslims must be separated from Islam itself. When women protested, they were objecting to people's actions, not to the religion. They
were protesting at what Omar, Abu Bakr, and Imam Ali [close associates of
the Prophet, and later caliphs] did, not at what the religion said. When they
asked, "why don't you take us to battle any more? Why do you limit our
actions?" it was because the Principle of women's participation in battle and
other activities was accepted by Islam; they were entitled to take part in
battle, as they had before. It's important that women weren't objecting to
Islam, as it didn't limit them, but to the actions of Muslims and rulers of
Muslim society.

ZMH: Why wasn't a verse revealed to the Prophet so that women too
could take part in battles?

SMS: Revelations don't address a specific sex; they address dutiful humans, who can be either men and women. Gender has no place in the divine
realm; gender is a relative matter; and it goes contrary to divine Justice and
God's glory if it becomes a basis. You must consider my arguments as a
system, I'm moving within a framework, and if you consider what I say

within that framework, there's no contradiction. I say that the subject in a divine Ruling is humankind, and prove that the use of masculine terms in Koranic injunctions doesn't mean they are solely addressed to men, but reflects Arabic grammatical rules according to which masculine forms are employed for more than two persons of different genders. In addition, general and fundamental injunctions in the Koran are in terms of *insan*, *nafs*, *nas*, which all denote humakind and are not gendered.[21] In feqh we have an extended discussion—too technical to go into here—as to whether the masculine gender in the Koran and hadith apply to both sexes or not. There are two views: some argue that the masculine gender indicates that men are the main addressees of God's command, others argue otherwise. Each side gives its own reasoning, and I have critically discussed each of these views, and made my own position clear.

ZMH: I know your position and arguments, which I find clear and coherent.[22] But what you now say suggests that even at the time of the Prophet, Koranic commands were to some extent bypassed; that is, the Prophet didn't implement them.

SMS: Yes, sometimes certain expediencies meant that the spirit couldn't be translated into practice. Again we must go back to what I said earlier: the three positions that the Prophet occupied [prophecy, leadership, and Muslim citizenship]. Even if the Prophet personally does something that contradicts the Revelation, we have the right to object, we can say, this isn't what the Koran tells us. I say this hypothetically, and the Jurists themselves have discussed the issue: when God says that the Prophet is in charge of the life and wealth of Muslims, this also has certain conditions.

ZMH: You say that the spirit, the Principle, was gender equality, even if the practice was not. What about polygamy? The Koran gives only man permission to practice it.

SMS: The Koranic positioning and the occasions of revelation must be heeded. The verse regarding polygamy has a definite positioning: it wanted to break the pre-Islamic traditions in which a man could take over a hundred wives. The Koran says, you cannot have more than four wives; that is, its intention is reform, to change gradually. This is very different from permitting and sanctioning polygamy. In fact, another verse makes this permission conditional and tells men to take more than one wife only if they are certain they can treat them justly, and then it says "you cannot be just."

ZMH: But the Prophet's practice does not support this; he took many wives; he left nine widows. It's argued that the Prophet became polygamous after Khadija's death—that is, when Islam was in power.

[21] Cf. Hassan 1988 and Wadud-Muhsin 1992.

[22] His earlier *Zanan* articles deal with: women's rights, in Shi'i law, to be judges and arbiters in court, and to be marja'; and with gender biases in family and penal laws; see Mir-Hosseini 1996b.

SMS: His practice in marriage stems from his personal position and isn't a model for Muslims to follow.

ZMH: But the Koran enjoins Muslims to follow the practice of the Prophet.

SMS: Not in this respect; both Koran and hadith explicitly say you can't follow the Prophet in this respect; it's discussed again in feqh literature. He had nine wives, but no other Muslim is allowed more than four. Women could marry the Prophet without mahr [dower], whereas a marriage without mahr is invalid in Islam.

ZMH: If we accept what you say, that Islam established gender equality but Muslims reversed it, the question is why and how? What did they have against women, as a group?

SMS: Since Muslims couldn't deny the Principle of equality and freedom, they had to contain it by turning exceptions into rules. When we look into it, we see limitations introduced one by one: first it was said that women shouldn't go to war, then that they shouldn't walk in the middle of the street, and finally that they shouldn't walk in the streets at all. The same with women's right to express their views. First it was said that women can talk with men, but not for very long, then not more than two words, and finally they shouldn't talk at all with unrelated men. I think there was a political edge to it. Women were among the early advocates of Islam, took part in wars, and played an important role in bringing it into power. Naturally they were going to ask for their share in the state that rules in the name of Islam, but this would undermine the interests of those who sought power, so women had to be marginalized. It was a question of power and worldly gain. These were the doings of Muslims, not Islam; and that's why women protested to the Prophet.[23]

ZMH: It seems that Imam Ali was among those who wanted women excluded; he has some very harsh words on women in *Nahj ol-Balagheh*.

SMS: As a Shi'i, I don't accept that these are the Imam's words, because the Prophet says, "haqq is with Ali," so Ali can't be separated from haqq [truth, justice]. I've said in the article that the Shi'a is here in a dilemma and must either accept that Imam Ali was a brutal man or deny these hadith. The Ali of *Nahj ol-Balagheh* is a brutal man, and we don't accept that image of him.[24]

ZMH: Where do you find the image of Imam Ali apart from *Nahj ol-Balagheh*?

SMS: On the basis of the Principles we have. Because what is there goes contrary to the Principles.

[23] Cf. Mernissi 1991.   [24] Sa'idzadeh 1995b, 109.

ZMH: My third comment is that some feminists have pointed to parallels in laws concerning women and slavery. Both negate the spirit of Islam and its Principle of human equality. In both, the individual's will is ignored: the slave and the wife are denied certain rights and choices because of their social position. Islam didn't sanction slavery but at the same time didn't ban it; Muslims were simply encouraged to free slaves. Can we say the same with respect to gender equality? History shows that if slavery is no longer practiced, this has nothing to do with Jurists' views or the Islamic position, but with the changed worldview, and the impact of the outside world on Muslims. Do you see parallels between the two? What is the feqh debate on the two? Have past Jurists compared the two or not?

SMS: Slavery is one of the issues that has always occupied my mind; there's no denying there are certain reflections of it in the laws of marriage in Islam and among Muslims. One of the theories that I say underlie marriage is that of slavery, that is, some of the assumptions of the jurists are premised on a theory of slavery. I agree with you up to this point, but not the rest. You seem to have forgotten what I've said many times—you even refer to it in your own paper—that there are three types of Rulings in Islam. The first is what we call *ta'sisi*, those "established" by Islam: they include prayers, and some (not all) Rulings on Pilgrimage. The second we call *emza'i*, those "signed," accepted, by Islam without modification: for instance, Islam accepted the Principle [not the form] of fasting in Judaism and other religions, and a number of social contracts and practices of the Jaheliyeh. The third we call *eslahi*, the Rulings that the religion intended to "reform": most social and political Rulings in Islam are of this kind, and it's here that questions of abrogation, generality and specificity, clarity or ambiguity of Koranic commands show themselves. For instance, slavery was widely practiced in the Jaheliyeh, and was an important element of its economy and culture; Islam intended gradually to change this practice, to reform it. It couldn't eradicate it all at once; it had to tolerate existing practices. But there's no evidence to indicate that Islam sanctioned it, accepted it, or established it. It never endorsed the Principle of slavery or encouraged its practice. The same is true with respect to women; Islam intended gradually to reform existing practices and to do away with all discriminations. For instance, women weren't entitled to inherit; Islam allocated them a share—not equal, because it intended to reform [things] in such a way that society would accept and people's opinion be taken into account.

The disparity you feel between Islamic Principles and Rulings stems from this. Among the Rulings established by Islam, all those upholding equality between the sexes are of the first kind, and any that you think contradict them are among the second or the third kind: either sanctioned or reformed but not established by Islam. The Rulings established by Islam are all based on the Principle of equality, including those concerning women.

ZMH: You haven't explained this in such a systematic way before, your writings are ambiguous. You see, I'm looking for a coherent and articulate system, something like that of Ayatollah Motahhari, but based on gender equality.

SMS: You must ask so that I can explain; I've worked out the whole argument in my mind like a computer, but I can't put it in this way in Iranian society—you know that there are limitations.[25] For instance, *Zanan* doesn't publish my material in the order I want. They don't understand my system; they have their own priorities.

As for your query why the Prophet didn't insist on implementing the Rulings established by Islam, I've dealt with that in the book—again implicitly. As long as the "forces of violation" were operating in society, the Prophet could not [insist]. We, the Shi'a, believe the Prophet wanted to designate Imam Ali as his successor, but didn't do it explicitly. It's there in the Koran, when it tells the Prophet: don't be afraid of the people, announce the Rulings.

ZMH: Are you suggesting that the Prophet, in implementing the terms of the divine Law, had to take the state of society into account?

SMS: Yes. I'm confident that, if the Prophet had lived longer, he'd certainly have implemented the Rulings, though gradually. We have evidence for this in both the Koran and hadith. There is a hadith that at the time of Jaheliyeh, in case of zena [sexual intercourse outside marriage], women were imprisoned for life; in the Koran this was first accepted, then abrogated. The hadith is narrated by Imam Sadeq, who says it was because the Prophet then feared the people; the penalty of one hundred lashes was introduced later when conditions became favorable. We accept this hadith—even though its authenticity is weak—since it's corroborated by the Koran.

What I've done that is still unfinished is that I've studied the Rulings of Islam from a historical perspective and compared them with Rulings in other religions. I hope to collect these in a separate book on *The History of Rules and Regulations of Religion*. I want to ascertain which Rulings are established, reformed, or accepted. When this is done, we can see how far Islam has reformed views, and the influence of other religions. Then we can judge whether or not the objections to Islam have any credibility.

[25] Almost three years later, in March 1998, Sa'idzadeh openly aired these views in an interview with *Iran-e Farda* (Iran Tomorrow), a monthly associated with the views of the Liberation Movement whose members were present in Bazargan's government, but were later excluded; see Sa'idzadeh 1998a.

But as for why the Rulings that Islam established gave rise to such a tendency [to gender inequality], this again involves the actions of Muslims. The gist of what I say in this book is that it was the Muslims who gave this color to the religion, added things that religion didn't necessarily say or even endorse. The Prophet himself had enlightened views, which don't agree with many opinions now expressed in the name of the religion. It is our views that give direction to Islamic cultures. . . . It is essential to separate individuals' thoughts from their actions; one of the problems is that the two are confounded when we talk about Islam.

ZMH: Can we really separate the two?

SMS: They can easily be separated; why not?

ZMH: Because people's thoughts are embedded in their actions; they don't exist or operate in a vacuum. One reflects the other . . .

SMS: Not necessarily. Taqiyeh isn't like this. Look, I believe men and women are equal in Iran, even if I act as though they are unequal. I do taqiyeh because I'm afraid of consequences. For instance, I think that men and women can shake hands, but in Iran you'd never see me shaking hands with any women. Something has come between my thought and my action.

ZMH: But you're aware of that something.

SMS: Yes, but when you say that actions reflect thoughts, I say not necessarily, because if you judge from my actions you may come to the wrong conclusion about my thoughts. My actions don't express equality—as I am doing taqiyeh—but my thought does. By separating one from the other you can understand the two, and then you understand why there's a contradiction between my thought and my action.

ZMH: But as you say, you are doing taqiyeh, you are hiding your thought. Your thought is embedded in your very taqiyeh, otherwise it would become something else. I mean that when a society bans shaking hands between sexes, this ban comes from a thought.

SMS: Of course, but it isn't necessarily a true reflection of that thought, it might even reflect its opposite. I agree with you. But the question is, who is to know that I'm doing taqiyeh? I want you to understand, when I insist on distinguishing Islam from the actions of Muslims, it's because I want to create this separation. When I say that distinctions must be made between ideas and individuals, between thoughts and actions, that Islam must not be confounded with views of Muslims, I am making a philosophical and logical assertion. I am trying to preempt and avoid the fallacy that arises when they are confounded.

ZMH: I differ from you here, because I really think the two can't be separated.

SMS: I accept that you can't separate them because you are trained that way. That's your art, your way of looking. But your view is only one, there are ten others, there are many other angles from which we must look. It depends on the glasses through which we choose to look. . . .

It was much later, after visiting Qom and learning more about the Houzeh milieu and values, that I realized why he insisted so much on separating "ideas from actions." For Saʿidzadeh, such a separation was necessary for establishing the system of women's rights within feqh frameworks, for broadening its focus from specific answers to new avenues for dealing with contemporary issues. I began to understand, too, why he disagreed with Sorush. His system of gender equality within feqh could not have emerged, I thought, without Sorush's approach to sacred texts and theory of the nature of religious knowledge, but unlike Sorush the intellectual, Saʿidzadeh the cleric held that the key to both understanding and solving Muslim women's issues was in feqh, as it is the most important among religious sciences.

Saʿidzadeh in 1997

In Tehran, in early 1997, I told Saʿidzadeh I was devoting a chapter to his ideas and asked him for a new piece of work. In May he gave me the text of an article he had just written on divorce, to show the working of his approach to feqh. Referring to himself in the third person, as though someone else were writing, he spells out the premises of what he now calls Modern Feqh (*feqh-e modern*), and introduces himself as its founder.[26] Here I give a complete translation of the text.

Feqh Premises of the Equality Perspective
Modern Feqh: the Case of Divorce

The presence of the Equality perspective in the arena of religious thought has shaken feqh theories. This new view, proposed exclusively by a researcher in the Qom Houzeh, rests on strong jurisprudential, theological, and legal foundations.[27]

This article deals briefly with one example of the application of this approach, and mentions some of its jurisprudential and legal bases.

Divorce has always been a problem for Muslim women. In the light of the new perspective the problem is no longer for women but for contemporary male jurists of Iran.[28]

---

[26] The article was published a year later in *Payam-e Hajar* (Saʿidzadeh 1998b).

[27] [SMS note: He has written over 150 articles on the issue, has ejazeh from several eminent Houzeh teachers, and is accepted in both Houzeh and university circles in Iran.] He is probably referring to his work with Shireen Ebadi, Mehrangiz Kar, and myself.

[28] [SMS note: If they are free from constraints and fear of their followers.]

In the Equality perspective, divorce cannot be considered separately from theories and assumptions made in feqh writings on marriage. Therefore, whatever we understand of marriage affects divorce. Based on terms employed in the Koran and the hadith, the Equality perspective has reached the conclusion that marriage rested on the "theory of unilateral protection." According to consensus of the Jurists, marriage is a customary affair and was a pre-Islamic tradition. The new religion accepted this tradition and, on the basis of the said theory, left divorce as it was. The modifications introduced by the new religion confined polygamy to four wives and limited the number of times a man could divorce [one woman].

With this brief overture, we now examine the basis of the Equality theory about marriage and its dissolution.

Identification of the subject is one of the difficulties and at the same time the ultimate manifestation of the Jurist's ability. The Jurist's first task is identification of the subject [of a Ruling], just as the physician's is to make a diagnosis. Once the illness is diagnosed, a cure becomes possible. The same is true in feqh. The error of previous Jurists (as regards marriage) lies in their identification of its subject.

The new perspective claims to find: 1. the subject of marriage, which is: the social/civil dimensions of [relations between] man and woman; in other words, man and woman are the subject of marriage and divorce, since both need each other and are parties to them; 2. and also the cause, which is a social theory reflecting the era of its origin. In the pre-Islamic era, only men were given social rights and responsibilities—and this was based on a set of ideas and assumptions that must be discussed and does not concern us here—and as a result the subject of the Marriage Ruling was understood to be men. With the marriage contract, women of the time came under the protection of the tribe (generally) and the husband (specifically), exactly like camels and sheep. Men could remove the protection any time and release the women, since women were not party to but subject of the contract. This unilateral protection was the basis of family links, and parts of this culture are still evident in the written sources and the idioms used. *Talaq*, in Arabic, means release, untether, from the tie of protection; it is used to refer to a camel which is untethered, no longer under the control of a driver, and free to graze where it wants; or a sheep which has left the herd and no longer has the protection of a shepherd. In this culture, the separation of a sheep from the herd is analogous to that of women from her kin-group and tribe; the driver's care is like being controlled and provided for by the husband. The same term, *emsak*, is used both for caring for and using an animal (its milk and back), and for caring for and sexual pleasures of women. These two examples reveal the importance of the "theory of protection" in the sphere of marriage and divorce.

Why Then Did Islam Accept It?

Islam accepted the Principle of protection, but left its form to [be defined by] the people. The new religion accepted that protection is a good and useful Principle, since unilateral protection was appropriate for people of that era, and since it was the way chosen by people themselves, [the religion] did not address it. But the silence of Law cannot be taken as acceptance of the form. While retaining the Principle, we can now change its form and solve the problem of talaq—since people demand it.

We accept the theory of Protection and believe it was this theory that is the cause for legislation of "accepted" laws of marriage and divorce in Islam. Having accepted this cause, we focus our discussion on unilaterality and bilaterality, and say:

The form of protection, its framework, and the manner of its application are relative, changeable, and subject to the demands of time and place. In every time and place people can alter the form of this theory; and since alteration in form (not nature) is permitted, then the product of this alteration is also permitted.

In the present era, protection can take any one of the following forms, as accepted by people:

- government protection of the family;
- men's protection of the family (generally) and of women (specifically);
- spouses' shared protection of the family;
- a combination of all the above.

Acceptance of each of the above forms will affect divorce in a different way. If we accept the first form, divorce will become governmental and will come under the control of the judge in charge, exactly like any other social contract, such as establishing and dissolving a company—the different form of judicial divorce stems from this. If we accept the second form, then divorce will be in the hands of women, exactly opposite to the form at present accepted by Muslim societies. If we accept the third form (which seems the most suitable for people of this era), then both men and women can divorce, and their rights in divorce become equal.

To be noted:

Protection is one the accepted principles in human societes. The basis for acceptance of this principle, in addition to custom, is people's social reason. Today too this principle governs all societies, and has a special role in government and among people. Asylum is based on the principle of protection, and depriving criminals and offenders of their rights [freedom] is the same as withdrawing protection from this group in society. In the view of this article, universal conventions and declarations are based on this theory.

Islam accepted the Principle of protection, but the form it took in the Islamic society of that era was only one instance. We cannot assume that only this instance among many other instances of protection is sanctioned by a religion which is based on revelation and absolute reason! Our explanation and analysis, therefore, is: since that instance was accepted by the people of that era and was useful for them, it was left as it was.

Religion is not concerned with outer forms, because religious Rulings are based on immutable roots, not on mutable branches![29]

Religion's silence, not criticizing the existing situation, does not mean approval of that situation. This is because reforms of Law are not placed on marriage and divorce, but place conditions on the man (the party who takes a woman and releases a woman), that is, they deal precisely with the form [of protection] mentioned.

In response to those who say that the Rulings of religion are eternal, immutable, and unchangeable, and therefore the above deduction cannot be accepted, I find it essential to add:

1. Eternity, immutability, and unchangeability all pertain to Principles and Rulings, not details and forms! We too consider the Rulings of Islam to be eternal, immutable, and unchangeable, but distinguish Principles from forms.

2. As for "discerning the cause"(*tanqih al-manat*),[30] the accepted views of the Shi'a have it that if the mojtahed Jurist knows or discerns what the cause of a Ruling is, or what the reasons were that influenced the creation of the Ruling, then he can give a fatwa on the basis of his understanding. In other words, Shi'i feqh views admit that once the cause of a Ruling becomes clear to the Jurist, by means of either rational or narrated proofs, he can act in accordance with his opinion. Feqh views in recent years are more inclined than their predecessors toward the validity and proof of this view.[31]

To prove its claim, the Equality perspective has resorted to the above procedure, and states:

The cause of legislating the divorce Ruling (in a unilateral form and for men) has been the theory of protection. Since we ascertained the cause and, on the other hand, since we made it clear that the cause of the Ruling was the theory of protection (not unilateral protection), it follows that forms of marriage and divorce are relative and subordinate to the will of the

---

[29] [SMS note: Shi'i feqh states that Law gives the Principles and the Jurist derives the branches. On this basis, in the case of marriage and divorce, the Principle is protection, the [current] form is protection by men. The jurists must thus, in accordance with the condition of the age, let go of this form and substitute another one for it.

[30] Technically the phrase means "connecting the new case to the original case by eliminating the discrepancy between them"; see Kamali 1991, 213. Literally, *tanqih* means purifying, *manat* means cause; it implies that a Ruling may have more than one cause, and the Jurist has to identify the proper one.

[31] [SMS note: Whether tanqih al-manat is the same as qiyas [analogy] or not, and if so, what sort of analogy is part of the issues related to this, needs to be discussed in conjunction with others in the osul al-feqh ("Absar al-Afkar," pp. 37–38, manuscript, Ja'fari College, Qa'en, Khorasan)].

people. The known form of this theory cannot be the concern and the cause of a Ruling.

The Law sanctions marriage and divorce (as based on the Principle of protection) and the prevailing practices (as among the useful and accepted forms of the time), but never considers them to be eternal.

Unlike Motahhari and those who still adhere to his discourse, Sa'idzadeh sees gender inequality in the shari'a not as a manifestation of divine justice, but as a mistaken construction by male jurists; and he argues that it goes contrary to the very essence of divine Will as revealed in the Koran. Likewise, he does not resort to Western scholarship to explain the reasons and necessity for the different treatment of women in Islam, but uses Islamic scholarship to argue for gender equality. There are also some interesting similarities between Sa'idzadeh's reading of the sacred texts and that of feminist writers such as Hassan, Wadud-Muhsin, and Mernissi. Although he starts from the same premises as the shari'a-based genre of literature on women in Islam, and uses the same mode of argumentation, he reaches conclusions similar to those of these writers: gender equality is a Principle in Islam and an inseparable part of the message of the Prophet, but in time Muslims bypassed and even inverted this message, and it is this inversion that is reflected in what came to be part of Islamic law.

These are instances of the rapprochement between the two genres that I wrote of in the Introduction, opening the way for a reconciliation between feminism and Islam at the level of interpretation. Although these writers' works (in particular Mernissi's) are read and taken seriously by feminists and in the West, they are more or less disregarded by Islamists and Jurists; Sa'idzadeh's work is beginning to make an impression among the latter: it remains to be seen whether it will find a readership among feminists abroad.

Conclusion _____

SINCE 1979, a combination of circumstance and design has initiated a quiet revolution in women's rights in Iran. I have sought, through the narratives in this book, to open a window on one of the internal debates that lie behind this revolution. What do the narratives tell us about Iranian women a generation after the Islamic Revolution?

First, they are evidence that the issue of women has become a central concern in the Islamic Republic at all three levels I identified in the Introduction: the interpretation and reinterpretation of the sacred texts, political ideology and rhetoric, and the social experiences of men and women. Women's issues are taken seriously at the seminaries in Qom, the center of religious knowledge and power. An ayatollah like Sane'i devotes his lessons to bringing about new interpretations relating to women; and an organization like the Islamic Propagation Office devotes one of its journals specifically to "the Women Question."

Why? One obvious, cynical answer is that the clerical establishment wants to define and monopolize the discourse on women. But the very fact that women's rights have become a battleground for at least three competing tendencies, all of them claiming legitimacy in Islam, makes monopoly impossible. When they were in opposition, the clerics, as guardians of Islam, could deal with practical issues at an abstract and generalized level, leaving it to the conscience of the believer to interpret and carry out the appropriate practices. Once in power, they have had to meet the challenges of the contemporary world, and this is transforming the ways in which women's issues are debated within an Islamic framework. The convergence of religious and political authority has opened a new door from within, which no longer can be closed.

What is unique to these debates in Iran, compared to those going on elsewhere in the Muslim world, is that their protagonists do not simply locate their discourses within Islam but operate within the parameters of a state in which one version of the Islamist vision has been realized. Women may not be taking part directly in feqh debates, and feqh is still the monopoly of male scholars who fix the terms of women's rights in religion; but we must remember that feqh is reactive, in the sense that it reacts to social and political realities, such as the extensive participation of women in the revolution and since then in political life. Society has become gender-aware and indeed the whole political process has become gendered.

Events in post-Khomeini Iran, in particular the Majles elections of 1996 and the presidential election of 1997, have showed the clerics that if they want to stay in power they cannot ignore popular demands for freedom, tolerance, and social justice. More women than before stood in the Majles elections, and some of them defeated candidates backed by conservatives, not only in Tehran and other large cities but also in smaller ones.[1] Among them was Fa'ezeh Hashemi, younger daughter of the previous president, who ran on a platform promoting women's participation in politics, society, and sport, and who was rumored to have polled even higher than Ali-Akbar Nateq-Nuri, the conservative choice for president. Although the number of women elected did not increase dramatically (thirteen deputies, compared to nine in the previous Majles)—and most of them are not Modernists—they have become much more vocal on women's issues, have presented a number of bills, and have set up a Women's Commission in the Majles. The way the women's press reports Majles debates on women has also changed. For instance, Zanan pilloried male deputies who spoke against a bill that further restricted men's right to divorce. When one cleric invoked a Koranic verse, Zanan printed his words, challenged his understanding of the sacred text, and warned that he risked losing women's votes.[2]

For the 1997 presidential elections, eight women nominated themselves as candidates, but the Council of the Guardians did not approve any of them. Since then, women's right to be president has been publicly debated. Some have interpreted rajul (Arabic "man"), the term used in the constitution, to mean "human," as in conventional English.[3] Women's votes were among the decisive factors in the election. No political figure can afford to alienate the new generation of women who have come of age during the Islamic Republic and are demanding equal opportunities under the shari'a on all fronts.[4]

There are signs that more women are joining the modernist tendency. Those who had previously considered women's issues unimportant have also joined the debate. Prominent among them is Jamileh Kadivar, who was the victim of a smear campaign when she stood for the Majles in Shiraz, because in one of her speeches she had questioned feqh wisdom on men's arbitrary right to divorce. This experience prompted her to publish a series of articles as a book, Zan (Woman).[5] Others who had toed the official line on gender are also breaking rank and finding their own voice. Ashraf Geramizadegan, who replaced Shahla Sherkat in 1992 as editor of Zan-e Ruz, resigned her post in Kayhan Publishing Institute in February 1997 "to keep the respect of her pen," as she

---

[1] See Kian 1997a.   [2] Zanan 32 (February 1997).
[3] The only woman candidate whose name became public was Azam Taleqani, director of the Islamic Women's Institute of Iran, and editor of its journal, Payam-e Hajar. In an interview with Zanan (34 and 35, April and July 1997) she said that she nominated herself to clarify the meaning of rajul. She asked for explanations; but the council has not yet come up with a response. See also Payam-e Hajar 227 (Spring 1997).
[4] See Kian 1996 and 1997b.
[5] Kadivar 1996. In her introduction, she quotes part of what Ayatollah Sane'i said in my interview with him, as published in Payam-e Zan.

put it to me.[6] In March 1998, the first issue of a new journal, *Hoquq-e Zanan* (Women's Rights), appeared, carrying her name as director and editor. July 1998 saw the launching by Fa'ezeh Hashemi of *Zan*, the first-ever women's newspaper in Iran, competing for readership with established dailies and inserting women into the very heart of the political struggle between Modernists and Traditionalists.

There have been further gains in the legal realm. In 1997, a law was passed requiring the mahr, dower, to be revalued in line with inflation, thus increasing the obstacles for men wishing to exercise their right to divorce. In April 1998, more women were appointed as judges; and in September the police officially recruited women. There have also been some setbacks. In May 1998, two bills were presented to the Majles: one proposed the adaptation of medical services to religious law, which would mean that doctors could treat only patients of the same sex; the second proposed, in defense of women's rights, to ban press "exploitation of women's images" and to outlaw "the creation of conflicts between men and women by propagating women's rights outside the legal and Islamic framework." Interestingly, the latter bill, clearly intended to tie President Khatami's hands in implementing the reforms promised at the time of his election, was prepared by conservative women members of the Majles.[7] Despite opposition by many modernists and some women's groups, in August the second bill became law.[8]

Meanwhile, the world in which Shi'i ulama live has changed beyond recognition. Qom is no longer a defended corner from which the new must be repulsed because of the "non-Islamic" nature of state and society. Fortunes have changed. After the revolution, it became an asset to have a cleric son-in-law; young clerics started to marry into families and environments that were closed to them before. The wives they married brought their own different life-styles and values with them, and have had a significant effect on life in the seminaries. In Qom, I was struck by the number of clerics I met, or heard of, whose wives had left them or were making their lives, as the men put it, "worse than hell." For the younger generation of clerics, women's presence in society as colleagues and counterparts is a fact of life; for them, unlike their elders, it is no sin to work alongside women.

A second lesson of this book is that the gender perspectives I have discussed—those of Inequality, Balance, and Equality—are not rigidly bounded,

[6] In a meeting at *Zan-e Ruz* in February 1997, on her last day in the office.

[7] Julian Borger, "New Laws Target Iranian Women," *Guardian*, 12 May 1998, 18. *Zanan* 42 (March/April 1998) devoted an editorial, "This Way Goes to Afghanistan," to objecting to this bill and rebuking the Majles women who proposed it.

[8] In June 1998 Sa'idzadeh was arrested. He was released five months later, after a closed trial; neither his crime nor the verdict were made public, but he was "unfrocked" and forbidden to publish. This appeared to be part of a general conservative clampdown on press freedom, which culminated in the closure of a number of newspapers.

and there is movement, dialogue, and interaction among their advocates. Not all of them are clerics or men, nor are their arguments and concepts derived solely from Islamic sources. Rather than separate entities, they should be seen as three stages in the unfolding debates over gender and power in the second decade of the Islamic Republic. Nor do individuals' perspectives on gender necessarily correlate with their other political views. Thus, a modernist Islamic intellectual like Sorush, who argues for a clear demarcation between politics and religion, can talk on gender from the same perspective as Ayatollah Javadi-Amoli, a staunch supporter of the velayat-e faqih.

Likewise, while representing two divergent political tendencies, the journals *Zanan* and *Payam-e Zan* agree on the principle of women's rights, and hold that Islam grants women these rights. Both want to change the present situation; but they differ over the details of what the rights are and the means of achieving them. *Payam-e Zan* rejects equality in rights and duties as implying similarity, and argues for equity as implying the notion of justice and balance in rights and duties, in an attempt to find a solution for women's problems within the parameters of Islamic jurisprudence. *Zanan* tries to bridge the old polarization between Islam and feminism, arguing for gender equality on all fronts. This difference means that a cleric like Saʿidzadeh, though he feels that his arguments are best appreciated in *Payam-e Zan*, finds *Zanan* the only forum in which he can air his views; it also allows secular feminists like Mehrangiz Kar to contribute to *Zanan*, keeping within the limits of gender discourses allowable in the Islamic Republic.[9]

For the ulama, "women" are now a "problem" for which a religious solution must be sought. But for male religious intellectuals this is not yet the case: gender inequality is not an issue urgent enough to address, but part of a larger problem, and they hope it will go away when their vision of Islam is realized. Thus they will not debate the issue with those ulama who are trying to modify the old rules, nor with women who are arguing for new ones. They avoid entering the domain of law, which is where gender inequality is maintained, and also where—I suggest—the potential for change lies. This potential, however, remains underexploited, with the exception of the work of young clerics like Saʿidzadeh—a "one-man-band" who carries little weight within Qom seminaries. The tyranny of the structure of learning and knowledge production is so entrenched, the pressure to comply with its inner rules and logic is so strong, that as Ayatollah Saneʿi reminded us, the founder of the Islamic Republic could not publicly articulate his own jurisprudential views on women's right to divorce.

It is such conformist pressures that have so far inhibited established scholars, such as Ayatollah Ebrahim Jannati and others known for their radical

---

[9] Hoodfar 1996b.

ideas, from publishing their views on gender relations.[10] Perhaps they are also the reason why scholars in al-Zahra, the most famous women's theological college, will not cooperate with *Payam-e Zan*. The use of pseudonyms must also be seen as a way of dealing with such pressures, indicating the emergence of a new public space in which the focus is on the argument, not on its advocate.[11] It also indicates the ways in which clerics are trying to reconcile their two worlds; while not risking their place in the scholarly world of Qom, they use their scholarship to try to change the world outside.[12]

A third lesson from the debates narrated in this book is not the specific answers they provide (and these should not be measured against the yardstick of current feminist theories), but the avenues they are opening for dialogue and change within the framework of Islam. They are making it possible for Muslim women to challenge the gender rules of their societies from within the Islamic framework; they are no longer forced, in Leila Ahmed's words: "to choose between betrayal and betrayal."[13] One can witness the makings of a new, still nascent, discourse on women in Islam which, unlike the old discourse, is not grounded on "nature theory"—does not reduce everything to regulating sexual relations between men and women—but opens a new space for the notion of women's social and human rights. This is an area of debate that has been more or less absent in classical Islamic legal texts, where women figure mainly in sections related to marriage and divorce.[14]

It is in this context that omissions and silences in the debates acquire their meaning. For example, although "the veil" is a major focus for Mernissi and some other feminists who address Western audiences or operate within the parameters of Western feminist discourses, the situation in Iran in the 1990s has prevented any serious debate on the issue, even in *Zanan*, which so eloquently champions women's rights to education, employment, and protection in marriage. Even Sa'idzadeh does not address hejab, whether for political considerations or because it is a matter of faith.

I found this silence understandable and usually maintained it in my own discussions with clerics. Unlike other issues, such as women's employment,

---

[10] In November 1997, Ayatollah Jannati discussed his views openly in an interview with a youth magazine (*Iran-e Javan*); he stated that all restrictions imposed on interaction between the sexes were due to certain mentalities and people's worldviews, not to Islam. Part of this interview was published in the daily *Iran*, which represents the modernist view within the government (no. 809, 13 November 1997, 8).

[11] I owe this point to Dale Eickelman (personal communication).

[12] Similarly, in an earlier generation, anthropologists would publish accounts of their fieldwork experiences as fiction, or using pseudonyms, so as not to jeopardize their academic status (see Tedlock 1991, 72).

[13] Ahmed 1984, 122.

[14] See Malti-Douglas 1992 for a textual analysis of how, in both classical and modern Arabo-Islamic discourse, women are tied to sexuality and the body.

education, and family law, there is no consensus among Iranian women on hejab, though many claim to speak for others. Hejab has its own payoffs, and enforcement of it can be empowering to women. Although it undoubtedly restricts some, it emancipates others by legitimizing their presence in public, which is still a male domain. Many women in Iran today owe their education, their jobs, their economic autonomy, and their public persona, to *compulsory* hejab. For many women, hejab is a marker of identity and the essence of their womanhood; it is what makes them acceptable in the eyes of society and eligible as partners in marriage. In this sense, wearing hejab is not so different from other dress statements made by women elsewhere.

Further, compulsory hejab paradoxically proved to be empowering for those it is particularly intended to restrain: so-called Westernized, middle-class women, now politically marginalized. The Traditionalists' obsession with enforcement as one of their key instruments gives these women a means of subverting it by exploiting its possibilities as a fashion statement. Such resistance—similar to what James Scott describes in his *Weapons of the Weak*—can be nothing more than individual acts of foot-dragging and evasion, lacking any kind of organization or planning, but may in the end make an utter shambles of the policies dreamed up by the powerful.[15] The Traditionalists cannot afford to show flexibility, precisely because of the power and threat of such mockery. There is too much at stake.

There is clearly a need for meaningful debate on the subject of hejab, but I could not see how to raise it. The gulf between Islamic and feminist notions of sexuality and social morality is still too wide to be bridged. I myself cannot accept certain interpretations of Islam, such as those of the Traditionalists and Neo-Traditionalists discussed in Parts One and Two; nor can I accept the kinds of sexual liberation and individualism advocated in certain Western feminist discourses. Yet I see hejab and family law as two sides of a coin: both focus attention on the sexual aspect of gender relations, that is, nature theory. Traditionalist feqh constructs both so as to deny women choice or voice, restricting women in the public domain by hejab, and subjugating them in private through family law, making them insecure in both domains.

Finally, to take these debates as narrated in this book at face value, and to expect them to inform us about the actual state of gender relations in post-revolutionary Iran, or about the scope of women's rights in Islam, is to misunderstand what they are about. These debates, one could argue on Foucauldian lines, must be seen as constituting what women's rights and gender equality in Islam are about, creating the very issue that they set out to investigate. They are making it possible to accommodate women's aspiration for equality, to question old assumptions, and to discuss women as not merely

---

[15] Scott 1985. Women's power to subvert the patriarchal order is well documented. For some examples, see Hatem 1986 and Kandiyoti 1988.

sexual but also social beings. Continuing silences, as well as the refusal of some women—including some female scholars in Qom and some secular feminists in Iran and abroad—to participate in the debates, are but moments in a process set into motion when the Islamic Republic was born. This process has—inadvertently—nurtured not only a new school of jurisprudence, which is slowly trying to respond to social realities, but also a new gender consciousness.

Glossary

Note: Macrons to indicate the long *a* are inserted here but not in the text.

ahkām — see *hokm*

ahādith — see *hadith*

asl (pl. *osul*) — Principle, of Islamic jurisprudence or law

āyatollah — 'sign of God', title of the highest-ranking Shiʻi clerics

chādor — specific Iranian veil

diyeh — compensation, blood money

ejtehād — (lit. exertion, effort), independent judgment, technically the effort a jurist makes in order to deduce a Ruling, which is not self-evident, from its sources; the process of arriving at judgments on points of religious law using reason and principles of jurisprudence

eshkāl — difficulty or ambiguity in the scope and applicability of a shariʻa mandate; see also *shobheh*

faqih — Jurist, expert in Islamic jurisprudence (see *feqh*)

feqh — Islamic jurisprudence

fetneh — (leading to) chaos, temptation to commit a forbidden act

gheibat — Occultation, concealment of the Twelfth Imam

gheirat — sexual jealousy, sense of honor

hadith (pl. *ahādith*) — traditions, sayings attributed to the Prophet Mohammad and the twelve Imams

halāl — lawful, permitted (contrast to *harām*)

haqq (pl. *hoquq*) — right, truth, justice

harām — unlawful, forbidden by shariʻa law

hejāb — barrier, covering for women, veil

hojjat ol-eslām — "proof of Islam," originally a title of high respect equivalent to contemporary "ayatollah," now devalued and used for middle-rank clerics

hokm (pl. *ahkām*) — Ruling, law

hokm-e sharʻi — religious Ruling, rule, divine Law

hokumat — government

Houzeh (-ye ʻelmiyeh) — theological college, the religious scholarly milieu

Imām — leader of the Shiʻi community of believers, one of the Twelve; now used to refer to Ayatollah Khomeini

Jāheliyeh — "ignorance," pre-Islamic period and culture

Jāmeʻat al-Zahrā — the largest theological college for female students in Iran

kalām — theology

kerāmat — human value, nobility

khādem — attendant at a shrine, servant at the house of an ayatollah

kholʻ — divorce initiated by a woman, in which she gives her husband a kind of compensation in return for his consent

khoms — "fifth," a religious tax of one-fifth on certain pecuniary and other gains, paid by Shiʻa to their marjaʻ.

mahr — dower, intrinsic part of every marriage contract, a sum of money or any valuable that a man gives or pledges to give the wife at the time of marriage

Majles — the Iranian parliament, composed of elected deputies

maqnaᶜeh — wimple-like headgear for women in contemporary Iran

marjaᶜ(-e taqlid) — "source of imitation," Shiᶜi clerical leader

marjaᶜiyat — institution of supreme authority in Shiᶜi Islam

mojtahed — a qualified (Shiᶜi) jurist who has reached the level of competence necessary to practice ejtehād

motᶜa, motᶜeh — temporary marriage (recognized in Shiᶜi law only)

nafaqeh — maintenance, the husband's duty in marriage and the wife's right

Nahj ol-Balāgheh — collection of Imam ᶜAli's sayings

nezām — order, regime, system, now used to refer to the Islamic Republic

osul al-feqh — the root sources of legal authority and the principles for deduction of feqh from those sources

rajul — man, person

reibeh — doubt, uncertainty, a feeling that one might commit a forbidden act

resāleh ᶜamaliyeh — practical treatise, a book of reference issued by a marjaᶜ-e taqlid for the religious guidance of his followers; it consists of legal rulings in all sections of applied feqh

seyyed (pl. sādāt) — descendant of the Prophet

sharᶜ — sacred Law

sharᶜi — in accordance with the sacred Law

shobheh — doubt, a question that comes into the mind of a believer which goes beyond the accepted body of religious knowledge

talāq — repudiation, unilateral divorce exercised by men

tamkin — obedience, submission, the wife's duty in marriage and husband's right

taqiyeh — dissimulation, Shiᶜi practice of concealing belief in order to protect self, family, or property from harm

taqlid — emulation, imitation, following the dictates of a *mojtahed*; see also *marjaᶜ*

vali-ye faqih — the "mandated jurist"; according to Khomeini, he should rule in the absence of the Hidden Imam

velāyat-e faqih — mandate of the jurist; see *vali-ye faqih*

zenā — sexual relations outside marriage

Bibliographic Essay _____

Women in Post-Revolutionary Iran

SINCE THE 1979 revolution in Iran, whatever concerns women, from their most private to their most public activities, has become part of public debate. Consciously or not, all Iranians, men and women, secular or religious, living inside or outside the boundaries of Iran, have been drawn into this debate and forced to take positions, which are reflected in the vast and varied literature that has been produced in the past two decades.

Rather than attempting an exhaustive review of this literature, this essay covers only a selection of works by and about women, pointing out some salient features and the major positions taken.

Iranian Publications

Works published in Iran fall—in terms of their authors' positions—into two broad categories: religious and secular. Farrokhzadi 1994 contains a fairly comprehensive list of 256 works by 178 women with a religious perspective, published between 1946 and 1992. Thirty-three of them appeared after the revolution and specifically deal with the issue of women; most were published by state-sponsored organizations, such as the Islamic Propagation Organization or the Qom Houzeh, whereas others were written just before the revolution. These writings are traditionalist or neo-traditionalist in approach and perspective. They include works by well-known scholars such as Nosrat Amin (1886–1983), the most renowned woman mojtahed of this century, and her student, Homayuni (b. 1917). Amin's only work on women (1990) gives women moral guidance on how to live an Islamic life but contains no legal argument. Homayuni 1992 deals with women's personality and place in creation. Other publications by women who teach in female seminaries include Ala'i-Rahmani 1993, dealing with Imam Ali's views on women, Gavahi 1990 and 1994 on women's legal rights, Gorji 1994 on the Koranic position on women, and Seffati 1997 on girls' puberty; unlike the first three authors, who argue for change, Seffati clearly endorses old feqh wisdoms.

The press regularly features interviews and speeches by politically active women. Some have close ties to the male political elite; for example, Jamileh Kadivar (wife of Ayatollah Mohajerani, minister of culture), Zahra Mostafavi (daughter of Ayatollah Khomeini), Zahra Rahnavard (wife of Mir Hosein Musavi, former prime minister), Azam Taleqani (daughter of Ayatollah Taleqani). Some of these women are regularly invited to speak at semiofficial meetings organized by women's organizations. Others are Majles deputies or government officials; for example, Shahla Habibi and Zahra Shoja'i, the former and current heads of the Women's Bureau in the President's Office. The main theme of their speeches, which are covered by the establishment press or published as conference proceedings, is defining the place of women in society from an Islamic perspective, and responding to criticism of the Islamic position on women.

Their views have been analyzed by a number of Iranian academics abroad, notably Afshar 1998 and Paidar 1995.

Women with a secular perspective air their views in the independent, nonestablishment press. Prominent among them are Shireen Ebadi and Mehrangiz Kar, lawyers and prolific writers who contribute to a variety of journals: Ebadi's articles appear regularly in *Jame'eh Salem*, and Kar's in *Zanan*. Kar has published books on women in society and law (1991) and in the labor market (1994), and on women's political rights (1997); see further Mir-Hosseini forthcoming.

Shahshahani et al. (1995) is a selective list of 488 publications by women with secular perspectives in the fields of social sciences and arts, including subjects as diverse as philosophy and cookery. Seventy-three are indexed under "women's issues."

Publications outside Iran

Most Iranians educated and living in the West who have written on women in postrevolutionary Iran left the country shortly after the revolution. Some never returned to Iran but followed events from a distance, continuing for many years to interpret them in the light of their experiences during the early phase of the revolution. Ironically, some of these writers seem to share, and thus help to perpetuate, the essentialist—and orientalist—terms of many Islamists' construction of gender in Islam, that is, as divinely ordained and immutable, not as changing and human and thus open to negotiation and modification (cf. Abu-Lughod 1993, 10–11). Like the Islamists, they implicitly sustain ahistorical understandings of Islam and gender, and resort to the same kind of sophistry, resisting a reading of Islamic law that treats it like any other system (see Mir-Hosseini 1998b).

The first wave of this literature, published in the early 1980s, reflected the reaction of middle-class and secular women to the early revolutionary discourse, arguing that Iranian women lost many rights. Prominent examples include three collections: Azari 1983a, Nashat 1983b, and Tabari and Yeganeh 1982. Articles in these volumes by Afshar 1982, Azari 1983b and 1983c, Nashat 1983a, Tabari 1982, and Yeganeh 1982 focus on Islamic ideology and its impact on women, as does Mahdavi 1985. On the women's movement and organization, see Afkhami 1984, Azari 1983b, Kian 1997b, Sanasarian 1982, Shahshahani 1984, and Tabari 1986. Notable among numerous politically oriented Persian-language publications abroad since the revolution are the feminist journal *Nimeh-ye Digar* and the proceedings of conferences of the Iranian Women's Studies Foundation.

The second wave, emerging in the 1990s, is less narrowly polemical and more willing to explore the complexities of the situation, often as a result of field research in Iran. Afkhami and Friedl 1994 contains several articles on aspects of women's situation in post-revolutionary Iran: in education, the labor market, and the law. Haeri 1993 discusses women's response to "fundamentalism" in Iran and Pakistan. Among others, Esfandiari 1997, Kian 1996, 1997a, 1997b, and 1998, Mir-Hosseini 1996a and 1996b, V. Moghadam 1988 and 1993, Ramazani 1993, Sanasarian 1992, Tohidi 1991, 1994, and Yavari-d'Hellencourt 1998 examine gender activism and the changing discourse on women in the second decade of the Islamic Republic. For accounts of the women's press in post-revolutionary Iran, see Kian 1997b, Mir-Hosseini 1996c, Najmabadi 1998, and Yavari-d'Hellencourt 1998. For differing analyses of the contentious issue of hejab, see Hoodfar 1995, Milani 1992, Mir-Hosseini 1996a, Najmabadi 1991 and 1994, Paidar 1995 and Tabari 1982a.

There are also a few anthropological studies of women and gender issues based on post-revolutionary field research. Adelkhah 1991 studied Islamist women in Tehran; Haeri 1989 temporary marriage; Hoodfar 1994a and 1996a changing policies and discourses on family planning; Kamalkhani 1998 women's religious practices and gatherings in Shiraz; Mir-Hosseini family courts in Tehran (1993), and gender discourses 1996a and 1996b; Torab 1996 and 1998 pious women in a neighborhood in Tehran.

Some of the most interesting new writing on women comes from those who were involved in the first wave of literature. Such writing shows a new maturity among Iranians based abroad, notably a new willingness to engage with feminist discourses generated within Iran, such as that of *Zanan*. They include Afkhami 1994, Afshar 1994, 1996, and 1998, Najmabadi 1991, 1994, and 1998 (Najmabadi wrote originally as Azar Tabari), Paidar 1995 and 1996 (Paidar wrote originally as Nahid Yeganeh), and Tohidi 1993, 1996, and 1998. Others of the first wave, however, maintain their original position, according to which there can be only a single reading of gender in Islam, as unable to accommodate women's demands; see for instance Chafiq 1991 and Moghissi 1993, 1994, and 1995.

Bibliography _____

Abbott, Nabia. 1942a. "Women and the State in Early Islam." *Journal of Near Eastern Studies* 1: 106–26.

————. 1942b. *Aishah: The Beloved of Mohammed*. Chicago: University of Chicago Press.

Abu-Lughod, Lila. 1993. *Writing Women's Worlds: Bedouin Stories*. Berkeley and Los Angeles: University of California Press.

Accad, Evelyne. 1991. "Sexuality and Sexual Politics: Conflicts and Contradictions for Contemporary Women in the Middle East." In *Third World Women and the Politics of Feminism*, edited by Chandra Mohanty, Ann Russo, and Lourdes Torres, 237–49. Bloomington and Indianapolis: Indiana University Press.

Adelkhah, Fariba. 1991. *La révolution sous le voile*. Paris: Karthala.

————. 1998. *Être moderne en Iran*. Paris: Karthala. English translation forthcoming. London: C. Hurst.

Afkhami, Mahnaz. 1984. "Iran: A Future in the Past: The 'Prerevolutionary' Women's Movement." In *Sisterhood Is Global*, edited by Robin Morgan, 333–41. Garden City, N.Y.: Anchor Books.

————. 1994. "Women in Post-Revolutionary Iran: A Feminist Perspective." In *In the Eye of the Storm: Women in Post-Revolutionary Iran*, edited by Mahnaz Afkhami and Erika Friedl, 1–18. Syracuse: Syracuse University Press.

Afkhami, Mahnaz, and Erika Friedl, eds. 1994. *In the Eye of the Storm: Women in Post-Revolutionary Iran*. Syracuse: Syracuse University Press.

Afshar, Haleh. 1982. "Khomeini's Teachings and Their Implications for Iranian Women." In *In the Shadow of Islam*, edited by Azar Tabari and Nahid Yeganeh, 75–90. London: Zed.

————. 1987. "Women, Marriage and the State in Iran." In *Women, State and Ideology: Studies from Africa and Asia*, edited by Haleh Afshar, 70–86. London: Macmillan.

————. 1989. "Women and Reproduction in Iran." In *Women—Nation—State*, edited by Nira Yuval-Davis and Floya Anthias, 110–25. London: Macmillan.

————. 1994. "Why Fundamentalism? Iranian Women and Their Support for Islam." Working Paper no. 2, Dept. of Politics, University of York.

————. 1996. "Islam and Feminism: An Analysis of Political Strategies." In *Feminism and Islam: Legal and Literary Perspectives*, edited by Mai Yamani, 197–216. London: Ithaca.

————. 1998. *Islam and Feminisms: An Iranian Case-Study*. London: Macmillan.

Ahmed, Leila. 1984. "Early Feminist Movements in the Middle East: Turkey and Egypt." In *Muslim Women*, edited by Freda Hussain, 111–23. London: Croom Helm.

————. 1991. "Early Islam and the Position of Women: The Problem of Interpretation." In *Women in Middle Eastern History: Shifting Boundaries in Sex and Gender*, edited by Beth Baron and Nikki Keddie, 58–95. New Haven: Yale University Press.

————. 1992. *Women and Gender in Islam: Historical Roots of a Modern Debate*. New Haven: Yale University Press.

Akhavi, Shahrough. 1996. "Contending Discourses in Shiʿa Law on the Doctrine of *Wilayat al-Faqih*." *Iranian Studies* 29, nos. 3–4: 229–68.

Akuchakian, Ahmad. 1995. "ʿEbrat-ha va Farakhaniha: Bardasht-ha va Taʾamollati dar-bareh-ye Konferans-e Jahani-ye Zan—Pekan Shahrivar 1374" (Lessons and Recollections: Notes and Thoughts on the World Women's Conference in Beijing September 1995). *Payam-e Zan* 44 (1374), 48–51 and 83; continued in issue 47 (1375), 30–35.

Alaʾi-Rahmani, Fatemeh. 1993. *Zan az Didgah-e Nahj ol-Balagheh* (Women from the Perspective of the Nahj ol-Balagheh). Tehran: Islamic Propagation Organization (1372).

Algar, Hamid. 1969. *Religion and State in Iran: 1785–1906*. Berkeley and Los Angeles: University of California Press.

———. 1985. *Imam Khomeini: Islam and Revolution and Writings and Declarations*. London: KPI.

Ali, Imam. 1981. *Nahjul Balagha: Sermons, Letters and Sayings of Imam Ali*. Qom: Ansariyan.

Altorki, Soraya, and Camillia Fawzi el-Solh, eds. 1988. *Arab Women in the Field: Studying Your Own Society*. Syracuse: Syracuse University Press.

Amin, Nosrat. 1990. *Ravesh-e Khoshbakhti* (The Way of Happiness). 5th ed. Qom: al-Zahra Press (1369).

Amini, Ibrahim. n.d. *Principles of Marriage: Family Ethics*. Qom: Ansariyan.

an-Naʿim, Abdullahi Ahmed. 1990. *Toward an Islamic Reformation: Civil Liberties, Human Rights, and International Law*. Syracuse: Syracuse University Press.

Appadurai, Arjun. 1988. "Introduction: Place and Voice in Anthropological Theory." *Cultural Anthropology* 3, no. 1: 16–20.

Arjomand, Said Amir. 1984. *The Shadow of God and the Hidden Imam: Religion, Poltical Order and Social Change in Shiʿite Iran from the Beginning to 1890*. Chicago: University of Chicago Press.

———. 1988. *The Turban for the Crown: The Islamic Revolution in Iran*. Oxford: Oxford University Press.

———. 1992. "Constitution of the Islamic Republic." *Encyclopaedia Iranica* 6: 151–58.

Azari, Farah. 1983a. *Women of Iran. The Conflict with Fundamentalist Islam*. London: Ithaca.

———. 1983b. "The Post-Revolutionary Women's Movement in Iran." In *Women of Iran: The Conflict with Fundamentalist Islam*, edited by Farah Azari, 190–225. London: Ithaca.

———. 1983c. "Islam's Appeal to Women in Iran: Illusions and Reality." In *Women of Iran: The Conflict with Fundamentalist Islam*, edited by Farah Azari, 1–71. London: Ithaca.

Azari-Qomi, Ahmed. 1993. *Sima-ye Zan dar Nezam-e Eslami* (Woman's Image in the Islamic Order). Qom: Dar ol-ʿElm (1372).

Badran, Margot. 1994. "Gender Activism: Feminism and Islamists in Egypt." In *Politics and Women: Cultural Reassertions and Feminisms in International Perspective*, edited by Valentine M. Moghadam, 202–27. Boulder: Westview.

———. 1995a. *Feminists, Islam and Nation: Gender and the Making of Modern Egypt*. Princeton: Princeton University Press.

———. 1995b. "Feminism." *The Oxford Encyclopedia of the Modern Islamic World* 2: 19–23.

———. 1997. "Towards Islamic Feminism: A Look at the Middle East." Paper delivered at conference, "Gender and Society in the Muslim World since 1800," Royal Holloway College, University of London, 3–4 July.

Baqeri-Bidhendi, Naser. 1992. *Banu-ye Mojtahed-e Irani* (An Iranian Mojtahed Lady). Qom: Islamic Propagation Office (1371).

Baron, Beth, and Nikki R. Keddie, eds. 1992. *Women in Middle Eastern History: Shifting Boundaries in Sex and Gender*. New Haven: Yale University Press.

Beck, Lois, and Nikki Keddie, eds. 1978. *Women in the Muslim World*. Cambridge: Harvard University Press.

Beeman, William O. 1986. *Language, Status and Power in Iran*. Bloomington: Indiana University Press.

Betteridge, Ann H. 1983. "To Veil or Not to Veil: A Matter of Protest or Policy." In *Women and Revolution in Iran*, edited by Guity Nashat, 109–28. Boulder: Westview.

Bodman, Herbert L., and Nayereh Tohidi, eds. 1998. *Women in Muslim Societies: Diversity within Unity*. Boulder, CO: Lynne Rienner.

Boroujerdi, Mehrzad. 1994. "The Encounter of Post-Revolutionary Thought in Iran with Hegel, Heidegger, and Popper." In *Cultural Transformations in the Middle East*, edited by Serif Mardin, 236–59. Leiden: E. J. Brill.

———. 1996. *Iranian Intellectuals and the West: The Tormented Triumph of Nativism*. Syracuse: Syracuse University Press.

Calder, Norman. 1995. "Marjaʿ al-Taqlid." *The Oxford Encyclopedia of the Modern Islamic World* 3: 45–48.

Chafiq, Chahla. 1991. *La femme et le retour de l'Islam: l'expérience iranienne*. Paris: Le Félin.

Clifford, James. 1988. *The Predicament of Culture: Twentieth-Century Ethnography, Literature, and Art*. Cambridge: Harvard University Press.

Clifford, James, and George Marcus, eds. 1986. *Writing Culture: The Poetics and Politics of Ethnography*. Berkeley and Los Angeles: University of California Press.

Cooper, John. 1998. "The Limits of the Sacred: The Epistemology of ʿAbd al-Karim Soroush." In *Islam and Modernity: Muslim Intellectuals Respond*, edited by John Cooper, Ronald L. Netter, and Mohamed Mahmoud, 38–56. London and New York: I. B. Tauris.

Dabashi, Hamid. 1993. *Theology of Discontent: The Ideological Foundation of the Islamic Revolution in Iran*. New York: New York University Press.

———. 1995. "Modern Shiʿa Thought." *The Oxford Encyclopedia of the Modern Islamic World* 4: 60–69.

de Groot, Joanna. 1996. "Gender, Discourse and Ideology in Iranian Studies: Towards a New Scholarship." In *Gendering the Middle East: Emerging Perspectives*, edited by Deniz Kandiyoti, 29–49. London: I. B. Tauris.

Doi, A. Rahman. 1989. *Women in the Shariʿa*. London: Ta-Ha.

———. 1993. *Women in the Quran and Hadith*. London: Ta-Ha.

Eickelman, Dale. 1992. "Mass Higher Education and the Religious Imagination in Contemporary Arab Soceties." *American Ethnologist* 19, no. 4: 643–55.

———. 1997. *The Middle East and Central Asia: An Anthropological Approach*, 3d ed. Upper Saddle River, NJ: Prentice Hall.

Eickelman, Dale. 1998. "Inside the Islamic Reformation." *Wilson Quarterly* 22, no. 1: 80–89.

Eickelman, Dale, and James Piscatori. 1996. *Muslim Politics*. Princeton: Princeton University Press.

El Guindi, Fadwa. 1981. "Veiling Infitah with Muslim Ethic: Egypt's Contemporary Islamic Movement." *Social Problems* 28, no. 4: 464–85.

El-Solh, Camillia Fawzi, and Judy Mabro, eds. 1994. *Muslim Women's Choices: Religious Belief and Social Reality*. Providence and Oxford: Berg Publishers.

Esfandiari, Haleh. 1994. "The Majles and Women's Issues in the Islamic Republic of Iran." In *In the Eye of the Storm: Women in Post-Revolutionary Iran*, edited by Mahnaz Afkhami and Erika Friedl, 61–79. Syracuse: Syracuse University Press.

———. 1997. *Reconstructed Lives: Women and Iran's Islamic Revolution*. Washington, D.C.: Woodrow Wilson Center Press; Baltimore and London: Johns Hopkins University Press.

Eshtehardi, Mohammad Mehdi. 1996. *Hazrat-e Ma'sumeh, Fatimeh-ye Dovvom* (Holy Ma'sumeh, the Second Fatima). Qom: 'Allameh Press (1375).

Fabian, Johannes. 1983. *Time and the Other: How Anthropology Makes Its Object*. New York: Columbia University Press.

Fahim-Kermani, Morteza. 1992. *Zan va Payam-avari* (Women and Prophecy). Tehran: Islamic Cultural Publication Office (1371).

———. 1995. *Chehreh-ye Zan dar Ayineh-ye Eslam va Qor'an* (The Face of Woman in the Mirror of Islam and the Koran). Tehran: Islamic Cultural Publication Office (1374).

Farrokhzad, Forugh. 1991. *Tavallod-e Digar* (Another Birth). 17th ed. Tehran: Morvarid (1370).

Farrokhzadi, Majid. 1994. *Ketab-shenasi-ye Asar-e Mazhabi-ye Zanan-e Irani (1306–1372)* (Bibliography of Religious Books by Iranian Women, 1927–1993). Tehran: Motahhar (1373).

Feiz, 'Ali Reza. 1995. *Mabadi-ye Feqh va Osul* (Foundations of Jurisprudence and Principles). Tehran: Tehran University Press (1374).

Ferdows, Adele K. 1983. "Women and the Islamic Revolution." *International Journal of Middle East Studies* 15, no. 2: 283–98.

———. 1985. "The Status and Rights of Women in Ithna 'Ashari Shi'i Islam." In *Women and the Family in Iran*, edited by Asghar Fathi, 13–36. Leiden: E. J. Brill.

Ferdows, Adele K., and Amir H. Ferdows. 1983. "Women in Shi'a Fiqh: Images through the Hadith." In *Women and Revolution in Iran*, edited by Guity Nashat, 55–68. Boulder: Westview.

Fernea, Elizabeth Warnock. 1985. *Women and the Family in the Middle East: New Voices of Change*. Austin: University of Texas Press.

Firuzi, 'Abbas. 1994. "Seir-e Tarikhi-ye Tashkil-e Shura-ye 'Ali va Modiriyat-e Houzeh" (The Historical Development of the Creation of the High Council and Management of the Houzeh). *Payam-e Houzeh*. 1, no. 1 (1373): 7–23.

Fischer, Michael. 1980. *Iran: From Religious Dispute to Revolution*. Cambridge: Harvard University Press.

Fischer, Michael, and Mehdi Abedi. 1990. *Debating Muslims: Cultural Dialogues in Postmodernity and Tradition*. Madison: University of Wisconsin Press.

Gavahi, Zahra. 1990. *Sima-ye Zan dar A'ineh-ye Feqh-e Shi'eh* (Woman's Image in the Mirror of Shi'i Jurisprudence). Tehran: Islamic Propagation Organization (1369).

———. 1994. *Barrasi-ye Hoquq-e Zanan dar Mas'aleh-ye Talaq* (Investigation of Women's Rights in the Issue of Divorce). Tehran: Islamic Propagation Organization (1373).

Gerami, Shahin. 1996. *Women and Fundamentalism: Islam and Christianity*. New York: Garland.

Ghoussoub, Mai. 1987. "Feminism—or the Eternal Masculine—in the Arab World." *New Left Review* 161: 3–19.

Göçek, Fatma Müge, and Shiva Balaghi. 1994. "Introduction: Reconstructing Gender in the Middle East through Voices and Experiences." In *Reconstructing Gender in the Middle East: Tradition, Identity and Power*, edited by Fatma Müge Göçek and Shiva Balaghi, 1–22. New York: Columbia University Press.

Göle, Nilüfer. 1996. *The Forbidden Modern: Civilization and Veiling*. Ann Arbor: University of Michigan Press.

Gorji, Monir. 1994. *Negaresh-e Qor'an bar Hozur-e Zan dar Tarikh-e Anbiya* (The Koranic View on Women's Presence in the History of Prophets). Tehran: Centre for Women's Studies (1373).

Haddad, Yvonne Yazbeck. 1985. "Islam, Women and Revolution." In *Women, Religion, and Social Change*, edited by Yvonne Haddad and Ellison Banks Findly, 275–306. Albany: State University of New York Press.

———. 1998. "Islam and Gender: Dilemmas in the Changing Arab World." In *Islam, Gender, and Social Change*, edited by Yvonne Yazbeck Haddad and John Esposito, 3–29. Oxford: Oxford University Press.

Haddad, Yvonne Yazbeck, and John Esposito, eds. 1998. *Islam, Gender, and Social Change*. Oxford: Oxford University Press.

Haeri, Shahla. 1989. *Law of Desire: Temporary Marriage in Iran*. London: I. B. Tauris.

———. 1993. "Obedience versus Autonomy: Women and Fundamentalism in Iran and Pakistan." In *Fundamentalisms and Society: Reclaiming Science, the Family, and Education*, edited by M. E. Marty and R. S. Appelby, 2: 181–213. Chicago: University of Chicago Press.

———. 1994. "Temporary Marriage: An Islamic Discourse on Female Sexuality in Iran." In *In the Eye of the Storm: Women in Post-Revolutionary Iran*, edited by Mahnaz Afkhami and Erika Friedl, 98–114. Syracuse: Syracuse University Press.

———. 1995. Review of *Marriage on Trial* by Ziba Mir-Hosseini. *International Journal of Middle East Studies* 27, no. 3: 350–52.

Haeri-Yazdi, Mehdi. 1995. *Hekmat va Hokumat* (Wisdom and Government). London: Shadi Press (1374).

Hassan, Riffat. 1988. "Equal before Allah? Woman-Man Equality in the Islamic Tradition." In *Dossier: Women Living under Muslim Laws* 5–6: 26–29. Original in *Harvard Divinity Bulletin* 7, no. 2.

———. 1996. "Feminist Theology: The Challenges for Muslim Women." *Critique: The Journal for Critical Studies of the Middle East* 9 (Fall): 53–65.

Hatem, Mervat. 1986. "The Politics of Sexuality and Gender in Segregated Patriarchal Systems: The Case of Eighteenth- and Nineteenth-Century Egypt." *Feminist Studies* 12, no. 2: 250–74.

Hermansen, M. K. 1983. "Fatima as a Role Model in ʿAli Sharʿiati." In *Women and Revolution in Iran*, edited by Guity Nashat, 87–96. Boulder: Westview.

al-Hibri, Azizah. 1982. "A Study of Islamic Herstory: Or How Did We Ever Get into This Mess?" *Women's Studies International Forum: Women and Islam*, edited by Azizah al-Hibri, 207–19. New York: Pergamon.

Higgins, Patricia. 1985. "Women in the Islamic Republic of Iran: Legal, Social and Ideological Changes." *Signs* 10, no. 3: 477–95.

Holy Quran. n.d. Translated by M. H. Shakir. Qom: Ansariyan.

Homayuni, Elviyeh. 1992. *Zan, Mazhar-e Khallaqiyat-e Allah* (Woman, Manifestation of God's Creativity). 3d impression, Isfahan: Neshat-e Esfahan (1371).

Hoodfar, Homa. 1994a. "Devices and Desires: Population Policy and Gender Roles in the Islamic Republic." *Middle East Report* 190 (September-October): 11–17.

———. 1994b. "Situating the Anthropologist: Personal Account of Ethnographic Fieldwork in Three Urban Settings: Tehran, Cairo, and Montreal." In *Urban Lives: Fragmentation and Resistance*, edited by Vered Amit-Talai and Henri Lustiger-Thaler, 206–26. Toronto: McClelland and Stewart.

———. 1995. "The Veil in Their Minds and on Our Heads: The Persistence of Colonial Images of Muslim Women." *Resources for Feminist Research* 22, nos. 3–4: 5–18.

———. 1996a. "Bargaining with Fundamentalism: Women and the Politics of Population Control in Iran." *Reproductive Health Matters* 8 (November): 30–40.

Hoodfar, Homa. 1996b. Interview with Mehrangiz Kar. *Middle East Report* 198 (January-March): 36–38.

Hoseini-Tehrani, Seyyed Mohammad Hosein. 1995. *Resaleh-ye Nekahiyeh: Kahesh-e Jamʿiyat, Zarbeh-ye Sahmgin bar Peikar-e Moslemin* (Marital Treatise: Population Decrease, a Massive Blow to the Body of Muslims). Qom: Hekmat (1374).

Hussain, Freda. 1984. *Muslim Women*. London: Croom Helm.

Jannati, Mohammad Ebrahim. 1991. *Manabeʿ-e Ejtehad* (Sources of Ejtehad). Tehran: Kayhan Publications (1370).

———. 1993. *Advar-e Ejtehad* (Cycles of Ejtehad). Tehran: Kayhan (1372).

———. 1995a. "Bolugh az Didgah-e Feqh-e Ejtehadi" (Puberty from the Perspective of Dynamic Fiqh). *Kayhan-e Andisheh* 61 (1374): 35–43.

———. 1995b. "Senn-e Noh Sal Mouzuʿiyat Nadarad" (The Age of Nine Is Not the Subject). *Farzaneh* 2, no. 5 (1374): 9–19.

Javadi-Amoli, ʿAbdollah. 1993a. *Zan dar Aʾineh-ye Jalal va Jamal* (Women in the Mirror of Glory and Beauty). Tehran: Rejaʾ Cultural Press (1372).

———. 1993b. *Ava-ye Touhid* (The Sound of Unity). Tehran: Institute for Editing and Publishing Imam Khomeini's Works (1372).

Johnson-Odim, Cheryl. 1991. "Common Themes, Different Contexts." In *Third World Women and the Politics of Feminism*, edited by Chandra Mohanty, Ann Russo, and Lourdes Torres, 314–27. Bloomington and Indianapolis: Indiana University Press.

Kadivar, Jamileh. 1996. *Zan* (Woman). Tehran: Ettelaʿat (1375).

Kamali, Mohammad Hashim. 1991. *Principles of Islamic Jurisprudence*. Revised ed., Cambridge: Islamic Texts Society.

Kamalkhani, Zahra. 1998. *Women's Islam: Religious Practice among Women in Today's Iran*. London and New York: Kegan Paul International.

Kandiyoti, Deniz. 1988. "Bargaining with Patriarchy." *Gender and Society* 2, no. 3: 274–90.

———. 1991. *Women, Islam and the State.* Philadelphia: Temple University Press.

———. ed. 1996. *Gendering the Middle East: Emerging Perspectives.* London: I. B. Tauris.

Kar, Mehrangiz. 1991. *Fereshteh-ye 'Edalat va Pardeh-ye Dozakh* (The Angel of Justice and the Curtains of Hell). Tehran: Roushangaran (1370).

———. 1994. *Zanan dar Bazar-e Kar-e Iran* (Women in the Labor Market of Iran). Tehran: Roushangaran (1373).

———. 1997. *Hoquq-e Siyasi-ye Zanan-e Iran* (Political Rights of Iranian Women). Tehran: Roushangaran (1376).

Keddie, Nikki, and Beth Baron, eds. 1991. *Women in Middle Eastern History: Shifting Boundaries in Sex and Gender.* New Haven: Yale University Press.

Khalatbari, Firouzeh. 1998. "L'inégalité des sexes sur le marché du travail: Une analyse des potentiels économiques de croissance." In *Les femmes en Iran: Pressions sociales et stratégies identitaires*, edited by Nouchine Yavari-d'Hellencourt, 95–118. Paris: Harmattan.

Khan, Maulana Wahibiddin. 1995. *Women in Islamic Shariah*, translated by Farida Khanam. New Delhi: Islamic Centre.

Kian, Azadeh. 1995a. "Gendered Occupation and Women's Status in Post-Revolutionary Iran." *Middle Eastern Studies* 31, no. 3: 407–21.

———. 1995b. "L'invasion culturelle occidentale: Mythe ou réalité?" *Cahiers d'Etudes sur la Méditerranée Orientale et le Monde Turco-Iranien* 20 (July-December): 73–90.

———. 1996. "Des femmes iraniennes contre le clergé: Islamiques et laïques pour la première fois unies." *Le Monde Diplomatique* (November): 8.

———. 1997a. "Women and Politics in Post-Islamist Iran: The Gender Conscious Drive to Change." *British Journal of Middle Eastern Studies* 24, no. 1: 75–96.

———. 1997b. "L'emergence d'un discours féminin independant: Un enjeu de pouvoir." *Les Cahiers de l'Orient* 47, no. 3: 55–72.

———. 1998. "La formation d'une identité sociale féminine post-révolutionaire: Un enjeu de pouvoir." In *Les femmes en Iran: Pressions sociales et stratégies identitaires*, edited by Nouchine Yavari-d'Hellencourt, 135–58. Paris: Harmattan.

Kondo, Dorinne. 1986. "Dissolution and Reconstitution of Self: Implications for Anthropological Epistemology." *Cultural Anthropology* 1, no. 1: 74–88.

Koran. See *Holy Quran*.

Lazreg, Marnia. 1988. "Feminism and Difference: The Perils of Writing as a Woman on Women in Algeria." *Feminist Studies* 14, no. 1: 81–107.

———. 1994. *The Eloquence of Silence: Algerian Women in Question.* London and New York: Routledge.

Lemu, Aisha, and Fatima Heeren. 1976. *Women in Islam.* London: Islamic Foundation.

Macleod, Arlene Elowe. 1991. *Accommodating Protest: Working Women and the New Veiling and Change in Cairo.* New York: Columbia University Press.

Madani-Tabrizi, Seyyed Yusef. 1989. *Minhaj al-Ahkam fi'l-Nikah wa'l-Talaq* (The Way of Rules in Marriage and Divorce). Qom: Isma'ilian (1412 HQ).

———. 1995. *Al-Masa'el al-Mostahdaseh Motabeq ba Fatwa-ye Hazrat-e Ayatollah al-ʿOzma Aqa-ye Seyyed Yusef al-Madani al-Tabrizi* (Newly Created Problems According to the Opinion of His Excellency . . .). Qom: Ismaʿilian (1416 HQ).

Mahdavi, Shirin. 1985. "The Position of Women in Shiʿa Iran: Views of the Ulama." In *Women and the Family in the Middle East: New Voices of Change*, edited by Elizabeth Warnock Fernea. Austin: University of Texas Press, 255–68.

Mahmood, Saba. 1996. "Feminism and Religious Difference." Paper presented at the Carsten Niebuhr Institute of Near Eastern Studies conference, "Women, Culture and Modernity," Copenhagen (18–21 February).

Makarem-Shirazi, Naser. 1993. "Emruz va Farda-ye Houzeh-ha" (Yesterday and Tomorrow of the Seminaries). *Payam-e Houzeh* Introductory Issue (Fall 1372): 81–92.

Mallat, Chibli. 1993. *The Renewal of Islamic Law: Muhammad Baqer as-Sadr, Najaf and the Shiʿi International*. Cambridge: Cambridge University Press.

Malti-Douglas, Fedwa. 1992. *Women's Body, Women's World: Gender and Discourse in Arabo-Islamic Writing*. Princeton: Princeton University Press.

Matin-asgari, Afshin. 1997. "ʿAbdolkarim Sorush and the Secularization of Islamic Thought in Iran." *Iranian Studies* 30, nos. 1–2: 95–115.

Mernissi, Fatima. 1975. *Beyond the Veil: Male-Female Dynamics in Muslim Society*. Cambridge, MA: Schenkman.

———. 1991. *Women and Islam: An Historical and Theological Enquiry*, translated by Mary Jo Lakeland. Oxford: Blackwell. (Also published as *The Veil and the Male Elite*, Reading, MA: Addison-Wesley, 1991. First published as *Le harem politique*, Paris: Albin Michel, 1987).

———. 1996. *Women's Rebellion and Islamic Memory*. London: Zed.

Mesbah, Mohammad Taqi, et al. 1985. *Status of Women in Islam*. Tehran: Islamic Propagation Organization.

Milani, Farzaneh. 1992. *Veils and Words: The Emerging Voices of Iranian Women Writers*. Syracuse: Syracuse University Press.

Mir-Hosseini, Ziba. 1993. *Marriage on Trial: A Study of Islamic Family Law: Iran and Morocco Compared*. London: I. B. Tauris.

———. 1996a. "Divorce, Veiling and Feminism in Post-Khomeini Iran." In *Women and Politics in the Third World*, edited by Haleh Afshar, 142–70. London: Routledge

———. 1996b. "Stretching the Limits: A Feminist Reading of the Shariʿa in Iran Today." In *Feminism and Islam: Legal and Literary Perspectives*, edited by Mai Yamani, 284–320. London: Ithaca.

———. 1996c. "Women and the Shariʿa in the Islamic Republic of Iran: A Changing Relationship." Paper presented at the Carsten Niebuhr Institute of Near Eastern Studies conference, "Women, Culture and Modernity," Copenhagen (18–21 February).

———. 1998a. "Mariage et divorce: Une marge de négociation pour les femmes." In *Les femmes en Iran: Pressions sociales et stratégies identitaires*, edited by Nouchine Yavari-d'Hellencourt, 95–118. Paris: Harmattan.

———. 1998b. "A Response to Shahla Haeri's Review of *Marriage on Trial*." *International Journal of Middle East Studies*. 30, no. 3: 469–71.

———. Forthcoming. "Feminist Movements in the Islamic Republic." *Encyclopaedia Iranica*.

Mo'men, Mohammad. 1993. "Sakhtar-e Modiriyat-e Houzeh" (The Management Structure of the Seminaries). *Payam-e Houzeh* Introductory Issue (Fall 1372): 93–102.

Moghadam, Fatemeh E. 1994. "Commoditization of Sexuality and Female Labor Participation in Islam: Implications for Iran." In *In the Eye of the Storm*, edited by Mahnaz Afkhami and Erika Friedl, 80–97. Syracuse: Syracuse University Press.

Moghadam, Valentine M. 1988. "Women, Work, and Ideology in the Islamic Republic." *International Journal of Middle East Studies*. 20, no. 2: 221–43.

———. 1993. *Modernizing Women: Gender and Social Change in the Middle East*. Boulder, CO: Lynne Rienner.

Moghissi, Haideh. 1993. "Women in the Resistance Movement in Iran." In *Women in the Middle East: Perceptions, Realities and Struggles for Liberation*, edited by Haleh Afshar, 158–71. London: Macmillan.

———. 1994. *Populism and Feminism in Iran: Women's Struggles in a Male-Dominated Revolutionary Movement*. London: Macmillan.

———. 1995. "Public Life and Women's Resistance." In *Iran after the Revolution*, edited by Saeed Rahnema and Sohrab Behdad, 251–67. London: I. B. Tauris.

Mohanty, Chandra Talpade. 1991. "Introduction: Cartographies of Struggle." In *Third World Women and the Politics of Feminism*, edited by Chandra Mohanty, Ann Russo, and Lourdes Torres, 1–47. Bloomington and Indianapolis: Indiana University Press.

Momen, Moojan. 1985. *An Introduction to Shi'a Islam: The History and Doctrine of Twelver Shi'ism*. New Haven: Yale University Press.

Mosaffa, Nasrin, ed. 1995. Special Issue on Women's Studies. *Foreign Policy 9*, no. 2. Tehran: Institute for Political and International Studies.

Motahhari. *See also* Mutahhari.

Motahhari, Morteza. 1991. *Nezam-e Hoquq-e Zan dar Islam* (System of Women's Rights in Islam). 15th impression, Qom: Sadra (1370).

———. 1994. *Pasokh-ha-ye Ostad be Naqd-ha'i bar Ketab-e Mas'aleh-ye Hejab* (The Master's Responses to Critiques of the Book *The Hejab Issue*). 5th impression. Qom: Sadra (1373).

———. 1995. *Ashna'i ba 'Olum-e Eslami 3: Osul-e Feqh–Fiqh* (Familiarity with Islamic Sciences 3: Principles of Jurisprudence–Jurisprudence). 12th impression, Qom: Sadra (1374).

Mottahedeh, Roy. 1985. *The Mantle of the Prophet: Religion and Politics in Iran*. Harmondsworth: Penguin.

———. 1995a. "Traditional Shi'ite Education in Qom." *Harvard Middle Eastern and Islamic Review* 2, no. 1: 89–98.

———. 1995b. "Wilayat al-Faqih." In *The Oxford Encyclopedia of the Modern Islamic World* 4: 320–22.

Murata, Sachiko. 1992. *The Tao of Islam: A Source-Book on Gender Relationships in Islamic Thought*. Albany: State University of New York Press.

Musavi, Kazem [Mohsen Sa'idzadeh]. 1994. "Sima-ye Zan dar Nezam-e Eslami!!" (Woman's Image in the Islamic Order). *Zanan* 17 (1373): 36–40.

———. 1995. "Maddeh-ye 1133-e Qanun-e Madani: Mard Mitavanad har Vaqt Bekhahad Zan-e Khod-ra Talaq Dehad" (Article 1133 of the Civil Code: A Man Can Divorce His Wife Whenever He Wants). *Zanan* 23 (1374): 46–57.

Musavi-Bojnurdi, Ayatollah Seyyed Mohammad. 1996a. "Rah-ha-ye Su'-e Estefadeh az Talaq-ra Bebandim" (Let Us Close Ways of Misusing Divorce). *Neda* 19–20 (1375): 11–16.

Musavi-Bojnurdi, Ayatollah Seyyed Mohammad. 1996b. "Taʿamol va Taʿaroz bein-e Feqh va Hoquq-e Bashar" (Compatibility and Conflict between Feqh and Human Rights). *Farzaneh* 3, no. 8 (1375): 7–14.

Mussallam, Bassim. 1983. *Sex and Society in Islam: Birth Control before the Nineteenth Century.* Cambridge: Cambridge University Press.

Mutaharri. *See also* Motaharri.

Mutahhari, Morteza. n.d. *Jurisprudence and Its Principles (fiqh and usul ul-fiqh)*, translated by Mohammad Salman Tawheedi. Elmhurst, NY: Tahrike Tarsile Qurʾan.

Mutahhari, Murtada. 1981. *The Rights of Women in Islam.* Tehran: World Organization for Islamic Service.

Nahj ol-Balagheh/Nahjul Balagha. See Ali, Imam.

Najafi, Mohammad Hassan. 1995. "Negahi be Mabani-ye Vojuh-e Sharʿi dar Hakemiyat-e Feqhi" (A Look at the Basis of Religious Taxes in the Rule of the Jurist)." *Feqh* 3 (Spring 1374): 5–24.

Najmabadi, Afsaneh. 1991. "Hazards of Modernity and Morality: Women, State and Ideology in Contemporary Iran." In *Women, Islam and the State*, edited by Deniz Kandiyoti, 48–76. London: Macmillan.

———. 1994. "Power, Morality, and the New Muslim Womanhood." In *The Politics of Social Transformation in Afghanistan, Iran and Pakistan*, edited by Myron Weiner and Ali Banuazizi, 366–89. Syracuse: Syracuse University Press.

———. 1998. "Feminism in an Islamic Republic: Years of Hardship, Years of Growth." In *Islam, Gender, and Political Change*, edited by Yvonne Yazbeck Haddad and John Esposito, 50–84. Oxford: Oxford University Press.

Nakanishi, Hisae. 1998. "Power, Ideology, and Women's Consciousness in Postrevolutionary Iran." In *Women in Muslim Societies: Diversity within Unity*, edited by Herbert L. Bodman and Nayereh Tohidi, 83–100. Boulder: Lynne Rienner.

Nashat, Guity. 1983a. "Women in the Ideology of the Islamic Republic." In *Women and Revolution in Iran*, edited by Guity Nashat, 195–216. Boulder, CO: Westview.

———, ed. 1983b. *Women and Revolution in Iran.* Boulder, CO: Westview.

Nasr, Seyyed Hossein. 1975. "Preface." In *Shiʿite Islam*, by ʿAllamah Sayyid Muhammad Husayn Tabatabaʾi, translated and edited by Seyyed Hossein Nasr, 3–28. Albany: State University of New York Press.

Nazlee, Sajda. 1996. *Feminism and Muslim Women.* London: Ta-Ha.

Nicholson, Reynold A. 1911. *The Tarjuman al-Ashwaq (Interpreter of Desires): A Collection of Mystical Odes by Muhyiʾddin Ibn al-Arabi.* London: Theosophical Publication House.

Omid, Homa. 1994. *Islam and the Post-Revolutionary State in Iran.* London: Macmillan.

Paidar, Parvin. 1995. *Women and the Political Process in Twentieth-Century Iran.* Cambridge: Cambridge University Press.

———. 1996. "Feminism and Islam in Iran." In *Gendering the Middle East: Emerging Perspectives*, edited by Deniz Kandiyoti, 51–68. London: I. B. Tauris.

Rahnema, Ali. 1994. *Pioneers of Islamic Revival.* London: Zed.

Ramazani, Nesta. 1993. "Women in Iran: The Revolutionary Ebb and Flow." *Middle East Journal* 47, no. 3: 409–28.

Richard, Yann. 1991. *L'islam chiʿite: Croyances et ideologies.* Paris: Fayard.

Rizvi, Sayyid Muhammad. n.d. *Marriage and Morals in Islam.* Qum: Ansariyan.

Robertson Smith, William. 1885. *Kinship and Marriage in Early Islam*. Cambridge: Cambridge University Press.

el-Saadawi, Nawal. 1980. *The Hidden Face of Eve: Women in the Arab World*. Translated by Sherif Hetata. London: Zed.

Sa'idzadeh, Seyyed Mohsen. 1987. *Hayat-e Ba'ad az Marg* (Life after Death). Qom: Naser Publications (1365).

———. 1990. *Bozorgan-e Qa'en* (The Notables of Qa'en). Qom: Private (1369).

———. 1992a. *Tarikh-e Qa'en* (The History of Qa'en). Qom: Private (1371).

———. 1992b. "Ketabshenasi-ye Hejab" (Bibliographical Study of Hejab). *Payam-e Zan* 8 (1371): 59–63; 9 (1371): 60–61.

———. 1992c, 1993a. "Zeib al-Nisa: Chehreh-ye Makhfi-ye Adab-e Farsi" (Zeib al-Nisa, the Hidden Face of Persian Literature). *Payam-e Zan* 10 (1371): 44–49; 11(1371): 44–49; 12 (1371): 44–47; 13 (1372): 45–48.

———. 1993b. "Gozari bar Pishineh-ye Tarikhi-ye Tahajom-e Farhangi" (A Passage over the History of Cultural Invasion). *Payam-e Zan* 17: 24–27; 18: 8–12; 19: 24–27; 20: 14–19; 21: 62–65 (1372).

———. 1993c. "Zanan, Tahsilat va Bardasht-ha-ye Dini" (Women, Education and Religious Assumptions). *Payam-e Zan* 19: 64–67; 20: 20–25; 22: 26–30 (1372).

———. 1994a. "Azadi-ye Zanan dar Doureh-ye Mohammad" (Women's Freedom at the Time of Mohammad). Unpublished manuscript (1373).

———. 1994b. "Tebq-e Kodam Qanun Hazineh-ye Darman-e Bimari-ha-ye Sakht-e Zan bar 'Ohdeh-ye Shouhar Nist?" (According to What Law Is a Husband Not Responsible for His Wife's Major Medical Expenses?). *Zanan* 18 (1373): 34–37.

———. 1994c. "Feqh, Zan, Arzesh-ha" (Feqh, Woman, and Values). *Zanan* 20 (1373): 44–51.

———. 1995a. "Feminizm: Tekrar-e Tajrobeh-ye Na-movaffaq" (Feminism: Repeat of an Unsuccessful Experience). *Payam-e Zan* 35 (1373): 22–27; 36 (1373): 16–21; 37 (1374): 12–19; 38 (1374): 28–33.

———. 1995b. "Tatbiq-e Feminizm ba Masa'el-e dini-ye Eslami" (Correspondence between Feminism and Islamic Religious Issues). In *Women, Gender and Islam*, proceedings of the Sixth Seminar of Iranian Women's Studies Foundation, 31–120.

———. 1998a. "Zarurat-e Enqelab dar Ravesh" (The Necessity for Revolution in Method). *Iran-e Farda* 41 (1377): 26–30.

———. 1998b. "Mabani-ye Feqhi-ye Didgah-e Barabari" (Jurisprudential Basis of Equality Perspective). *Payam-e Hajar* 233 (1377): 50–53.

Sabbagh, Suha, ed. 1996. *Arab Women: Between Defiance and Restraint*. New York: Olive Branch Press.

Said, Edward. 1978. *Orientalism*. New York: Pantheon Books.

Salehi-Najafabadi, Ne'matollah. 1996. "Qezavat-e Zan dar Feqh-e Eslami" (Women's Judgment in Islamic Feqh). In *Majmu'eh-ye Asar-e Kongreh-ye Bar-rasi-ye Mabani-ye Feqhi-ye Hazrat-e Emam Khomeini* 12: 230–67. Tehran: Institute for Editing and Publishing Imam Khomeini's Works (1375).

Sanasarian, Eliz. 1982. *The Women's Rights Movement in Iran*. New York: Praeger.

———. 1986. "Political Activism and Islamic Identity in Iran." In *Women in the World: 1975–1985, the Women's Decade*, edited by L. B. Iglitzen and R. Ross, 207–24. Santa Barbara: ABC-Clio.

Sanasarian, Eliz. 1992. "Politics of Gender and Development in the Islamic Republic of Iran." *Journal of Developing Societies* 8, no. 1: 56–68.

Sanders, Paula. 1991. "Gendering the Ungendered Body: Hermaphrodites in Medieval Islamic Law." In *Women in the Middle Eastern History: Shifting Boundaries in Sex and Gender*, edited by Beth Baron and Nikki Keddie, 74–95. New Haven: Yale University Press.

Schirazi, Asghar. 1997. *The Constitution of Iran: Politics and the State in the Islamic Republic*. Translated by John O'Kane. London and New York: I. B. Tauris.

Scott, James C. 1985. *Weapons of the Weak: Everyday Forms of Peasant Resistance*. New Haven: Yale University Press.

Seffati, Zohreh. 1997. "Senn-e Bolugh-e Shar'i-ye Dokhtaran" (The Legal Age of Maturity of Girls). In *Bolugh-e Dokhtaran*, edited by Mehdi Mehrizi, 379–90. Qom: Islamic Propagation Office (1376).

Shaheed, Farida. 1994. *Controlled or Autonomous: Identity and the Experience of the Network Women Living under Muslim Laws* (Occasional Paper no. 5). Grabels, France: Women Living Under Muslim Laws.

Shahshahani, Sohila. 1984. "Religion, Politics and Society: A Historical Perspective on the Women's Movement in Iran." *Samya Shakti* 1–2: 100–20.

Shahshahani, Soheila, Zhila Hoda'i, and Fahimeh Sepehr-Sadeqian. 1995. *Inja Iran, Man Zan* (*This Is Iran, I Am a Woman*). Tehran: Modabbar (1374).

Shari'ati, Ali. 1979. *On the Sociology of Islam*, translated by Hamid Algar. Berkeley: Mizan Press.

———. 1980. *Fatima Is Fatima*, translated by Laleh Bakhtiar. Tehran: Shari'ati Foundation.

———. 1994. *Zan: Majmu'eh-ye Asar 21* (Women: Collected Works 21). 6th impression, Tehran: Chap-pakhsh (1375).

Shirazi, Fariba. 1995. "Ejlas-e Pekan: Gami Movaffaq va Tajrobe'i Geranbaha baraye Zan-e Irani" (Beijing Conference: A Successful Step and a Valuable Experience for Iranian Women). *Payam-e Zan* 44: 42–47; continued for 12 installments, concluding in *Payam-e Zan* 56 (November 1996).

Shryock, Andrew. 1997. *Nationalism and the Genealogical Imagination: Oral History and Textual Authority in Tribal Jordan*. Berkeley and Los Angeles: University of California Press.

Siddiqi, Muhammad Muzheruddin. 1952. *Women in Islam*. Lahore: Institute of Islamic Culture.

Skovgaard-Petersen, Jakob. 1994. "Never Change your Sex in Cairo: Islamic Reactions to Some Modern Surgery." Paper presented in workshop on "Cases and Contexts in Islamic Law," University of Michigan (3–4 December).

Smith, Jane. 1985. "Women, Religion and Social Change in Early Islam." In *Women, Religion, and Social Change*, edited by Yvonne Yazbeck Haddad and Ellison Banks Findly, 19–35. Albany: State University of New York Press.

Sonbol, Amira el-Azhary, ed. 1996. *Women and the Family and Divorce Laws in Islamic History*. Syracuse: Syracuse University Press.

Sorush, 'Abdol Karim. 1977. *Nehad-e Na-aram-e Jahan* (The Dynamic Nature of the World). Tehran: Sarat Cultural Institute (1356).

———. 1992. *Razdani va Roushan-fekri va Dindari* (Augury and Intellectualism and Piety). Tehran: Sarat Cultural Institute (1371).

———. 1994a. *Tafarroj-e Son': Goftar-ha'i dar Ma'qulat-e Akhlaq va San'at va 'Elm-e Ensani* (Essays on Ethics, Arts and Human Sciences). Tehran: Sarat Cultural Institute (3d ed. 1373; first published 1366).

———. 1994b. *Tazad-e Dialektiki* (Dialectical Antagonism). Tehran: Sarat Cultural Institute (4th ed. 1373; first published 1357).

———. 1994c. *Ide'uluzhi-ye Sheitani* (Satanic Ideology). Tehran: Sarat Cultural Institute (5th ed. 1373; first published 1359).

———. 1994d. *Qabz va Bast-e Te'urik-e Shari'at* (Theoretical Contraction and Expansion of the Shari'a). Tehran: Sarat Cultural Institute (3d ed. 1373; first published 1370).

———. 1994e. *Farbehtar az Ide'uluzhi* (Sturdier than Ideology). Tehran: Sarat Cultural Institute (2d ed. 1373; first published 1372).

———. 1994f. *Qesseh-ye Arbab-e Ma'refat* (The Tale of the Masters of Knowledge). Tehran: Sarat Cultural Institute (2d ed. 1373; first published 1373).

———. 1995a. *Ousaf-e Parsayan* (Attributes of the Pious), 3d ed. Tehran: Sarat Cultural Institute (1374; first published 1371).

———. 1995b. "Horriyat va Rouhaniyat" (Liberty and the Clergy). *Kiyan* 24 (1374): 2–11.

———. 1995c. *Hekmat va Ma'ishat* (Wisdom and Life), vol. 1. Tehran: Sarat Cultural Institute (2d ed. 1373; first published 1373).

———. 1996a. "Zehniyat-e Moshavvash, Hovviyat-e Moshavvash" (Confused Mentality, Confused Identity). *Kiyan* 30: (1375): 4–9.

———. 1996b. "Tahlil-e Mafhum-e Hokumat-e Dini" (Analysis of the Concept of Religious Rule). *Kiyan* 32 (1375): 2–13.

———. 1997a. *Hekmat va Ma'ishat* (Wisdom and Life), vol 2. Tehran: Sarat Cultural Institute (1376).

———. 1997b. *Modara va Modiriyat* (Tolerance and Governance). Tehran: Sarat Cultural Institute (1376).

Spellberg, Denise A. 1991. "Political Action and Public Example: 'A'isha and the Battle of the Camel." In *Women in the Middle Eastern History: Shifting Boundaries in Sex and Gender*, edited by Beth Baron and Nikki Keddie, 45–57. New Haven: Yale University Press.

Stern, Gertrude. 1939. *Marriage in Early Islam*. London: Royal Asiatic Society.

Stowasser, Barbara. 1993. "Women's Issues in Modern Islamic Thought." In *Arab Women: Old Boundaries, New Frontiers*, edited by Judith E. Tucker, 3–28. Bloomington: Indiana University Press.

———. 1994. *Women in the Qur'an: Traditions and Interpretations*. New York: Oxford University Press.

———. 1998. "Gender Issues and Contemporary Quran Interpretation." In *Islam, Gender, and Social Change*, edited by Yvonne Yazbeck Haddad and John Esposito, 30–44. Oxford: Oxford University Press.

Tabari, Azar. 1982a. "The Enigma of the Veiled Iranian Women." *MERIP* 103 (February): 22–27.

———. 1982b. "Islam and the Struggle for Emancipation of Iranian Women." In *In the Shadow of Islam*, edited by Azar Tabari and Nahid Yeganeh, 5–25. London: Zed.

———. 1986 "The Women's Movement in Iran: A Hopeful Prognosis." *Feminist Studies* 12, no. 2: 342–60.

Tabari, Azar, and Nahid Yeganeh, eds. 1982. *In the Shadow of Islam*. London: Zed.

Tabataba²i, ʿAllamah Sayyid Muhammad Husayn. 1975. *Shiʿite Islam*, translated and edited by Seyyed Hossein Nasr. Albany: State University of New York Press.

———. n.d. *Taʿaddod-e Zoujat va Maqam-e Zan dar Eslam* (Polygyny and the Status of Women in Islam). Qom: Azadi.

Taleqani, Azam. 1991. "Faʿaliyatha-ye Dah-Saleh-ye Mo²assaseh-ye Eslami-ye Zanan-e Iran" (Ten Years of Activities of the Islamic Organization of Iranian Women). *Daftar-e Dovvom: Masa²el-e Zanan*. Tehran: Islamic Organization of Iranian Women (1370).

Tedlock, Barbara. 1991. "From Participant Observation to Observation of Participation: The Emergence of Narrative Ethnography." *Journal of Anthropological Research* 47, no. 1: 69–94.

Tedlock, Dennis. 1987. "Questions Concerning Dialogical Anthropology." *Journal of Anthropological Research* 43, no. 4: 325–37.

Tohidi, Nayereh. 1991. "Gender and Islamic Fundamentalism: Feminist Politics in Iran." In *Third World Women and the Politics of Feminism*, edited by Chandra Mohanty, Ann Russo, and Lourdes Torres, 251–67. Bloomington and Indianapolis: Indiana University Press.

———. 1993. "Iranian Women and Gendered Relations." In *Irangeles: Iranians in Los Angeles*, edited by Ron Kelly et al., 175–83. Berkeley and Los Angeles: University of California Press.

———. 1994. "Modernity, Islamization, and Women in Iran." In *Gender and National Identity: Women and Politics in Muslim Societies*, edited by Valentine Moghadam, 110–47. London: Zed.

———. 1996. *Feminizm, Demokrasi va Eslam-gera²i* (Feminism, Democracy, and Islamism in Iran). Los Angeles: Ketabsara.

———. 1998. "The Issues at Hand." In *Women in Muslim Societies: Diversity within Unity*, edited by Herbert L. Bodman and Nayereh Tohidi, 277–94. Boulder, CO: Lynne Rienner.

Torab, Azam. 1996. "Piety as Gendered Agency: A Study of *Jalaseh* Ritual Discourse in an Urban Neighbourhood in Iran." *Journal of the Royal Anthropological Institute* (N.S.) 2, no. 2: 235–52.

———. 1998. "Neighbourhoods of Piety: Gender and Ritual in South Tehran." Ph.D. dissertation, School of Oriental and African Studies, University of London.

Tucker, Judith. 1993. *Arab Women: Old Boundaries, New Frontiers*. Bloomington: Indiana University Press.

Vafa²i, ʿAbdol Vahid. 1996. *Sima-ye Qom* (Portrait of Qom). Tehran: Islamic Propagation Organization (1375).

Vakili, Valla. 1996. *Debating Religion and Politics in Iran: The Political Thought of Abdolkarim Soroush* (Studies Department Occasional Paper Series, no. 2). Washington, D.C.: Council on Foreign Relations.

Wadud-Muhsin, Amina. 1992. *Qur²an and Women*. Kuala Lumpur: Penerbit Fajar Bakti SDN. BHD.

Watt, W. Montgomery. 1988. *Islamic Fundamentalism and Modernity*. London: Routledge.

Wright, Robin. 1996. "Islam and Liberal Democracy: Two Visions of Reformation." *Journal of Democracy* 7, no. 2: 64–75.

Yavari-d'Hellencourt, Nouchine. 1995. "La difficile réémergence d'une presse indépendante en Iran: *Kyàn*, une revue en quête de modernité islamique." *Cahiers d'Etudes sur la Méditerranée Orientale et le Monde Turco-Iranien* 20 (July-December): 91–114.

————. 1998. "Discours islamiques, actrice sociales et rapports sociaux de sexe." In *Les femmes en Iran: pressions sociales et stratégies identitaires*, edited by Nouchine Yavari-d'Hellencourt, 190–229. Paris: Harmattan.

Yazdi, Mohammad. 1994. "Moruri bar yek Naqd" (Going Over a Review). *Zanan* 19 (1373): 7–8.

Yeganeh, Nahid. 1982. "Women's Struggles in the Islamic Republic of Iran." In *In the Shadow of Islam*, edited by Azar Tabari and Nahid Yeganeh, 26–74. London: Zed.

Yeganeh, Nahid, and Nikki R. Keddie. 1986. "Sexuality and Shiᶜa Sexual Protest in Iran." In *Shiᶜism and Social Protest*, edited by Juan R. I. Cole and Nikki Keddie, 108–36. New Haven: Yale University Press.